ALL IN THE DAY'S WORK

Photograph by *Alfred Cheney Johnston*

Ida M. Tarbell

At 70

ALL
IN THE DAY'S WORK

An Autobiography

BY IDA M. TARBELL

With An Introduction
by Linda Simon

G.K.HALL &CO.
Boston, Massachusetts
1985

First G.K. Hall printing, 1985
Introduction copyright © 1985   Linda Simon

Library of Congress Cataloging in Publication Data

Tarbell, Ida M. (Ida Minerva), 1857–1944.
  All in the day's work.

  Reprint. Originally published: New York : Macmillan, 1939.
  Includes index.
  1. Tarbell, Ida M. (Ida Minerva), 1857–1944. 2. Journalists—
United States—Biography. I. Title.
PN4874.T23A33   1985   070'.92'4 [B]   85-8486
ISBN 0-8398-2881-0

To

SARAH A. TARBELL
My Sister and My Loyal Friend

CONTENTS

INTRODUCTION
by Linda Simon

"IT HAS been said that Miss Tarbell is the most popular woman in America," declared a magazine editorial in 1904. "Her exposé of the Standard Oil Trust is a brave and brilliant piece of work, and, in the literature of revolt, marks a new departure.... She is one of those women with whom a profession is not a tentative thing, but a life business." By 1904 the forty-seven-year-old Tarbell had been a working journalist for more than a quarter of a century. In 1906, when Theodore Roosevelt included her in his epithet of "muckraker," she was considered a reformer of national renown. Yet Tarbell was no radical. "My point of attack," she said, "has always been that of a journalist after the fact," not "the advocate of a cause or a system." She was, she admitted, a "student of the times," a historian of her world.

All in the Day's Work stands with the autobiographies of Ray Stannard Baker, Lincoln Steffens, William Allen White, and S. S. McClure as a rich source of information about the reform movement that received such noisy publicity in the first decade of the century. Tarbell recreates here a sense of the commitment and urgency shared by writers on the staff of *McClure's Magazine,* and later at the *American,* two of the most influential journals of the time. She provides sensitive portraits of her colleagues and associates—including Theodore Roosevelt, Jane Addams, John D. Rockefeller, Alexander Graham Bell, and Louis Pasteur. Most important, she helps us to understand the motivations and goals of those men and women who worked to change the consciousness of their age.

These motivations, even some eighty years later, are not easily separated from myths and legends cultivated by muckrakers themselves or generated by some historians.

Were the muckrakers revolutionaries? idealists? anarchists? Had they been so deeply disillusioned about America that they were hopeless and despondent? Were they socialists? Were the women outspoken feminists? What, in short, did they want?

Tarbell's memoir offers what, to many, may be startling revelations. We find that Tarbell, like her fellow writers, came from a strong religious background that sustained her later on and informed her judgments of the world she observed. Although Tarbell, as an adult, no longer practiced the strict religion of her family, her Methodist upbringing instilled in her a sense of discipline and purpose that never was lost. As she grew increasingly involved in political and economic issues, she identified as an essential problem the conflict between "Commercial Machiavellianism and the Christian code." Wishing that the world could be guided by the moral principles of her youth, she agreed with John S. Phillips, the colleague she most respected, that "The only way to improve the world is to persuade it to follow the Golden Rule."

We find, too, that in the age of Roosevelt, it was Lincoln whose values seemed most relevant to America and its problems. Tarbell's abiding respect for Lincoln was shared by many of her colleagues, and her monumental biography not so much spurred, but reflected, a new surge of interest in the martyred president. Ray Stannard Baker recalled that once, at an editorial meeting, he and Lincoln Steffens were depressed by the state of the country. "It was a bleak world we saw that morning," he said later, "nowhere in America any great leadership; nowhere, apparently, any vision." It was Tarbell who quickly helped lift that depression. "Remember," she said earnestly, "that we have had great leadership in the past: we shall have it again in the future. Keep looking back to Abraham Lincoln."

These men and women, though accused by Roosevelt of never letting in "light and air," were, in fact, optimistic, believing strongly in the efficacy of justly applied laws and the inherent integrity of the American political system. They had firm faith in the ultimate triumph of the good. "All that we can do," said Tarbell in one of her articles, "is temporarily to accelerate or to delay the stream of righteousness." Certainly these hard-driving intellectuals wanted to hasten the coming of "righteousness," and saw in journalism an effective way to influence their society.

Earlier in her life, however, Tarbell had found that defining a role for herself was doubly hard because she was both an intellectual and a woman. For a time, she struggled with the idea that women might be imbued with a special sense of morality, and so might offer to society a "quality of service" unique to their sex. It was this idea, in part, that caused her to leave an editorial job at the *Chautauquan* and go to Paris: she was intent on becoming a writer—a historian and biographer—and in focusing specifically on Madame Manon Philipon de Roland, a Frenchwoman active during the Revolution of 1789. Through Madame Roland, she thought, she could explore this problem of "service" and also better understand her own feelings as a woman who sought control over her own life, wished never to marry, venerated the family, and felt decidedly uncomfortable with the women's rights movement in late-nineteenth-century America. Eventually she evolved a special brand of feminism that mystified the likes of Jane Addams and Anna Shaw: she advocated social reform in the workplace, but was against women's suffrage; she believed that women's essential role was in the home, raising a family, yet she herself, voicing no regrets, rejected this role. She was, it seems, not so much interested in feminism as she was in justice, independence, and free will.

These interests guided her work and her life, earning her respect and admiration. Colleagues described her as a woman of integrity and virtue, a center of calm and sanity in the frenetic *McClure's* offices. Lincoln Steffens remembered her as "sensible, capable, and very affectionate. . . . When we were deadlocked we might each of us send for her, and down she would come to the office, smiling, like a tall, good-looking young mother, to say, 'Hush, children.' " She easily could break through petty squabbles; her interest was always in the good of the magazine. Baker remembered her capacity for hard work, her diligence, and her dedication. "No one could have been more exacting than she was as a studious inquirer," he said, "or more devoted to the truth of the matter. . . . And no one was ever more determined as a fighter for the things she believed in, and lived for. She was steady and sound, never sensational in the manner of her writing or in the way she lived. . . . Ida Tarbell was the best of us."

She was disappointed at being branded a muckraker, insisting that she was only a reporter and that her sources substantiated all she wrote about John D. Rockefeller and his giant corporation. If, in writing her history of the oil trust, she brought notoriety to herself and shame to Rockefeller, she could have done nothing else. "I didn't make the Standard Oil History, you know," she told an interviewer after her series had appeared. "I merely wrote it."

Tarbell was eighty-two when *All in the Day's Work* was published, and had agreed to write her autobiography, she said, because she needed money. Always reticent, she had no intention of providing the sensational rendering of her world that her publishers had hoped for; nor did she divulge intimate details about her inner life. "I have often found it difficult to explain myself to myself, and I do not often try," she once told a friend. Her diaries, housed now at the Allegheny College library, are hardly more revealing than this book. Ida Tarbell lived a public life, and it is this life that is presented here, with grace and dignity. On her eightieth birthday, Tarbell told a reporter that she was writing her memories of "five stirring decades." Indeed they were, and she was not merely an astute observer, but an eager and enthusiastic participant.

For more information on Ida Tarbell: "Idarem," as she was affectionately called by her colleagues at *McClure's,* appears in many of their memoirs: Baker's *American Chronicle* (Scribner's, 1945), Steffens's *Autobiography* (Harcourt, Brace, 1931), and McClure's *My Autobiography* (Stokes, 1914). Peter Lyon's *Success Story: The Life and Times of S. S. McClure* (Scribner's, 1963) offers a well-researched and thorough presentation of Tarbell's role at the magazine and her relationship with McClure and his staff. A succinct overview of Tarbell's life is found in Mary E. Tomkins's monograph *Ida Tarbell* (Twayne, 1974). The most recent biography is by Kathleen Brady (Putnam's, 1984).

Linda Simon, author of biographies of Alice B. Toklas, Thornton Wilder, and Lady Margaret Beaufort, is currently at work on a history of the year 1906. She teaches writing at Harvard.

ALL IN THE DAY'S WORK

MY START IN LIFE

IF IT had not been for the Panic of 1857 and the long depression which followed it I should have been born in Taylor County, Iowa. That was what my father and mother had planned. In fact, however, I was born in a log house in Erie County, Pennsylvania, on November 5, 1857. It was the home of my pioneering maternal grandfather Walter Raleigh McCullough. No home in which I have ever lived has left me with pleasanter memories of itself. It was a Cape Cod house, a story and a half high, built of matched hewn logs, its floors of narrow fitted oak planks, its walls ceiled, its "upstairs" finished, a big fireplace in its living room. There were spreading frame outbuildings to accommodate the multiple activities of a farm which was in my time a going concern. I remember best the big cool milk room with its dozens of filled pans on the racks, its huge wooden bowl heaped with yellow butter on its way to the firkin, its baskets piled with eggs, its plump dressed poultry ready for market.

Like all young married people of pioneer ancestry and experience having their way to make, my parents wanted land. Land of their own, combined with what my father could earn at his profession as a teacher and his trade as a joiner, meant future security. It was the proved way of the early American.

After much looking about in northwestern Pennsylvania where the families of both were settled, they had decided that the West offered greater opportunity and so in the spring of 1857, a year after his marriage, my father, Franklin Sumner Tarbell by name, started out to find a farm. He had but little money in his pocket, and the last one hundred fifty miles of his search were made on foot. How enthusiastic he was over the claim he at last secured! His letters tell of the splendid dome of sky which covered it, of the far view over the prairie, of marvelous flowers and birds, of the daily passing along the horizon of a stream of covered wagons, settlers bound for California, Pikes Peak, Kansas, Nebraska; and some of them, he found, were earlier Iowa settlers, leaving the very state which for the moment seemed to him the gate to Paradise.

He set himself gaily at breaking land, building the house for mother, working in a sawmill to pay for the lumber. He did it alone, even to the making of window frames and doors. I know how he did it—whistling from morning till night, mischief and tenderness chasing each other across his blue eyes as he thought of my mother's coming, their future together.

The plan they had made provided for her going west with their household goods in August. The money was arranged for, so they thought; but before it was taken from the bank the panic came, and every county bank in Pennsylvania was closed. There was no money anywhere, nothing for my mother to do but stay where she was while my father struggled to earn by teaching and carpenter work the money which would bring us on. But the panic reached Iowa, dried up its money supply. People were living by barter, my father reported. What a heartbreaking waiting it was for them, coming as it did after an engagement of six years every week of which they had both found long!

The fall and winter of 1857, the spring and summer of 1858 passed. Still there was no money to be had, and then in the fall of 1858 father started out to *teach* his way to us. Before he found a school he had walked one hundred and eighty miles—walked until his shoes and clothes were worn and tattered. It was "shabby and broke," as he had written it would be, that he finally in the spring of 1859, when I was a year and a half old, made his way back to my mother still living in the log house in Erie County.

According to the family annals I deeply resented the intimacy between the strange man and my mother, so far my exclusive possession. Flinging my arms about my mother, so the story went, I cried, "Go away, bad man."

The problem for my father now was to earn money to take us back to Iowa, for my mother to continue her patient waiting. For a dozen years before her marriage she had taught in district schools in Erie County, as well as in a private school of an aunt in Poughkeepsie, New York. She was a good teacher, but she was married! She must stay with her family then until her husband had a home ready for her; so ruled my grandmother, chock-full as she was of the best and severest New England rules for training girls to be ladies. You might live in a log house. You were reminded loftily that many of the "best families" had done that while "settling the country," but you must "never forget who you are!" "Remember that your father is a McCullough of an ancient and honored Scotch clan, his mother a Raleigh of Sir Walter's family, that I am a Seabury, my great-uncle the first Episcopal Bishop in the United States, my mother a Welles, her father on Washington's staff." It was a litany her four daughters all had to learn!

Exciting employment waited my father. For six or seven years before his marriage, when he was earning his way through the Academy of Jamestown, New York, he spent his summers running a fleet of three or more flatboats of merchandise to be delivered at trading points on the Allegheny and the Ohio River—always as far south as Louisville, sometimes even up the Mississippi. "Captain Tarbell," his small and jolly crew called him. The River was the chief highway of a great country. To its waters came the pioneer and trader, the teacher, the preacher, the scientist, the prophet, as well as every species of gambler, charlatan, speculator, swindler, cutthroat. My father's stories of what he saw were among the joys of my childhood: a great fleet of steamboats burning at Pittsburgh, a hanging, river churches and preachers and show boats, children who never knew other homes than a boat, towns, cities, and what he loved best of all—nights floating quietly down the great Ohio, the moon above. Not strange that after those cruel months of working his way back to us he should have seized this opportunity again to take charge of his Jamestown friend's river enterprise.

The trip went well, and at the end of August, 1859, he turned back, money in his pocket to take us to Iowa. But as he journeyed eastward he was met everywhere by excitement. A man had drilled a well near a lumber settlement in northwestern Pennsylvania— Titusville it was called—drilled for oil and found it, quantities of it. My father, like most men who traveled up and down the Allegheny and Ohio in those days, was familiar with crude petroleum. He had used it to grease creaking machinery and, too, as a medicine, a general cure-all, Seneca oil; used it for the colds, the fever and ague, the weak lungs which had afflicted him from boyhood. He knew, too, that there were those who believed that if rock oil, as it was called, could be found in sufficient quantities it would make a better light than the coal and whale oils then in common use. The well near Titusville producing twenty-five to one hundred barrels a day—nobody knew how much—proved that if other reservoirs or veins could be opened by such drilling there would be oil to light the world.

Rumors were exciting and grew in the telling. The nearer he came to Erie County, the bigger the well. He met men on foot and horseback making their way in. Something to look into before he started back to Iowa. He looked into it, not merely at Titusville with its first well, but down the stream on which the first well stood and where other wells were already drilling. Oil Creek, it was called. What if they continued to get oil? my father asked himself. Where would they put it? They would need tanks, tanks in numbers. He believed he could build one that would hold five hundred or more barrels. He said as much to the owner of a well drilling down the creek near the mouth of a tributary called Cherry Run. "Show me a model that won't leak, and I'll give you an order." He lost no time in making his model and got his order.

Here was a chance for a business if oil continued to be found, a business with more money in it than he had ever dreamed of making. Moreover, he knew all the elements of that business, had had experience in handling them. Tank building called for his trade, that of the joiner. Iowa could wait.

By the summer of 1860 he had his shop going at the mouth of Cherry Run near the well for which he had received his first order. The shop running, he built what was to be my mother's first home of her own, the one for which with infinite confidence and infinite pain she had been waiting since her marriage four years and a half before.

It was in October of 1860 that my father drove his little family over the Allegheny foothills some forty miles. There were two of us children now, for in July of 1860 my brother William Walter Tarbell, named from his two grandfathers, had been born. Close beside his shop father had built a shanty. It had a living room with an alcove, a family bedroom with trundle beds for us children, and a kitchen. A covered passage led into the shop, which was soon to be the joy of my life for here were great piles of long odorous curly pine shavings into which to roll, to take naps, to trim my gown, and in which to search day in and day out for the longest, the curliest.

But these shavings and my delight in them were a later discovery. My first reaction to my new surroundings was one of acute dislike. It aroused me to a revolt which is the first thing I am sure I remember about my life—the birth in me of conscious experience. This revolt did not come from natural depravity; on the contrary it was a natural and righteous protest against having the life and home I had known, and which I loved, taken away without explanation and a new scene, a new set of rules which I did not like, suddenly imposed.

My life in the log house had been full of joyous interests. There were turkeys and ducks and chickens, lambs and colts and calves, kittens and puppies—never could I be without playmates. There were trees and woods and flowers in summer—a great fireplace with popcorn and maple candy in winter, and I an only grandchild the center of it all. But what had I come to? As mother realized, a place of perils, a creek rushing wildly at the side of the house, great oil pits sunken in the earth not far away, a derrick inviting to adventurous climbing at the door. No wonder that warnings and scoldings and occasional switchings dogged my steps. Moreover, I was no longer the center of the circle: a baby filled her arms—"my" arms! A man still strange gave me orders and claimed her—"my" mother.

It was not to be endured, and so one November day just after my third birthday I announced I was going to leave. "Going back to Grandma." "Very well," my mother said. I knew the way the men went when they walked away from the shop, and I followed it, but not far. Across the valley in which we lived ran an embankment. To my young eyes it was as high as a mountain, and the nearer I came the higher it looked, the higher and blacker. And then suddenly as I came to its foot I realized that I had never been on the other side, that I did not know the way to Grandma's. I knew I was beaten, and sat down to think it over. Never in all these years since have I faced defeat, known that I must retreat, that I have not been again that little figure with the black mountain in front of it, a little figure looking longingly at a shanty dim in the growing night but showing a light in the window.

Finally I turned slowly back to the house and sat down on the steps. It seemed a long time before the door opened and my mother in a surprised voice said:

"Why, Ida! I thought you had gone to Grandma's."

"I don't know the way," I said humbly.

"Very well. Come in and get your supper."

Respect for my mother, her wisdom in dealing with hard situations, was born then. I was not to be punished; I was not to be laughed at; I was to be accepted. Years later she told me of the unhappy hour she spent watching me go off so sturdily, to come back so droopingly, watching with tears running down her cheeks, but determined I must learn my lesson. It was a bit of wisdom she never ceased to practice. My mother always let me carry out my revolts, return when I would and no questions asked.

In the three years we spent in the shanty on the flats there was but one other episode that had for me the same self-revealing quality as this revolt. It was my first attempt to test by experiment. The brook which ran beside the house was rapid, noisy, in times of high water dangerous for children. Watching it, fascinated, I observed that some things floated on the surface, others dropped to the bottom. It set me to wondering what would happen to my little brother, then in dresses, if dropped in. I had to find out. There was a footbridge near the house, and one day when I supposed I was unobserved I led him onto it and dropped him in. His little skirts spread out and held him up. Fortunately at that moment his screams brought a near-by workman, and he was rescued. I suppose I was spanked; of that I remember nothing, only the peace of satisfied curiosity in the certainty that my brother belonged to the category of things which floated.

What I really remember of these early days concerns only my personal discoveries, discoveries of the kind of person I was, of the nature of things around me which stirred my curiosity. Whether a childish experience was deep enough to etch itself on my memory or I only know of it from hearing it told and retold, I always decide by this test: if I really remember it, the happening is set in a scene—a scene with a background, exits, entrances, and properties. I know I remember my revolt and defeat because I always see it as an act on a stage, every detail, every line clear.

Of the pregnant, bizarre, and often tragic development going on about me I remember nothing; yet the uncertainties and dangers of it were part of our daily fare.

Whether there was oil in the ground in sufficient quantities to justify the prodigious effort being made to find it, nobody could know. If not, the shop and shanty were a dead loss—another long

delay on the road to Iowa. All that winter of 1860 and 1861 my
father was asking himself that question; but in 1861 it was answered when up and down Oil Creek a succession of flowing wells
came in, wells producing from three hundred to three thousand
barrels a day—"fountain wells," "gushers," "spouters," they
called them from the great streams which rose straight into the
air one to two hundred feet, to fall in an oily green-black spray
over the surrounding landscape.

Deadly, dangerous, too, as the Oil Region learned to its sorrow
by a disaster almost at the doorsteps of our Cherry Run home. It
was the evening of April 17, 1861. The news of the Fall of Sumter
had just reached the settlement, remote as it was from rail and
telegraph connections, and all the men of the town had gathered
after supper at one place or another to discuss the situation. What
did it mean? What would the President do? My father was sitting
on a cracker barrel in the one general store. As he and his friends
talked a man ran in to tell the company that a fresh vein of oil
had been struck in a well on the edge of the town. Its owner, Henry
Rouse, had been drilling it deeper; the oil was spouting over the
derrick. Great news for the community still uncertain as to the
extent of its field. Great news for my father. It meant tanks.
Everybody jumped to run to the well when the earth was rocked
by a mighty explosion. A careless light had ignited the gas which
had spread from the flowing oil until it had enveloped everything
in the vicinity. Before my father reached the place nineteen men,
among them his friend the well-owner Henry Rouse, had been
burned to death. How many had escaped and in what condition,
nobody knew.

Late that night as my father and mother grieved they heard
outside their door a stumbling something. Looking out, they saw
before them a terrible sight, a man burned and swollen beyond
recognition and yet alive, alive enough to give his name—one of
their friends. My mother took him in—the alcove became a hospital. For weeks she nursed him—the task of the woman in a

pioneer community, a task which she accepted as her part. Thanks
to her care, the man lived. The relics of that tragedy were long
about our household—comforts and bedquilts she had pieced and
quilted for Iowa stained with linseed oil, but too precious to be
thrown away.

But all this is as something read in a book, something which has
become more poignant as the years have gone by and I am able
to feel what those long weeks of care over that broken man meant
to my mother.

The business prospered, the shop grew. Little do I remember
of all this, or the increased comforts of life or moving into the
new home on the hillside above the town by this time known as
Rouseville. But the change in the outlook on the world about me,
I do remember. We had lived on the edge of an active oil farm
and oil town. No industry of man in its early days has ever been
more destructive of beauty, order, decency, than the production
of petroleum. All about us rose derricks, squatted enginehouses
and tanks; the earth about them was streaked and damp with the
dumpings of the pumps, which brought up regularly the sand and
clay and rock through which the drill had made its way. If oil
was found, if the well flowed, every tree, every shrub, every bit of
grass in the vicinity was coated with black grease and left to die.
Tar and oil stained everything. If the well was dry a rickety
derrick, piles of debris, oily holes were left, for nobody ever
cleaned up in those days.

But we left the center of this disorder, went to the hillside,
looked down on it; and as for me I no longer saw it, for opposite
us was a hillside so steep it had never been drilled. It was clothed
with the always changing beauty of trees and shrubs, the white
shadflowers and the red maples, the long garlands of laurel and
azalea in the spring, the green of every shade through the summer, the crimson and gold, russets and tans of the fall, the frost-
and snow-draped trees of the winter. I did not see the derricks
for the trees. The hillside above our house and the paths which

led around it became a playground in which I reveled. I was not the only one about to forget the ugliness of the Valley and remember through life the beauty of those hillsides. Years later I was to know fairly well one of the great figures in the development of oil, Henry H. Rogers, then the active head of the Standard Oil Company. We discovered in talking over the early days of the industry that at the very moment I was beginning to run the hills above Rouseville he was running a small refinery on the Creek and living on a hillside just below ours, separated only by a narrow ravine along each side of which ran a path. "Up that path," Mr. Rogers told me, "I used to carry our washing every Monday morning, go for it every Saturday night. Probably I've seen you hunting flowers on your side of the ravine. How beautiful it was! I was never happier." That reminiscence of Henry H. Rogers is only one of several reasons I have for heartily liking as fine a pirate as ever flew his flag in Wall Street.

Soon after we went to the home on the hill the oil country, at that moment suffering a depression, was stirred by the news that a great well had been struck ten miles from Rouseville at Pithole, an isolated territory to which the veterans in the business had never given a thought. The news caused a wild scramble. A motley procession of men with and without money, with and without decency, seeking leases, jobs, opportunity for adventure, excitement and swindling travelled on foot or horseback up the Valley of Cherry Run in full view from our house.

Father was one of the first to take advantage of the Pithole discovery, putting up his tank shops there and doing a smashing business during the short life of the field. Its "bottom fell out" in 1869. He rode back and forth from his shop on a little saddle horse—Flora, beautiful creature—usually with considerable sums of money in his pocket. The country was full of ruffians, and stories of robbery were common. When he was very late in returning mother would walk the floor wringing her hands. I could never go to bed those nights until he had returned, not because I felt her anxiety but because of the excitement and mystery of it. I carried a dramatic picture of him in mind, a kind of Paul Revere dashing along the lonely road, the rein on Flora's neck, his pistol in hand. But he always came home, always brought the money he had collected, which he must keep in the tiny iron safe in his office annexed to the house until he could carry it to Oil City where he banked.

My life became rapidly more conscious now that I had left the flats behind, experience deeper. Here was my first realization of tragedy. It was the spring of 1865. Father was coming up the hill, mother and I were watching for him. Usually he walked with a brisk step, head up, but now his step was slow, his head dropped. Mother ran to meet him crying, "Frank, Frank, what is it?" I did not hear the answer; but I shall always see my mother turning at his words, burying her face in her apron, running into her room sobbing as if her heart would break. And then the house was shut up, and crape was put on all the doors, and I was told that Lincoln was dead.

From that time the name spelt tragedy and mystery. Why all this sorrow over a man we had never seen, who did not belong to our world—*my* world? Was there something beyond the circle of hills within which I lived that concerned me? Why, and in what way, did this mysterious outside concern me?

I was soon to learn that tragedy did not come always from a mysterious beyond. What a chain of catastrophes it took to teach the men and women who were developing the new industry the constant risk they ran in handling either crude or refined oil. They came to our very door, when a neighboring woman hurrying to build a fire in her cookstove poured oil on the wood before she had made sure there were no live coals in the firebox. An awful explosion occurred and she and two women who ran to her assistance were burned to a crisp. I heard horrified whisperings about me. The refusal to tell me what had happened aroused a terrible curiosity. I gathered that the bodies were laid out in a house not far away and, when nobody was looking, stole in to look at them. Broken sleep for me for nights.

The mystery of death finally came into our household. There had been a fourth child born in the house on the hill—"little Frankie," we always called him—blue-eyed like my father, the sunniest of us all. For weeks one season he lay in the parlor fighting for life—scarlet fever—a disease more dreaded by mothers in those days than even smallpox. Daily I stood helpless, agonized, outside the door behind which little Frankie lay screaming and fighting the doctor. I remember even today how long the white marks lasted on the knuckles of my hands after the agony behind the closed door had died down and my clenched fists relaxed.

Little Frankie died, became a pathetic and beloved tradition in the household. My little sister, who had made a terrible and successful fight against the disease, told me how she could not understand why father and mother cried when they talked of Frankie.

"If they want to see him," she thought, "why do they not put a ladder from the top of the hill up to the sky into heaven and climb up? If Frankie is there God would let them see him."

I have said that my first recollection of Lincoln was the impression made by the tragedy of his death. That this was so was not for the lack of material on him in our household. My father was an ardent Republican. Back in '56 he had written from his river trip, "Hurrah for Frémont and Dayton." As soon as he had had more money than the actual needs of the family required, he had subscribed to *Harper's Weekly*, *Harper's Monthly*, the New York *Tribune*, began to buy books. Of all of these I remember only the *Weekly* and *Monthly*. My brother and I used to lie by the hour flat on our stomachs, heels in the air, turning over the exciting pages of the War numbers; but none of it went behind my eyes—none concerned me. Only now when I go back to the files of those old papers there is a whispering of something once familiar.

Of the *Monthly* I have more distinct recollections. It was in these that I first began to read freely. Many a private picnic did I have with the *Monthly* under the thorn bushes on the hillside above Oil Creek, a lunch basket at my side. There are still in the family storeroom copies of *Harper's Monthly* stained with lemon pie dropped when I was too deep into a story to be careful. Here I read my first Dickens, my first Thackeray, my first Marian Evans, as George Eliot then signed herself. My first Wilkie Collins came to me in the *Weekly*. Great literature—all pirated, I was to learn much later. My friend Viola Roseboro tells me that at this time she was reading Harper's pirated paper-bound copies of Dickens. It was much later that they came my way.

However, all the reading I was doing was not so respectable. On the sly I was devouring a sheet forbidden to the household— the *Police Gazette*—the property of the men around the house, for we had men around the house, men of various degrees of acceptability to my mother, but all necessary to my father's enterprises. The business had grown; it meant a clerk, bosses, workmen. In a pioneer community like ours it was hard to find comfortable living quarters for single men. My father and mother, both brought up on farms, accepted as a matter of course the housing and feeding of hired men. So it was in line with their experience as well as with the necessities of the case that our household was arranged to take care of a certain number of men connected with my father's business. For sleeping quarters a bunkhouse was built on the hillside; mornings and evenings, they sat at the family table. This accepting men of whose manners and ways she often heartily disapproved was distasteful to my mother; but she had not been a schoolteacher for nothing, and she applied her notions of discipline. She would not have swearing, drinking, rough manners, and certainly she would not have had the *Police*

Gazette in the house. But the men had it, and now and then when my brother and I played about the bunkhouse it was easy for me to pick up a copy and slip it away where my dearest girl friend and I looked unashamed and entirely unknowing on its rough and brutal pictures. If they were obscene we certainly never knew it. There was a wanton gaiety about the women, a violent rakishness about the men—wicked, we supposed, but not the less interesting for that.

One reason the *Police Gazette* fascinated me was that it pictured a kind of life I knew to be flourishing in a neighboring settlement, a settlement where my father had shops run by a boss who, as well as his sister, was a family friend, and where I was often allowed to visit. This settlement, Petroleum Center, had by something like general consent become Oil Creek's "sink of iniquity."

The discovery of oil, the growing certainty that it was the beginning of a new industry, that money was flowing into the Oil Region quickly brought an invading host of men and women seeking fortunes. It was a new and rich field for tricksters, swindlers, exploiters of vice in every known form. They were soon setting up shops in every settlement and, to the credit of the manhood of the Oil Region, usually being driven out by self-directed vigilantes.

At Rouseville a "joy boat" which made its way up the Creek that first winter and tied up near my father's shop was cut loose in the middle of the night after its arrival. Its visitors found themselves floating down the Allegheny River the next morning and obliged to walk back. From that time open vice shunned the town. But when wealth poured out of the ground at Petroleum Center there was too great excitement to think of order, decency. Before it was realized, the town was alive with every known form of wantonness and wickedness. By the time I was allowed to visit our friends there, I saw from the corner of my eye as I walked sedately the length of the street saloons, dance halls, brothels; and

I noted many curious things. The house where I visited stood on a slope overlooking one of the most notorious dance halls of the Oil Region—Gus Reil's. Often I left my bed at night and watched that long low building from which rose loud laughter, ribald songs, shouts, curses. Later horror was added to Gus Reil's fascination, for here a Rouseville boy was shot one night.

If Petroleum Center was giving me an opportunity to feed my curiosity about things in the world of which I was not supposed to know, it happened also to be the indirect means of awaking my interest in the stars, one of the most beautiful interests of my youth. My father had seen the early passing of the wooden oil tank, the coming of the iron tank, and had used his capital to become an oil producer. One of his first investments had been in an oil farm on the hills above the wicked town which so excited my curiosity. His partner in this venture, M. E. Hess, lived on this farm with his family. In that family was a daughter about my age and bearing my name—Ida. We became friends and visited back and forth as chance offered. My chance came often when Mr. Hess, riding with a companion over the hills to Rouseville to consult with father, dropped his companion and took me back with him, usually at night. A fine pair of saddle horses he had—"High Fly" and "Shoo Fly." My first experience in horseback riding was following him on "Shoo Fly" over the hills after dark.

Mr. Hess was an altogether unusual man, educated, with a vein of poetry in him. As we rode he would stop every now and then to name the stars, trace the constellations, repeat the legends. My first consciousness of space, its beauty, its something more than beauty, came then.

Not a bad counterbalance for what I was gathering in the town below the farm on the hill and seeing reproduced in the *Police Gazette*, which so perfectly pictured its activities.

But there were other correcting forces at work on me. The men who formed the vigilante committee to make Rouseville difficult for commercialized vice (my father one of them) set themselves early to establishing civilizing agencies—first a church.

It was decided by the men and women who were to build and support this church that it should be of the denomination of which there were the largest number in the community. The Methodists had the numbers, and so my father and mother who were Presbyterians became and remained Methodists. Their support was active. We did not merely go to church; we stayed to class meeting; we went to Sunday school, where both father and mother had classes; we went to Wednesday night—or was it Thursday night?—prayer meeting. And when there was a revival we went every night. In my tenth or eleventh year I "went forward" not from a sense of guilt but because everybody else was doing it. My sense of sin came after it was all over and I was tucked away in bed at night. I had been keenly conscious as I knelt at the Mourners' bench that the long crimson ribbons which hung from my hat must look beautiful on my cream-colored coat. The realization of that hypocrisy cut me to the heart. I knew myself a sinner then, and the relief I sought in prayer was genuine. I never confessed. It wasn't the kind of sin other converts talked about. But it aroused self-observation; I learned that often when I was saying the polite or proper thing I was thinking quite differently. For a long time it made me secretly unhappy thinking that in me alone ran an underground river of thought. Later I began to suspect that other people were like this, that always there flowed a stream of unspoken thought under the spoken thought. It made me wary of strangers.

A side of my life which moves me deeply now, as I think back, was the continuous effort of my father and mother to give me what were called advantages, to use their increasing income to awaken and develop in me a taste for things which they had always been denied. They wanted music in the household and our grandest possession became a splendid Bradbury square piano—

a really noble instrument—with one of the finest, mellowest tones
that I have ever heard in a piano.

A music teacher turned up in the community and I was at
once set at five-finger exercises, and I was kept at them and all
that follows them for many years; but I found no joy in what
I was doing. It is possible that with different teachers from those
available there might have been a spring touched, for untrained
as I am I am not without a certain appreciation of music.

I mastered the mechanics of piano playing well enough, however, to become later one of the regular performers in the high
school in the town to which we were to move—Titusville, Pennsylvania. I remembered nothing of this until two of my old friends
in Titusville, school chums, told me that I was one of the three
or four who played the piano for the morning exercises, that I
sometimes played my show pieces, and that on one occasion I was
an actor in a scene which they recalled with glee. They told me
I was playing a duet with a classmate. We either lost our place
or did not agree as to time—stopped entirely, argued the matter
out, began over, and this time went through without dissension;
but I have only this secondhand memory of my contribution to
the musical life of the Titusville High School.

I remember the efforts of my father and mother to show me
something of the outside world much more clearly than I do
those to awaken my interest in books and music. There were little
trips, once as far as Cleveland—the whole family—the marvel of
the "best hotel," of new hats and coats and armfuls of toys.
There were summers at the farm, only thirty miles away. Best
remembered and most enjoyed were the all-day-excursion picnics.
No one can understand the social life of a great body of the
American people in the latter part of the nineteenth century
without understanding the hold the picnic had on them. The
Tarbell household took the picnic so seriously that it had a special equipment of stout market baskets, tin cups and plates, steel

knives and forks, tin spoons, worn napkins (the paper ones were then unheard of). The menus were as fixed as that for a Thanksgiving dinner: veal loaf, cold tongue, hard-boiled eggs—"two apiece"—buttered rusks, spiced peaches, jelly, cucumber pickles, chowchow, cookies, doughnuts (we called them fried cakes), and a special family cake. And you ate until you were full.

Our grandest picnic excursions in those days were to Chautauqua Lake, a charming sheet of water only some fifty miles from home. Near the head of the lake lay an old Chautauqua County town, Mayville; at its foot, Jamestown where my father for several years had been a student in the Academy, and from which in vacations he had gone on his annual trips down the Ohio. Loaded with big baskets of lunch, we took an early train to Mayville, changed there to a little white steamer: zigzagged the length of the lake, twenty or so miles, stopping at point after point. We ate our lunch en route, and at Jamestown went uptown to drink a bottle of "pop." And then came the slow return home, where we arrived after dark exhausted by pleasure.

Three or four miles from Mayville on the west side of the lake jutted a wooded promontory—Fair Point—the site in those days of a Methodist camp meeting; and here we sometimes stopped for the day. We never liked it so well as going to Jamestown; neither did father.

I DECIDE TO BE A BIOLOGIST

FIVE years went by in the house on the hill, and then in 1870 when I was thirteen I found myself in Titusville, Pennsylvania, in a new house my father had built. How characteristic of the instability of the oil towns of that day, as well as of the frugality of my father, was this house! From the beginning of the Pithole excitement he had, as I have said, made money—more than he could ever have dreamed, I fancy; and then about 1869 practically without warning the bottom fell out, as the vernacular of the region put it. The end shut up my father's shops there, but it also gave us the makings of a home. In that rapid development, only four years long, a town of some twenty thousand had grown up with several big hotels—among them, one called the Bonta House. It had features which delighted my father—long French windows, really fine iron brackets supporting its verandahs, handsome woodwork. The Bonta House was said to have cost $60,000, but its owners were glad to take the $600 father offered when the town "blew up." He paid the money, tore down the building, loaded its iron brackets and fine doors and windows, mouldings and all, and I suppose much of its timber, onto wagons and carted it ten miles away to Titusville where, out of it, he built the house which was our home for many years.

Titusville was not like Rouseville, which had suddenly sprung from the mud as uncertain as a mushroom of the future. It had been a substantial settlement twenty years before oil was found there, small but sturdy with a few families who had made money chiefly in lumber, owning good homes, carefully guarding the order and decency of the place.

The discovery of oil overran the settlement with hundreds of fortune seekers. They came from far and near, on foot, horse-back, wagon. The nearest railroad connection was sixteen miles away, and the roads and fields leading in were soon cut beyond recognition by the heavy hauling, its streets at times impassable with mud.

The new industry demanded machinery, tools, lumber—and the bigger it grew, the greater the demand. Titusville, the birth-place of all this activity, as well as the gateway down the Creek, must furnish food and shelter for caravans of strangers, shops for their trades, offices for speculators and brokers, dealers in oil lands and leases, for oil producers, surveyors, and draftsmen—all the factors of the big business organization necessary to develop the industry. In 1862 the overflow was doubled by the arrival of a railroad with a connection sixteen miles away with the East and West. The disbanding of the Army in June of 1865 brought a new rush—men still in uniform, their rifles and knapsacks on their backs. Most of this fresh inflow was bound to the scene of the latest excitement, Pithole.

Stampeded though she was, Titusville refused to give up her idea of what a town should be. She kept a kind of order, waged a steady fight on pickpockets, drunkards, wantons; and in this she was backed by the growing number of men and women who, having found their chance for fortune in oil, wanted a town fit for their families. After churches, the schools were receiving the most attention. It was the Titusville schools which had deter-mined my father and mother to make the town their permanent home.

But school did not play a serious part in my scheme of things at the start. I went because I was sent, and had no interest in what went on. I was thirteen, but I had never been in a crowded room before. In a small private school the teacher had been my friend. Here I was not conscious my teacher recognized my exist-ence. I soon became a truant; but the competent ruler of that schoolroom knew more than I realized. She was able to spot a truant, and one day when I turned up after an unexplainable absence she suddenly turned on me and read me a scathing lecture. I cannot remember that I was ashamed or humiliated, only amazed, but something in me asserted itself. I suppose that here a decent respect for the opinions of mankind was born; at least I became on the instant a model pupil.

A few months later I passed into high school; and when at the end of the year the grades were averaged at a ceremony where everybody was present I stood at the head of the honor roll. Nobody could have been more surprised. I had not been working for the honor roll: I had simply been doing what they expected me to do as I understood it, and here I was at the top. I remember I felt very serious about it. Having made the top once, I knew what would be expected of me. I couldn't let my father and mother or my teachers down, so I continued to learn my lessons. It was a good deal like being good at a game. I liked to work out the mathematics and translations—good puzzles, but that they had any relation to my life I was unconscious. And then suddenly, among these puzzles I was set to solve, I found in certain textbooks the sesame which was to free my curiosity, stir desires to know, set me working on my own to find out more than these books had to offer. The texts which did all this for me were a series I suspect a modern teacher might laugh at—Steele's Fourteen Weeks in Zoology, Geology, Botany, Natural Philosophy, Chemistry.

Here I was suddenly on a ground which meant something to me. From childhood, plants, insects, stones were what I saw when I went abroad, what I brought home to press, to put into bottles, to "litter up the house." The hills about Rouseville were rich in treasures for such a collector, but nobody had ever taught me more than their common names. I had never realized that they were subjects for study, like Latin and geometry and rhetoric and other such unmeaning tasks. They were too fascinating. But here my pleasure became my duty. School suddenly became exciting. Now I could justify my tramps before breakfast on the hills, justify my "collections," and soon I knew what I was to be—a scientist. Life was beginning to be very good, for what I liked best to do had a reason. No doubt this uplift was helped by the general cheerfulness of the family under our new conditions of life.

Things were going well in father's business; there was ease such as we had never known, luxuries we had never heard of. Our first Christmas in the new home was celebrated lavishly. Far away was that first Christmas in the shanty on the flats when there was nothing but nuts and candy and my mother and father promising, "Just wait, just wait, the day will come." The day had come—a gorgeous Christmas tree, a velvet cloak, *and* a fur coat for my mother. I haven't the least idea what there was for the rest of us, but those coats were an epoch in my life—my first notion of elegance.

This family blossoming was characteristic of the town. Titusville was gay, confident of its future. It was spending money on schools and churches, was building an Opera House where Janauschek soon was to play, Christine Nilsson to sing. More and more fine homes were going up. Its main street had been graded and worked until fine afternoons, winter and summer, it was cleared by four o'clock for the trotting of the fast horses the rich were importing. When New Year's Day came every woman received—wine, cakes, salads, cold meats on the table—every man went calling. That is, Titusville was taking on metropolitan airs, led by a few citizens who knew New York and its ways, even spoke familiarly of Jay Gould and Jim Fisk, both of whom naturally enough had their eye on us. Did not the Erie road from which they at the moment were filling their pockets regard oil as one of its most profitable freights? We were grain for their mill.

There was reason for confidence. In the dozen years since the first well was drilled the Oil Creek Valley had yielded nearly thirty-three million barrels of crude oil. Producing, transporting, refining, marketing, exporting, and by-products had been developed into an organized industry which was now believed to have a splendid future.

Then suddenly this gay, prosperous town received a blow between the eyes. Self-dependent in all but transportation and locally in that through the pipe lines it was rapidly laying to shipping points, it was dependent on the railroads for the carrying of its crude oil to outside refining points and for a shipping of both crude and refined to the seaboard—a rich and steady traffic for which the Oil Region felt the railroads ought to be grateful; but it was the railroads that struck the blow. A few refiners outside the region—Cleveland, Pittsburgh, Philadelphia —concocted a marvelous scheme which they had the persuasive power to put over with the railroads, a big scheme by which those in the ring would be able to ship crude and refined oil more cheaply than anybody outside. And then, marvelous invention, they would receive in addition to their advantage a drawback on every barrel of oil shipped by any one not in the group. Those in the South Improvement Company, as the masterpiece was called, were to be rewarded for shipping; and those not in, to be doubly penalized. Of course it was a secret scheme. The Oil Region did not learn of it until it had actually been put into operation in Cleveland, Ohio, and leaked out. What did it mean to the Oil Region? It meant that the man who produced the oil, and all outside refiners, were entirely at the mercy of this group who, if they would, could make the price of crude oil as well as refined. But it was a plan which could not survive daylight. As soon as the Oil Region learned of it a wonderful row followed. There were nightly antimonopoly meetings, violent speeches, processions; trains of oil cars loaded for members of the offending corporation were raided, the oil run on the ground, their buyers turned out of the oil exchanges; appeals were made to the state legislature, to Congress for an interstate commerce bill, producers and refiners uniting for protection. I remember a night when my father came home with a grim look on his face and told how he with scores of other producers had signed a pledge not to sell to the Cleveland ogre that alone had profited from the scheme —a new name, that of the Standard Oil Company, replacing the name South Improvement Company in popular contempt.

There were long days of excitement. Father coming home at night, silent and stern, a sternness even unchanged by his after-dinner cigar, which had come to stand in my mind as the sign of his relaxation after a hard day. He no longer told of the funny things he had seen and heard during the day; he no longer played his jew's-harp, nor sang to my little sister on the arm of his chair the verses we had all been brought up on:

> Augusta, Maine, on the Kennebec River,
> Concord, New Hampshire, on the Merrimack, etc.

The commotion spread. The leaders of the New York Petroleum Association left out of the original conspiracy, and in a number of cases (as was soon to be shown) outraged chiefly for that reason, sent a committee to the Oil Region to see what was doing. The committee was joyfully welcomed, partly because its chairman was well known to them all. It was my Rouseville neighbor, Henry H. Rogers.

Mr. Rogers had left the Creek in 1867 and become a partner in the Pratt firm of refiners and exporters of Brooklyn, New York. He and his associates saw as clearly as his old friends in the Oil Region that—let the South Improvement Company succeed in its plan for a monopoly—everybody not in the ring would be forced to go out of business. The New York men seem to have been convinced that the plans for saving themselves which the organized producers and refiners were laying stood a good chance of success, for back in New York Mr. Rogers gave a long interview to the *Herald*. He did not mince words. Cleveland and Pittsburgh were "straining every nerve to create a monopoly." They would succeed if their control of the railroads continued. He and his fellows felt as the men in the Oil Region did, that the breaking up of the South Improvement Company was a "necessity for self-existence." They were as bold in action as in words, for when a little later the president of the Standard Oil Company of Cleveland, John D. Rockefeller (to date, the only beneficiary of the South Improvement Company), sought an interview in New York with Mr. Rogers and his committee he was treated cavalierly and according to the newspapers retreated after a brief reception "looking badly crestfallen."

Thus was the Henry H. Rogers of 1872.

Out of the long struggle begun as a scrimmage came finally a well developed cooperative movement guaranteeing fair play all around. It was signed by the Standard Oil Company's representative and all the oil-carrying railroads. The railroads indeed were the first to succumb, knowing as they did that what they were doing was contrary to the common law of the land, and being thundered at as they were by the press and politicians of all the country. "I told Willie not to go into that scheme," said old Commodore Vanderbilt; and Jay Gould whined, "I didn't sign until everybody else had."

Out of the alarm and bitterness and confusion, I gathered from my father's talk a conviction to which I still hold—that what had been undertaken was *wrong*. My father told me it was as if somebody had tried to crowd me off the road. Now I knew very well that, on this road where our little white horse trotted up and down, we had our side, there were rules, you couldn't use the road unless you obeyed those rules, it was not only bad manners but dangerous to attempt to disobey them. The railroads— so said my father—ran through the valley by the consent of the people; they had given them a right of way. The road on which I trotted was a right of way. One man had the same right as another, but the railroads had given to one something they would not give to another. It was wrong. I sometimes hear learned people arguing that in the days of this historic quarrel everybody took rebates, it was the accepted way. If they had lived in the Oil Region through those days in 1872, they would have realized that, far from being accepted, it was fought tooth and nail. Everybody did not do it. In the nature of the offense everybody could not do it. The strong wrested from the railroads the privilege of preying upon the weak, and the railroads never dared give the privilege save under promise of secrecy.

In walking through the world there is a choice for a man to make. He can choose the fair and open path, the path which sound ethics, sound democracy, and the common law prescribe, or choose the secret way by which he can get the better of his fellow man. It was that choice made by powerful men that suddenly confronted the Oil Region. The sly, secret, greedy way won in the end, and bitterness and unhappiness and incalculable ethical deterioration for the country at large came out of that struggle and others like it which were going on all over the country—an old struggle with old defeats but never without men willing to make stiff fights for their rights, even if it cost them all they ever hoped to possess.

At all events, uncomprehending as I was in that fine fight, there was born in me a hatred of privilege—privilege of any sort. It was all pretty hazy to be sure, but still it was well, at fifteen, to have one definite plank based on things seen and heard, ready for a future platform of social and economic justice if I should ever awake to my need of one. At the moment, however, my reflection did not carry me beyond the wrongness of the privilege which had so upset our world, contradicting as it did the principle of consideration for others which had always been basic in our family and religious teaching. I could not think further in this direction, for now my whole mind was absorbed by the overwhelming discovery that the world was not made in six days of twenty-four hours each.

My interest in science, which meant for me simply larger

familiarity with plants and animals and rocks, had set me looking over my father's books. Among them I found Hugh Miller's
"Testimony of the Rocks," and sat down to read it. Gradually
I grasped with a combination of horror and amazement that,
instead of a creation, the earth was a growth—that the creative
days I had so clearly visualized were periods, eons long, not to be
visualized. It was all too clear to deny, backed as it was by a
wealth of geological facts. If this were true, why did the Bible
describe so particularly the work of each day, describe it and
declare, "And the evening and the morning were the first day,"
etc., and end, "and he rested on the seventh day"? Hugh Miller
labored to prove that there was no necessary contradiction between Genesis and Geology. But I was too startled to accept what
he said. A Bible that needed reconciling, that did not mean what
it said, was not the rock I had supposed my feet were on; that
words could have other meaning than that I had always given
them, I had not yet grasped.

I was soon to find that the biblical day was disturbing a great
part of the Christian world, was a chief point of controversy in
the church. I had hardly made my discovery when Genesis and
Geology appeared in the pulpit of the Methodist Church of
Titusville, Pennsylvania. Filling this pulpit at that time was a
remarkable and brilliant man, Amos Norton Craft. Dr. Craft
was an indefatigable student. It was told of him to the wonder
of the church that he laid aside yearly $200 of his meager salary
to buy books. Like all the ministers of those days, he was obliged
to face the challenges of science. Many of his fellows—most of
them, so far as my knowledge went—took refuge in heated declarations that the conclusions that science was making were pro-
fane, godless, an affront to divinity. Not so Dr. Craft. He accepted them, strove to fit them into the Christian system. He
startled his congregation and interested the town profoundly by
announcing an evening course of lectures on the reconciliation
of Genesis and Geology. The first of the series dealt with the

universe. I had never known there was one. The stars, yes. I could name planets and constellations and liked nothing better than to lie on my back and watch them; but a universe with figures of its size was staggering. I went away from those Sunday night lectures fascinated, horror-stricken, confused—a most miserable child, for not only was my idea of the world shattered, not only was I left dizzily gyrating in a space to which there was no end, but the whole Christian system I had been taught was falling in a general ruin. I began to feel that I ought to leave the church. I did not believe what I was supposed to believe. I did not have the consolation of pride in emancipation which I find youth frequently has when it finds itself obliged to desert the views it has been taught. Indeed, I doubted greatly whether it was an emancipation. What troubled me most was that if I gave up the church I had nothing to put in place of something it had given me which seemed to me of supreme importance; summed up, that something was in the commandment, "Do as you would be done by." Certainly nothing which Hugh Miller or Herbert Spencer, whom I began to read in 1872 in the *Popular Science Monthly*, helped me here. They gave me nothing to take the place of what had always been the unwritten law of the Tarbell household, based as I knew upon the teachings of the Bible. The gist of the Bible, as it had come to me, was what I later came to call the brotherhood of man. Practically it was that we should do nothing, say nothing, that injured another. That was a catastrophe, and when it happened in our household—an inarticulate household on the whole, though one extraordinarily conscious of the minds and hearts of one another—when it happened the whole household was shadowed for hours and it was not until by sensitive unspoken efforts the injured one had been consoled, that we went on about our usual ways.

This was something too precious to give up, and something for which I did not find a substitute in the scientific thinking and arguing in which I was floundering. The scientists offered me nothing to guide me in human relations, and they did not satisfy a craving from which I could not escape; that was the need of direction, the need of that which I called God and which I still call God. Perhaps I was a calculating person, a cautious one. At all events I made up my mind to wait and find out something which better took the place of those things which I so valued. It cost me curious little compromises, compromises that I had to argue myself into. The chief came in repeating the creed.

I could repeat, "conceived of the Holy Ghost, born of the Virgin Mary," because for many years I did not know what that meant. It was the resurrection that disturbed me. I could not accept it, nor could I accept the promise of personal immortality. That had become a grave doubt with me when I first grew dizzy with the consciousness of the vastness of the universe. Why should I expect to exist forever as a conscious mind in that vast emptiness? What would become of me? I did not want to think about it, and I came then to a conviction that has never left me: that as far as I am concerned immortality is not my business, that there is too much for me to attend to in this mortal life without overspeculation on the immortal, that it is not necessary to my peace of mind or to my effort to be a decent and useful person, to have a definite assurance about the affairs of the next world. I say this with humility, for I believe that some such assurance is necessary to the peace and usefulness of many persons, and I am the last to scoff at the revelations they claim.

And yet it was hard to give up heaven. Among the books on our shelves—many of them orthodox religious books—was one that had a frontispiece which I had accepted as a definite picture of the heaven to which I was to go. Jehovah sat on a throne, cherubim and seraphim around him, rank upon rank of angels filling the great amphitheater below. I always wondered where my place would be, and whether there would be any chance to work up in heaven as there seemed to be on earth, to become a cherub.

But giving up this heaven was by no means the greatest tragedy in my discovery that the world was not made in six days of twenty-four hours each. The real tragedy was the birth in me of doubt and uncertainty. Nothing was ever again to be final. Always I was to ask myself when confronted with a problem, a system, a scheme, a code, a leader, "How can I accept without knowing more?" The quest of the truth had been born in me— the most tragic and incomplete, as well as the most essential, of man's quests.

It was while groping my way, frightened like a lost child, I found a word to hold to—evolution. Things grew. What did they grow from? They all started somewhere. I was soon applying the idea. Nothing seemed to matter now, except to find the starting point of things and, having that, see why and how they grew into something else. How were you to go to work to find the start of life? With a microscope. And I soon was in the heat of my first intellectual passion, my first and greatest—that for the microscope. With a microscope I could perhaps get an answer to my mystification about the beginning of life, where it started; and then, I believed, I should find God again.

I was a practical person apparently, for I at once began to save my money and soon had enough to put into a small instrument. The house in Titusville, like many of its period, had a tower room, a steep staircase running up to it. This room was surrounded on three sides with big double windows. I begged to have it for my own. Here I was allowed to set up shop; here I had my desk, my papers, and my microscope; here I was alone with my problems. That little microscope had a good deal to do with my determination to go to college. If I was to become a microscopist—I had already adopted that word—I must study, get an education.

This determination of mine to get an education, go to college, was chiefly due, no doubt, to the active crusade going on in those days for what we called woman's rights. Ours was a yeasty time, the ferment reaching into every relation of life, attacking and remodeling every tradition, every philosophy. As my father was hard hit by the attack on his conception of individualism in a democracy—freedom with strictest consideration for the rights and needs of others—as I was struggling with all the handicaps of my ignorance, with the nature of life, a search for God, so my mother was facing a little reluctantly a readjustment of her status in the home and in society. She had grown up with the Woman's Rights movement. Had she never married, I feel sure she would have sought to "vindicate her sex" by seeking a higher education, possibly a profession. The fight would have delighted her. If she had gone to Iowa she surely would have soon joined the agitation led there in the late fifties by Amelia Bloomer, the inventor of the practical and ugly costume which still carries her name, the real founder of dress reform. We owe it to Amelia Bloomer that we can without public ridicule wear short skirts and stout boots, be as sensible as our feminine natures permit—which is not saying much for us when it comes to fashions. But my mother found herself a pioneer in the Oil Region, confronted by the sternest of problems which were to be settled only by immediate individual effort and good will.

The move to Titusville, however, soon put my mother in touch with the crusade for equal political rights which was taking the place of the earlier movement for woman's rights. The Civil War had slowed up that agitation; indeed, many of its best talking points had been conceded and were slowly going into practice. Most of the militants had thrown themselves into war work and, after the war, into the campaign for negro suffrage; but the passing of the Fourteenth Amendment in 1868, for the first time introducing the word "male" into the Constitution, aroused a sense of outrage, not only in the advocates of equal rights but in many women who had not approved of previous agitations. Elizabeth Cady Stanton and Susan B. Anthony, the greatest of the early leaders, failing to keep the humiliating distinction out

of the Amendment, began a tremendous national crusade for
woman's suffrage. They marshaled a group of splendid women
and undertook an intensive campaign meant to reach every woman
in the country. It reached us in Titusville, even reached our home
where my father and mother, always hospitable to crusaders,
opened their doors to them. I remember best Mary Livermore
and Frances Willard—not that either touched me, saw me; of
this neglect I was acutely conscious. I noted, too, that the men
we entertained did notice me, talked to me as a person—not
merely as a possible member of a society they were promoting.
There was Neal Dow—father by this time was a prohibitionist—
who let me show him our Dante with Gustave Doré's pictures.
Men were nicer than women to me, I mentally noted.

As the struggle for equal rights grew in heat I became aware
that it was far from a united struggle, that as a matter of fact
leaders and followers were spending almost as much time disap-
proving of one another's methods as fighting for their cause. The
friction came largely from the propensity of Mrs. Stanton and
Miss Anthony to form alliances shocking to many of their oldest
and wisest friends. Before the war they had, rather recklessly
from a political point of view, supported easier divorce. As one
of their friends wrote them, they had in so doing broken the heart
of the portly *Evening Post* and nearly driven the *Tribune* to the
grave. Time had not cooled their ardor for strange bedfellows.
They made an alliance now of which I heard no little talk by my
mother and her friends; it was with the two most notorious women
in the eye of the public at the moment. "Hussies," conservative
circles in Titusville, Pennsylvania, called them—Victoria Woodhull and Tennessee Claflin.

It was not difficult for even a girl of fifteen to pick up some
idea of what these women were, so well did they advertise themselves, and so delightedly did the press back them up in their
doings. Beginning their careers as clairvoyants, they had developed professionally their undoubted powers until they were in

the sixties—the two best known and best paid trance-physicians of their day. Victoria claimed to have raised a child from the dead, and Tennessee, the harder worker of the two, made enough money to keep thirty-five relations in comfort. "If I am a humbug sometimes, look at the dead beats I have to support," was her answer to those who accused her of abusing her talents. Both women frankly advocated free love, and so it was believed quite as frankly practiced it.

With this equipment they entered Wall Street in the eighteen-sixties as consultants. The "lady brokers," they were called. They quickly built up a profitable business. Old Commodore Vanderbilt was so tickled by their combination of beauty and effrontery, talents and ambitions, that he is said to have proposed marriage to Victoria. He was more valuable as a friend. She kept his picture on the wall of the salon where she received her clients, and under it the framed motto, "Simply to thy cross I cling."

In 1870 Victoria Woodhull announced herself as a candidate for President in 1872. So successful was she in attracting and holding big audiences, and so brilliantly did she present the arguments for equal rights, that Mrs. Stanton and Miss Anthony threw scruples to the wind and took her into their camp—from which promptly there was a considerable exodus of scandalized ladies. Not only did Victoria win the countenance of these two great leaders, but she involved them in the Beecher-Tilton scandal, which for months she worked steadily to force before the public.

The reverberations of the conflict inside the suffrage party, together with what I picked up about the Beecher trial (I read the testimony word by word in our newspapers), did not increase my regard for my sex. They did not seem to substantiate what I heard about the subjection of women, nor did what I observed nearer home convince me. Subjection seemed to me fairly divided. That is all: I saw there were "henpecked men," as well as "downtrodden women." The chief unfairness which I recognized was in the handling of household expenses. Women who must do the spending were obliged to ask for money or depend on charging. My mother had not been trained to live on as generous a scale as was now possible, but my father never said, "We have so much and no more to spend." They worked often at cross purposes. So I gathered as I listened to intimate talks between women, listened to suffrage speakers, read the literature; so did many American husbands and wives. I felt no restraint myself, for I always had at least a little money and I, too, could charge. This foolish practice led me into funny expenditures.

I had no sense of the appropriate in clothes. Often I had an ardent desire for something fitted only for grown-ups, and I always had a keen ambition to fit myself out for occasions. Some time in the early seventies Clara Louise Kellogg came to town. My father and mother were in the West, but they had arranged that I was to hear her. It seemed as if some kind of regalia was necessary, so I charged a wide pink sash and a pair of yellow kid gloves.

Out of the agitation for rights as it came to me, two rights that were worth going after quite definitely segregated themselves: the right to an education, and the right to earn my living —education and economic independence.

The older I grew, the more determined I became to be independent. I saw only one way—teach; but if I was to teach I must fit myself, go to college. My father and mother agreed. I had a clear notion of what I wanted to teach—natural science, particularly the microscope, for I was to be a biologist. I made my choice—Cornell, first opened to women in 1872; but at the moment when the steps to enter Cornell were to be taken, there appeared in the household as an over-Sunday guest the president of a small college in our neighborhood, only thirty miles away, Allegheny. Among the patrons of that college was the Methodist organization known as the Erie Conference, to which the Titusville church belonged. I had heard of it annually when a representative appeared in our pulpit, told its story and asked for support. The president, Dr. Lucius Bugbee, was a delightful and entertaining guest and, learning that I was headed Cornellward, adroitly painted the advantages of Allegheny. It was near home; it was a ward of our church. It had responded to the cry of women for educational opportunity and had opened its doors before the institution I had chosen.

Was not here an opportunity for a serious young woman interested in the advancement of her sex? Had I not a responsibility in the matter? If the few colleges that had opened their doors were to keep them open, if others were to imitate their example, two things were essential: women must prove they wanted a college education by supporting those in their vicinity; and they must prove by their scholarship what many doubted—that they had minds as capable of development as young men. Allegheny had not a large territory to draw from. I must be a pioneer.

As a matter of fact the only responsibility I had felt and assumed in going to college was entirely selfish and personal. But the sense of responsibility was not lacking nor dormant in me. It was one of the few things I had found out about myself in the shanty on the flats when I was six years old and there was a new baby in the family.

The woman looking after my mother had said, "Now you are old enough to make a cup of tea and take it to her." I think, in all my life since, nothing has seemed more important, more wonderful to me than this being called upon by an elder to do something for mother, be responsible for it. I can feel that cup in my hand as I cautiously took it to the bed, and can see my mother's touching smile as she thanked me. Perhaps there came to her a realization that this rebelling, experimenting child might one day become a partner in the struggle for life so serious for her at the moment, always to be more or less serious.

But to return to Dr. Bugbee and his argument; before he left

the house I had agreed to enter Allegheny in the fall of 1876.
And that I did.

What did I take with me? Well, I took what from my earliest
years I had been told was necessary to everyone—a Purpose,
always spelled with a capital. I had an outline of the route which
would lead to its realization. Making outlines of what was in my
mind was the one and only fruit that I had gathered so far from
long terms of struggle over grammar, rhetoric, composition.
Outlines which held together, I had discovered, cleared my mind,
gave it something to follow. I outlined all my plans as I had
diagramed sentences. It was not a poor beginning for one who
eventually, and by accident rather than by intention, was to earn
her living by writing—the core of which must be sound structure.

One thing by choice left out of the plan I carried from high
school was marriage. I would never marry. It would interfere
with my plan; it would fetter my freedom. I didn't quite know
what Freedom meant; certainly I was far from realizing that it
exists only in the spirit, never in human relations, never in human
activities—that the road to it is as often as not what men call
bondage. But above all I must be free; and to be free I must be
a spinster. When I was fourteen I was praying God on my knees
to keep me from marriage. I suspect that it was only an echo of
the strident feminine cry filling the air at that moment, the cry
that woman was a slave in a man-made world. By the time I was
ready to go to college I had changed my prayer for freedom to
a will to freedom. Such was the baggage I carried to college,
where I was soon to find several things I had not counted on.

3

A COEDUCATIONAL COLLEGE
OF THE EIGHTIES

WHEN I entered Allegheny College in the fall of 1876 I made my first contact with the past. I had been born and reared a pioneer; I knew only the beginning of things, the making of a home in a wilderness, the making of an industry from the ground up. I had seen the hardships of beginnings, the joy of realization, the attacks that success must expect; but of things with a past, things that had made themselves permanent, I knew nothing. It struck me full in the face now, for this was an old college as things west of the Alleghenies were reckoned—an old college in an old town. Here was history, and I had never met it before to recognize it.

The town lay in the valley of a tributary of the Allegheny River—French Creek. Its oldest tradition after the tales of Indians was that George Washington once drank from a spring on the edge of the campus. Certainly he passed that way in 1753 when he came up the river valley from Fort Duquesne (Pittsburgh), following the route which led to Fort Le Bœuf near Lake Erie. He comments in his diary, published the year after his trip, on the extensive rich meadows through which he had passed, one of which "I believe was nearly four miles in length and considerable wider in some places." To this particular "rich meadow" a few years later came one David Mead and laid out a town and sold land. Here soon after came the representative of the Holland Land Company, colonizers of first quality. Good men came, distinguished names in Pennsylvania's history, and they wanted a college. The answer to their wish came in 1815 when one of the most scholarly men of that day, Timothy Alden of Massachusetts, heard their call and, picking up all his worldly possessions, made the two months' trip by coach and boat to the settlement called Meadville.

Timothy Alden, like many of his fellows, was fired by a deep belief that through Christian democracy alone could men arrive at the better world towards which he, scholar that he was, knew they had been groping from their earliest beginnings. But men could only come to an understanding of their individual and collective responsibilities to democracy through education. Therefore, as men spread westward he and others like him must follow them with education.

But once in Meadville how little he found with which to carry out his project—a log courthouse for a schoolhouse, and little or no money, though of what they had men gave freely. Now Timothy Alden knew that throughout the East were men of scholarly traditions convinced as was he that democracy would work only if men were trained to understanding and sacrifice. He believed that they would help his Western venture. In 1816 he went East to find out. He was not wrong in thinking there would be sympathy for the young college. Out of their meager store men gave—this one, fifty cents; that one, five dollars; few, more—and men gave books, one, two, five. The list of donors now in the college archives shows many of the best known names of the day—Lowell, Adams, Tucker, Parkman, Channing in Boston and twenty-nine fine New York names. Friends were made for Allegheny in every town and city where its brave story was told. Timothy Alden came back with $361 in money and with books, more needed than money, estimated to be worth $1,642.26.

From that time he kept the undertaking steadily before the East, promoted it by every method known to the times. A great response to his passionate effort came in 1819 when the college world of the East was shocked by learning that William Bentley of Salem, Massachusetts, had left his famous collection of "clas-

sical and theological books, dictionaries, lexicons and Bibles"
to a college in the wilderness of northwestern Pennsylvania, a
college without a home, still doing its work in a log courthouse.
That gift, long a bitter drop in the cup of Harvard, it is said,
made a home of its own necessity for Allegheny, and in 1820 the
corner stone of Bentley Hall, named for the donor, was laid.
It took many years to complete it; but, when done on the lines
Timothy Alden had himself laid down, it was one of the most
beautiful buildings in the country. Today it easily stands after
Independence Hall as the most perfect piece of Colonial architecture in the state of Pennsylvania. For me Bentley Hall was
an extraordinary experience. It was the first really beautiful
building I had seen, a revelation, something I had never
dreamed of.

Fifty-six years had passed since the corner stone of Bentley
Hall was laid, and not one of them without disappointments
and sacrifices. More than once it had seemed as if the brave attempt must fail. Two buildings only had been added in these
years: Culver Hall, a frame boarding house for men; Ruter
Hall, a grim uncompromising three-story rectangular brick
structure, fifty by ninety feet in size, a perfect reflection of the
straitened period to which it belonged. The "Factory" was our
slighting name for Ruter Hall, but in this stern structure I was
to find a second deep satisfaction—the library; in a room on
the top floor, ninety feet long and at least sixteen in height was
housed not only the splendid Bentley collection, but one even
more valuable, that of Judge James Winthrop of Cambridge,
Massachusetts, rare volumes from the great presses of Europe,
three tons of books brought overland in wagons by Boston team-
sters in 1822. They lined the great unbroken inside wall, as well
as every space between openings. From the window seats one
looked out on the town in the valley, its roofs and towers half
hidden by a wealth of trees, and beyond to a circle of round-
breasted hills. Before I left Allegheny I had found a very pre-

cious thing in that severe room—the companionship there is in the silent presence of books.

Allegheny did not of course admit women at the start; but the ferment caused by the passing of the Fourteenth Amendment making it clear that only men were to be regarded as citizens stirred the Allegheny constituents mightily. Its chief patron, as I have said, was the Methodist Church. Now the Methodist Church was a militant reformer. The greatest of its bishops, Matthew Simpson, had backed Mrs. Stanton and Miss Anthony and their colleagues at every step. Leaders among Methodist women had been abolitionists, aggressive temperance advocates, and now they became militant suffragists. Their influence began to tell. In 1870, with misgivings in not a few minds the admission of women was voted. This was the same year that the University of Michigan opened its doors to women, and two years before Cornell. In the six years before I entered ten women had graduated. When I came there were but two seniors, two juniors, no sophomores. I was a lone freshman in a class of forty hostile or indifferent boys. The friendly and facetious professor charged with the care of the "young ladies" put it that I was "Lost in the Wilderness of Boy."

From the first I was dimly conscious that I was an invader, that there was abroad a spirit of masculinity challenging my right to be there, and there were taboos not to be disregarded. My first experience was that of which Virginia Woolf speaks so bitterly in "A Room of One's Own"—the closing of the college green to her at Oxbridge. Nearly fifty years before her book was written I was having at Allegheny the same experience.

The sloping green of the campus below Bentley Hall was inviting. Between classes I made my way one day to a seat under a tree only to hear a horrified call from the walk above, "Come back, come back quick." An imperative summons from an upperclass woman. "You mustn't go on that side of the walk, only men go there."

It was not so simple to find a spot where you could go and be comfortable. If Bentley Hall, where all the classes were held, was a beautiful piece of architecture, its interior could hardly have been more severe. The rooms were heated with potbellied cast-iron stoves, seated with the hardest wooden chairs, lighted by kerosene lamps. In winter (and the winters were long) the snow tracked in kept the floors wet and cold. Often one wore a muffler in chapel. But of all that I was unheeding. My pioneer childhood served me well. Moreover, I realized at the start that I had found what I had come to college for, direction in the only field in which I was interested—science. I found it in a way that I doubt if Cornell could have given me at the moment, shy and immature as I was: the warming and contagious enthusiasm of a great natural teacher, one who had an ardent passion for those things which had stirred me and a wide knowledge which he fed by constant study and travel—Jeremiah Tingley, the head of Allegheny's department of natural science.

Professor Tingley was then a man of fifty, sparkling, alive, informal. Three years before, he had been one of the fifty chosen from many hundred applicants to spend the summer with Louis Agassiz on the island of Penikese in Buzzards Bay. Agassiz had planned with enthusiasm for the Penikese Summer School, and for those privileged to enter who could understand and appreciate it was an unforgettable experience; certainly it was for Jeremiah Tingley. He carried there Agassiz's faith in observation and classification, as well as his reverence for Nature and all her ways. For both men the material world was but the cover of the spirit. Professor Tingley would quote Agassiz sometimes: "Nature always brings us back to absolute truth whenever we wander."

This fervent faith had a profound and quieting effect on my religious tumult. I learned a new word: Pantheism. Being still in that early stage of development where there must be a definite word by which to classify oneself, I began to call myself a pantheist—and I had a creed which I repeated more often than the creed I had learned in childhood:

> Flower in the crannied wall,
> I pluck you out of the crannies,
> I hold you here, root and all, in my hand
> Little flower—but *if* I could understand
> What you are, root and all, and all in all,
> I should know what God and man is.

It reassured me; I was on the right track, for was I not going to find out with the microscope what God and man are?

Professor Tingley's method for those he found really interested in scientific study was to encourage them to look outside the book. There was where I had already found my joy; but I suspected it was the willful way, that the true way was to know first what was in the books. Here in Professor Tingley's classes you were ordered to go and see for yourself. He used to tell us a story of his first experience at Penikese. A stone was put before him, a round water-washed stone, on which he was to report. He looked at the stone, turned it over. There was nothing to report. "It is not the outside, it is the inside of things that matters," said Agassiz. And in the laboratory that became our watchword: Look inside.

Discovering my interest in the microscope, I was not only allowed, I was urged to use the magnificent binocular belonging to the college, was given the free run of the laboratory along with a few as crazy as myself. Here my most exciting adventure apart from what I found under the microscope came from actually having my hands on a "missing link." Evolution, to which I was clinging determinedly, could only be established, I realized, by discovering the links. There was one peculiar to the waters in our valley, the *Memopomo Alleghaniensis,* a creature twelve to fifteen inches long with gills and one lung, able to live in the water or mud as circumstances required. The mud puppy, as it was appropriately called, was slimy, loathsome, but I worked over it with awe. Was I not being admitted into the very workshop of Nature herself—seeing how she did it?

Professor Tingley took his little group of laboratory devotees into his home circle. He and Mrs. Tingley were housed in a wing of Bentley Hall—big rooms built for classrooms. They had no children, and in the years of their study and travel they had gathered about them things of beauty and interest. The atmosphere of those rooms was something quite new and wonderful to me. It was my first look into the intimate social life possible to people interested above all in ideas, beauty, music, and glad to work hard and live simply to devote themselves to their cultivation.

And such good talks! Much of it was concerned with fresh scientific thought, the inventions and discoveries which were stirring the world. An omnivorous reader of the scientific publications of Europe and America, Professor Tingley kept us excited, not only by what had been done but what it might mean. There was the telephone. I had been in college but a few weeks when my father asked me to go with him and my brother to the Centennial Exposition of 1876. President Bugbee, who had made me his special care for a time—Mrs. Bugbee even taking me into their home until an appropriate boarding place could be found— was heartily in favor of my going. I went, and when I returned Professor Tingley's first question was, "Did you see the telephone?" I hadn't even heard of it. Two exhibits only of that exposition made a deep enough impression on me to last until today—my first Corot and the Corliss engine. Professor Tingley was greatly disappointed, and I did not understand why until a few weeks later he called the student body together to explain and illustrate the telephone by a homemade instrument. "You'll talk to your homes from these rooms one day," he told us. "New York will talk to Boston." He didn't suggest Chicago. "Dreamer," the boys said. "Dreamer," my father and his Titusville friends

said a little later when an agent of the Bell Associates, the first
company to attempt putting the new invention within reach of
everybody, came to town selling stock. How often I heard it said
later, "If I'd bought that telephone stock!"

Years later I told Alexander Graham Bell of my introduction
to the telephone. "Nobody," he said, "can estimate what the
teachers of science in colleges and high schools were doing in those
days not only to spread knowledge of the telephone but to stir
youth to tackle the possibilities in electricity."

What I best remember is not the telephone but Professor Tingley's amazing enthusiasm for the telephone. This revelation of enthusiasm, its power to warm and illuminate was one of the finest
and most lasting of my college experiences. The people I had
known, teachers, preachers, doctors, business men, all went
through their day's work either with a stubborn, often sullen
determination to do their whole duty, or with an undercurrent of
uneasiness, if they found pleasure in duty. They seemed to me
to feel that they were not really working if they were not demonstrating the Puritan teaching that labor is a curse. It had never
seemed so to me, but I did not dare gloat over it. And here was a
teacher who did gloat over his job in all its ramifications. Moreover, he did his best to stir you to share his joy.

But while I looked on what I was learning in the laboratory as
what I had come to college for, while each term stiffened my
ambition to go deeper and deeper into the search for the original
atom, science was not all that interested me. The faculty, if
small, was made up largely of seasoned men with a perspective
on life. There was not only deep seriousness but humor and toler-
ance, and since we were so small a college the student was close
enough to discover them, to find out what each man as an individual had to offer him. As I learned the power of enthusiasm
from Jeremiah Tingley, I learned from another man of that
faculty the value of contempt. Holding the chair of Latin was
one of the few able teachers I have known, George Haskins,

father of that sound scholar of international repute, the late
Charles Homer Haskins, at the time of his death Professor
Emeritus of Medieval History at Harvard University. What deep
satisfaction his career gave his father, himself a man of many
disappointments!

George Haskins labored, usually in vain, to arouse us to the
choiceness of Latinity, the meaning of Rome's rise and fall, the
quality of her men, the relation of that life to ours. Professor
Haskins' contempt for our lack of understanding, for our slack
preparation, was something utterly new to me in human inter-
course. The people I knew with rare exceptions spared one another's feelings. I had come to consider that a superior grace;
you must be kind if you lied for it. But here was a man who
turned on indifference, neglect, carelessness with bitter and caustic contempt, left his victim seared. The sufferers lived to say,
some of them at least: "I deserved it. He was never unjust, never
inappreciative of effort."

"Cherish your contempts," Henry James advised me once
when he had drawn from me a confession of the conflict between
my natural dislike of saying anything unpleasant about anybody
and the necessity of being cruel, even brutal, if the work I had
undertaken was to be truthful in fact and logic. "Cherish your
contempts," said Mr. James, "and strength to your elbow." If
it had not been for George Haskins I doubt if I should have
known what he meant; nor should I ever have become the steady,
rather dogged worker I am. The contempt for shiftlessness which
he inspired in me aroused a determination to be a good worker.
I began to train my mind to go at its task regularly, keep hours,
study whether I liked a thing or not. I forced myself not to waste
time, not to loaf, not to give up before I finished. If I failed at
any point in this discipline I suffered a certain mental and
spiritual malaise, a dissatisfaction with myself hard to live with.

In spite of my painful efforts to make a regular worker out
of myself, life at college was lightened by my discovery of the

Boy. Incredible as it seems to me now, I had come to college at eighteen without ever having dared to look fully into the face of any boy of my age. To be sure, I had from childhood nourished secret passions for a succession of older individuals whom I never saw except at a distance, and with whom I never exchanged a word. My brother and his friends, my father and his friends—these I had always hobnobbed with; but those who naturally should have been my companions, I shunned. I was unable to take part in those things that brought the young people of the day together. I did not dance—the Methodist discipline forbade it. I was incredibly stupid and uninterested in games—still am. I had no easy companionable ways, was too shy to attempt them. I had my delights; the hills which I ran, the long drives behind our little white horse, the family doings, the reading of French regularly with my splendid friend Annette Grumbine, still living, still as she was then a vitalizing influence in the town and state for all that makes for a higher social life—these things and my precious evening walks, the full length of Titusville's main street, alone or with some girl friend while we talked of things deepest in our minds.

But in all this there was no boy. I was not long in discovering him when I reached Allegheny, for the taboos I encountered at the start soon yielded under the increased number of women, women in college, in special courses, in the Preparatory Department. They swept masculine prohibitions out of the way—took possession, made a different kind of institution of it, less scholastic, gayer, easier-going. The daily association in the classrooms, the contacts and appraisements, the mutual interests and intimacies, the continual procession of college doings which in the nature of things required that you should have a masculine attendant, soon put me at my ease. I was learning, learning fast, but the learning carried its pains. I still had a stiff-necked determination to be free. To avoid entangling alliances of all kinds had become an obsession with me. I was slow in laying it aside when I began to take part in the social life of the college, and because of it I was guilty of one performance which was properly enough a scandal to the young men.

There were several men's fraternities in the college; most of the boys belonged to one or another. It was an ambition of the fraternities to put their pins on acceptable town and college girls. You were a Delta girl, or a Gamma girl or a Phi Psi girl. I resented this effort to tag me. Why should I not have friends in all the fraternities? And I had; I accumulated four pins and then, one disastrous morning, went into chapel with the four pins on my coat. There were a few months after that when, if it had not been for two or three non-Frat friends, I should have been a social outcast.

I spent four years in Allegheny College. Measured by what I got instead of by what I did not get and was obliged to learn later, I regard them as among the most profitable of my life. I find often that men and women accuse the college of not opening their minds to life as it is in the world. For a mind sufficiently developed to see "life as it is" I cannot conceive a more fruitful field than the classics. If I had been sufficiently mature I could have learned from George Haskins' teachings of Cicero and Tacitus and Livy more than I know today about the ways of men in their personal and their national relations, more of the causes of war, of the weaknesses of governments. But I was not ready for it. Life is the great teacher, and she leads us step by step. It is not the fault of the human teacher that his pupil must learn to climb by climbing.

It was in the spring of 1880 that I graduated. I still carried the same baggage with which I had entered—a little heavier to be sure, a little better packed, a little better adapted to the "Purpose." The only difference which threatened disturbance was that I had added an item which I had refused to bring with me in 1876. Then I was not willing to believe I would ever marry— now I thought possibly some day I might; but the item was not heavy, not heavy enough at least to prevent my rejoicing over the fact that I was graduating with a job. I had signed a contract with an institution of which I had never heard until the negotiations leading to it opened. After frequent communications with the faculty a representative of the Poland Union Seminary of Poland, Ohio, with some misgivings had employed me to serve as its Preceptress—$500 a year "and board yourself." I was jubilant. It meant economic independence—the first plank in my platform. I would use my leisure to work with the microscope; I would save my money; I would one day go abroad and study with some great biologist. I would never abandon my search for the beginning of life, the point where I expected to find God.

It was then with entire confidence in the future that I started out in August of 1880 for the town of Poland on the Western Reserve of Ohio, to begin what women were then talking of in more or less awed tones as a Career.

4

A START AND A RETREAT

IF I had been going on my honeymoon I should scarcely have been more expectant or more curious than I was in August of 1880 when I left home to take my first position: "Preceptress of Poland Union Seminary, Poland, Mahoning County, Ohio— $500.00 a year and board yourself"! Poland was not a long journey from my home—four or five hours.

I found the village delightful. It had the air of having been long in existence, as it had. Here there was no noise of railroads, no sign of the coal and steel and iron industries which encircled it but had never passed its boundaries. Here all people seemed to me to live tranquilly in roomy houses with pleasant yards or on near-by farms where there were fine horses and fat blooded sheep, and where planting and harvesting went ahead year in and year out in orderly fashion.

The chief and only industry of Poland was its seminary, now about thirty years old. It was a community enterprise started in 1848 by Mr. B. F. Lee, the financial agent who had hired me. Everybody in the village had subscribed to its endowment, practically every church had at one time or another been its patron. The long depression of the seventies had crippled its finances sadly; but times were better now, and the well-to-do Presbytery of Mahoning County had agreed to take it under its care. But I was soon to learn that Poland Union Seminary in spite of the patronage of the Presbytery lived on a narrow and worn shoestring. Moreover, I at once divined, kind as were those who were responsible for my being there, that I had been injected into a situation of which Mr. Lee had given me no hint strong enough to penetrate my inexperience. It was serious enough, as on the very day the school bell first rang for me the villagers began to let me know. Men and women would stop me on the street to say:

"So it's you that's taking Miss Blakeley's place. You have no idea how badly we feel about her resigning. I went to school to her, my father and mother went to school to her. I had hoped all my children would go to her. She was a wonderful teacher, a beautiful character. You look pretty young; you haven't had much experience, have you?"

I was not long in learning that the devotion of the community to Miss Blakeley was deserved. The village was right in honoring her, in mourning her. It no doubt felt a certain satisfaction in letting me know at the start it in no way regarded me as an adequate substitute. Its insistence was such that, before the end of my first fortnight, I was ready to resign.

My morale would hardly have been so quickly shaken if I had not at once discovered to my consternation that there was an important part of my duties which was in danger of proving too much for me. The worst of it was that it concerned the largest block of pupils in an institution where every pupil counted, where Mr. Lee regarded it as of vital importance that every pupil be given what he wanted. Here he advertised you could prepare for college, here you could have special advanced work in anything you wanted. And Mr. Lee was right if the seminary was to live as a cog in the country's educational wheel.

Somebody ought to write, perhaps somebody has written of the passing of this once valuable institution. It came before the college and the high school and for a time did the work of both; but when the high school began to prepare students for the college and the colleges added preparatory departments and at the same time offered special courses the seminary slowly realized that it must either go out of business or combine with one or another of its healthy growing rivals.

In a few places, as in Poland Village, the seminary was hanging on tenaciously, trying to demonstrate that it was still a better man than these new undertakings, these high schools, these colleges with their preparatory schools.

The faculty which was to make the demonstration at Poland was made up of three persons: in order of rank, the President, the Preceptress, her assistant. The acting President insisted on all the perquisites of his title. His chief duty he regarded as conducting the chapel with more or less grandiloquent remarks. When my assistant and I complained of too much work he would scowl and say that his executive duties made it impossible for him to take on more classes. The result was that I started out with two classes in each of four languages—Greek, Latin, French, and German, as well as classes in geology, botany, geometry, trigonometry. In addition there was my threatened Waterloo, the two largest classes in the school: one in what was called "verb grammar," the other, "percentage arithmetic"—so named from the points in the textbooks where the term's work began. From time immemorial these two classes had been conducted in the interests of the district schoolteachers of the territory. It was the custom for these teachers to spend one term a year in the seminary, where, regardless of the number of years they had been teaching, the number of times they had treated themselves to a period of study, they always (so I was told) insisted on their verb grammar and their percentage arithmetic. It was like a ritual. As they were the numerical backbone of the institution, there was nothing so important in the judgment of management as their satisfaction.

It was a killing schedule for one person, but I was so eager, so ridiculously willing, so excited, and also so fresh from college that I did not know it. Indeed, as I look back on it I think I did fairly well, all things considered. I should have had no great alarm about my success if it had not been for the grammar and the arithmetic. From the first day I realized I was on ground there which, once familiar, was now almost unintelligible. I could and did teach my geometry and "trig" with relish; I could and did pilot fairly advanced classes in four languages so that the pupils at least never discovered that in one of them I was far beyond my depth, and that in all of them I at times knew myself to be skating on thin ice; but these district schoolteachers, several of them older than I, were not to be deceived or bluffed. They had had experience—I had not; and like the villagers of Poland they proposed to make me realize that no college diploma could make up for inexperience. Experience in "percentage arithmetic" and "verb grammar" came from doing the same examples and diagraming and parsing the same sentences year after year and going back to teach them in their communities. Many of these examples were tricky. Many of the sentences were ambiguous. They had learned solutions for both, solutions which had the backing of tradition. I was soon terrified lest I be trapped, so scared I would wake up in the night in cold sweats. This was my state of mind when one day the most important man in the Village, Robert Walker, the local banker, stopped me on the street.

"Sis," he said—he was to always call me Sis—"Sis, you are following a fine teacher." I could have wept—the same old story. "But don't worry, what you must do is keep a stiff upper lip."

"Oh, thank you, sir," I said as I hurried on lest I cry in the street.

But that "keep a stiff upper lip," coming from the man it did, restored me; and I resolved, cost what it would, to find a way to master my district schoolteachers. True, it took me two months to discover the weak place in their armor. Finally I learned they were solving problems and parsing sentences not according to principles but according to answers they had learned. The reason they insisted on going over them year after year at the seminary was to keep the solutions in their memory. I had no skill in solving puzzles, but I did know something about the principles and determined to try them on problems and sentences that were not in their books or any books to which they had access.

And so one day, luckily for me before they had a chance to demonstrate my incapacity as two or three of them I am confident were expecting to do, I casually put on the board two or three rather tough examples from outside arithmetics, two or three not simple sentences from grammars I felt sure they had never seen. I always recall with satisfaction the perplexity with which the two or three young men I most feared looked at what I had set for them, their injured protest. "But those examples are not in our books." "What difference does that make? The only important thing is that you know the principles. If you can't apply them, why learn them?"

After a month of excursions into territory unfamiliar to them I had them humbled and slowly grasping certain new ideas. I knew I was regarded with respect. It was the one conquest in the two years I spent as the Preceptress of the Poland Union Seminary of which I was proud.

Before these two years were up Mr. Lee must have realized he would never get from me the help he needed in his ambition to preserve the school as a seminary, that I would never become another Miss Blakeley. He wanted some one ambitious to make teaching a life work. I was not. Teaching was a mere stepping-stone in my plan of life, and at Poland Union Seminary it had proved a slippery stone. From the time I bounded out of bed in the morning—for in those days I did bound out of bed—until I dropped into it at an early hour, dead tired, I had no time for my microscope. It had become dusty on the table, but the passion for it and what it might reveal was still strong in me. My confidence that I could save money to continue my studies on five hundred dollars a year had proved illusory. I found myself coming out short, obliged to borrow from my father. There came to be a mutual, if unspoken, agreement between Mr. Lee and me that I should resign. Neither of us was getting what he had hoped, and so at the end of the second year, June, 1882, I gave up teaching as a stepping-stone.

So far as I could then see or did see for a long time, this first effort at an independent self-directing life was an interlude which had no relation to what I wanted at the time to do or what, as it turned out, I did do.

The most lasting impressions and experiences in this Poland interlude had little or nothing to do with my work in the seminary. They came from the friendships I formed while that work went on, centering in the family of the understanding gentleman who had at the outset stopped me on the street to say, "Keep a stiff upper lip."

I was soon to realize that this shrewd bit of advice was instigated by his daughter Clara, who was to become and who remains one of my dearest friends. Indeed, it was due to her understanding and affection that my two years in Poland, quite apart from the professional disappointment in them, were the gayest, most interesting, and in many ways the happiest of my life up to that time.

Clara Walker, or "Dot," as high and low in and about Poland called her, was a fine example of the out-of-door girl of the eighties, the girl who had revolted against lacing, high heels, long skirts, and substituted for them an admirable uniform of independence—tailor-made coat and skirt, high-neck shirtwaist with four-in-hand tie, flat heels. This outfit suited Clara Walker's sturdy figure, her vigorous and free movement. Her eyes suited her costume, for they were grey, direct, merry, looking unwaveringly on everybody and everything.

Dot was close-mouthed, but when she sensed possible unfairness in a situation which interested or concerned her she had her own wordless way of dealing with it. It was she who realized the determination of the villagers of Poland to make me feel that I never could fill Miss Blakeley's place to their satisfaction. She was loyal as they to the old teacher, but she wanted me to have my chance and, the first week of school, announced herself my champion by appearing at the door of the seminary as I was making my weary way out at the end of the day.

"Wouldn't you like to take a drive?" she said.

And there stood her smart turnout. What an escape from verb grammar and percentage arithmetic and my growing inferiority complex! From that time she never lagged in her determination to help me conquer my problem by taking me away from it. She apparently took real pleasure in showing me the country. Never a week that we did not go somewhere: Into town for the theater—the first time I saw Mary Anderson, then the most be- loved actress as well as the most beautiful woman in the country, was in Youngstown in "Pygmalion"; to big farms with great flocks of blooded sheep and horses and ponies; to coal mines and iron mills; to little old towns and run-down settlements skipped, like Poland, by the invasion of industry.

Clara peopled all these various places with the unadorned realistic tales of living and dead men and women. She had been born and had grown up in Mahoning County. She had a widely scattered family connection, but most important was her gen- uine interest in all human beings and theirs in her. She was a perfect listener, never prying. People liked to talk to her; she never forgot, related things, judged shrewdly and kindly, with the result that she had in her mind a map of the human life of the country, quite as reliable as a road map—a map in warm humorous colors.

Years later I realized that in those two years in Poland I had had under my eyes a vivid picture of what happens to the farmer, his home, his town, his children when industry invades his land.

This Mahoning country had been so rich, so apparently stable. The men and women so loved what they and their forebears had done that they yielded slowly to the coal miner and the mill man, but they were giving way in the eighties. The furnace was in the back yard of the fine old houses with their ample barns; and the shaft of the coal mine, in the richest meadows. The effort to reconcile the two was making, but industry was conquering: the destruction of beauty, the breaking down of standards of conduct, the growth of the love of money for money's sake, the grist of social problems facing the countryside from the inflow of foreigners and the instability of work—all this was written for him who could read. I could not read then, but I gathered a few impressions which I realize now helped shape my future interests and thinking.

It was on these long drives I first learned that not cities alone but all communities have dregs, slums. Strange that it should be in such a place as Poland, but here it was—a disreputable fringe where a group of men and women had long been living together with or without marriage. You heard strange tales of incest and lust, of complete moral and social irresponsibility, and they were having a scandalously jolly time of it. Why I was not more shocked, I do not know; probably because incest and lust were almost unknown words to me in those days.

And there were indelible impressions of the industrial world. When we drove into Youngstown, ten miles away, we passed between iron furnaces lying along the Mahoning River. After the long depression of the seventies they were again busy, and into the valley were coming hundreds and hundreds of foreigners brought from Europe by the news that there was once again work in the United States. It was in passing through the very heart of this furnace district one night returning from the theater that I first learned of the terrible dangers that lie in the smelting of ore. A furnace had burst; men had been trapped by the molten metal, and their charred remains were being carried across the road. Unforgettable horror.

And it was on one of these chance drives that I first saw what women can do in moments of frenzied protest against situations which they cannot control, first had my faith challenged in the

universally peaceful nature of my sex. I learned the meaning of
Maenads, Furies, as we came upon a maddened, threatening
crowd rushing towards the offices of the mills which had been
shut down without warning. It was led by big robust shrieking
women, their hair flying, their clothes disheveled. It was a look
into a world of which I knew nothing, but like the charred bodies
carried across the road as I rode from the theater it was an
unforgettable thing.

There were other introductions to the industrial world less horrifying. It was while in Poland that I first went into a coal mine—
a deep old-fashioned coal mine, a subsidiary to a farm. Under
some of these great farms with their blooded sheep, their fine
orchards and fields, their horses and ponies, coal had been found.
And it was being mined as a side line of the farm, a new kind
of crop. Near the head of the shaft were little houses for the
miners; and when dull times came and the mine was shut down
the farmers took on their care. There was a slaughter of an immense number of pigs, the putting down of barrels of pork, the
smoking of an incredible number of hams, the making of sausages
and headcheese.

"But why, why all this?" I asked.

"Oh," said my hostess, "mining is unstable business. When
there are long shutdowns we must help the miners out, see that
they have food."

The intimacy with Dot Walker gave me a home. Mrs. Walker
treated me as a daughter, and as for Robert Walker, who still
called me "Sis," he liked to have me around and to give me a
word of wise counsel now and then. It is because, in those months,
I learned him to be as kindly, shrewd, honest, simple-minded a
man as I have ever known that I must interrupt my narrative
long enough to put in here the story of one of the cruelest episodes of which I personally have known in the fifty years that I
have been a more or less understanding observer of our national

political life. The story is of Robert Walker and his one-time friend William McKinley, the twenty-fifth President of the United States.

When I became an intimate of the Walker household a person I often heard mentioned by its head was "the Major"—Major McKinley. Now it was not in 1880 a name unfamiliar to me. I had met it already at Allegheny College, where McKinley had once been a student. When the Civil War broke out he had joined the exodus of students who volunteered at the first call. He had come out of the war a major, studied law, and settled in Canton, Ohio, only sixty or seventy miles from Poland and in the same Congressional District. Here in 1876—the Mahoning district as it was called—had sent him to Congress. It was a matter of interest in Allegheny in my time to have one of its former students turn out a Congressman, its usual crop being teachers, preachers, and missionaries.

When I came to Poland I learned quickly that McKinley had lived there as a boy, had attended the seminary, and was their proudest example of "the boy who had made good." For four years he had been their Congressman. How they boasted of him! How solidly they voted for him!

I was not long in the Walker household before I sensed something more in Robert Walker than a citizen's pride in McKinley. It was that species of adoration a modest, honest-minded man often has for his leader—his leader who can do no wrong. I realized this when I first saw them together. The Major had come to our seminary commencement in June of 1881. I remember nothing at all of the speech he made, but the scene on the wide green in front of the village church after the exercises were over remains vivid. Scattered about were scores upon scores of girls and women in the frilly white gowns, the long white feather boas, the flower-trimmed hats, the gay parasols of the period; and in and out wound the Major, shaking hands, smiling, exchanging friendly greetings—all together at home, no back slapping, no kissing of babies. It was all so gentle, so like a picture of an English garden party where the politics are hidden beneath the finest of social veneers. And there was Robert Walker almost effulgent.

"Well, Sis," he asked me later, "what do you think of the Major?" A remark to which he expected no answer. What answer other than his could there be?

What I did not know then was that from the beginning of William McKinley's political career Robert Walker had been his chief—and for a time, I think, his only—financial backer. Beginning with his first campaign for Congress in 1875 Mr. Walker had advanced the Major $2,000 for expenses. He continued equal advances before each successive campaign, the understanding being that $1,000 a year was to be paid on the debt.

Along with this financial support went a staunch support of all the Major's political ideas. These ideas were those of the Republican party, and for men like Robert Walker the party was hallowed. It was "the party of Lincoln." Loyalty to Lincoln required loyalty to all that was directly or indirectly connected with him.

"Is Robert Lincoln a dude?" one of my Mahoning County acquaintances asked me years later when I told him that I had been talking with Robert Lincoln about his father.

"Is he a dude?"—by which he meant, as I took it, a kind of Ward McAllister.

"No, no, not that," I assured him.

"Well," he said reflectively, "even if he was a dude I would vote for him for President because he is Abraham Lincoln's son."

The chief test of loyalty to the party of Lincoln in Ohio was the degree of support given to the high protective tariff. William McKinley's support was devout and unqualified. He looked on a duty so low that it allowed importations as a species of treason. There was tin plate, for example.

The year that I went to Poland, 1880, McKinley first espoused a duty on tin plate. There was strong opposition among iron and steel manufacturers. They felt they already had all they could look after in Congress; but when they told this to McKinley his answer was that unless they supported tin plate he would not support their tariffs. Naturally they yielded, and tin plate was added to their list of protégés. McKinley felt so sure of ultimate victory for the duty that he evidently did not hesitate to advise his friends to get ready for its coming. At all events he encouraged Robert Walker, suggested to him in fact that he establish in Youngstown, Ohio, a stamping plant for the making of tinware, taking with him as partner his brother-in-law Andrew J. Duncan. As Andrew Duncan had no money to invest the Major gave to Mr. Walker a sheaf of signed notes to be used whenever he had need of money.

Now Robert Walker was not a manufacturer; he was a farmer and a good one—a coal operator—the banker of the Village of Poland and the surrounding country, but it was not in Robert Walker's nature to refuse to help the Major or his relatives in their ambitions, as he had already frequently proved. Indeed, at that time he was backing McKinley's brother Abner in a business venture which was soon to fail with loss of all he had put in. But Robert Walker's faith in McKinley's wisdom was such that he could not conceive of failure in anything he advised.

The plant was started in 1890. There could not have been a more unlucky moment to launch a new industry. The long depression of the nineties was beginning. Iron and steel were already seriously affected. Money was tight. Robert Walker found himself almost at once forced to use the Major's notes. He found only too soon that he had embarked on a hopeless undertaking, and in February of 1893 the works were closed.

Now at that moment Mark Hanna and his colleagues on the National Republican Committee were counting on William McKinley to win the Presidential election for them in 1896. The announcement that he was involved in the Walker failure to the tune of some one hundred thousand dollars, more than the combined fortune of himself and wife, was a cruel blow to their plan. McKinley was straightforward with them. He had signed the notes; he must give up politics, go back to the law, and pay his honest debts. But that could not be permitted. He was too important—one hundred thousand dollars was a small sum compared to what the Republican Committee expected from his election. The money was raised—not so quietly. It became necessary to explain how McKinley had become involved to this amount, and the explanation which McKinley's political friends put out was that he was a victim of "a man named Walker," as Mark Hanna's able biographer, Herbert Croly, calls him—a man whom he had trusted, and who had deceived him as to the amount of money he was raising on his notes. That is, the Republican committee deliberately put on Robert Walker the stigma of fraud, presented him to the public as a man who had betrayed confidence, and William McKinley never denied their presentation.

I have it from Robert Walker and from his daughter that no note of William McKinley was ever cashed without consulting him, and I believe them. Moreover, Andrew Duncan was in this enterprise and knew what was going on. It is an interesting fact that when my friend Clara Walker, who kept the accounts for the McKinleys and her father, went the morning after the announcement of the failure to her office in Youngstown, all her books had disappeared along with many papers which belonged to the firm.

I had been living abroad for two years when all this happened, but just before I had left America I had talked with Robert Walker about his venture—the money he was trying to raise on McKinley's notes. His confidence was untarnished.

"The Major knows, Sis. He will see this thing through. I'd do anything to back him."

And he did. When on my return I went to see my friends I

found they had given up practically everything, and Robert Walker himself was utterly broken by the ignominy heaped on him.

I begged him to give me his side of the story, let me tell it, told him I would never rest until I had an opportunity to put down what I knew of his long support of the Major's ambitions, what I believed of him as a man of unselfish integrity. He absolutely and finally refused. "Nobody would ever believe the Major could do anything wrong. I didn't."

But the Major had allowed the oldest and most loyal friend he had in his public life to be ruined not only in fortune but in reputation. Now that Robert Walker and Mrs. Walker are both gone and reviving the episode can no longer give them pain, it gives me a certain solace to put down the story as I believe it.

I was leaving Poland, but what was I to do? Today, with my passion for the microscope still undimmed, I would naturally seek a place in one of the many laboratories now open to women. Hundreds of women in the country bent on scientific research are now in industrial, institutional, or governmental laboratories, but in 1882 there was almost nothing of that kind open to women. The change is due, first, to the tremendous advance in scientific research; second, to the way women have proved their adaptability to laboratory work. No doubt the great majority of them are, like the majority of women in offices, laboratory wives, but we have inspired workers among them; probably, all things considered, as large a proportion as among men.

If things had been as they were in 1876, when I asked my father if he could put me through college and he had so cheerfully and happily, I think, agreed, I could have asked to be financed for higher studies. But things were not as they had been, and it would have been quite out of the question in 1882, when I decided that my first step towards economic independence was mistaken, for him to finance me—the country was coming into a new depression, that of '83 and '84, and the oil business was in a serious state for those who produced the oil.

But my home was open, wide open. I think it was this fact that is at the bottom of my strong conviction that the home is an essential link in the security of men and women. After one has gone forth on his own there frequently comes a time when he is shelterless as far as his own resources go. To have a refuge of which he is sure is one of the most heartening and stabilizing experiences in a life. If my Poland venture was a failure professionally it did not throw me on the street; I had a place to go and think it over. When I asked my mother if it would be all right for me to come home, her answer was what it always was to be in the future when I was obliged (more than once) to make the request: "Of course, that is your right." That is, my father and mother looked on the home they had created not as something belonging only to them—a place they had for their comfort and privacy, it was a place for all of those in the family procession who had no other place to go. In turn I saw that home opened to grandmother and grandfather, aunts and uncles, children and grandchildren, quite regardless of the extra burden it put on their resources, limitations on their space, the irritations and complications that are always bred by the injection of extra persons, however beloved and close, into a settled group.

It was in June, 1882, that I went back home, dusted my desk in the Tower room now shared with my sister's playhouse and dolls—set up my microscope and went to work on the Hydrozoa. But not for long.

5

A FRESH START—
A SECOND RETREAT

It was the custom of the Tarbell household to do its part in entertaining the Methodist ministers and presiding elders who periodically "filled the pulpit" of our church. In the winter after my return from the Poland venture we had a guest, an important local personage, Dr. Theodore L. Flood, a preacher who had retired from active ministry to take the editorship of a magazine called *The Chautauquan*, published in the town thirty miles from Titusville where I had so recently spent four years—Meadville, the home of Allegheny College.

On this visit Dr. Flood asked me to "help him out" for a month or two in a new department in his magazine. I was quick to accept, glad to be useful, for I had grown up with what was called the Chautauqua Movement. Indeed, it had been almost as much a part of my life as the oil business, and in its way it was as typically American. If we had a truer measure for values we would count it more important.

This Chautauqua Movement had grown out of a Methodist camp meeting held annually at Fair Point on the pleasant lake which in my childhood had been the terminus of our most ambitious all-day excursions. The president of this Association by 1870 was a man justly respected in all that part of the world for his good deeds, as well as his business acumen—Lewis Miller, a manufacturer of Akron, Ohio. Mr. Miller was to be known nationally as the father-in-law of Thomas Edison, but old-time Chautauquans put it the other way: "Edison is Lewis Miller's son-in-law." That was enough recommendation for Edison in their minds.

Lewis Miller's interest in Chautauqua went beyond the annual camp meeting. He saw the opportunity to build up there a summer home where parents could give their children healthy out-of-door amusement, protection from the evil ways of the unregenerate, and sound modern instruction in the Bible. Sympathy with this program induced a half-dozen families in the Titusville Methodist Church to join in the purchase of a lot on the outskirts of the grounds and start a Titusville settlement—a cottage with a mess hall and a few rooms—tents serving as sleeping quarters for extras. Father joined the colony soon after we moved to Titusville. We had a tent and a flat-bottomed boat.

Through the years I have been recalling, the years in high school, college, as Preceptress of Poland Union Seminary, part of all my summers had been spent at Chautauqua. Lewis Miller's laudable attempt to furnish attractive instruction in the Bible meant little or nothing to me at first; the flat-bottomed boat meant a great deal. But in 1874 something happened that dragged me away from the water. Lewis Miller had persuaded the most eminent advocate of the Sunday school in America, Dr. (afterwards Bishop) John H. Vincent, to select Fair Point as the home of a National Interdenominational Sunday School Institute which he and those who saw with him had been for some time planning. The first session of this new organization was held in 1874 under the name of the Chautauqua Assembly. It was recognized at once as a revolution upsetting the old order.

The most spectacular feature of the revolution was the Chautauqua platform, making as it did stirring, challenging contacts with current intellectual life. There one heard the great speakers of the day on all sorts of subjects. There fine concerts were given. It was the scientific lectures which caught me, particularly those of Dr. R. Ogden Doremus of New York. His platform experiments, in which two skillful women assisted, excited me as I had never been before. But what aroused me most were certain demonstrations with a magnificent microscope which they were giving in a little building at one side. Nothing in the world seemed to matter to me so much as to be able to talk with these women, to ask their advice about the work I was beginning with the little instrument bought with my own carefully saved money. Perhaps, oh, perhaps, I dreamed, they would let me look through the great beauty they handled so deftly, focus it, watch the life which went on in its field. So one day I hung around after the talk was over, slipped up to them, steeled myself to tell them that I was going to be a microscopist, begged them to give me a few lessons, advise me. The two ladies smiled down from their height, so plainly showing they thought me a country child with a queer behavior complex. "Quite impossible," they said, and turned back to their conference with Dr. Doremus.

Abashed, humiliated, but luckily too angry to cry I made my way back to my flat-bottomed boat. I would show them, I re-solved, clenching my fists!

It was years before I attempted again to get from a Chau-tauqua undertaking more than it was offering to the public at large. There were many of these undertakings. Dr. Vincent saw to that. A man better fitted by experience, conviction, and per-sonality to persuade a half-asleep, wholly satisfied community to accept a new order could not have been found in the America of the eighties. John Vincent was forty-two years old when he came to Chautauqua—handsome, confident, alert, energetic, radi-ating well-being. And he was an orator, and orating at Chau-tauqua made men tolerant even of heresy. He went about his business of organizing the work of the Assembly with a skill which commanded the admiration of everybody, even those hostile to the secularization of their beloved camp meeting. As a plat-form manager I never have known his equal. He had magnetism, but he knew when and how to turn it on; he was shrewd, cun-ning, pungent. He pricked bubbles, disciplined his audience. The Chautauqua audience came to be one of the best behaved out-of-door audiences in the country. The fact that we were out of doors had persuaded us that we were free to leave meetings if we were bored or suddenly remembered that we had left bread in the oven, or that the baby must have wakened. When the performance had been stopped once or twice to "give that lady a chance to go out without further disturbing the speaker" we learned to stay at home or to sit out the lecture.

There is only one word to describe what Lewis Miller and Dr. Vincent now did to Chautauqua, and that is "electrification." The community was made up mainly of hard-working men and women who wanted a vacation in surroundings where they would not "have to worry about the children." Certainly if high fences with gates through which you could not pass in or out after ten P.M.—never pass without your ticket, and not even with one on Sundays—if watchful guards and ten o'clock curfew, if a mass public opinion on the part of elders in support of these restrictions, could have suppressed all the mischief and lawlessness in the youth which swarmed Chautauqua, parents were right in sleeping tranquilly. As a matter of fact I never knew of any serious offenses, though there probably were many which I was still too much of a little girl to recognize. The worst mischief in which I personally assisted was playing tag up and down the relief model of Palestine, which skirted the lake as Palestine does the Mediterranean. It was spotted with plaster-of-Paris models of towns from Damascus to Bethsaida. I remember one rule of our game was that you could not be tagged if you straddled Jerusalem. The most serious vandalism of which I knew and in which I had no part was stealing Damascus or Nazareth or Tyre and carrying it away bodily.

Dr. Vincent did not change the restrictions, but he made them more endurable by the fresh interest he put into our lives. His effect on the community physically was immediate. It began to grow. The sound of the hammers nailing together the, for the most part, flimsy cottages was never still. The result was very like what Mark Twain found in the summer colony of Onteora in

the Catskills in its first year—"the partitions so thin you can hear
the women changing their minds."

Housekeeping improved. It had been as sketchy as the cottages—picnic housekeeping. You saw them at it, out in the rear
of their cottages, over an old wood stove or stone fireplace, the
men in their shirt sleeves, the women in big aprons, if not wrap-
pers. Planks on sawhorses for tables, mats (we had not learned
to say "doilies" yet), benches for seats. The natural practice of
bringing discarded furniture from home to furnish the cottages
led to the only distinctive piece of Chautauqua furniture I recall
—a long high-backed bench made from an old-fashioned four-
post bedstead. There were few garrets in all the country about
Chautauqua that did not harbor one or more such bedsteads.
They had been hidden away when families could afford the new-
styled quartered-oak or walnut bedroom suites. Some ingenious
mind had seen that by shortening the sidepieces of a four-poster
to seat width, using the headboard for a back, you had a commodious and, with cushions, a comfortable seat, even couch. They
were scattered all over the place.

With the coming of Dr. Vincent, Chautauqua rapidly developed a Promenade along the south end of the lake front. Cottages here were lathed and plastered, had wicker chairs on their
verandahs, and the residents soon were taking their meals at
the really stately Athenaeum Hotel. It was in this front row that
Dr. and Mrs. Vincent came to live in a tent, a tent de luxe with
a real house—so it looked to us—behind it.

Sometimes when we were properly dressed and shod we walked
past the hotel and the cottages housing our aristocrats, and if
by chance we saw Dr. or Mrs. Vincent or, best of all, the "Vincents' little boy"—George, we later learned his name to be—
why, then we boasted of it at the supper table as one might say
today, "I saw President Roosevelt, Mrs. Roosevelt, Sistie, Buz-
zie."

Dr. Vincent kept the place on its toes not only by the steady improvement of its platform, its amusements, in the quality of the people who came to teach and preach, but by a steady flow of new undertakings. He planned incessantly to stir not only our souls but our minds. We came to expect new ideas at each successive session and were never disappointed if sometimes a little bewildered. Behind all these various undertakings was the steadying hand of Lewis Miller, the silent partner, who had begun by spying out the land, establishing a community, laying the foundations for the Institution as it exists today—a center of democratic, Christian culture.

Dr. Vincent's masterpiece, as I always thought, came in 1878 when he laid before his Chautauquans a plan which had been long simmering in his never quiet mind. He did this in the finest of what we call inspirational talks that I ever heard—at least it stirred me so deeply that I have never forgotten the face of the orator nor, more important, the upturned faces of his hearers. He announced a scheme for a four-year course of home reading under the direction of the Chautauqua management adapted to men and women who had missed a college education, but who felt a deep desire for knowledge and were willing to adopt any practical plan which would give them a college outlook. It was to be called the Chautauqua Literary and Scientific Circle.

Now this does not sound exciting; but as a matter of fact it was deeply exciting, for the speaker was pouring out his heart. He had never had a college education; he had never ceased to feel the lack of what he believed it would have given him. He had struggled to make up for his loss by persistent, systematic daily reading and study. Establishing the habit as a boy, he had never abandoned it. It had given him deep satisfaction, supplied, he thought, the college outlook. He believed there were thousands of men and women in the United States, scores, possibly hundreds, in his audience, who had been forced, as he had been, to sacrifice their early ambitions for education. They had hidden the hunger in their hearts where at times it still gnawed. He was offering them the same help he had found, and confidently, glow-ingly, he outlined the course of home reading which Dr. John H. Finley has so aptly named the American Adult Education Pioneer.

The uplifted faces all about me told the story, particularly the faces of the women of thirty or more. Women of that genera-tion had had their natural desire for knowledge intensified by the Woman's Rights movement, in which the strongest plank had been a demand for the opportunity for higher education. These women were now beyond the day when they could go to college, but here was something which they saw intuitively was practical.

The immediacy of their response was in a degree accounted for by their devotion to Dr. Vincent. I suppose most of the women who frequented Chautauqua were more or less in love with him, the worship a man of overflowing sentiment receives from the benches, but most of his audience would have preferred to die rather than reveal their secret passion.

Well, it was a great emotional experience with large and imme-diate practical results, for, before the summer session was over, eight thousand people had joined the Chautauqua Literary and Scientific Circle.

They had joined, and they were buying the books chosen. The most important volume in that first year's course was Green's "Short History of the English People"—in my judgment the most important book save one that the Chautauqua Literary and Scientific Circle ever included, that exception being W. C. Brownell's "French Traits." The sudden demand for so large and expensive a volume as Green's History, outside of regular trade channels, followed as it was by spectacular sales of other books from which neither publisher nor writer had expected any-thing out of the normal, set the whole publishing world agog, and naturally raised the question, "How are we to get in on this new market?"

There were many approaches, all legitimate enough so far as I know. I found a rather amusing proof of one not long ago in Marjorie Wiggin Prescott's fine collection of manuscripts and rare books—a volume of Lew Wallace's "Ben Hur" enriched by a letter to the publisher, signed by Mrs. Wallace and dated November 24, 1884. The letter, which is self-explanatory, is reproduced here with Mrs. Prescott's permission.

Crawfordsville, Nov. 24, 1884.

Dear Sir

Because of inquiries of correspondents as to the *number* of *wives* Gen. Wallace has had, I have thought best to instruct you to add to the dedication of *Ben-Hur*, making it:

To
The Wife of My Youth
who still abides with me

This with Gen. Wallace's consent.

Several literary clubs have made it a handbook for study in connection with Roman History. If by some means you could have it adopted by the Chautauqua Club, which numbers twenty thousand members, it might be worth while to try. Pardon the suggestion.

May I ask you to furnish me a report of the sales of *Ben-Hur*, year by year, from the beginning?

With high regard,

Very truly yours
SUSAN E. WALLACE.

As the Chautauqua Literary and Scientific Circle grew, there came increasing necessity of a steady sympathetic administration. To help in this task it was decided in 1880 to establish a monthly organ—*The Chautauquan*, it was to be called—in which portions of the required readings could be published more cheaply than in book form, and through which by counsel and suggestions the leaders could keep in closer touch with the readers—better meet their needs. Dr. Vincent was quick to sense weak places in the organization, and ingenious in devising ways to take care of them. It was to try out one of his devices that Dr. Flood was now asking my temporary help.

Here was the situation that had been uncovered—hundreds of those who had joined the great circle and bought its books were without dictionaries, encyclopaedias, explanatory helps of any kind, and they lived too far away—on the Plains, in the mountains, on distant farms—to reach libraries. Headquarters were inundated with questions: How do you pronounce this word, translate this phrase? Who was this man, this woman? What does this or that mean?

"Could not *The Chautauquan* take care of this difficulty," suggested Dr. Vincent, "by annotating the portions of the various texts to be read in that particular month? Let some one try it out."

As I happened to be the "some one" within reach when Dr. Flood received the suggestion, the attempt was put up to me— temporary trial, I was made to understand. Now I had known from childhood homes and towns where there were practically no books beyond the Bible and the children's spellers. As books had always come after bread in our household I naturally pitied those who did not have them; so I undertook the notes with the determination to make them as helpful as I could.

To my surprise and delight Dr. Vincent sent word to me that I had caught his idea, and that he had advised Dr. Flood to ask me to prepare similar notes each month.

"Will you do it?" asked Dr. Flood.

I jumped at the chance, calculating that it would take not over two weeks of my month, give me pin money, and leave time for the microscope—that my future was in it, I did not dream.

But my task required better equipped libraries than Titusville offered; Meadville, only thirty miles away, headquarters for *The Chautauquan*, had them, and so I arranged to do my work there, remaining until I had read the proofs—an exacting job which never ceased to worry me. What if the accent was in the wrong place? What if I brought somebody into the world in the wrong year? Something of the kind happened occasionally, and when it did I quickly discovered that, while there might be many Chautauqua readers who did not have books of reference, there were more that did and knew how to use them.

Once in touch with the office of *The Chautauquan* I began to see things to do. Dr. Flood had little interest in detail. The magazine was made up in a casual, and to my mind a disorderly, fashion. I could not keep my fingers off. A woman is a natural executive: that has been her business through the ages. Intuitively she picks up, sets to rights, establishes order. I began at once to exercise my inheritance, proved useful, was offered a full-time job, and threw myself heartily into an attempt to learn how to make up a magazine in the way I suspected a magazine should be made up.

When the long-suffering foreman of the printing office discovered I was in earnest he undertook my education, taught me the vocabulary—the only galley I had heard of up to that time was a war vessel of the Middle Ages—suggested dummies, and offered a model. He installed a proper respect for the dates on which copy was to be in, and forms closed: showed me the importance of clean copy by compelling me to see with my own eyes the time it took to make a correction, trained me until I could stand over the closing of the last form and direct the necessary changes to be made in order to make room for a three-line advertisement which had just arrived, and which, such was the need of *The Chautauquan* for advertising, must under no consideration be thrown out. When I could do that nonchalantly I felt as if I had arrived. And this training I owed to as fine a craftsman as there was in the trade at the time; as well, he was a courteous and patient gentleman—Adrian McCoy, long the head of the pressroom where *The Chautauquan* was printed.

My willingness to take on loose ends soon brought to my desk much of the routine office correspondence—letters to be answered by a more or less set form, signed with Dr. Flood's name and mailed without troubling him to read them.

In this grist were many letters from readers, women chiefly, who laid their troubles and hopes on our shoulders, confident of understanding and counsel. Dr. Flood's answers to such communications were courteous but formal. Probably he appreciated as I did not that there lay safety. I felt strongly that such an appeal or confidence should have a personal, sympathetic letter, and I began producing them, pouring out counsel and pity. I shudder now to think of the ignorant sentiment I probably spilled. But my career as a professional counselor was checked suddenly by the unexpected result of a series of letters to a contributor. This gentleman, a foreign lecturer and teacher, had been chilled by the lack of understanding by Americans of his ideals. And all of this he was expressing in letters to the office after our acceptance of one or two of his articles. I was deeply touched by his outpourings and answered in kind—of course signing my editor's name. Then one day Dr. Flood received a letter saying that on such a day the gentleman would be in Meadville. He must see the one who so understood him. And come he did. Poor Dr. Flood did not know what it was all about.

"But these letters," the visitor exclaimed. "Oh," Dr. Flood said, "Miss Tarbell wrote those. We'll speak to her."

And so he was presented—letters in hand—Dr. Flood looking sternly at me and leaving me to my fate.

"Did you write these letters?" the bewildered and disappointed stranger asked.

All I could say was, "Yes, I wrote them."

"And Dr. Flood never saw them?"

"No," I said, "he never does."

"I might have known it was a woman," he groaned, and fled. And that was the last we ever saw or heard of him. But it made a vast difference in my editorial correspondence.

I was not satisfied, however, with setting things to rights and counseling the unhappy. Having convinced my editor-in-chief that I could keep his house in better order than he had been interested in doing, I became ambitious to contribute to its furnishing, to extend its field beyond matters purely Chautauquan. I began by offering contributions to what was called the Editor's Table—the Editor's Note Book. I began to write articles, even went off on trips to gather information on subjects which seemed to me to be fitting.

The first and most ambitious of these undertakings was an investigation made in the Patent Office in Washington of the amount of inventing the records showed women to have done. I had been disturbed for some time by what seemed to me the calculated belittling of the past achievements of women by many active in the campaign for suffrage. They agreed with their opponents that women had shown little or no creative power. That, they argued, was because man had purposely and jealously excluded her from his field of action. The argument was intended, of course, to arouse women's indignation, stir them to action. It seemed to me rather to throw doubt on her creative capacity. Power to create breaks all barriers. Women had demonstrated this, I believed, again and again while carrying on what I as an observer of society was coming to regard as the most delicate, complex, and essential of all creative tasks—the making of a home. There was the field of invention. At the moment it was being said in print and on the platform that, in all the history of the Patent Office, women had taken out only some three hundred patents.

I had seen so much of woman's ingenuity on the farm and in the kitchen that I questioned the figures; and so I went to see, feeling very important if scared at my rashness in daring to penetrate a Government department and interview its head. I was able to put my finger at once on over two thousand patents, enough to convince me that, man-made world or not, if a woman had a good idea and the gumption to seek a patent she had the same chance as a man to get one. This was confirmed by correspondence with two or three women who at the time were taking out patents regularly.

These dashes into journalism, timid and factual as were the results, gave my position more and more body, began slowly to arouse my rudimentary capacity for self-expression. At the same time my position was enriched by a novel feature of our undertaking, one that any editor of a monthly journal can appreciate. We published but ten issues, suspending in July and August in order to get out on the grounds at Chautauqua an eight-page newspaper—the Chautauqua Assembly *Daily Herald*. This meant moving our Meadville staff bodily to the Lake late in June.

I was soon contributing two columns of editorials a day to the *Herald*, comments on the daily doings of the Assembly, and making many stimulating acquaintances in doing it. Among them I valued particularly Dr. Herbert B. Adams and Dr. Richard T. Ely of Johns Hopkins University, men who were stirring youth and shocking the elders by liberal interpretations of history and economics. We felt rather proud of ourselves at Chautauqua that we were liberal enough to engage Dr. Adams and Dr. Ely as regular lecturers and teachers, and that our constituency accepted them, if with occasional misgivings.

It was not only the faculty of Johns Hopkins which was adding to my friends. One who remains today among those I most value came from its student body—Dr. John H. Finley. Dr. Finley gave several summers to the Assembly *Herald*, reading its copy and its proofs among other things. It was he who read my two columns and, no doubt, kept me out of much trouble; but once there did slip by him a misquotation over which he still chuckles when we talk of Chautauqua days. I made it a practice to head my first column with a digest of the day's happenings—a line to an event and, as a starter for the paragraph, a quotation. I had been rather pleased one day to select a line from James Thomson:

The meek-eyed Morn appears, mother of dews.

A copy of the paper was always thrown on the verandah of my upstairs room around five o'clock in the morning, and I hopped out of bed to see what had happened to my column. That morning something dire had happened, for my quotation ran:

The *weak*-eyed *Worm* appears, mother of dews.

Eminence came from across the water annually and gave color and importance, so we thought, to our doings. A foreign visitor with whom I had a pleasant acquaintance running over some years was Dr. J. P. Mahaffy of the University of Dublin. Dr. Mahaffy had contributed a series of delightful articles to the required readings in *The Chautauquan*—"Gossip About Greece" —and in the summer of 1889 he came over for two or three courses of lectures at the Assembly. A distinguished figure, he was, and such a contrast in his tweeds, his free movements, his spirited wide-ranging talk to most of us.

My acquaintance grew out of our mutual interest in the flora of any spot where we happened to be. One day as I came in from a botanizing expedition outside the grounds carrying stocks of the lovely field lilies common in the region, Dr. Mahaffy seized my arm: "You care for flowers and plants? I thought American women had no interest in them." A libel I quickly hooted. In defense of my sisterhood I went diligently to work to show him our summer flora. But he cared for nothing as much as our summer lilies, begged me after the flowering was over to send him bulbs, which I proudly did. In exchange I received from his Dublin garden seeds of a white poppy which, he wrote me, he had originally gathered in the shadow of the statue of Memnon in Egypt. Those poppies have always gone with me; they flourished in my mother's garden in Titusville—now they flourish in my Connecticut garden.

My life was busy, varied, unfolding pleasantly in many ways, but it also after six years was increasingly unsatisfactory, so unsatisfactory that I was secretly, very secretly, meditating a change.

I was scared by what *The Chautauquan* seemed to be doing to the plan I had worked out for the development of my mind. I had grown up with a stout determination to follow one course of study to the end, to develop a specialty. The work I was doing demanded a scattering of mind which I began to fear would unfit me for ever thinking anything through. I realized that an editor of value must have made up his mind about more things than had I, feel himself ready to fight for those things if necessary. I had no program in which *The Chautauquan* was interested. Moreover, I did not want to be an editor.

But to break with *The Chautauquan* meant sacrificing security. I had always had a vision of myself settled somewhere in a secure corner, simple, not too large. I never had wanted things; I always had a dislike of impedimenta, but I wanted something cheerful and warm and enduring. There I could work over that which interested me, day in and day out, with no alarm for my keep. Now *The Chautauquan* was a secure berth; so far as I could figure, it would last through my time at least. To give it up meant complete economic insecurity. I probably should not have been willing to sacrifice what I think I had honestly earned if there had not been growing upon me a conviction of the sterility of security. All about me were people who at least believed themselves materially secure. They lived comfortably within their means, they were busy keeping things as they were, preserving what they had. They were the most respectable people in town, but secretly I was beginning to suspect their respectability.

One day, listening to a fine elderly Scotch Presbyterian minister who had in his congregation a large group of these stable, secure, best citizens, I was startled when he leaned over his pulpit and, shaking his fist at us, shouted, "You're dyin' of respectability." Was that what was happening to me? I saw with increasing clearness that I could not go beyond a certain point on *The Chautauquan*, mentally, socially, spiritually. If I remained, it was to accept a variety of limitations, and my whole nature was against the acceptance of limitations. It was contrary to the nature of things as I saw them; to be happy, I must go on with fresh attempts, fresh adventuring. The thing that frightened me earlier in my youth came to the top now: that thing that made me determine I would never marry because it meant giving up freedom, was a trap. It was clear enough that I was trapped—comfortably, most pleasantly, most securely, but trapped.

As time went on I realized that this security to which people so clung could not always be counted on. They might think so, but had I not seen beautiful homes sold under the hammer in Titusville, homes of those whom the town had looked on as impregnable financially? In my years on *The Chautauquan* in Meadville I had been a shocked observer of one of the many dramatic political failures of the eighties, the defeat of the Republican candidate for Governor of Pennsylvania at a critical moment—a Meadville banker, Wallace Delamater. I was too much of a mugwump to sympathize with the Republican platform, but I liked Wallace Delamater. I believed him, as I think the records show, to be a tool of a past master of machine politics—Matthew Quay. Taken up by Quay, the resources of the Delamater bank and of allied banks in Meadville at the call of his party, he made a campaign which was called brilliant. There was no doubt of the result in Meadville.

I went to bed early, the night of the election, expecting to be aroused by the ringing of bells, the blowing of whistles, for there was to be a celebration. When I awakened with a start it was broad daylight. Had I slept through the celebration? A sense of doom hung over me; I dressed hurriedly, went down to get the paper. Wallace Delamater was defeated. Promptly the Delamater bank closed and, one after another, four banks of the town followed. There was a heavy run on the one remaining, the one where I had my little deposit. The panic in the town was desperate; everything was going. I don't think I have ever been more ashamed of anything in my life connected with money than I was when I took my bank book and went to my bank to ask for my deposit. It was all the money I had in the world—times were bad. But I have always continued to be a little ashamed that I yielded to the panic, the more because my bank didn't fail!

No, the security men flattered themselves they had achieved was never certain. Moreover, my security was costing more in certain precious things than I was willing to pay. Take the matter of making something professionally sound, useful, justifiable, out of myself, which is the only one of these "precious things" that I am talking about! I could do no more towards it where I was. To begin with, I at last knew what I wanted to do. It was no longer to seek truth with a microscope. My early absorption in rocks and plants had veered to as intense an interest in human beings. I was feeling the same passion to understand men and women, the same eagerness to collect and to classify information about them. I find the proofs of this slow and unconscious change of allegiance in an accumulation of tattered notebooks tucked away for years, forgotten and only brought out after I had set myself this curious task of tracing the road I have traveled through my eighty years, trying to find out why I did this thing and not that, getting acquainted with my own working life.

I seem to have begun to enter observations on human beings soon after I had settled down to learn how to put a magazine together in an orderly fashion. I applied the same method that I had used for so many years in collecting and classifying natural objects which excited my curiosity. Take leaves, on which I was always keen. I started out in high school to collect them from all the flora in my territory, classifying them by shapes, veins, stalks, color. Rarely do I take up a family book of those early years that there do not fall out from between the pages leaves of one thing or another that I had pressed to help me carry on my scheme of classification. I suspect that I did not get much beyond a glib naming of parts.

Something analogous happened when I recognized that men and women were as well worth notes as leaves, that there was a science of society as well as of botany.

What had happened was undoubtedly that the tumults, the challenges of my day had finally penetrated my aloofness, and that I was feeling more and more the need of taking a part in them. The decade I spent in Poland and on *The Chautauquan* had a background not so unlike that of the present decade. At its beginning we were only fifteen years from a civil war which had left behind not only a vast devastated region with the problem of its reconstruction, but the problem of a newly freed people. It had left bitterness which in intensity and endurance no war but a civil war ever leaves. We had had our inflation, a devastating boom followed by seven years of depression, outbreaks of all the various forms of radical philosophy the world then knew. Youth talks glibly of communism today as if it had just appeared in the country; but Marxian Communists transferred the headquarters of the International to New York City in the seventies. More conspicuous than the Communists were the Anarchists. Every city in the United States had its little group, preaching and every now and then practicing direct action. Indeed, they were a factor in all the violent labor disturbances of the period.

In 1879 prosperity had come back with a whoop, and, as she usually does after a long absence, had quickly exhausted herself by fantastic economic excesses. By the time I undertook to annotate the Chautauqua Literary and Scientific Circle's readings the country had begun to suffer again from its wanton speculation and reckless overbuilding of railroads. Factories and mines and mills shut down; and when work stopped disorder began, particularly on the railroads of the Southwest, the awful massacre of Chinese in Wyoming—more awful, the Haymarket riot in Chicago followed as it was by the execution of four men, all counselors of violence to be sure, but no one of them found guilty either of making or of throwing the bomb.

The eighties dripped with blood, and men struggled to get at causes, to find corrections, to humanize and socialize the country; for then as now there were those who dreamed of a good world although at times it seemed to them to be going mad.

The Chautauquan interested itself in all of this turbulent and confused life. Indeed, it rapidly became my particular editorial concern. We noted and discussed practically every item of the social program which has been so steadily developing in the last fifty years, the items which have crystallized into the Square Deal, the New Freedom, the New Deal.

The present argument for high wages, we made in the eighties. We called it "the new economic coefficient in our industrial life." "It is the well-paid workman," said *The Chautauquan*, "who is a relatively large consumer. We are built upon a foundation of which this well-paid workman is an important part."

As for hours and conditions, we were ardent supporters of the eight-hour day, organized labor's chief aim in the eighties, and we were for contracts between labor and capital, each being held responsible for his side of the bargain. We were for education, arbitration, legislation, the program of the Knights of Labor rather than the program of force which the growing American Federation of Labor was adopting. We discussed interminably the growing problem of the slums, were particularly strong for cooperative housing, laundries and bakeshops; we supported the popular Town and Country Club, seeking to keep a healthy balance between the two; we were advocates of temperance but shied at prohibition—largely, I think, because it had become a political issue, and we did not like to see our idealists going into politics, as Bellamy and Henry George and the leaders of many causes were doing.

That is, in the decade of the eighties we were discussing and thinking about the same fundamentals that we are today.

My realization of the stress of the period began at home. Titusville and all the Oil Region of Pennsylvania were struggling to loosen the hold of the mighty monopoly which, since its first attack on the business in 1872, had grown in power and extent until it owned and controlled over 90 per cent of the oil industry outside of the production of the raw crude. The region was divided into two hostile camps—the Independent Producers and Refiners, and the Standard Oil Company. Their maneuvers and strategy kept town and country in a constant state of excitement, of suspicion, of hope, and of despair.

There was a steady weakening of independent ranks both by the men worn out or ruined by the struggle, and those who saw peace and security for themselves only in settling and gave up the fight.

In those days I looked with more contempt on the man who had gone over to the Standard than on the one who had been in jail. I felt pity for the latter man, but none for the deserters from the ranks of the fighting independents. Those were the days when the freeing of transportation, the privilege which had more to do with the making of the monopoly than anything else, more even than the great ability of its management, was the aim of all reformers. For years the Independents had worked for an interstate commerce law which would make rate discrimination a crime. To me such a law had come to have a kind of sanctity. It was the new freedom, and when it was passed in 1887 I felt an uplift such as nothing in public life, unless I except Mr. Cleveland's tariff message of the year before, had ever given me.

But it was not the economic feature of the struggle in the Oil Region which deeply disturbed or interested me. It was what it was doing to people themselves, to the people I knew, to my father and mother and their friends. It was the divided town, the suspicion and greed and bitterness and defeats and surrenders. Here was a product meant to be a blessing to men—so I believed; and it was proving a curse to the very ones who had discovered it, developed it.

I began to fill pages with notes of things seen and heard, and finally I decided I should write a novel about it. Very secretly indeed, I went at it, assembling a cast, outlining a plot, writing two or three chapters. Poor stuff. Luckily I soon found out I was beyond my depth and gave it up.

From my notebooks I judge that I abandoned my novel the more readily because I had conceived what I called "a more fundamental research"! This was nothing less than a Science of Society to be illustrated by my own observations on men and women. Looking over it now, I see that the framework came from reading the voluminous discussions of the nature of society then flooding the public. I took my framework where I found it, but I filled it in with observations, gathered on all sides, of people I knew, heard about, particularly read about in the newspaper.

But this ambitious work soon met the same fate as the novel. It broke off at the end of the third chapter because I had concluded I could not construct society as it was until I knew more about woman. I suspected she had played a larger part in shaping society than she realized or perhaps was willing to admit. I was questioning the argument that this is entirely a man-made world. I had found too many woman-made parts in it to accept the characterization at its face value. My science of society would not be honest, I concluded, if the only part woman was allowed to play in it was that of doormat, toy, and tool. I was troubled, too, by the argument that women must be given suffrage if society was to be improved. Man had made a mess of the world, I was told; woman must take his tools and straighten things up. I did not feel the confidence of my courageous friends. "Why should we expect them to do better with the vote than men have done?" I asked. "Because they are women," I was told. But they were human beings, like men, and they were human beings with no experience of the tools they wanted to use; and I had enough sense of the past to believe that experience counted, and that it would be wise for all men and women to consult it when they tried new ventures.

There had been women in public life in the past. What had they done? I had to satisfy myself before I went further with my science of society or joined the suffragists. It was humiliating not to be able to make up my mind quickly about the matter, as most of the women I knew did. What was the matter with me, I asked myself, that I could not be quickly sure? Why must I persist in the slow, tiresome practice of knowing more about things before I had an opinion? Suppose everybody did that. What chance for intuition, vision, emotion, action?

My notebooks show that I began my plodding by making out a list of women who seemed to offer food for reflection. The group that excited me most were the women of the French Revolution. I made little studies of several, wrote little pieces about them, and these little pieces I submitted to the editor of *The Chautauquan;* he published several of them—a study of Madame de Staël, of Marie Antoinette, of Madame Roland. But soon I became heartily ashamed of my sketches, written as they were from so meager an equipment. I felt this particularly about Madame Roland. I made up my mind that I was going to know more about this woman, that she probably would teach me what sort of contribution might be expected from a woman in public life.

That meant research. How was I to carry it on? Whatever studying I did depended on my ability to support myself while doing it; whatever studying I did while on *The Chautauquan* must be turned into something available for the magazine. My time and strength belonged to it. Obviously, I could not do sufficient research and continue my position; it was as impossible as

it had been to act as preceptress of the Poland Union Seminary
and at the same time carry on my study with the microscope.
Where was I to carry on this research? There was but one place
—Paris. And how was I to finance myself in Paris—a strange
country and a strange tongue—long enough to write a book?
I did not consider the possibility of getting a regular job: I did
not want one. I wanted freedom, and I had an idea that there
was no freedom in belonging to things, no freedom in security.
It took time to convince myself that I dared go on my own. But
finally I succeeded.

Coming to a decision has a loosening, tonic effect on a mind
which has been floundering in uncertainty. Liberated, it rushes
gaily, hopefully, to the charting of a new course. I had no sooner
resolved to strike out on my own than my mind was bubbling with
plans. I forgot that I was thirty-three years old and, according
to the code of my time and my society, too old for new ventures;
I forgot that outside of my very limited experience on *The
Chautauquan* I knew nothing of the writing and publishing
world, had literally no acquaintance among editors; I forgot that
I was afraid of people, believed them all so much greater and
more important than they often turned out to be that it cost me
nervous chills to venture with a request into a stranger's presence.

Dismissing all these real handicaps, I plunged gaily into planning for a career in journalism, self-directed, free-lance journalism. Surely I could find subjects enough in Paris to write about,
subjects that would interest American newspapers. We were in
the thick of a great agitation over the condition and the conduct
of American cities. *The Chautauquan* had touched it occasionally. How did Paris keep house? I planned a syndicate of my
own which would answer all questions. Out of my newspaper
work might not articles grow for magazines? I thought so, and
books, beginning of course with my study of Madame Roland.
So long as I told nobody about my plans, they worked beautifully, carried me upward and onward into a new and happier,

more profitable, more satisfying world. But when I announced my decision, laid out what I proposed to do, all the glow and confidence went out of me, all the weaknesses in my venture came again to the top. There were friends who said none too politely: "Remember you are past thirty. Women don't make new places for themselves after thirty." There were friends who resented my decision as a reflection on themselves. A woman whose friendship I valued said bluntly: "You are one of us. Aren't we good enough for you?" My act was treason in her eyes. The whole force of the respectable circles to which I belonged, that respectable circle which knew as I did not the value of security won, the slender chance of replacing it if lost or abandoned, was against me and so out of friendliness.

When I told my editor-in-chief I was leaving, going to Paris to study, he was shocked. "How will you support yourself?" he asked, really anxious, knowing that I must depend on my own efforts.

"By writing," I said.

"You're not a writer," he said. "You'll starve."

He had touched the weakest point in my venture: I was not a writer, and I knew it. I knew I never should be one in the high sense which I then and still more now give to that word. I had neither the endowment nor the passion nor the ambition to be a writer. I was rather a student, wanting to understand things quite regardless of how I could use that understanding if I reached it. There was much selfishness in my wanting to know for the sake of knowing, much of a dead scholar in me; and that dead scholar has always hung, more or less a weight, about my neck.

But if I was not a writer I had certain qualifications for the practice of the modest kind of journalism on which I had decided. I counted no little on my habit of planning in advance what I was going to do, and I had a strong conviction that a plan of my own was worth more than any plan which was made for me.

Again, if I could not write, I did have a certain sense of what mattered in a subject and a strong conviction that it was my sense of what mattered, and not somebody else's, that would give my work freshness and strength if it was to have any.

Then there was my habit of steady, painstaking work—that ought to count for something. And perhaps I could learn to write. If I were to do so, could I do better than soak myself in French prose? I had read French steadily from my school days; I had done not a little translating of articles from the big reviews for *The Chautauquan*. If I could live with the language, might I not master something of what seemed to me its essential qualities, those which gave it both body and charm? These qualities were the soundness of structure, the way it held together, and the beautiful clarity of expression. At least I could try for them.

But when I tried to explain all this to my critical friends they continued frankly skeptical, indignant. It was my father and mother who backed me up, though I think they were both puzzled and fearful. "I don't know what you can do, Ida," my father said, "that's for you. If you think you can do it, try it." But in the end it took all the grit I had to go ahead.

Breaking up established relations is not easy. You begin by pulling up deeply rooted things, rooted in your heart; you abandon once cherished purposes. When I left *The Chautauquan* I was no longer the eager and confident young woman who ten years before had started out for herself in Poland, Ohio; I was ten years older, and I was keenly conscious that I had in those ten years accumulated a fairly complete collection of shattered idols. That I could forget them as quickly and as completely as I did, I owe to the Paris of the nineties. I had scarcely passed her gates before I had fallen under her spell. At once I was experiencing all the amazing rejuvenation that comes from falling in love, whatever the object. It was not to be "See Paris and die," as more than one friend had jeered. I knew with certainty it was to be "See Paris and live."

6

I FALL IN LOVE

FALLING in love with Paris at first sight—a *coup de feu*, it was—in no way dimmed the energy and the care with which on the day of my arrival I began to put into operation the cautious and laborious Plan for self-support I had brought along. It rather intensified it. As I must begin at the bottom to build up contacts with strangers on the other side of the ocean, and as there was but $150 in my pocket, there was no time to waste.

In the ten years I had been trying to support myself I had learned that the art of spending money is quite as important in a sound financial program as the art of earning it. I had been going on the theory, as I still am—practice is another story—that what I earned must cover my expenses and leave a surplus for emergencies and expansion. I had applied my principles to my small salary on *The Chautauquan*—never over $100 a month —well enough to get myself to Paris and have this little reserve to care for myself while I was proving or disproving that I could convince a few American editors whom I had never seen that my goods were worth buying.

The first step, obviously, in carrying out my program was cheap living. Luckily for me, two of my associates on *The Chautauquan*, excited by my undertaking, had decided to join me. One, Josephine Henderson, was a friend of Titusville days and like myself a graduate of Allegheny College. Jo, as we called her, was a handsome woman with a humorous look on life—healthy for me. I have never had a friend who judged my balloons more shrewdly or pricked them so painlessly. With us was a beautiful girl, Mary Henry, the daughter of one of the militant W.C.T.U. workers of that day, a neighbor and a friend as well as a co-

89

worker of the great temperance leader Frances Willard. At the steamer a friend of Mary's appeared, announcing that she, too, was going along. This meant four of us to share rent and food.

Back in Titusville I had picked on the Latin Quarter as at once the cheapest and the most practical place in Paris for one to live who must go on the cheap. Then, too, the University was in the Latin Quarter, and we were all planning to take lectures. I was even flirting with the idea that I might find time to take a degree.

So on arrival, putting our bags in the little room of the cheap hotel on the Right Bank to which we had gone, we headed at once for the Latin Quarter. I had picked on the neighborhood where I wanted to settle, near the Musée de Cluny. Not that I knew a thing about the Musée or what was in it; simply Cluny was one of the words that had always pulled me. This magic was largely responsible for our settling in the Rue du Sommerard almost next door to the spot in the city which save one was to have the greatest fascination as well as the deepest consolation for me.

But finding these quarters was no easy task. My friends gulped as I did at the stuffiness, the dinginess, the primitive sanitation, the obvious fleas, and the suspicion of other unmentionable pests in the places at which we looked. But settle I would, and so with groans they consented finally to the taking of two tiny bedrooms, a salon, along with the use of a kitchenette in one of the four apartments controlled by a Madame Bonnet. Our selection was not as unwise as it looked at the moment. Indeed, as it turned out, Madame Bonnet remained my landlady throughout the coming three years.

As quickly as we had found our lodging we established relations with the little shops in the neighborhood where one could for a few sous buy all the makings of a meal. You bought exactly what you needed and no more—a single egg, one roll or croissant, a gill of milk, two cups apiece of café au lait, never having a drop left in the pot. Brought up as we had all been at loaded tables, the close calculation shocked us at first as something mean, stingy. "Why, the very scraps from a meal at home would feed us here." And that was true—more shame to our bringing up. But we learned to buy as our thrifty neighbors did and to like it, and we learned how to order at the cheap and orderly little restaurants of the Quarter so as to get a sufficient meal of really excellent food for a franc (then nineteen cents or, as we carelessly reckoned it, twenty—one hundred centimes to a franc). Only on grand occasions did we allow ourselves two francs.

The pleasantest and most profitable part of the experience was the acquaintances we made with the women who kept the little shops, the little restaurants. As soon as they were convinced of our financial responsibility and our social seriousness, they became friendly—a friendliness not based on the few sous we were spending so carefully but on interest and curiosity. We were new types to them; but, once convinced we were what we pretended to be, they treated us with a deference quite different from the noisy greetings they gave the people of the neighborhood or their rather contemptuous familiarity with the occasional cocotte who strayed in. That is, we were very soon placed by the shopkeepers of the vicinity. It was my first lesson in the skill, almost artistry with which all classes of the French people classify those with whom they are thrown in contact, notably foreigners. Later I was to observe this in the more highly developed classes where I established professional relationship.

I was a stranger seeking information—an American journalist, a student, so I told them. But what kind of person was I? What was there in me they could tie to, depend upon?

Obviously I was not rich. If I had been, there would have been quickly gathered around me a group to offer entertainment as well as treasures to buy; but it was clear I had little money, so that was out of the question. There are other things by which the French label you, a woman particularly—charm, beauty, chic, *l'esprit*, seriousness, capacity to work, intelligence, *bonté*. Those with whom I had dealings for any length of time hit perfectly on my chief asset. I was a worker. "A *femme travailleuse*," they said to one another, and if they passed me to an acquaintance that was the recommendation. No people believe more than the French in the value and dignity in hard work. I was treated with respect because of my working quality. It was not saying that I should not have gone farther and faster if I had been a beauty, if I had had what they call charm and the fine secret of using it, but they were willing to take me for what I had. Being a worker, the chances were I was serious. I might or might not prove intelligent, but here they gave me the benefit of the doubt and waited for a final answer. That which they were slowest in making up their minds about was goodness—*bonté*. They were not willing to accept anything but natural unconscious goodness, and it takes time to make sure about that.

While we were finding our way about, I was at work. If I did not have the documents to prove it I would not believe today that just a week after arriving, and in spite of the excitement and fatigue of settling, I had written and mailed two newspaper articles.

Enamored as I was of the city, no work could have been more satisfying than that I had laid out for myself. My little self-directed syndicate concerned itself with the practical everyday life of the city. One is always keen to know all the common things about the thing or person one loves. How did Paris keep herself so clean? What did she eat and drink, and where did she get it? How much did it cost her? Where did she go for fun? How did she manage it that even her very poor seemed to know how to amuse themselves, that her beggars were a recognized institution? There were a multitude of things I thirsted to know about her. And if I could get my bread and butter in finding out, what luck! What luck!

At once I became an omnivorous reader of the newspapers, and

I found to my joy that many of them felt as I did about the Parisian scene. They carried paragraphs as captivating as those that our *New Yorker* unearths for its fascinating editorial department on the city to which it belongs. Another discovery which surprised me was that my best source for illustration was the illustrated catalogues of the French Salons of recent years. I wanted pictures of markets, of rivers, of beggars, of marriages, of all the things that people were doing as they went about their business. And what rejoiced me was that many French artists seemed to love the streets and what went on there in much the same way that I did. They loved to see Paris at her daily toil, meeting her daily problems, and every year they turned out pictures showing her at it.

Later I was to discover that this daily life of the Parisians of different classes has always been material for able artists. The best illustrations I found for my Madame Roland in her youth were those of Chardin in the Louvre.

My manner of living, the contacts and circumstances attending the gathering of my material for my newspaper articles brought me for the first time in my life into daily relations with that greatest segment of every country's population—those whom we call the poor, and of whom if we are well-to-do or if we are rich we are so curiously unconscious. I had belonged all my conscious life to the well-to-do, those who spent a dollar without seriously weighing it. Society had seemed to me to be chiefly made up of such people. Of course there were the rich, but they were so few in number as to be negligible—at least they had never counted in my life; nor had the poor counted as a permanent class. I had the American notion that the chief economic duty of the poor was to become well-to-do. The laborer, the clerk, the man who worked for others should save his money, put it into the business, or start out for himself, no matter how hard, how meager the return. Dignity and success lay in being your own master, owning your own home—I am sure my father would rather have grubbed corn meal and bacon from a piece of stony land which was his own than have had all the luxuries on a salary. One of his complaints against the great oil trust was that it was turning the men of the Oil Region into hired men—mighty prosperous hired men, some of them, but nevertheless taking orders, even orders as to what to say, for whom to vote.

To his way of thinking this was failure for an American. I suspect his philosophy working in me was at least partially responsible for my revolt against the kind of security I had achieved on *The Chautauquan*. I was a hired girl.

But in the society where I found myself in Paris there was no such contempt for the fixed job. On the contrary, it was something for which you were responsible, to which you owed an obligation. Serious workers in Paris seemed to me to give to the job the same kind of loyalty that serious men and women in America gave to the businesses they owned. You respected yourself and were respected in proportion to your fidelity to it. You might be advanced, but more probably not. Opportunity did not grow on every bush as at home, and if it came a Frenchman's way he weighed it—at home you seized it, trusting to luck. Here luck seemed to me to have little or no standing in a business enterprise, big as it counted in the lotteries in which everybody took part. To my surprise I found these people, working so busily and constantly, were not restless like the Americans; nor were they generally envious. I had a feeling that my concierge, who never had been across the Seine to the Right Bank, who lived in a room almost filled by her huge bed and its great feather puffs, who must have looked long at a sou before she spent it, would not have changed places with anybody in Paris. Were not the lodgers on whom she kept so strict a watch kind, generous, and regular with fees? Had she not friends in the street? Might she not win a slice of a fortune one day from the fraction of a lottery ticket which she annually found a way to buy? And who had so magnificent a cat? The pride of the House. What more could she ask?

Certainly there was more interest in the tasks, less restlessness, less envy, than in the same class in America. Was it my father's philosophy which made the difference? Was it your duty if you were poor to struggle to be well-to-do, and if well-to-do struggle to be rich? It meant you were always trying to be somebody else. If it was your duty to be discontented, could you escape envy? Was it not necessary, if you were to keep yourself up to the effort, to feed yourself on envy as in war men must be fed on hate if they are to kill with vigor and gusto?

It was too much to believe that the content, the fidelity to the job were universal. Nevertheless, it was sufficient to cement the laborious poor into a powerful and recognized class, a class with traditions, customs, recognized relations to other classes, having its own manner of homes, amusements, worship; a class self-respecting, jealous of its prerogatives, and able in need to protect itself.

But the multitude of hard-working and fairly satisfied men and women were not all the poor with whom I came close. There were those who could find no work; there were many of them, for the long world depression of the nineties was on its way. The winter of '91 and '92 was a cruel one, and the museums, libraries, lecture rooms, churches where I went about my daily duties were swarmed with poor souls trying to deceive the guardians into thinking that they had come to study pictures, read books, listen to lectures, to confess their sins or listen to mass. The guardians only saw them when they became a crowd or attempted to camp for the day. Most pathetic to me were their efforts to make furtive toilets, taking a comb from a pocket to smooth tangled hair, scissors to cut the fringe from a frayed cuff.

There were soup kitchens to keep them from starving, though many a one starved or froze or ended his misery in the Seine that winter. At one of these kitchens I officiated for a brief time. It was run by the McAll Mission in the Faubourg Saint-Antoine. I was not there as a Samaritan but as a reporter looking for copy. What could I do for them but tell Americans what a few Americans were doing in Paris to ease the vast misery? It might bring a few sous for soup. I believe it did.

But they pulled less strongly on my sympathy than a class of the poor which I found to be in our Quarter—men and women no longer young, past the employing age, who lived alone on tiny incomes, sometimes the fruit of their own past thrift, sometimes an inheritance, again the gift of a friend. I watched and speculated about how they did it, the more seriously because I asked myself if the day might be coming when I should belong to this class. If I ever did, I hoped I could carry it off with as much dignity as the one called the Countess on our street. She lived *sous les toits* in a high house opposite me, a tall, erect, white-haired woman in a gown and cape of faded and patched silk which still showed its quality as did its wearer. More than once I watched her stop late at night at the garbage can on the sidewalk opposite, turning over its contents. Many of the tradespeople seemed to feel that she honored them when she came in to buy an occasional egg or apple. She was so gracious, so completely *grande dame*. One day I heard the woman from whom I bought my café au lait say: "Will not Madame honor me by trying my coffee? It is still hot." She was pouring out a cup as she said it, and the Countess with a benignant smile said, "If that will give you pleasure, my good Marie." She needed it. Marie knew that, but Marie was more than paid by that smile. "It is a great honor," she told me lest, being a foreigner, I did not understand the Countess, "to have so great a lady come into one's shop." There it was again, another standard than money, the standard of class, breeding, cultivation, the grand manner.

The more I saw of the gallant poor of Paris, the more convinced I was if they could get on so could I, learning to live on what I could make. And I was going to make something. My doubt about that was set at rest some six weeks after my arrival when I received a check for my first syndicate article—$5.00. It was quickly followed by checks from two more of the six papers to which I had submitted my syndicate proposition—50 per cent was not a bad percentage and they were good papers, the Pittsburgh *Dispatch*, the Cincinnati *Times-Star* and the Chicago *Tribune*. These three papers remained faithful to me until the election of 1892 compelled them to give all their space to politics, so they explained. I believed them, for they had all written me kind letters about my stuff and the *Times-Star*, unsolicited, raised my pay to $7.50!

Then the unbelievable happened. In December, a little less than three months after my arrival in Paris, *Scribner's Magazine* accepted a story—a grand Christmas present indeed, that news. Fiction was not in the Plan, but one of the first pieces of work that I did after arriving in Paris was a story born of a delightful relationship with an old French dyer of Titusville, Monsieur Claude. As soon as I had finally determined that I would burn all bridges and go to Paris for study, I had set about my preparation in thorough fashion. There was the language. I had read it fluently for years—but speak it? No. Could I master enough in the few months I had before sailing to find my way about? If so, I must have some one to talk with. The best the town afforded was Monsieur Claude and his mouselike wife. They were flattered by my request. Three times a week I went, and we talked and studied until they both were sure I could make myself understood in common matters. In this delightful association I discovered that the passion of Monsieur Claude, the longing of his heart, was to see France before he died. He had insisted that I learn and almost daily repeat Béranger's "France Adorée." Once in Paris, I understood him, wrote his story, sent it—a trial balloon—to *Scribner's Magazine*.

The selection was made on a principle which young writers too rarely consider when they attempt to place their wares, and that is understanding of the tastes and prejudices and hobbies of periodicals. Useless in 1890 to send a story on "France Adorée" to a magazine which was interested purely and simply in realistic literature; but the inexperienced writer frequently does not realize that. Naturally I had learned in my work on *The Chautauquan* something of the pet interests of the leading publishing houses. I knew that *Scribner's* enjoyed French cultivation, French character, French history. I hoped my sentimental title "France Adorée" would not antagonize the editor of *Scribner's Magazine*.

But I had expected nothing from it, being in that state of mind where I had ceased to expect, only to accept. So that when I received a friendly letter from Mr. Burlingame, the editor of the magazine, saying that he liked the story, that he accepted it, I felt as one must who suddenly draws a fortune in the sweepstakes.

In due time a check for $100 arrived. What excitement in our little salon when I showed my companions that check! "Now," declared our beautiful Mary, "we can move to the Champs Elysées." And she would have done it, for she was one of those who always see spring in a single sparrow. We stayed where we were, I requiring a whole flock of sparrows to convince me that it was spring.

The influence of the story on my fortunes was all out of proportion to its value. Most important was the courage it gave me. If I, a stranger, could do something that a great editor of a great magazine thought good enough to accept, why, after all, I might work it out. That which moved me most deeply, gave me joy that made me weep, was that now I should have something to show to my family. I had felt a deserter. Times were hard in the Titusville household in these early nineties. My father's and brother's experiences in the oil business—of which I want to speak later—were more than discouraging; they were alarming. My sister was ill and in the hospital; my mother's letters were saturated with anxiety. And here was I—the eldest child in the family, a woman of years and of some experience, who had been given an education, whose social philosophy demanded that she do her part in working out family problems—here was I across the ocean writing picayune pieces at a fourth of a cent a word while they struggled there. I felt guilty, and the only way I had kept myself up to what I had undertaken was the hope that I could eventually make a substantial return. If any one of the family felt that I should have been at home there never was a hint of it. From them I had unwavering sympathy and encouragement.

But if in three months' time I could do what I had done, and I made the most of it in my letters home, why, then they would see some hope for the future. Not only would the story help them to believe in me, it would give something more imposing to show to inquiring friends than the newspaper articles which had been their only exhibit.

When the story appeared in the following spring the reverberations in my Paris circle were encouraging and useful. I even heard of it from "the other side," as we called the Right Bank, for Theodore Stanton (at that time the head of the Associated Press in Paris) came with Mrs. Stanton to call on me and tell me he liked the story.

The most important fruit was that Mr. Burlingame looked me up when he made his annual spring visit to Europe. Here was my chance to tell him about Madame Roland, to ask if he thought his house would be interested in such a biography if it turned out to be a good piece of work. "The suggestion would have to be considered in New York," he replied. But he promised me it would be considered. And it was, for not long afterwards he wrote me that the house was interested in my project, certainly wanted to see the manuscript.

This was enough to settle finally a struggle that had tormented me for many weeks. I had come to Paris determined to fit myself for magazine work along historical and biographical lines; but once close to the world of the scholar, surrounded by men and a few women who lived stern, self-denying lives in order to master a field however small I was seized with an ambition to be a scholar. It was a throwback to my old passion for the microscope. I would specialize in the French Revolution—I would become a professor.

But Mr. Burlingame's answer to my inquiry as to whether the Scribner company would be friendly to a biographical study of my lady settled the matter; which shows, I take it, how shallow my scholarly ambitions really were.

The Scribner connection was not the only one putting heart into me. Among my early trial balloons was one marked for McClure's Syndicate, New York City. It carried an article of two thousand words with a catchy title—"The King of Paris"— cribbed from a French newspaper. It was the story of Jean Alphand and his services to the city. The balloon reached its destination. The article was promptly accepted with a promise of $10 when it was published, also a suggestion that they would be glad to consider other subjects if I had them to offer—which I did. Indeed, I gave them no time to forget me; not that they took all I hustled across the Atlantic, but they took enough to make me feel that this might be a stable and prosperous market for short and timely articles. When suggestions finally began to come from them I felt the ground firmer on my feet. One of these suggestions led me into an especially attractive new field, and in the long run had important bearing on my major interest, Madame Roland. It was that I try a series of sketches of French women writers. There was a respectable group of them, and I asked nothing better than to look them up.

I began with a woman who at that time was introducing leading contemporary English and American writers to the French through the *Revue des deux Mondes*—Madame Blanc, her pen name Théodore Bentzon, a person of rare distinction and of gallant soul. She had been a lady in waiting at Napoleon III's court, had made an unfortunate marriage, was now living on a small income and what she could earn by writing. In her salon there was a portrait taken in her young womanhood which charmed me, but when I spoke of it she shook her head as if she did not want to remember it. "Une femme qui n'existe plus," she said.

Hard worker as Madame Blanc was, she found time to start me on my rounds among the French women writers. I doubt if there was an American writer of our day who would have had both the kindness of heart and the sureness of herself to take so much trouble for an unknown woman. She started me off, and I turned out ten or a dozen little pieces before I was through. With one of my subjects I had an amusing flirtation—I think I may call it a flirtation. This was Madame Dieulafoy who with her husband had done eminent work in archaeology, and who had a roomful of exhibits in the Louvre to her credit—a very great person indeed. Madame Dieulafoy was the only woman I had ever seen at that time who wore men's clothes. It had been found necessary to put her into trousers for excavating work, and she liked them so well and Monsieur Dieulafoy loved her so in them that they had obtained permission from the French Government for her to wear them in Paris. From more than one source I heard of the sensation she created among servants when she came to call. They abandoned their duties to peep from dark places at the woman in men's clothes.

Madame Dieulafoy and I grew friendly over the history of the exploits of women in the world, and it took no time at all for me to decide to write the history of women from Eve up, as if I had not already enough on my hands. She applauded my idea, gave me many suggestions, but it never went any further than my few visits, which as I say were more or less flirtations. She was such a pretty little man, so immaculate (the best tailors in Paris did her, I was told), that I could not keep admiring eyes off her. She used her eyes, too, and loved to pat me on the knee, partly I suppose because I always blushed when she did it. It was an amusing acquaintance and a profitable one to me, for she was as interested in my plans for articles as if I had been one of her own.

Another woman who interested me greatly was Judith Gautier. My interest was stirred by my indignation that her name had been left off the list of living women distinguished in French literature sent to the Chicago Exposition of 1893. There was much speculation among my friends as to how it happened. My own conclusion was that it was because of her long and impassioned devotion to the music of Richard Wagner.

The first Wagner opera to be given in Paris was "Tannhäuser." This was in the early sixties, when Judith Gautier was about fourteen years old. She went to the opera with her father —Théophile Gautier—and was enthusiastic although the house received it coldly. As they were walking home a little fellow with hollow cheeks, eagle nose, and very bright eyes joined them. He rejoiced with cheerful violence over the failure of the opera. The girl, angered, forgot her manners and blurted out, "It is clear, sir, that you know you have heard a masterpiece, and that you are talking of a rival."

"Do you know who that was, saucebox?" her delighted father asked as they passed on.

"No, who?"

"Hector Berlioz."

It was the beginning of a lifelong devotion. Wagner was to her not only the master musician but a species of divinity. In 1882 she published a volume on him—valuable for its reminiscences.

Early in the winter of 1892 "Lohengrin" was announced for the season of Grand Opera. I was amazed at the loud and bitter protests. Among the few lovers of Wagner who had courage to come to the defense of the master was Judith Gautier. She was abused for it. As this was my first realization that political hatred ever influences the judgment in matters of art, I took the incident very much to heart. I could understand why people might dislike Wagnerian music, but that the soldiers should be called out to protect the Opera House when one of his greatest works was to be given shocked me. You could then so hate an enemy that beauty herself was outraged!

It was easy for me to conclude that Judith Gautier's name had been left off the list of writing women sent to the Chicago Exposition because the committee wanted to punish her for defending the works of a great artist in whom she profoundly believed.

The opening up of opportunities so much more quickly than I had dared dream spurred me to longer and harder hours at work. There were few mornings that I was not at my desk at eight o'clock; there were few nights that I went to bed before midnight, and there was real drudgery in making legible copy after my article was written. It was all done by longhand—careful and painstaking handwriting, it was. I was to find later that Mr. McClure's partner in the Syndicate, Mr. J. S. Phillips, trying to estimate the possibilities in this correspondent bombarding them with articles and suggestions, set me down from my handwriting as a middle-aged New England schoolteacher.

But if life was hard and life was meager, and if down at the bottom of my heart it was continuously in question to which class of the poor I would finally belong, life to my surprise was taking on a varied pattern very different from the drab existence of hard work and self-denial that I had planned and was prepared to endure to the end. It began at the Rue du Sommerard, where at the outset we stumbled on what turned out to be the most colorful, unusual, and frequently perplexing association that had ever come the way of any one of us.

When we took our rooms from Madame Bonnet she had told us that one room in the apartment was reserved for an Egyptian

Prince who came only for the week ends. He was *bien comme il faut, très riche, très* everything desirable. He would not disturb us, we might never see him. Upon inquiry we discovered that all Madame Bonnet's rooms save those we were taking were occupied by Egyptian students of law or medicine or diplomacy. The Prince, himself, a cousin of the Khedive, was in the military school at Saint-Cyr. He kept a room at Madame Bonnet's to spend an occasional holiday or Sunday with his compatriots, all of his age and all of the upper classes.

We all shared the American flutter over titles, and when we caught a first glimpse of the Prince and his friends we were still more excited. They were quite the most elegant-looking male specimens so far as manners and clothes went that any one of us had ever seen. Here was more in the way of flavor than we had bargained for. We had come to study the French and had dropped into an Egyptian colony.

We soon discovered that they were as curious about us as we were about them, for hardly were we settled when Madame Bonnet came to say that the *messieurs* were all in her salon. Wouldn't we come in and make their acquaintance? Of course we went. They wanted us to dance. Now it was Sunday, and we had all been brought up under the Methodist discipline. Sunday was a day of rest and worship and no play, no amusement of any kind. In my household at least I was supposed to play only hymns on the piano as we were supposed to read only religious books. My mother and I compromised at last on Gottschalk's "Last Hope"; she, being moved by the story of its composition, thought that it must be religious, but "Martha" and "Poet and Peasant," my two other show pieces, were forbidden.

Indeed, when I was forty years old my father, catching me reading a volume of a certain Congressional trust investigation on a Sunday afternoon, reproved me in his gentle way. "You shouldn't read that on Sunday, Ida." I quickly exchanged it for

"Pilgrim's Progress," which is not without suggestion for a student of the trust.

My young companions were particularly shocked at the Egyptians' invitation to dance. I think it had never occurred to them that all people did not keep Sunday. "No," we said a little severely, "we don't dance on Sunday." I had the satisfaction of hearing them whisper soberly to one another, "*très religieuses.*" It was just as well, I thought, they should have that idea to start with; better than starting with the degree of intimacy they might see in our dancing in their landlady's salon on a first meeting.

But we had what was for us an exciting evening, and when we left and they all begged "Come again" we promised that we would.

It was the beginning of a weekly party. Madame Bonnet gave the Egyptians their dinners. We agreed to take dinners once a week with her. We couldn't afford more, and besides we wanted to be on the safe side in our relations. There must be no question in their minds about our entire respectability—respectability as we understood it. What interested me particularly was that at once they wanted to understand our conventions, social and religious and political. Nothing disturbed them more, I found, than a feeling that perhaps they had not quite understood, that unintentionally they had infringed on our customs. Once convinced of this, we could go with entire freedom to our weekly Egyptian evenings. As I recall them they were happy evenings much like children's parties at home, for the Egyptians loved games, tricks, charades, play of any sort. They laughed and shouted and, if something went wrong, flew into a rage like children.

The meat of the connection was the talk which sometimes ran far into the night. All of these young men were in training for some kind of professional or official position. Two or three of them had taken from three to four years at German gymnasia or English universities. All of them spoke three or four languages. The Prince's English was perfect, and no one of us could ever hope to approach the French of the group, learned for the most part in Switzerland as children. They had much more curiosity and real information about the social customs of other countries than we had. They were eager to know all about our ways, particularly the life of women, their relation to men before and after marriage.

There were would-be reformers of Egyptian marriage customs among them; especially did they resent the convention which prevented them looking at the face of the bride before the marriage ceremony. One of the group had made a vow never to marry as long as that custom existed and was urging his compatriots to join him. Nearly all of them insisted that they would never marry more than one woman. They asked with a frankness startling to our ears about the way monogamy worked in the United States. They were curious to know the position of the mistress, and when we were shocked and insisted that a good man never had a mistress they were frankly incredulous. It would never work out, they insisted. One wife they understood; but one wife and no mistress seemed entirely impractical.

Politics interested them profoundly. Particularly did they hate England—how deeply and bitterly I did not realize until in January of '92 news of the death of the Khedive, Tewfik Pasha son of Ismail Pasha, great-grandson of Mehemet Ali, came to the Rue du Sommerard. Madame Bonnet came in at once to tell us how sorrowful our friends were and to ask that we dine with them that night. We found them very grave. "He was a good man," they insisted, "our friend." What was going to happen now? I took it they feared changes in government which might make their own futures uncertain. They were uneasy, frightened and wanted us to understand the reason behind their anxiety.

After dinner a large number of their compatriots filed into

the room. We were begged to stay. They evidently wanted us to understand better their suspicion of what England might do in this crisis. The longer the talk, the more bitter they grew.

"Down with England!" they began to cry.

Indignation and enthusiasm are qualities as contagious as disease. Before I realized it, I shared their anger and was drinking repeatedly in *l'eau sucrée*—good Mohammedans that our Egyptians were, they never touched wine—drinking repeatedly to loud and angry roars of "A bas l'Angleterre!"

The Egyptians were not only a picturesque and enlivening feature in our life: they had a social value which they never suspected. We used them rather shamelessly to impress wandering Americans who looked with badly concealed scorn on the Latin Quarter and particularly on our narrow and stuffy rooms. "A Prince was our neighbor," we said loftily, and to prove it we could show an autographed photograph which the Prince on his own notion had given me. I kept it on the mantel in the little salon. When we felt particular need of asserting ourselves we told of our weekly dinners and they lost nothing of their gaiety and interest in our telling. There was so much more flavor in them, we always assured those who tried to high-hat us, than ordinary sight-seeing offered!

I have always felt rather proud of the way we handled ourselves in that year, keeping the entire respect of our Egyptians. It was not always so easy. It fell into my awkward hands to handle one rather violent love affair. A pretty and vivacious young girl had joined our party at the request of her brother: "Will you look after her?" The Egyptians were delighted with her, and she treated them as she might a group of American boys, could see no reason why she should not go out with them. Only our combined disapproval, our insistence that if she did she soon would be classed in the Quarter as little better than the gay little girls who swarmed about, and with whom we occasionally out of the corner of our eyes saw our Egyptians: she must not run that risk. But while that was managed the inevitable stir of youth could not be managed, and it was not long before I had one of the nicest of the boys begging me on his knees to let him pay his addresses to my little friend, insisting that he would marry her, never take another wife. He wept and pleaded, but I held my ground until finally the young girl who loved his suit but not the boy was safely on the ocean.

A long time afterwards I had proof that we did look after ourselves. When a couple of our party were going to Italy one of these young men gave them a letter of introduction to an Egyptian friend in Milan. The letter was not presented, and not opened until two or three years later, when my friend showed me the postscript. It read: "Surtout soyez convenable avec ces dames."

After the Egyptians came our French professor, a woman of forty, buxom, competent, gay-hearted, an able teacher. I have never known man or woman more shrewd in gauging character or more expert in turning the qualities she found to her own advantage. If she respected or admired them she took no more than she gave—frequently, as in my case, much less. But if she found a pupil lazy or dishonest or stingy or rich and irresponsible, she took mercilessly. "Such people deserve nothing—nothing," she declared once when I protested.

She respected me because I worked, but she always told me frankly that although I read French easily and wrote it *pas mal* I should always speak it with the "detestable" English accent. "No ear—too old." However, I could be made more fluent, my vocabulary enlarged, my grammar perfected. And to that end she bent all her efforts, establishing several useful exchange relations. The chief of these was her most intimate friend, Monsieur X, a man who I suppose had been for many years her lover.

Monsieur X had no superior intelligence; but he was industrious and *bon enfant*, and partly at least through the help of Madame A had come to hold an excellent official position. She kept him busy improving his chances. At the moment she took me on she had him translating a big volume on the English system of handling the unemployed and the helplessly poor, an acute problem for France in the early nineties. As she already had pried out of me full information of all I was trying to do, she saw at once the possibility of a trade. If I would help him in translating, he would secure reports and information on subjects in which I was interested. It seemed a good thing for me at any rate, and the arrangement was made.

I continued to help with the book until it was published. It was well received, even *couronné* by the Academy of Science. To my astonishment I found then that Madame A's interest in this book and its success was that it would help her in making a more profitable marriage for Monsieur X. They had settled on a wife —that, I knew—but, as she told me, his position was so much improved by the success of his book that he was worth a much larger dot. Therefore, she set out with his help, I suppose, to find another wife. They succeeded, and the affair was arranged.

I was deeply disturbed by the matter. I believed, as I still do, that the only safe basis for a happy marriage is a compound of physical harmony, capacity for companionship combined with understanding and acceptance of each other's ideals. I could see little chance where it was a matter chiefly of balanced income. But Madame A had no sympathy with my idealistic attitude towards marriage.

Of course it left her high and dry. The little dinners which the three of us had shared almost every week became dinners *à deux*. The first night I was torn with sympathy.

"Will you never see him again?" I asked.

"Of course, not now, later perhaps. These things arrange themselves, mademoiselle."

But I noticed she ordered a double cognac that night.

Madame A rendered one very great service to our group, one which we could never repay. We had been but a short time in

Paris before we realized that one of our duties was to be helping out American girls and women who had come to Europe to study a little, sight-see a little, travel a little, expecting easily to form congenial relations with the people of the country, and who for one reason or another had never been able to do this. They were disappointed and unhappy. The four of us standing together made a nucleus they envied. We made it a rule to do our best to help them out; but at least in one case it involved us in serious trouble.

Among those who had attached themselves to us was a woman of some forty or more years with a curiously repellent personality. I have never known a person to produce a more melancholy effect on strangers. I have seen our little salon empty itself if she dropped in on our evening at home. Even Madame Bonnet's little black dog Riquet, who had adopted us, would slink around the edge of the room and beg to be let out if she came in. What was the matter? We could not imagine. More than once she threw herself into my arms and sobbed that she was unhappy, in great trouble, of which she could not speak.

Miss C had been some three months in the house when we came home from a week-end trip to be met by an outraged Madame Bonnet. Miss C, she told us, had been arrested, arrested for stealing at the Bon Marché and the Louvre. She was in Saint-Lazaire. There was a note for me. I must do something. Think of the disgrace to her establishment!

The note told me only where she was, that she had engaged a lawyer, asked me to see him. I did, and found him of the type which I suppose hangs around all prisons into which great cities dump women of the street and petty criminals. His only interest was in a possible retainer. How much would I pay him for taking the case? Nothing, I assured him, until I had talked to the American authorities. I went to the consulate, where an irate and worried official swore loudly at the faculty of American women for getting into trouble in France.

"Here I am," he said, "saddled with a girl who is going to have a baby and who swears she'll kill herself if I don't arrange for her to have it so her family will never know.

"I was afraid she would do it too, and then there would be another nasty scandal to hush up, so I got the man here and told him he must put up the money to see her through.

"He laughed at me; but I pulled this revolver out of the drawer" (suiting the action to the word) "and told him I thought I ought to shoot him, but that if I didn't I'd send for the girl's brother and see that he did. Well, he settled for ten thousand francs. But that does not let me off. What am I going to do with the baby? And now here you are with one of the nastiest kind of cases for a French court. They can't stand foreigners stealing from them."

"But what am I to do?" I wailed.

"She'll have to stand a public trial. You must impress the judges. Find out if she's got friends. Get cablegrams. Show she has relatives willing to help her. Read her letters. See if they don't show what is behind this, and when the trial comes have all the pretty girls and prosperous-looking men you know present. They'll look at you, and they'll think twice. Put on a campaign, woman."

And so I started out to put on a campaign. I began by reading her letters. I did not go far before I had the story—a tragic one. Miss C was well born, her family prosperous and important in her state, she a graduate of a great university. She had been a successful teacher, was to have been married to a man whom she had loved for years with passion and depth. For reasons I never knew the engagement was broken. In an attempt to forget, patch up her shattered hopes, she had come to Europe for study and travel; but she couldn't forget, and every week for months she had written the man long letters and every week they had come back to her unopened.

Her despair became so black that, as she told me later, "I had to do something." And so, as when one bites on a sore tooth, she had begun to steal. The proofs of it were all there in her room: a pathetic collection of articles, not worth stealing, slipped mainly from bargain counters. Among them there were at least seventy pairs of gloves of every size and color—none of them any one of us would have worn. There were some fifty pen knives; there were a pile of half-bolts of ribbon and lace, innumerable spools of silk and cotton, packages of pins and needles. All taken not because she wanted them, only to hurt herself in another spot, take her mind from the original wound.

Understanding her wretchedness, I could sympathize with her folly. I began my campaign by telling Madame of our trouble. She detested Miss C, thought her crazy, though she admitted she was a better pupil than any one of us, but here was excitement, also an opportunity to serve us. What the consul had not suggested, she did.

There was a long wait. Our prisoner was transferred to the Conciergerie, where I went to see her. A gruesome trip under the very windows from which I knew Madame Roland had looked in the days before she mounted the cart and took her last ride along the quay to the guillotine.

When the trial came the sympathizing claque was a grand success. At Madame A's suggestion we dressed for it in the best we had, bought new flowers for our hats and fresh gloves, brought over two or three handsome young women from the Champs Elysées Quarter. As for Madame A herself, she made a toilette which even a judge would see and hear.

I had suggested that Monsieur X, being an important person, might impress the judge. She was horrified. "Drag a member of the Government into such a stupid affair! No, you Americans must do it. I'll bring the rich American."

And she did. The rich American was a wealthy idler who for several winters had taken lessons from her, largely, I think, because he found her so pungent and amusing. He treated her royally as to fees and kept her in flowers and candy. He looked his part of important man of affairs. No one could have added more to our display, for one could see even the judges eyeing enviously the elegance of his clothes.

Petty larceny cases were at that time, and I suppose still are, taken into a courtroom perhaps forty by twenty, with seats for friends and the public. On a mounted platform at the end sat three judges in their robes. A dossier of each case lay before them; they had for our friend a rather impressive collection of documents, cablegrams from her family, proofs that her father was or had been a man of importance in public affairs, her college diploma, her check book and a letter of credit showing her to have ample funds.

When all was ready seven prisoners were brought in, six men half degenerate petty thieves and our poor pale tired friend between them. Nothing more incongruous could have been seen than this well dressed woman of evident breeding flanked by these hopeless derelicts.

After looking over the papers in her dossier the judges looked at her and then at us, now paler than she and praying for mercy with eyes and clasped hands. They were perplexed and annoyed. Was there an international angle to the case?

"What are you doing in Paris?" asked one of them harshly.

"Studying," Miss C answered.

"You take a queer way to do it," he said tartly. "Why did you do this?" he asked more gently.

With a weary shake of her head she said, "Je ne sais pas."

It was Madame A who won the case, for it was to her the judges turned as one who, they knew at a glimpse, talked their language. She sailed down the aisle to take her stand before them, and I never have seen any one, man or woman, to whom one could so aptly apply the old figure, "like a full-rigged ship." They let her talk. She told how *comme il faut* we all were—as they could see. We were important, serious, rich. Yes, rich. Then she said candidly: "This woman is crazy. Send her home to her friends."

She had solved their problem, told them their duty, and they followed her advice, adding a fine of five hundred francs and an order that she leave France in a week after her dismissal, and never return.

Madame A had saved Miss C, but she wanted no thanks from her, wouldn't see her; nor would Madame Bonnet let her come into the house save to gather up her things. She had been a fool and got caught. To steal the *riens* as she had! It was a disgrace and respectable people like them could not afford to have her cross their doorways.

Luckily for us, our association with American women was not confined to problem cases. There was a disturbing number of them compelling me to ask myself again and again if this break for freedom, this revolt against security in which I myself was taking part was not a fatal adventure bound to injure the family, the one institution in which I believed more than any other, bound to produce a terrible crop of wretchedness and abnormality. Had not even the few successes I saw about me been paid for by a hardening of heart, a suppression of natural human joyousness that was uglier even than the case of my poor Miss C?

But I was saved from too much perplexity over what freedom might be doing to my compatriots by a gradual drifting into rather close companionship with a number of Americans like ourselves taking lectures at the Sorbonne, and the Collège de France. It was a great piece of luck for us since these Americans were all students of more experience and attainment than any one of us. There was Dr. John Vincent of the History Department of Johns Hopkins University, and along with him his wife who spent hours of every day making beautiful copies of canvases in the Luxembourg. There were Fred Parker Emery of the English Department of Massachusetts Institute of Technology and his wife. There was a younger man, Charles D. Hazen, a Hopkins graduate—a man who was to make a distinguished career for himself in French history, and now Professor Emeritus of History at Columbia, the author of many valuable books.

Serious work did not dull our new friends' curiosity about French life in general nor prevent a humorous detached view of things. We soon were dining together every week in restaurants of the Quarter into which we had never ventured before. Here for one franc, fifty (thirty cents) we got a decent dinner—*vin compris*, as well as a gay company of students and their girls. They were so merry, so natural in their gaiety that none of us were anything but amused over their little ways. It was in one of these restaurants that for the first time in my life I saw a girl take out a compact, straighten her hat—her head had been on her cavalier's shoulder and it was out of plumb—straighten her hat and powder her nose. That the day would come when the manners and customs of the Latin Quarter of the nineties would be the manners and customs of American girls in practically every rank of life would have been unthinkable to me then.

Our new friends added greatly to the pleasure of the weekly sight-seeing excursions which had been one of the features of The Plan. "Every week end, go somewhere"—I had laid down. So every Saturday we were taking a *bateau mouche* or train or tram journey costing only a few of our precious sous—to Saint-Denis, the September fête at Saint-Cloud, Versailles. If the weather was bad we went to the museums, the churches, the monuments. Our new friends liked the idea. When spring came our promenades took on a wider range. There were week-end trips to Fontainebleau and to one after another of the great cathedral and château towns—Chartres, Beauvais, Rheims, Pierrefonds, Compiègne.

Week ends in company as genial, unaffected and intelligent as that of our new friends proved were a rare experience. When the time came for a final break-up of the crowd in August of 1892—my first companions had already gone back to America—those left of us decided to take a farewell vacation together.

The difficulty was to settle on a place. Here was something not on my schedule. We considered Etaples, Beuzeval-Houlgate, Belle-île and finally at the last moment took tickets to Mont-Saint-Michel—a glorious spot; but after watching the tide come in for two successive days, after climbing to the top and descending to the bottom of the château, sitting out sunsets on the wall and eating omelettes at Madame Poulard's until we were fed to the full we pushed on to Saint-Malo and exhausted it as quickly as we had Mont-Saint-Michel. As we listened bored to the orchestra in the square a poster on a wall suddenly caught our collective eyes. It told us to go to the Island of Jersey. With one accord we said "Let's," packed our bags and caught the steamer all within an hour. At Jersey we walked into lodgings: rooms, plenty of them; a salon looking on the sea; such sea fish and vegetables and fruit as only that island offers. We thought it was costing a fortune, but when the bill came—house, housekeeper, maid, and food such as we had not had for a year—it totaled just eighty cents apiece for a day.

That vacation put a gay finish on my first year in Paris. I began the second in deep depression, for several good reasons. First, I had exhausted my reserve. I think I came back from my vacation with twenty francs in my pocket. All my American associates were gone or going soon. I had a new address, for Madame Bonnet had moved from the neighborhood of the Musée Cluny to the more somber neighborhood of the Panthéon and, hardest of all, I knew now that instead of one year more I must have at least two to finish my undertaking. The homesickness and hunger for my family had never been appeased. I had lived on their letters. If they did not come regularly I scolded and wailed; I begged for details of their daily life. My mother was an intimate letter writer, delightfully frank about her neighbors and about the family. She told who was at church, fretted because father spent so much time with his precious Sunday school class of girls, described every new frock, told what they had for Sunday dinner, announced the first green corn in the garden, the blossoming of her pet flowers—snowdrops and primulas and iris in the spring, roses in the summer, anemones in the fall, cactus in the winter. Occasionally she would apologize for her homely details, particularly after I had written a long guidebookish epistle home describing some ancient monument I had been visiting. How I must have bored them sometimes! But home details—"I live off them," I told her. "You can't tell me too much about your daily doings."

This feeling about my family made me a sensitive receiving plate and accounts, I suppose, for the only proof I personally have ever had of the possibilities in telepathy. This came the first Sunday of June, 1892. I had hardly taken my coffee when I fell prey to a most unaccountable alarm. What it was about, I did not know. I could not work and finally went to the street. For hours I walked, not able to throw off the black thing that enveloped me. It was late in the afternoon when I returned to find a compatriot with a letter of introduction waiting. As he was leaving the apartment after his call I picked up my daily copy of *Le Temps* and as I always did turned first to the news from *les Etats Unis*. It was to read that the city of Titusville and its neighbor Oil City had been utterly destroyed by flood and fire. The only buildings left in my home town were said to be the railroad station and a foundry. A hundred and fifty persons had been drowned or burned to death—the inhabitants had taken to the hills.

At that moment my caller came back for his umbrella. I seized him roughly: "Read, read. What shall I do?"

He was a sensible man. "Steady, steady," he said. "Put on your hat, and we'll go out and get other papers." We were soon back with the last editions of all the English and French journals. They all gave space to the disaster, each more distressing and unsatisfactory than the one before.

This explains my black day, I told myself. The family is dead

—our home gone. It was useless to cable, for the newspapers all spoke of broken communications. But the next morning as I was dressing, Madame Bonnet came in with a cablegram. Hardly daring to open it I backed into the corner of the room to feel the support behind me of the walls while my friend Mrs. Vincent, still with me, watched with white face. The telegram was from my brother, and it had just one word. "Safe."

When finally a letter came, I found I had justification for my day of horror. For many hours there had been but little doubt in the minds of my father and brother that the family would have to take to the hills. But they were safe, our home was standing. The experience left me more nervous than ever about them, and now that my friends were gone it took all the resolution I could summon to keep my foolish alarms under control.

Although I was beginning my second year with no money in the bank I had friendly relations with two publishing firms that seemed to see a possible something in my work. There was *Scribner's Magazine*, a relation of which I was justly proud; not only had they encouraged me about my book, but they had asked me to let them consider magazine subjects that interested me and that I was doing. But, while it was the relation on which I hoped to build serious work in the future, at the moment I must share it with something of quicker return; and that seemed to be the McClure Syndicate. I felt surer of this after my first meeting with its founder, S. S. McClure. That meeting had been just before my vacation in the summer of 1892; Mr. McClure had dropped into Paris in the meteoric fashion I found was usual with him, and came by appointment to see me at my new address in the Rue Malebranche. This crooked and steep passage off the Rue Saint-Jacques was unknown to half the *cochers* of Paris, but Mr. McClure found it and arrived bareheaded, watch in hand, breathless from running up my four flights—eighty steps.

"I've just ten minutes," he announced; "must leave for Switzerland tonight to see Tyndall."

A slender figure, S. S. McClure, a shock of tumbled sandy hair, blue eyes which glowed and sparkled. He was close to my own age, a vibrant, eager, indomitable personality that electrified even the experienced and the cynical. His utter simplicity, outrightness, his enthusiasm and confidence captivated me. He was so new and unexpected that practical questions such as, "Would you be interested in articles on . . ." and "How much will you pay?" dropped out of mind. Before I knew it I was listening to the story of his struggle up. How as a peddler he had earned money for college—who could have let him go without buying? —his vast schemes of learning undertaken when a freshman at Knox College, one of which was to study every word in the English dictionary, its start, its development, its present stage, its possible future, his beautiful romance with Hattie, his wife, the story of the Syndicate and of John—always John this, John that, and last a magazine to be—soon. And here I was to come in. While he talked I was managing somehow to tell him the story of my life and hopes and to fit things together.

What was to have been ten minutes stretched to two hours or more. "I must go," he suddenly cried. "Could you lend me forty dollars? It is too late to get money over town, and I must catch the train for Geneva."

"Certainly," I said. I had forty dollars there in my desk, the sum set aside for my farewell vacation. It never occurred to me to do anything but give it to him.

"How queer," he said, "that you should have that much money in the house!"

"Isn't it?" I replied. "It never happened before." But I didn't mention the vacation.

I had some bad moments after he was gone. "Will-of-the-wisp," I said, "a fascinating will-of-the-wisp. I'll never see that money. He'll simply never think of it again. I'll have to give up that vacation. Serves me right."

I did see the money promptly, for Mr. McClure did not forget as I expected him to do, but wired his London office that night to send me a check.

What the new magazine would want from me, I gathered in my long and exciting interview with Mr. McClure, was articles on the achievements of the great French and English scientists. Not history, not literature, not politics, but science, discoveries, inventions, and adventures.

Here I was back to my college days. I found my natural enthusiasm for the physical world and its meanings which Professor Tingley had directed was not dead, only sleeping. I found that, little as I knew of all these things, I still had something of a vocabulary and knew enough to find my way about by hard work. There was Pasteur; there was Janssen, who was building an observatory on Mont Blanc; there was Bertillon, the inventor of the system of criminal identification then attracting the attention of the world. It took all my courage to talk with these gentlemen, but I was soon to find they were the simplest and friendliest of people. For two years I kept on hand popular scientific articles whose success depended on interviews with distinguished specialists, and in that time I met with only one rebuff; but that was a very contemptuous one. It was not from a man but from a gifted American woman who was doing valuable special work in one of the great French scientific institutions. The effect of scholarship on a woman, I told myself. She doesn't ripen, she hardens. I know better now. It happens, but by no means to all women. Take Dr. Florence Sabin, a great human being as well as a great specialist.

The contacts I made on this work left me precious memories. There was my acquaintance with Madame and Monsieur Pasteur. One of the first articles Mr. McClure asked for was on the Institute, then but eight years old. Of course that meant an interview with Pasteur if it could be managed. It turned out to be easy enough.

The Pasteurs lived in a spacious apartment in the Institute:

big rooms with heavy furniture, heavy curtains, dark soft rugs of the period. It was not until I was actually in the library where Madame Pasteur led me that I realized how sadly Pasteur was crippled by the paralysis of his left side which he had suffered twenty-five years earlier after three years of incessant and exhausting labor on the diseases of the silkworm. He moved with difficulty, he hesitated painfully over words; but his eyes were bright, curious, interested.

After a few more or less stumbling explanations on my part we fell to talking naturally. They made it so easy. Mr. McClure was insistent at that moment on what were called human documents, series of portraits of eminent people from babyhood to 1893. I must have a Pasteur series. Monsieur and Madame were delighted with the idea. The old albums were brought out, and the three of us bent over them exactly as we did now and then at home when the question of W. W. T. at one, S. A. T. at two, I. M. T. at three came up. Again and again they stopped to say: "Tiens! Voilà Pierre, comment il est drôle!" "Marie, comme elle est jolie!"

When the album was closed and we had talked long of his early life I made an effort to get some idea of what he was thinking of now, but he said: "No science. If you want that, go see Monsieur Roux." And so reluctantly I went down the stairs that led from the apartment, the kindly old faces watching me, for Monsieur and Madame Pasteur had done me the honor to see me off, and Monsieur kept repeating as I went down, "Look out, the stairs are dark."

When finally the article came out, in the second issue of *McClure's Magazine*, September, 1893, I took a copy to him. He was as pleased as a boy with the pictures. On a later visit he complained that one of his colleagues had carried off the copy. Could I get him another? When I took this to him it was with the request that he write a maxim for the January, 1894, issue of the magazine.

Mr. McClure had had the happy idea of asking from leaders of science, industry, religion, literature a paragraph or two embodying their convictions as to the outlook for the world's future, their hopes for it. There was need enough of encouragement. The world had been going through as bad a year as often comes its way, a year of despair, uncertainty, hopelessness. What was ahead? The replies which filled eighteen pages of the magazine included letters and sentiments from Huxley, Tyndall, Max Müller, Henry Stanley, Julia Ward Howe, Cardinal Gibbons, and a score of others: noble collection. It was published under the heading "The Edge of the Future." It raised my interest in the venture to a high pitch of enthusiasm. It was for me the spirit, the credo of the new magazine. It meant something more than I had dreamed possible in magazine journalism.

For the "Edge of the Future" undertaking I was asked at a last moment to collect all the sentiments I could from distinguished Frenchmen. Pasteur, certainly, and he was easy. "Of course I will do it," he said. "Come back, and I'll have it ready." But when I went back I found him in a flurry. He had written his *pensée*, and it was lost.

"Never mind," comforted Madame Pasteur. "She'll come back when you have it ready for her."

And so I did; but it was unfinished, and Madame Pasteur had to stand over him, encouraging him with tender *très biens* and little pats while he wrote. He was peevish as a child; he didn't like the looks of it, tried again, and finally with a pathetic look said: "I'm afraid you don't want either. But if you do, take your choice." And so I did.

What he had written was:

"In the matter of doing good, obligation ceases only when power fails."

Before the time limit was up I had autographed sentiments from Alphonse Daudet, Zola, Alexandre Dumas, François Coppée and Jules Simon, as well as a collection of impressions still clear. There was Zola.

I carried away from my visit with him an impression of a man agitated, confused, sulky, an impression emphasized by the amazing conglomeration of furnishings of all ages and all countries which cluttered the entry, stairway, and big salon of his house. I had to wind my way between suits of armor, sedan chairs, Chinese lacquered tables and seats, carved and painted wood to reach him standing at the end of the room. The whole house was like that, as is shown in a series of sketches McClure published in one of the early numbers. He talked long and violently about his enemies, defended his realism, hinted that he was a latter-day Balzac, also a great collector spending his leisure in Paris at art sales, which accounted for my difficulty in finding him in his own salon. The sentiment he gave me was a reflection of his talk and of the point of view of his school.

"War," he wrote, "is the very life, the law of the world. How pitiful is man when he introduces ideas of justice and of peace, when implacable nature is only a continual battle field."

Dumas *fils* was the only serene person in the group and was very courteous, the quietest Frenchman I ever met.

Jules Simon touched me deeply by what he wrote:

> "Faire le bien
> Récolter l'ingratitude
> Se confier à Dieu."

7

A FIRST BOOK—
ON NOTHING CERTAIN A YEAR

Now that *McClure's* was really started, I felt that on what I could do for them and the two or three articles in which I had interested *Scribner's* I could live, and that I might drop everything else and devote the bulk of my time to my real business— a study of the life of Madame Roland. She had never been out of my mind. Soon after my arrival I had found to my joy that my daily walks to and from the National Library, where I was spending most of my time, could be laid through the very Quarter in which her father had carried on his trade of goldsmith and past the house in which she had been born, the church where she had taken her first communion, the prison where she had spent her last days, along the route she followed to the guillotine.

"What luck, what luck," I used to say, "that I should be taking the very walks she took!" It was amazing how little things had changed. The house where Madame Roland was born still stands at the western point of the Ile de la Cité looking down on the statue of Henry IV and the busy Seine, and to the right the Pont-Neuf, in her day the heart of Paris and still to me one of its most fascinating spots.

As she slowly came to life something more important began to take shape, something which had been little more than a set of dates and events in my mind. I began to see the Revolution already well on its way when she was born; I saw it rising around her, sucking her in, using her when she thought it had gone far enough and should check its excesses, throwing her over without her head while true to type it went the whole way, finally falling exhausted into the hands of a dictator equipped with guns.

124

The physical scars of all this long train of violence could be seen on my daily walks or studied in the Musée Carnavalet where Paris has gathered documents and relics of what she has destroyed as well as of what she has achieved. But besides the scars of Madame Roland's time were other scars dating from the centuries, scars of revolutionary outbreaks of the same type hardly to be distinguished from those of the period I was trying to visualize; and the more you knew of these explosions, the more they seemed to fit together. You could not bound Madame Roland's Revolution as I had supposed. What I had called the French Revolution was only an unusually violent episode in the lifelong struggle of Paris to preserve herself as a free individual, the slave of no man or group of men. Revolution had always been her last resort in making herself what she was, in forcing kings to do her bidding, tolerating them when they fed her well, beautified her, protected her, but throwing them over when they asked too much money for the job they did.

The marks were all over the city. How could I understand Madame Roland until I understood the elemental force which for centuries had been sweeping Paris in big or little gusts? Did these who sought to loosen the force suppose that they created it or could control it, once loosened? Had Madame Roland, confident as she had been of her ability to act as Providence, frank as she was in saying that no role but that of Providence was suited to her powers, been anything more than a revolutionary tool and victim?

It had always been at work and still was. I must find out about it, and it looked at the moment as if I were going to have a good opportunity to watch a revolutionary revival—of what proportions no man could tell.

The Panama affair had disgusted all self-respecting Frenchmen. "Is the Republic to be a failure?" they were asking. Nothing so gives heart to the leaders of lost causes, disappointed political groups, advocates of panaceas and particularly to the radical-minded, as a rousing political scandal. Panama stirred all the parties of France to action—Bourbons and Bonapartists, extreme conservatives, socialists of all the many varieties, and particularly the anarchists.

There were four groups of the latter, no one of which would have anything to do with any of the others. It was the Independents who now went into action. Members of this group worked alone, letting not even their fellows know what they had in mind. A branch of the order existed in the United States, and it was one of them, Alexander Berkman, who attempted this same year, 1892, to assassinate Henry Frick in Pittsburgh. The Independent who acted first in Paris was Jules Ravachol by name, a man some thirty-three years old, a dyer by trade, with a courageous but not a criminal face. So I thought when, a little later, I secured his photograph and measurements from the Criminal Identification Bureau for *McClure's Magazine*.

Ravachol began by blowing up various houses. It was like a tocsin. All over France similar outrages followed, and they continued at intervals for two or more years—the crowning one a bomb thrown in the Chamber of Deputies in December of 1893 by a notorious anarchist known as Auguste Vaillant. Several Deputies and eighty or more spectators in the gallery were wounded seriously. It was a ghastly affair.

The outbreaks and the rumors of outbreaks as well as the actual destruction had a bad effect on the nerves of many of the French. There was Alphonse Daudet.

Madame Daudet had offered to get me a *pensée* for the collection I was making for *McClure's Magazine*, and arranged for me to call for the copy. After we had tea she took me to the library to see how "Alphonse was getting on." It was my first glimpse of him: a little man, with a shock of straight black hair which stood out rather ferociously at the moment, evidently from running his fingers through it. His face was pale, his eyes astonishingly black and bright. He had lost two or three teeth, and the remaining ones were not very good. He was terribly excited. He had not finished his *pensée*, he said, because he had just had a visit from an anarchist. The servant had let in a man who had demanded twenty francs to buy a wagonload of dynamite to blow up the Hôtel de Ville. He grew more and more excited as he talked.

"I really expected the man to kill me," he said, "and I got out this revolver which I always keep in the drawer." And he pulled it out to show it to me. "A pretty affair," he said, "if while you two were visiting in there a tragedy had gone on in here."

I so shared the general nervousness that, more than once when I saw a man on the omnibus carrying a package, I feared a bomb and abruptly descended; yet along with all my nervousness I was always nosing around, hoping to see a bomb go off. It seemed to me that was my journalistic duty, but I never saw anything more than the ruins they had caused. I did see a pretty good revolution, one that had all the earmarks that I had been finding in my attempted study of Revolution. It was in July of 1893. This time it was youth in revolt, the youth of the Latin Quarter and the Beaux Arts. From start to finish the revolt went on practically under my windows.

The Annual Ball of the Beaux Arts in the winter of 1893 had scandalized Paris. As I remember, the exhibit which outraged was a lady who promenaded with no other covering than a mosquito net. The protest finally reached the Chamber of Deputies, where a member—Berenger—took it up in a serious way and proposed a restrictive law which angered the students. It was, they said, an interference with their right to amuse themselves. Immediately long and picturesque *monômes*—single lines of men, one hand on the shoulder of the man in front, the other grasping a hand of the one behind—threaded their way up and down the boulevards, particularly in the vicinity of the Luxembourg, chanting at the top of their voices, "Conspuez Berenger!" "Conspuez Loze [Chief of Police]!" "Down with the puritans!"

The demonstration began on a Saturday, and that night a great crowd centered in a café in my neighborhood. The place was packed inside and out with youths noisier and noisier as the hours went on. Finally the crowd became so unruly that a squadron of police charged them. There was a great hubbub and in the mêlée somebody hurled one of the heavy white match boxes which were used on all the tables in the Latin Quarter restaurants—a dangerous missile. It hit an innocent spectator who had come to see the fun—a young man of twenty-two or twenty-three from the other side of the river—and killed him. The students were wild with rage, and all that night and all next day they tore up and down the streets, pulling up trees, knocking over kiosks, breaking windows.

The shopkeepers of Paris, having the experience of centuries of revolutionary outbreaks behind them, knew when to retire; and before Monday night the heavy wooden shutters with which they protect their fronts were all up, their doors closed, and the Quarter was alive with soldiers and mounted police. The center of the disturbance that day, however, was not the Latin Quarter but the streets around the Chamber of Deputies, where a great band of angry students kept up a tumult. There were funny incidents. A big group of deputies came out to look over the demonstration, and on the instant the air rang with the jingling of hundreds of big copper sous pitched on the pavements to cries of "Panama, Panama."

The Dahomans were pets of Paris in those days, a picturesque addition to the population. Handsomer creatures never were seen. It happened a carriageful, naked to the waist, attempted to pass through the crowd. At once the students set up the cry, "Berenger, Berenger, bring 'em a figleaf, bring 'em a figleaf."

By Tuesday the Latin Quarter had begun to look sinister. The inevitable had happened.

A popular disturbance never remains long in the full control of those who start it. Advocates of all sorts of systems and causes join it, seize it, if one of them can produce a real leader. A students' revolt can easily become an anarchist raid, with looting and arson on the side by professional lawbreakers, who always come out of their hiding places when anarchy breaks out. As the to-be-expected invasion of the Latin Quarter from without began, destruction increased. Omnibuses were seized and, at strategic points, piled up as barricades.

But the rioters never succeeded in making a stand. Steadily and quietly, night and day, platoons of mounted police moved up and down the boulevards and into the Quarter. I tried at first to go on my usual round, hoping to learn something of revolutionary technique, but after I had been caught in a crowd the cavalry was driving from the Place de la Sorbonne, had heard bullets whistling over my head, been forced to take refuge in the portal of the church, I was content to stay at home. However, there was excitement enough there.

Our street was narrow and steep. When the cavalry charged, it would fill up with the rioters. The movement was amazingly quiet—no shouting, no shots, the only noise the clatter of the horses' feet as they drove the mass ahead.

This invasion of our street produced panic among the foreigners in the house. There were a couple of middle-aged American women on the floor below me out seeing the world; but they had not bargained for a Revolution, and during the three or four days our Revolution was going on they shut themselves night and day in their room.

The Egyptians were in a worse panic. They whispered horrible stories of what happened in revolutions, and one night when fires had been set in our neighborhood and the firemen were out, they were sure we were all going to be burned alive. "Here we are, fourth floor," cried one of them, "too high up to get out. We'll all be dead by morning."

A week was as long as the students could hold out in the torrid weather. There were too many cavalry, too many soldiers, too

alert a police force, and also there were the apaches, the anarchists. It was no longer their revolution. They gave up; and by the
end of the week kiosks were replaced, trees replanted, windows
and doors opened, and we were all going on in our normal way.

Over, all quiet, nevertheless it was a pretty fine little revolution while it lasted. Was it not like Ravachol and Vaillant, a
symptom, the kind of symptom by which the rise of the revolutionary fever always announces itself? Were there those who
would nourish these symptoms as carefully as Madame Roland
and her friends had nourished them in her day? If so, you would
get your explosion. And for what good, I was asking myself.

Madame Roland had lost her head because she was not content
with a first Revolution which had given the country a Constitution. She wanted to get the King and Queen and the highborn of
all varieties out of the way. She wanted a Republic. She lost her
head to those who were not satisfied with getting King and Queen
out of the way, who wanted her and her followers out of the way
as soon as they began to cry for order. Her Republic had collapsed under Napoleon Bonaparte. There had come a return to
the Bourbon, then a Republic, then a return to a Bonaparte and
again her Republic. But was this corrupt and vulgar Republic
I was hearing about any better than the corrupt and scandalous
court she hated and helped overthrow? Was the affair of the
diamond necklace any worse than the affair of Panama? Was the
Bastille a more ghastly prison than the spot where they were now
sending political prisoners—the Devil's Island of the Tropics?

I did not have the consolation of a fixed political formula to
pull me out of my muddle. It is very easy to put everything in
its place when you have that and are armed with its faith and
its phrases. But here was I with a heroine on my hands whose
formula and methods and motives I was beginning to question as
I was questioning the formula, the methods and motives of
France of the moment.

What kept me at my task, prevented me from throwing up

Madame Roland and going on a blind research for the nature and roots of revolution, was the brilliant and friendly intellectual circle into which my quest of Madame Roland had led me.

Among the names I had been advised to include in my series on the writing women of Paris was that of A. Mary F. Robinson, an Englishwoman of the pre-Raphaelite school, a poetess of delicacy and distinction who had married one of the eminent scholars of France, James Darmesteter, a Hebrew and a cripple. One had only to look into his face to know that here was a great soul. And what interested me so was that this something in his face, his remarkable head, wiped out all sense of incongruity between the mating of this slender and exquisite woman with this man of alien race and crippled body. I never felt for a moment an incongruity.

When Monsieur Darmesteter learned I was after Madame Roland he was immediately helpful. "You must know Léon Marillier of the Ecole des Hautes Etudes. He is a great-great-grandson of Madame Roland. He has papers which have never been given to the public. I will write you a letter." Which he did, a letter which brought me an invitation to dinner.

This dinner was the gate to a whole new social and intellectual world. Here was a French academic household of the best sort, simple, hard-working, gay. Léon Marillier was an excellent and respected scholar. Jeanne, his wife, a sister of the Breton poet, Anatole Le Braz, was not only a skillful household manager but, like the wives of many French scholars, her husband's amanuensis, copy and proof reader, and general adviser. She had particular charm among Parisians, for she was a Bretonne who loved her *pays* and kept its distinguishing marks without being provincial. Here I found, too, eager to go over the papers which Léon Marillier spread out after dinner for my inspection, one who was to prove a most helpful and delightful friend, Charles Borgeaud the eminent Swiss scholar, a friend of my friends the Vincents now back at Johns Hopkins.

But this was not the end of it. There was a closer connection, Léon Marillier's mother, the great-granddaughter of Madame Roland, and they quickly passed me on to her.

Here again I was invited to dinner, and here I discovered a circle different from anything I had ever known, a household of brilliant men presided over by Madame Marillier, a most gracious woman, of fine intelligence, freed and mellowed by a tragic life, as I was to learn. More than any woman I have ever known, Madame Marillier came to stand in my mind and heart as the personification of that quality which the French hold so high—*bonté*.

The leader of the group of men was a Sorbonne professor of history—Charles Seignobos. He was a learned man who carried his learning not as an accomplishment but as a social utility. Seignobos was a not too dogmatic socialist and materialist, a good pianist, a marvelous talker, a lovable and pungent personality. Around him there gathered every Wednesday evening for dinner at Madame Marillier's table a number of young men—all serious students, liberal minds, hard workers. After dinner six or eight more habitués of the house were sure to drop in for coffee and for talk.

Among these regular habitués was Lucien Herr, who at that moment was seeking to convert to socialism the two men who in the years since have done most to make the doctrine an impregnable factor in political life in France—Jean Jaurès and Léon Blum, the recent premier of France. Herr at that time was the librarian at the Ecole Normale, as well as managing editor of the *Revue de Paris*. In both positions he met many young would-be scholars and writers. When one of them seemed to him to have the makings of a liberal thinker he worked over him as a missionary works to save a soul. He was so working in the early nineties over Jean Jaurès and Léon Blum.

Occasionally Lucien Herr brought to the Seignobos circle one of those whom he was seeking to convert. If Jaurès and Blum were ever among them they made no particular impression on me, much as I dislike to think so. They were simply a couple of Lucien's young men.

Although Herr believed the socialistic state he sought would and could come by a peaceful evolution, the thing I remember best about him was an exhibit of indifference to bloodshed which shocked me to the core. The night that Vaillant threw the bomb in the Chamber of Deputies the group was dining with Madame Marillier; Lucien was late, not an unusual happening. We were halfway through when he came in, pale, exalted. We all turned in our seats as he standing told us how he had been in the Chamber when the bomb was thrown, of the explosion in mid-air, of the wounded all about him. He had no word of the suffering, only of the political bearings of the deed.

"But the wounded, Lucien," broke in Seignobos, who could not endure the thought of pain.

"Cela ne me fait rien," said Lucien.

His opposition to bloodshed was intellectual, not emotional like that of Seignobos.

On the face of it nobody could have been less at home in such a group than I, a tongue-tied alien, all eyes and ears, contributing nothing but my presence; yet it came about before many weeks that "Mademoiselle Mees," as Seignobos called me, had a place at the weekly dinners. Undoubtedly the friendship that sprang up quickly between Madame Marillier and me, as well as the fact that I asked nothing but to listen, explained it. I could afford to listen; I had never heard such talk. There was nothing on earth that was foreign or forbidden. Opinions were free as the air, but they had to fight for their lives. There was a complete absence of pretense, and sophistry was thrown as soon as it came to its feet. That it was a friendly circle, its acceptance of me was proof enough.

Friendliness began at the door when I arrived Wednesday evening. It was always Seignobos who came rushing to meet me, seized my hand, helped me off with my wraps, danced about me asking eager boyish questions about what I had been doing since I was there last. The talk begun, I was forgotten unless by chance he suddenly recalled me. Then he would jump up, run over, demand, "What do you think of that?" Half the time I was thinking less about what they were saying than about their exciting personalities. They seemed to be vividly related to life, but much of their talk was based on something that was not life— abstract literature, learning, speculation. I realized this when they talked of America. Seignobos saw it only as he had read about it in books. It seemed to him not to be producing that intellectual élite on which he felt the salvation of society depended—a group capable of doing the thinking and planning for a world of lesser men. It was the lesser men who were coming to the top in America. Confronted with superiority from America, he refused to believe it native. One summer I presented to him a friend of mine, a woman of exquisite mind and manner. "She is not American?" he said. "They do not produce that kind in America. Where was she born—where was she educated?"

"In Kansas," I said. He bounded out of his chair like a ball. "It couldn't be, it couldn't be. Kansas is only a half-settled state. One has only to look to see this is a rare type that you have brought here. She never came out of Kansas."

I never saw him more outraged than one day when pressure was brought to bear on him to accept a position in the University of Chicago at a handsome salary. Jumping up, he raced around the room. "Chicago! What can a man of intelligence find there? You can't build an intellectual center on money and organization. It is a growth. Five hundred years from now Chicago may be fit for scholars, but not now."

He mistrusted the intelligence of the United States, but less than that of England. Americans were not stupid: Englishmen were. He wanted none of them in his circle. I met this prejudice head-on when I asked permission to introduce to him a brilliant young English friend, H. Wickham Steed.

I had never known a young man who was surer of what he wanted to do in life or who was preparing for it in a more thorough and logical fashion than Steed. His ambition was to become a foreign correspondent of the London *Times*. He knew that for this it was necessary for him to be familiar with the languages, the history, the men, the politics of the leading countries of the Continent. He began by taking some two years in Germany. Now he was acquainting himself with the French language, literature, politics, leaders. I found Steed especially interesting on a subject of which I knew little, although we were having reverberations in the United States. This was the philosophy of Karl Marx. Steed was familiar with its then status in Germany, knew its leaders—Liebknecht and Engels. He envied me my relations with the group at Madame Marillier's, envied me my Wednesday night dinner, as he might very well.

"Could you not present me?" he asked.

I knew how jealous they were of their circle, and knew, too, they thought the English a stupid bigoted race and wanted none of it. But Steed was certainly not stupid. Besides, he was young, and I had a feeling that nothing would be better for him than contact with these enlightened friends of mine. And so with some hesitation I told Seignobos about him and asked him if I might bring him.

"Never! The English are stupid."

"You are wrong about Steed," I argued. "You ought to be willing to give him the benefit of the doubt."

After some arguments I was allowed to present my protégé. As I expected, they pounced on him mercilessly. It was fine to see the way he held his own and a relief when, after an hour or more of baiting, Seignobos came to my corner and in a tone of surprise and wonder said, "Mademoiselle Mees, your Englishman is intelligent."

When they came to that conclusion they took Steed in, and from that time on he was welcome. All through the years of his brilliant career as a correspondent and later through the war as foreign editor of the London *Times*, the association with Seignobos continued. In his recollections, "Through Thirty Years," Steed tells of his introduction to the circle—"a sort of entrance examination" which convinced his examiners he was less stupid than he ought to have been.

This then was the group in which my interest in Madame Roland had landed me. As the weeks went on, the intimacy grew greater. Whatever occurred to them that might help me in my work, they suggested. It was through their introduction that I was given every opportunity in the manuscript room of the National Library to work over the large collection of Roland manuscripts which had just been catalogued. Indeed, I was the first person to work on them in the Library.

Delightful as well as important to my enterprise was the invitation Madame gave me in the spring of 1893 to go with her for a fortnight to Le Clos, a country estate which had been in the Roland family for at least a hundred years before the Revolution. After the death of Monsieur and Madame Roland in 1793 Le Clos had passed to their daughter. It now belonged to Madame Marillier, who managed it, giving special care to its chief yield, grapes—made into wine on the place.

Le Clos lay in the Beaujolais, some thirty miles north of the city of Lyons and close to a hamlet called Theizé. Here Madame Roland had spent some four years while her husband served as inspector of manufactures at Lyons. The château was little changed, so Madame Marillier told me. The activities were what they had been a hundred years ago. It was a rare chance to see my heroine in a different role, busy with other duties than those of student, tuft-hunter, political diplomat, Providence to a Nation. I needed to see her in a more natural and helpful environment, for I was beginning to mistrust her.

The journey to Le Clos with Madame Marillier, taken in May, was an adventure for both of us. How much she had jeopardized her position in her own family by traveling with a foreigner and a Protestant, I did not realize until the day we spent sightseeing at Dijon. She left me for an hour to visit an important and ancient aunt. "I should not dare take you with me," she said, "my aunt would cast me out if she knew I was traveling with a heretic."

To reach Le Clos we left the railroad at Villefranche and climbed in a horse-cart for an hour and more, steadily up hills, across valleys, a high broad country, striped by many colored ribbonlike farms, dotted by stout buildings of dull yellow, the stone of the country, sprinkled with splendid trees, vineyards and orchards. Theizé, the hamlet we sought, lay high. We drove between its walls, turned into a lane, and stopped before a big gate in a yellow wall. Behind it lay Le Clos, a little white château of Louis XIV's time with corner towers and red-tiled roofs, a court on one side, a garden on the other. From this garden one looked out over a magnificent panorama of hills, mountains, valleys, stretching to the Swiss Alps in the east. On clear evenings the snowcaps were visible and now and then the round crown of Mount Blanc glowed on the sky line like an immense opal.

Within the château there had been little outward change from Madame Roland's time. There was the same great dark kitchen, with its stone floor, its huge fireplace (although now a stove helped out), the same shining copper vessels on the walls. There was the same brick floor in the billiard room with its ancient table, its guns and caps of successive generations of soldiers on the walls. The brightest place within the house was the salon, done in yellow plush, family portraits on the walls, a piano, books.

I had an apartment to myself looking out on the garden and beyond to the mountains: a bedroom, toilet and workroom, severe as a nun's cell with its uncovered floor, its unadorned walls, but containing every necessary comfort and a wealth of books—five hundred or more in my workroom, including several magnificent sets. Among them, Voltaire complete in seventy volumes. They nearly all bore eighteenth century dates, and some of them the name of Roland himself. Indeed, the home was rich in books of value. In Madame Marillier's library there were two thousand or more; but these were only "what was left." From the collection she had inherited she had given Léon Marillier complete early sets of Voltaire, Rousseau, Diderot; she had made a collection of scientific books for Louis Lapique, one of the members of her Paris household, and another of historical books for Charles Seignobos, and still there were all these hundreds, many of which I had the right to believe Madame Roland herself had handled. We ransacked them for marginal notes and hunted through the drawers of old desks and bureaus for papers, finding not a few small bits which were grist for my mill.

Books were about all the original possessions of Le Clos that the Revolutionists of the seventeen-nineties had not made away with. The château itself had not suffered seriously, though there were still some slight scars; but, books aside, it had been completely stripped of furnishings. Even today, so Madame Marillier told me, it was not unusual when inquiry was made about the origin of some interesting old piece in a Beaujolais farmhouse to be told, "Oh, that came from Le Clos a hundred years ago."

The Revolution stripped Le Clos of its possessions and all but ended the family. But it did not succeed in convincing all the Beaujolais of its beneficence. There was not a little outspoken antirevolutionary feeling still abroad. The Marseillaise was never played in Theizé, I was told. The curé and the municipal council would not permit it, nor would they allow the 14th of July to be celebrated. While I was at Le Clos there was a sharp dispute in a neighboring hamlet on the playing of the "Marseillaise." The bandmaster refused to lead when it was asked. It was put up to the band who voted yes. Thereupon the master laid down his

baton and went off in a huff. Madame Roland's Revolution was
not ended.

But I did not think much of such dark matters at Le Clos.
They did not belong to the years I had come there to relive.
Those were only gay, happy, useful years. I knew from her letters before me she could and did fill the role of a local Providence,
adjusting her activities and reforms to what her constituency
understood and was willing to accept. She filled her time as I
saw my friend Madame Marillier filling hers, busy from morning
until night with the affairs of the estate, visiting the people,
prescribing remedies for man and beast, vegetables and vines,
arranging a marriage for this pair, making an invalid more comfortable, taking care of some peasant's wayward son, climbing up
the steep hillside to early mass to set a good example, discharging naturally and intelligently that responsibility to the family,
the estate, the dependent countryside, which the Frenchwoman
seems to accept as her contribution to the state. It makes her
something steady, wise, superior, a strong factor in the economic,
social, and religious stability of France.

I had never seen anything which seemed to me more useful
than what Madame Marillier was doing, and I had opportunity
to judge, for everywhere she went she took me with her. Her in-
variable card of introduction to these natural-born skeptics of
the value of all persons not born and raised in France was,
"Mademoiselle comes from the same country as your vines." That
was enough for them. Their vines had been devastated by repeated visitations of the phylloxera, and it was not until the
introduction of American roots that the vineyards had recovered.
They were looking well now. I was welcome at once; they treated
me as if I were the benefactor, yet I doubt if any of them knew
where America was. Most of them with whom I talked placed it
somewhere in Africa. Africa they did know, as a name at least,
because many of their sons went there for military service. One
of the most surprising things to me among the French, high and

low, was their utter indifference to the geography of the rest of the world. Why should they bother about the rest of the world? There was only one land about which they should know: that was France, and that they should know to the last corner. Even many educated people I met did not distinguish North from South America. In Madame Darmesteter's drawing room I met cultivated people who believed that all Americans carried weapons in their pockets, and that Indians walked the streets of Chicago. When I protested that it was against the law to carry a revolver, and that the only Indians in Chicago were those that were imported as they imported the Dahomans, they smiled incredulously.

Many of them, I concluded, got their notions of what America was like from the exhibits in a certain public hall on the Grand Boulevards. Here you paid a sou or two to look through stereoscopes at amusing and sometimes very improper pictures. Here the walls were decorated with illustrated newspapers from different countries, and among them were always copies of the *Police Gazette*. As a matter of fact it was in this hall of the Grand Boulevard of Paris that I saw the first copy of the *Police Gazette* that I had seen since those days back in Rouseville when my friend and I carefully studied the underworld in the sheets that we could slip away from the bunkhouse of my father's workmen.

The visit to Le Clos with its grist of impressions, the conviction that I had seen Madame Roland herself, in her happiest as well as her most useful days, completed the study of source material for her life on which I had been working as I found time through the twenty months I had been in Paris. It rounded out the woman she was, softened the asperity which I was beginning to feel for her; also it strengthened my suspicion that while a woman frequently was a success as the Providence of a countryside she did no better than a man when she attempted to fill that function for a nation.

Now I was ready to write my book. Of course while I was doing this I must keep the wolf from the door, and it was not so easy in the year 1893 for a stray journalist in Paris to get out of the distracted American market orders or pay for orders. The depression of the nineties, now in its third year with five years more to go, was working havoc everywhere. It was hard to get your money even if your debtors consented you had earned it. I was depending at the moment largely upon the new magazine, *McClure's*. It had started in the summer of 1893, an undertaking which only the young and innocent and the hopelessly optimistic would ever have dared. It has always been a marvel to me that Mr. McClure and Mr. Phillips were able to hold on through that dreadful year; but they did, and with a resourcefulness, even gaiety, that nobody but those who saw it can appreciate.

I knew perfectly well that if the magazine lived I should get all the money I earned, but in the summer of 1893 they did not have it. It came to a serious pass with me, a point where I did not have a sou or anybody to whom I could confide my predicament. Not for the world would I have told my devoted Madame Marillier that there was no money in my purse; not for the world would I have confided it to Madame A; and, as for the Americans on the scene, I was bent on impressing them with the fact I was really getting on. At all events it must not go back to Titusville or Meadville, Pennsylvania, that this questionable venture of mine had brought me so low.

And so one warm summer day I took my sealskin coat, which really was a very good one quite out of keeping with the rest of my wardrobe—by this time close to scandalous—I took the coat and marched over town to the Mont de Piété. They were polite to me; but I was a foreigner, that coat might be stolen, probably was. What credentials did I have, whom could I give as reference? There was nobody in the town that I was willing to have know what I was doing. But did I have documents to prove my identity?

Yes, I said, I had; and I would bring them. So I left my coat and raced back to the Left Bank for my credentials. And what were they? What did I have? There were letters from my publishers; there was my checkbook—exhausted but nevertheless a checkbook. Without thinking it would be of any particular use I took my Allegheny College diploma. The inspector passed lightly over the letters of editors, the stubs in my checkbook, but the diploma impressed him; and so it was on my Allegheny College diploma I made the loan which helped me over the bad months of 1893 while I was waiting for a check from a land in the grip of one of the most serious money famines that it had ever known.

Although there might be anxious moments over money I was freer to work on my book than I had ever been. And work I did, as hard as I could, all that terrifically hot summer. My friend Madame Marillier had gone to Brittany. She begged me to come along; but I had used up all my vacation money in my trip to Le Clos—a trip I had extended to Switzerland and to a chain of French towns where there were beautiful things I wanted to see, to Bourg, Mâcon, Cluny, Autun. There was nothing that I wanted to do more except finish up and go home.

But the finishing up was not so easy. I had undertaken the study of this woman in order to clear up my mind about the quality of service that women could give and had given in public life, particularly in times of stress. I had hoped to come out with some definite conclusions, to be able to say: "The woman at this point will be a steady, intuitive, dependable force. She will never lend herself to purely emotional or political approaches to great social problems; she knows too much of human beings. Her business has always been handling human beings. Building families has been her job in society. You can depend upon her to tell you whom to trust, whom to follow, whom to discard. These intuitions of hers about people are born of centuries of intimate first-hand dealing with human beings from babyhood on—they are among the world's greatest values. And she will be no party to violence. She knows that solutions are only worked out by patient coopera- tion, and that cooperation must be kindly. She knows the danger of violence in the group as she knows the danger of selfishness. She has been the world's greatest sufferer from these things, and she has suffered them in order that she might protect that thing which is her business in the world, the bearing and the rearing of children. She has a great inarticulate wisdom born of her ex- perience in the world. That is the thing women will give."

That was what I had hoped to find Madame Roland giving; and I had found a politician with a Providence complex. I had also found what I had been trying to shove aside, as women do, new proof of that eternal and necessary natural law that the woman backs up her man. Madame Roland had been Royalist, Republican, Revolutionist, according to the man she loved. She had served her man with unyielding conviction, would not temper or cooperate, intolerant, inflexible.

But what woman in America seeking the vote as a sure cure for injustice and corruption would listen to such a message? That, of course, was no affair of mine. My affair was clearing my own mind. So far I had only succeeded in adding to its confusion, even in destroying faiths I had held. There was the ancient faith that you could depend upon the woman to oppose violence. This woman had been one of the steadiest influences to violence, will- ing, even eager, to use this terrible revolutionary force, so bewil- dering and terrifying to me, to accomplish her ends, childishly believing herself and her friends strong enough to control it when they needed it no longer.

The heaviest blow to my self-confidence so far was my loss of faith in revolution as a divine weapon. Not since I discovered the world not to have been made in six days of twenty-four hours each, had I been so intellectually and spiritually upset. I had held a revolution as a noble and sacred instrument, destroying evil and leaving men free to be wise and good and just. Now it seemed to me not something that men used, but something that used men for its own mysterious end and left behind the same relative proportion of good and evil as it started with.

Never did I so realize my ignorance of life and men and society as in the summer of 1894, when I packed up the manuscript of my life of Madame Roland to take it back to America for its final revision in the peace of my home.

Of course, I told myself, I would go through with it. I would put down what I had found as nearly as I could, even if I had not got what I came for. And then came the question, Can I get what I came for? Is it to be found—the real answer to my question about woman in society, the point or position where she can best serve it? Can I find an answer to this other question that has so disturbed me—the nature of revolution? Apparently, I told myself, as I packed my bag finally to go back to America, you have only begun; but at least you have a new starting point. Cheer up, make a new plan. And I was making a new plan. I had been making one for some time. It was laid down economically, professionally, and socially with as much precision as the plan with which I had come to Paris in 1891. It was a plan for my return to Paris.

I would go home, get my book into shape, try to convince the Scribners that it was worth their publishing. I would get a good long visit with my family, the only thing I felt now to be worth while in life. I wanted to be sure they were there, that the house was there, that my father's chair stood by the living-room center table under the drop gas reading light, that the family Sunday dinner was what it had always been. I wanted to hear my father ask the blessing at the table, to sit with my sister and mother afternoons out on the shady side of the lawn. I wanted all the home flowers I could gather—and it was queer what a big place flowers took in my dreams of home. My mother was one of those women for whom, they say, "anything will grow." And she had had flowers, summer and winter. One of the deprivations of not having money in Paris had been that I could not buy flowers. I had to content myself with lounging around the flower markets on the Square of Notre Dame. I lingered there almost as much as I did over the bookstalls along the Seine. But at home I could gather all I wanted.

I would come back to France on different terms. My friendly publishers would give me work. I had schemes for books and articles which I felt sure would interest the Scribners, that history of women, for instance. Then there was this lively, friendly, aggressive, delightful *McClure's.* There were plenty of things I could write for them.

I would take an apartment in the Latin Quarter up high where I could look over the roofs, see the sky. I would have a salon like Madame Marillier's. She would find me a *bonne à tout faire,* and I could have people in to dinner—Madame Marillier, Seignobos, and perhaps Lucien Herr and Louis Lapique and Charles Borgeaud would come. The summer would bring over my precious American friends—the Vincents, Emerys, Hazens, and my sister must join me. Life would be full and satisfying while I cleared up my mind on women and revolution and continued my search for God in the great cathedrals.

It was with this baggage and a terrible thirst for a long drink of family life that in June, 1894, I said "Au revoir" to my friends. I felt so sure it was Au revoir.

The first two months after I reached America I spent at home convincing myself that my family in spite of the trials it had been suffering was unchanged in its ways, its loyalties, and its philosophy. If life was not as easy materially for my father and mother as their long years of labor and self-denial gave them the right to hope, I found that they were enjoying that most precious experience, the evidence of the continuity of their lives. My brother and his fine wife with their children, two girls and a boy, lived only a few doors away, and the grandchildren were as much in one home as in the other. They gave, I found, a continual fresh zest to the household and its doings. My father again had the legitimate excuse for going to the circus which our growing up had taken from him: "The children want to go." My mother had as strong a justification for family picnics and birthday celebrations on which she tired herself out: "The children enjoy them so."

For me those children were a challenging experience. Three years had made the youngsters keen observers, and I found them appraising me in the fashion of natural unspoiled children. Launched on one of the long narrative monologues to which I am addicted with intimates I would suddenly be checked by the cool impersonal stare of nieces or nephew. They did not know they were doing it, but I knew they were taking my measure. They were not only an unending interest and joy to me but a salutary correction, as they have continued to be to this day.

But before I was really sure of my standing with them, though quite reassured as to that with their elders, and just as I had put the finishing touches to my Madame Roland, I was snatched away from Titusville by a hurried letter from Mr. McClure. I must come at once to New York and write a life of Napoleon Bonaparte.

8

THE NAPOLEON MOVEMENT
OF THE NINETIES

When I reached New York I found that the situation behind the hasty call to come on and write a life of Napoleon was pressing. The Napoleon Movement, which I had been following in Paris for two years, had reached the editorial desk of *McClure's Magazine* in the form of a permission to reproduce a large and choice collection of Napoleon portraits, the property of a distinguished citizen of Washington, D.C.—Gardiner Green Hubbard. Mr. Hubbard was popularly known as the father-in-law of Alexander Graham Bell, the inventor of the telephone. He was as well the father-in-law of the telephone since it was largely through his faith in the invention before it was recognized as a practical utility, and his shrewd and indefatigable work in securing patents, in enlisting supporters, and in fighting rival claimants, that the telephone had been developed and secured for Mr. Bell and his family.

Mr. Hubbard had long been a Napoleon collector. The revival of interest in the man in the early nineties had made him feel that his collection ought to be reproduced for the public. But he insisted a suitable text—that is, one he liked—must go with the pictures. Mr. McClure had secured something well written from an able Englishman, Robert Sherard, a great-grandson of Wordsworth; but it was so contemptuously anti-Napoleon that Mr. Hubbard would not allow his pictures to go with it. And here it was August, and Mr. McClure with the headlong speed in which he conducted affairs had announced the first installment for November.

I was both amazed and amused by the idea that a popular

147

American magazine would think of such an undertaking. Why? I asked myself. I had seen the Napoleon Movement start and grow in Paris in 1892 and 1893. I had read everything that came along in the way of fresh reminiscences, of brilliant journalism, particularly that of *Figaro,* and I had tucked away in my clippings a full set of the Caran d'Ache cartoons which so captivated Paris; but I looked on the Movement as political, an effort of the Bonapartists to revive the popular admiration for the country's most spectacular figure. If the revulsion against the Panama brand of republicanism could be kept alive, fed, might there not be a turning to Bonaparte? Just as the anarchists took advantage of the situation by hurling bombs, so the Bonapartists turned to blazoning France with the stories of the glory that had been hers under the Little Corporal. It is an amazing record of achievement, and one had to be a poor Frenchman, or poor human being for that matter, not to feel his blood stir at its magnificence.

But write a life of Napoleon Bonaparte? It was laughable. And yet how could I refuse to try?

In passing through New York in June I had given Mr. McClure the right to call upon me, promising to join his staff after my vacation. He would give me forty dollars a week—more money than I had ever expected to earn. With care I could save enough to carry me back to Paris, and at the same time I could learn more of the needs of the McClure organization.

The forty dollars a week was a powerful argument. Moreover, I had been talking largely about devoting myself to French Revolutionary history. If this wasn't that, what was? But there was something else. This man had pulled France out of the slough where she lay when Madame Roland lost her head. I had a terrific need of seeing the thing through, France on her feet. Napoleon had for a time set her there and brought back decency, order, common sense.

I would try, I told Mr. McClure, at his expense, but I should

have to go back at once to Paris. Where else could I get sufficient
material? That idea of getting to Paris encouraged me to try,
but first we all agreed I must go to Washington and talk with
Mr. Hubbard, look over the collection. Promptly an invitation
came from Mrs. Hubbard to come at once to their summer home
out Chevy Chase way on Woodley Lane not far from the Rock
Creek Zoo. President and Mrs. Cleveland had their summer home
on the Lane, and the Maclean place, where Admiral Dewey was
to go when he returned the conquering hero from the Philippines,
was across the way. Twin Oaks, as the Hubbard place was called
from two big oaks just in front of the house, was the finest country estate in the Washington district, as well as the most beautiful home into which I had ever been admitted. Mrs. Hubbard
herself was a woman of rare taste and cultivation, a really great
lady, and what she was showed from end to end of that lovely
sunny house. Maids, butler, gardener, all took on something of
her dignity and gentleness.

Mr. Hubbard was a man of some seventy years then, wiry,
energetic, putting in every moment of his time serving his friends
and family and in worshiping Mrs. Hubbard. I think he tried
her preference for quiet and dignity and for people of her own
kind. It must have made her a little uneasy to have a strange
woman with a meager wardrobe and a preoccupied mind drop
into her carefree, gaily bedecked society; but she took it all in
the best nature and with unvarying kindness and understanding.
I liked her particularly for the way she accepted Mr. McClure
in the days to come. He would burst unexpectedly into the house
at any moment which suited his convenience, his bag loaded with
proofs of the Napoleon prints, and almost before he had made
his greeting the bag was open and the proofs spread helter-
skelter over the carpet. Being very much on my good behavior
I was a little horrified myself, and then I did so want them to
like and appreciate Mr. McClure. When I tried to apologize for
the dishevelment he wrought Mrs. Hubbard laughed. "That

eagerness of his is beautiful," she said, "I am accustomed to geniuses." And so she was, as I was to find.

It did not take me long to discover that there was plenty of material in Washington for the Napoleon sketch. Mr. Hubbard had the latest books and pamphlets. It was easy to arrange that I have proofs from Paris of two or three volumes of reminiscences that had been announced. In the State Department I found the full Napoleonic correspondence published by the order of the French Government. Files of all the leading French newspapers of the period were in one library or another. In the Congressional Library there was a remarkable collection of books gathered by Andrew D. White when he was minister to Germany from 1879 to 1881, the bulk of them in German, French, and English. An item of this collection not to be duplicated was some fifty volumes of pamphlets in several different languages made in Germany during the Revolution and covering the Napoleonic era. They were for the most part the hasty agitated outbreaks of *vox populi*—protests, arguments, prophecies, curious personal adventures—but among them were rare bits. Taken as a whole they reflected the contemporary state of mind of the people of Europe as did nothing I had ever seen.

Convinced of the adequacy of material, I reluctantly gave up Paris and settled down to work in the Congressional Library. It was not so easy to find a writing table there in the early nineties, and it took some persuasion to convince the ruler of the place, Ainsworth Spofford, that I was worth the effort, that is that I was there to use his books day in and day out until my task was done. Certain of that, he tucked me in, though stacks of books rising from floor to ceiling had to be moved to find room.

I wonder if students in the United States know how much they owe to this man. He gave his life to making a library first to serve Congress, for he held the firm conviction that Congressmen generally needed educating, and that books handy in which he could find materials for their committee work and their speeches would contribute to the process. He made it his first business to provide them as near on the instant as possible with what he thought they needed. In return for this service he used every opportunity to wheedle, shame, beg money from them, money for books, equipment, an increased staff, and always for better accommodations; for Mr. Spofford had a great vision of a national library, educating not only Congress but the people. To realize that vision he had become what he was when I knew him, a devoted, domineering, crabbed czar of his realm. He worked incessantly, doing everything, knowing everything. He paid little attention to the irritated criticisms of those who saw only the inconveniences and dust and overcrowding of the old rooms, and who charged him with inefficiency and tyranny. His mind was on the arrangement and administration of the marble pile already under way across the square. This was what he had been working for—a worthy place for books. His sharp, irritated, "There, maybe you can find something in that," banging a dusty volume on my table, has often sounded in my ears as in later years I worked at the commodious desks of the library he had dreamed, and which to my mind is a monument to him more than to any other man—naturally enough since he was the only man I ever knew who had anything to do with its existence.

Six weeks, and I had my first installment ready. I had done it with my tongue in my cheek. Impudence, it seemed to me, to write biography on the gallop. I had kept myself to it by repeating in moments of disgust: "Well, a cat may look at a king. I'll sketch it in, and they can take or leave it." But Mr. Hubbard liked what I had done, and that meant Mr. McClure hurried it to the printers while I in hot haste went ahead with my sketching.

I expected nothing for myself from it more than the forty dollars a week, and the inner satisfaction of following the thrilling drama from the terror of '93 down to St. Helena. That satisfied me. But to my surprise I did get the last thing in the world I had expected, the approval of a few people who knew the field. John C. Ropes wrote me he liked the treatment: "Come and lunch with me when you are in Boston and see my Napoleon collection." I couldn't believe my eyes. Of course I went.

Charles Bonaparte, the grandson of Jerome Bonaparte, and Mrs. Bonaparte invited Mr. Hubbard and me to lunch with them in Baltimore to see their collection. Curious the little things one remembers of long-ago experiences! Out of that visit I recall only that Mrs. Bonaparte told me that in the garret when she came into the house where Jerome and his American wife, Elizabeth Patterson, had lived, there were literally barrels of string, short lengths neatly rolled, accumulated by the sister-in-law of Napoleon. Why remember that when the home was full of treasures on my subject? Probably because I have never been able to throw away a string without a pang.

Something better worth remembering was the startling resemblance to Napoleon in a certain pose of Charles Bonaparte. As he stood talking unconsciously, hands behind his back, slightly stooped, he was the counterpart of Raffet's Napoleon, the most natural of them all.

A bit of consolation for my hasty work came from the last source I would have expected: William Milligan Sloane, the author of an elaborate study, the outcome of years of research, recently published by the *Century Magazine*. That was the way biography should be written, I told myself: years of research, of note-taking, of simmering and saturation. Then you had a ripened result. I said something of this once to Mr. Sloane.

"I am not so sure," he replied, "that all the time you want to take, all the opportunity to indulge your curiosity and run here and there on bypaths, to amuse yourself, to speculate and doubt, contribute to the soundness or value of a biography. I have often wished that I had had, as you did, the prod of necessity behind me, the obligation to get it out at a fixed time, to put it through, no time to idle, to weigh, only to set down. You got something that way—a living sketch."

I couldn't have listened to more consoling comment. There must have been something in his characterization of "living," for now, over forty years since it first appeared in book form, I still receive annually a small royalty check for my "potboiling" Napoleon!

What really startled me about that sketch was the way it settled things for me, knocked over my former determinations, and went about shaping my outward life in spite of me. It weakened my resolve never again to tie myself to a position, to keep myself entirely footloose; it shoved Paris into the future and substituted Washington. It was certainly not alone a return to the security of a monthly wage, with the possibility that the wage would soon grow, that turned my plans topsy-turvy, though that had its influence. Chiefly it was the sense of vitality, of adventure, of excitement, that I was getting from being admitted on terms of equality and good comradeship into the McClure crowd.

The "Napoleon" had given the magazine, now in its second year, the circulation boost it needed. My part in it was not exaggerated by the office or by me. We all agreed that it was the pictures that had done it, but the text had framed the pictures, helped bring out their value, and it had been done at a critical moment.

The success of the "Napoleon" sketch did me a good turn with the Scribners, who had had my manuscript of "Madame Roland" for some time. They were hesitating about publishing it. There was no popular appeal. I was entirely unknown, but the "Napoleon" work gave me sufficient backing to persuade them. At least that was the explanation the literary head of the concern, William C. Brownell, gave me. Thus my first book was my second to appear. My reward for writing it came from my interest in doing it, what I learned about how to go at a serious biographical study, certainly not in royalties. My first check was for forty-eight cents. I had used up my share of the small sales in corrections of the proofs and gift copies.

I must stay with them, declared Mr. McClure. And the more I saw of Mr. McClure and his colleagues, the more I wanted to stay. Of my first impression of S. S. McClure in Paris I have spoken. Closer views emphasized and enlarged that impression. He was as eager as a dog on the hunt—never satisfied, never quiet. Creative editing, he insisted, was not to be done by sitting at a desk in a comfortable office. It was only done in the field following scents, hunts. An omnivorous reader of newspapers, magazines, books, he came to his office primed with ideas, possibilities, and there was always a chance that among them was a stroke of genius. He hated nothing so much in the office as settled routine, wanted to feel stir from the door to the inner sanctum. And he had great power to stir excitement by his suggestions, his endless searching after something new, alive, startling, and particularly by his reporting.

He stood in awe of no man, but dashed back and forth over the country, back and forth to Europe interviewing the great and mighty. He brought back from his forays contracts with Stevenson, Conan Doyle, Anthony Hope, Kipling. It was something to find yourself between the covers of a book printing a Jungle story. They all came out in *McClure's* in those years and were followed by "Captains Courageous" and "Stalky" as well as many of the greatest of the short stories and poems—"The Ship That Found Herself," "The Destroyers," the "Recessional" —things that left you breathless and gave to a number the touch of genius for which the office searched and sweated.

Mr. McClure was always peering over the Edge of the Future. It was this search for what was on the way that brought to *McClure's* the first article in an American magazine on radium, the X-ray, Marconi's wireless, Lilienthal's and Octave Chanute's gliders, Langley's steam-driven air-runner and in time the first article on the Wrights' flying machine.

In my field of biography and history the Edge of the Future meant to Mr. McClure the "unpublished" or the so poorly published that its reappearance was equal to a first appearance. The success of a feature spurred him to effort to get more of it, things which would sharpen and perpetuate the interest. He was ready to look into any suggestion, however unlikely it might seem to the cautious-minded. He was never afraid of being fooled, only of missing something.

His quick taking of a hint, his warm reception of new ideas, new facts, had its drawbacks. If they were dramatic and stirring Mr. McClure was impatient of investigation. He wanted the fun of seeing his finds quickly in print. At one point in the publication of the Napoleon he caused me real anxiety by his apparent determination to print a story for which I could find no authority.

Among the contributors to the Syndicate at that time was a picturesque European with a title and an apparently endless flow of gossip. He pretended to have been a member of the Court of Napoleon III and in the confidence of the Emperor. This relation accounted for his having been invited to join a strange secret party made up by the Emperor, who was worried over a rumor that the body of Napoleon I did not lie under the dome of the Invalides. It was not known who did lie there or what had become of Napoleon. To reassure himself the Emperor decided to go with a few chosen friends and open the tomb. They gathered in the dead of night. The tomb was opened. There lay Napoleon, unchanged. The Emperor's mind was at rest. He swore the group to secrecy, but took affidavits to be used in case of political necessity. The fall of the Empire seems to have made the gentleman feel that his oath was no longer binding, and that he could cash in on his adventure.

I did not believe the story, but when I expressed my doubt all I could get out of Mr. McClure was a severe, "What a pity you do not know something about Napoleon!" No new idea to me, since it was the first thing I was thinking every morning when I went to work. What I did not know, as I worried over the possible publication of what I believed a fake, was that in spite of his quick and enthusiastic acceptance of a good story, S. S. McClure cared above all for the soundness, the truthfulness of the magazine. Good stories—yes. But they must hold water, stand the scrutiny of those who knew. Moreover, he knew what I did not as yet, that he could go the limit in his enthusiasms since he had at his side a partner on whom he counted more, I think, than he then realized to balance his excitements.

This happened now. The story was in type, scheduled. Mr. McClure was going to Europe. "While you're over there, Sam," said his partner quietly, "you better verify that Napoleon story. We'll hold it until we hear from you."

A few weeks later came a laconic postal card. "Don't publish the story of the opening of Napoleon's tomb. It wasn't opened."

I never heard the matter referred to after that. By the time he returned he had forgotten what to me was a near tragedy, to him a joyful bit of editorial adventure.

I came later to feel that this quick kindling of the imagination, this untiring curiosity, this determination to run down every clue until you had it there on the table, its worth or worthlessness in full view, was one of Mr. McClure's greatest assets; but it was an asset that would have landed him frequently in hot water if it had not been for the partner who had saved him from the Napoleon hoax, John S. Phillips—J. S. P. as he was known in the office.

Living in Washington as I had been doing, I had seen little of Mr. Phillips, only heard of him, for his name was the one oftenest on Mr. McClure's tongue. His calm and tactful handling of the "General," as the office called Mr. McClure, in the ticklish Napoleon story delighted me.

"Here's a man," I told myself, "who has a nose for humbugs as well as one who knows the power of patience when dealing with the impatient."

As time went on and I spent more and more of it in New York, finally settling there at the end of the decade, I had better opportunities to watch Mr. Phillips in action. I was not long in learning that he was the focus of every essential factor in the making of the magazine: circulation, finance, editing. Into the pigeonhole of his old-fashioned roll-top desk went daily reports of bank balances, subscriptions received, advertising contracts to be signed, books sold. I doubt if he ever went home at night without having a digest of those reports in his head. He knew their relation to the difficult problem of putting the undertaking on its feet.

It was largely Mr. Phillips' love of fine printing and his habit of keeping track of the advances in printing processes that led *McClure's* late in the nineties to set up its own plant. It included all of the new miraculous self-feeding machines, automatic presses, folders, binders, stitchers.

It was the first magazine plant of the kind in the country and had many visitors. Among them was Mark Twain. Mr. Phillips tells an amusing story of his visit. As they stood watching the press perform, a sheet went awry on the bed. The press at once stopped and rang a bell calling for the pressman, who immediately came and helped the big automat out of its plight.

"My God, man!" cried Mark Twain, "That thing ought to vote."

It did more than cast votes for *McClure's*. It saved the money which finally balanced the budget—and then some.

To those of us on the inside it was always a marvel that John Phillips found time to be an editor, as well as a focusing center for everything that went on. At the bottom of his constant editorial supervision was, I think, a passion for the profession. He was unmistakably the most intellectual, as well as the best intellectually trained, person in the office. After graduating at Knox College in Illinois he had taken a degree at Harvard and later spent two years studying literature and philosophy in the University of Leipzig. When he came to the magazine he put all his training into the professional problem.

He was an invaluable aid to the group of staff writers the magazine was building up. He was no easy editor. He never wheedled, never flattered, but rigidly tried to get out of you what he conceived to be your best, taking it for granted that you wanted to make the most of your piece and it was his business to help you. I never had an editor who so quickly and unerringly spotted weaknesses, particularly in construction. He had a fine feeling, too, for the right word, took the trouble to search for it, often bringing in a penciled memo of suggestions long after you had decided to let it go as it was. He knew the supreme value of naturalness, detested fake style. "A kind of disease," I have heard him say, quoting somebody.

It always disturbed a few of us that nobody outside of the office knew what an important part in the making of *McClure's* John Phillips played. He had that rare virtue—the willingness and ability to keep out of the picture if thereby he could make sure the picture was not spoiled in the making.

The one member of the staff besides Mr. McClure whom I knew, when I began to find myself so to speak absorbed, was already by virtue of his unusual gift for comradeship a friend as well as a species of boss—that was Auguste F. Jaccaci, a brilliant artist and art editor as well as one of the most versatile and iridescent personalities I have ever known. I first met Jac, as he was called by everybody, in Paris, when as an advance agent of the new magazine he was sounding out possibilities for writers and illustrators. He took me out to dinner and paid the *addition*. We talked until late, then he simply put me on my omnibus and let me go back to the Latin Quarter alone. Here was established the *modus operandi* for our frequent visiting in the future, in Paris, in New York, in Washington—with one revision. After that first dinner I paid my share of the check, save on special occasions when Jac, a knowing epicure, selected the dinner and treated me.

It was he who showed me the first copy of *McClure's*, that of August, 1893, showed it to me at five-thirty in the morning, at a café across the square from the Gare Saint-Lazare where he had ordered me by cablegram from London to meet him. For nobody in the world excepting a member of my family should I have been willing at that hour to cross Paris. But I couldn't afford to show a lack of interest. Moreover, I must confess that this preposterous order flattered me a little. It was taking me man to man, I said to myself. And so I was there. He had to bully the garçon to get a table out on the sidewalk and make us coffee.

All this was a good basis for a comradeship which lasted to his death. It lives in my memory as something quite apart in my relations with men. Jac had a certain superior appreciation and wisdom never quite put into words, but which you felt. I for my part was always straining to understand, never quite reaching it. Part of his charm was his confidence in his own superiority and his anxiety lest we didn't quite realize it. And then there were his rages. They came and went like terrible summer thundershowers. He would roar down the corridor of the office while I sat and watched him enthralled. Those rages, whether directed at me or somebody else, never made any other impression on me than that of some unusual natural phenomenon.

Here then were the leaders in the crowd to which I had been admitted by virtue of a hasty sketch of Napoleon Bonaparte done on order.

Thank God I had sense enough to realize that here were three rare personalities, and that to miss such associations would be sheer stupidity. Also to know that I was an unusually lucky woman to be accepted.

Then there was the magazine they were making. There was something youthful, gay, natural about it which captivated me. Often, too, it achieved a most precious thing. Mr. Phillips called it a "lift." To be youthful, gay, natural with a "lift"—that was an achievement.

And then I found the place so warmly and often ridiculously human. Mr. McClure was incapable of standing up before a hard-luck story, with the result that he brought into that overcrowded office a string of derelicts ranging from autocratic scrub ladies to indigent editors—brought them in and left them for J. S. P. to place. But J. S. P. was not far behind in his sympathy for those who were down and out. I watched him more than once rescue an author who perhaps out of sheer discouragement had taken to drink and landed in jail. Mr. Phillips saw that he was bailed out, his debts paid, work given him. I never ceased to wonder that these two men loaded with work and responsibility should seemingly consider it part of their daily job to rescue the wastrel and the disheartened.

There was reason enough for me to stay with *McClure's*.

9

GOOD-BYE TO FRANCE

THE Napoleon sketch had not been finished before Mr. McClure
was urging me into a new job—not writing this time, but editing,
editing according to his recipe. "Out with you—look, see, report." Abraham Lincoln was the subject. My heart fell. "If you
once get into American history," I told myself, "you know well
enough that will finish France. It will also finish your determination to solve the woman question and determine the nature of
revolutions. They will go the way of the microscope and your
search for God. Are you to spend your life running, now here,
now there, never follow a path to its end?" Or was I taking my
ambitions too seriously? It seemed probable. However, I was to
have five thousand a year if I went along. There was no question
in my mind but it was my duty to earn that money.

Lincoln was one of Mr. McClure's steady enthusiasms. I once
saw him, in puzzled efforts to find the reason for the continued
life of a certain great American magazine, going through the
file from the Civil War on, solely to find out what attention had
been given to Lincoln. "Not a Lincoln article in this volume, nor
in this," he cried. "It is not a great magazine, it has overlooked
the most vital factor in our life since the Civil War, the influence
of the life and character of Abraham Lincoln."

His insight told him that people never had had enough of
Lincoln. Moreover, he believed that there was to be had for the
seeking a large amount of "unpublished" reminiscences. It was
on this conviction that he started me off.

He was right about "unpublished" material. Lincoln had been
dead only about thirty years, and hundreds of those who had
known him in one connection or another were still living. His

161

secretaries Nicolay and Hay had finished their great documentary life of their chief. They should have personal material not in their volumes. There were members of his Cabinet still living, members of Congress of his time, editors like Joseph Medill of the Chicago *Tribune*, Horace White of the Chicago *Tribune* and later of the New York *Evening Post*, Colonel McClure of the Philadelphia *Inquirer*. There were scores of men in Illinois towns who had traveled the circuit with him, for whom he acted as counsel, scores of people who had as a youth heard the Lincoln-Douglas Debates, and had been stirred to say, "Lincoln's got it right." They had followed him in his fight against the extension of slavery and later into the war to save the Union. There was indeed no point of his short trail from birth to death where living men and women had not known him as colleagues, friends, opponents, critics.

Also, there had never been a time from the day he had become a Presidential candidate to the hour of his assassination that his life had not been under scrutiny. Yet it had been difficult to find out much about him. "There is not much of me," he told a friend searching for biographical material. But there had been enough always to touch deep springs in American hearts and consciences. Men like William Dean Howells and J. G. Holland, later to occupy high places in our literary life, had written campaign lives of him. Hardly was he in his coffin before his brilliant, if unstable, law partner William Herndon was gathering from all sources reminiscences, estimates, documents on his life up to the Presidency; and from his gathering Herndon made a story of extraordinary vitality and color. Most important—always to remain most important—was the collection of his Letters and Speeches and the ten-volume "Abraham Lincoln: A History" by Nicolay and Hay.

Why do more? What was there to be had? Mr. McClure insisted that there was plenty if one searched.

I went to talk it over with John Nicolay, who as well as his fine daughter Helen was an honored member of the famous old Washington Literary Society where I was a frequent guest. I told him what Mr. McClure proposed. Did he not have something he could give me? He was emphatic in saying there was nothing of importance to be had. The collection of letters and speeches he and Mr. Hay had made was complete; they had told all there was worth telling of Lincoln's life. He would advise me not to touch so hopeless an assignment. I think Mr. Nicolay never quite forgave me for going ahead. Later when the results of my search began to appear and gradually to shape themselves into a Life of Lincoln he came to me one evening to protest. "You are invading my field. You write a popular Life of Lincoln and you do just so much to decrease the value of my property."

I was deeply distressed. He thought me a poacher. I told him I believed he was mistaken. I pleaded that if I could write anything which people would read I was making readers for him. To know a little of Lincoln was for the serious a desire to know more. He and Mr. Hay had written something that all students must have. I could never hope to make an essential lasting contribution. But he went away unconvinced.

Mr. Nicolay's point of view, if not generous, was certainly honest. I understand it better now than I did then. He had lived through the great years of the Civil War always at Lincoln's elbow. He had been the stern, careful, humorless guardian of a man who carried his mail in his hat and a laugh on his lips. His reverence for him was a religion. He had given years of conscientious hard labor to the editing of the "Complete Works" and the writing of the history, and now he was retired. Lincoln was his whole life. We all come to rest our case on the work to which we have given our best years, frequently come to live on that, so to speak. When the time comes that our field is invaded by new workers, enlarged, reshaped, made to yield new fruit, we suffer shock. We may put up a "No trespassing" sign, but all to no use.

Mr. Nicolay's tragedy was in not having found a fresh field. How different it was with his colleague John Hay, whose secretaryship with Lincoln had been an episode in a diplomatic career of unusual distinction and usefulness! In 1894 everybody recognized that he had a greater future before him. His part in the Life of Lincoln had been but one of many contributions to the literature of his day. His social circle was the choicest, and he was rich. Hay had everything; Nicolay, only Lincoln, and he looked on all who touched his field as invaders.

Mr. Nicolay's rebuff settled my plan of campaign. I would not begin at the end of the story with the great and known, but at the start in Kentucky with the humble and unknown; I would follow the trail chronologically; I would see for myself what sort of people and places those were that had known Lincoln, reconstruct the life of his day as far as living men and women backed by published records furnished reliable material. I would gather documents as I went, bits of color, stories, recollections; I would search in courthouses and county histories and newspapers; I would pick up pictures as I went, a picture of everything that directly or indirectly touched on what I was after. I would make sure if among these people who had known him there might not be letters not in the "Complete Works"; and, if I were lucky, somewhere on the trail I might turn up the important unpublished reminiscences which Mr. McClure was so certain existed. It was a gamble, the greater because I was so profoundly ignorant of American life and history.

It was in February of 1895, the Napoleon work still unfinished, though far enough ahead to give me a month for a preliminary survey, that I started for the Lincoln country of Kentucky to begin work on this program. It was characteristic of Mr. McClure, as he saw me off in the deadly cold, to take sudden alarm for my comfort. "Have you warm *bed socks?*" he asked anxiously. "We'll send you some if not. It will be awful in those Kentucky hotels."

It was—Louisville aside—awful in more than one hotel and train in my first month of Lincoln hunting.

The results were not exciting. They were too fragmentary: bits of unrecorded recollections, a picture, a letter, a newspaper paragraph, a court record which had passed notice. What was to be done with them? Here was no smashing new contribution such as an article of unpublished recollections from Mr. Nicolay might have been, but here were bits of value if you were to enlarge and retouch the popular notion of the man Lincoln. It was soon clear to Mr. McClure and Mr. Phillips that what I was collecting must be dovetailed into the published records; and that, they told me, was my business. Before I knew it I was writing a Life of Lincoln, though the first three chapters carried the legend, "Edited by Ida M. Tarbell." The office seemed gradually to conclude that the editor had become the author, though I think they were ahead of me in this decision.

We had a lucky break at the start which launched the undertaking even better, I think, than the big article we were looking for. Among my Washington acquaintances was a delightful Chicago woman, Mrs. Emily Lyons. She belonged to the group of early settlers who were still at this time in the thick of the exciting struggle to make the city the richest, the finest physically and socially in the country. Their energy, their daring, their confidence, their eagerness to learn, to adapt, was one of the social phenomena of the day. Now Mrs. Lyons' husband was important in the wealth-producing class as she was in the social. She knew practically everybody. When she learned that I was interested in new material on Lincoln she said at once: "Come to Chicago. I'll see that you meet Robert Lincoln, and I'll see that he gives you something." Too good to be true. But Mrs. Lyons kept her promise when I reached Chicago on my first expedition, producing Mr. Lincoln at once.

"Now, Robert," she ordered as she filled our cups, "I want you to give her something worth while."

To be drinking tea with the son of Abraham Lincoln was so unbelievable to me that I could scarcely take note of his reply. I searched his face and manners for resemblances. There was nothing. He was all Todd, a big plump man perhaps fifty years old, perfectly groomed, with that freshness which makes men of his type look as if they were just out of the barber's chair, the admirable social poise of the man who has seen the world's greatest and has come to be sure of himself; and this in spite of such buffeting as few men had had—the assassination of his father when he was twenty-four, the humiliation of Mary Lincoln's half-crazed public exhibition of herself and her needs, the death of his brother Tad, the heartbreaking necessity of having his mother committed for medical care, and more recently the loss of his only son. Robert Lincoln had had enough to crush him, but he was not crushed. At the moment he looked and felt, I think, that he had arrived where he belonged. The Republican party would have been happy, no doubt, to make him its leader if he had shown political genius recalling that of his father. They tried him out. Garfield and Arthur made him Attorney General, Harrison named him minister to the Court of St. James's, but nothing happened. He was not political timber, but by this time big business wanted him. It was his field. He was now president of the Pullman Company.

I devoured him with my eyes. He was very friendly. To Mrs. Lyons' order to do his best for me he laughingly replied, "Of course if you say so, Emily." But he went on to say he was afraid he had little that would help me. Herndon had taken all his father's papers from the law office. I think he used the word "stolen," but I am not sure; at least I knew he *felt* they were stolen. He had protested, but was never able to get anything back. As for the Presidential period, all the correspondence was packed away in Washington, but it had been fully used by Nicolay and Hay. However, he had what he believed to be the earliest portrait made of his father—a daguerreotype never published. I could have that.

I held my breath. If it was true! I held my breath still longer when the picture was finally in my hands for I realized that this was a Lincoln which shattered the widely accepted tradition of his early shabbiness, rudeness, ungainliness. It was another Lincoln, and one that took me by storm.

Of course we made it the frontispiece to our first installment, and the office saw to it that those whose opinions were of value had fine prints of it. It called out some remarkable letters. Woodrow Wilson wrote that he found it "both striking and singular— a notable picture." He was impressed by "the expression of the dreaminess, the familiar face without its sadness." Charles Dudley Warner wrote that he found it "far and away the most outstanding presentation of the man" he had ever seen. "To my eyes it explains Mr. Lincoln far more than the most elaborate engraving which has been produced." A common enough comment was that it "looks like Emerson." Edward Everett Hale wrote us that he had shown the picture to "two young people of intelligence who each asked if it was not Waldo Emerson."

A valuable and considered comment came from John T. Morse, the author of a Life of Abraham Lincoln, as well as editor of a series on leading American statesmen:

I have studied this portrait with very great interest [wrote Mr. Morse]. All of the portraits with which we are familiar show us the man as made; this shows us the man in the making. And I think every one will admit that the making of Abraham Lincoln presents a more singular, puzzling, interesting study than the making of any other man in human history. I have shown it to several persons without telling them who it was. Some say a poet; others a philosopher, a thinker, like Emerson. These comments also are interesting, for Lincoln had the raw material of both these characters very largely in his composition though political and practical problems so overlaid them that they show only faintly in his later portraits. This picture, therefore, is valuable evidence as to his natural traits.

Robert Lincoln was almost as proud as I was of the character of the comment. If he felt, as he well may have done, that he was taking a chance in responding so generously to his friend Mrs. Lyons' order, he was rewarded by the attention the picture received from those whose opinions he regarded highly. Always thereafter he was quick to see me when I took a Lincoln problem to him, as I did when I had exhausted all other sources. He was always frank and downright. One puzzle I brought amused him no little. It was the recurring rumor that Abraham Lincoln had written a letter to Queen Victoria early in the war begging her not to recognize the Confederacy. He was said to have sent it direct. Now no hint, however unlikely, no clue, however shadowy, was passed by in what had become in the McClure office a veritable bureau of Lincoln research. "Anything is possible," was our watchword. I was carrying on a widespread correspondence and continually dashing in one direction or another on what turned out often to be wild-goose chases, but also not infrequently brought in valuable game. Mr. McClure was especially excited over this letter. The State Department pooh-poohed the idea; the curator of documents in London was noncommittal. I interviewed people who were in position to know what was going on, but learned nothing. Finally I went to Chicago to see Robert Lincoln. His eye seemed harder to me in his office than over Mrs. Lyons' tea table, but he quickly put me at ease. I was certain that my quest was going to seem ridiculous to him; indeed, it had become a little so to me. But he didn't throw it aside. He picked it up and played with it. He had never heard of such a letter and doubted if it had been written.

"If father had done that," he said with emphasis, "and Mr. Adams"—Charles Francis Adams, then minister to Great Britain—"had learned of it, he would have resigned. Father knew of course that all communication between governments must be carried on by the credited ambassadors."

And then he fell to talking laughingly of his own experiences at the Court of St. James's. He said he had received all sorts of things to be presented to the Queen—patchwork quilts, patent medicines, books, sheet music. "I suppose," he said, "that lots of Americans fancy that their ambassador smokes cigarettes awhile every morning after breakfast with the Queen. They take it for granted he can drop in for tea any time and present quilts. Of course such people see no reason why a President cannot write a Queen direct." And he laughed until the tears came.

That interview put an end for the time being to the search for "the letter to the Queen," as the item had come to be called in the office.

When the Life was finally complete Mr. Lincoln wrote me: "It seemed to me at first that the field had been too many times gleaned to hope for much from the work you were undertaking, and I must confess my astonishment and pleasure upon the result of your untiring research. I consider it an indispensable adjunct to the work of Nicolay and Hay."

Mr. Nicolay, however, never agreed.

If Robert Lincoln was always friendly he threw me once into the greatest panic I suffered in the course of my Lincoln work, though this was long after the Life was published. I had gone to him to ask if he would arrange for me to consult the collection of Presidential papers. "Impossible," he said. "They are in the safety vault of my bank. I won't allow anybody to see them. There is nothing of my father's there, that is of value—Nicolay and Hay have published everything; but there are many letters *to* him which if published now would pain, possibly discredit able and useful men still living. Bitter things are written when men are trying to guide a country through a war, particularly a Civil War. I fear misuse of those papers so much that I am thinking of destroying them. Besides, somebody is always worrying me about

them, just as you are, and I must be ungenerous. I think I will
burn them."

I was scared; I feared he would do it, but Herbert Putnam,
the head of the Congressional Library, had already seen to that.
He did not burn them; the Library got them finally, but with
the condition that they were not to be opened until twenty-one
years after Robert Lincoln's death. He died in 1926. The papers
will not be available to students until 1947, which probably lets
me out!

The early portrait set the key for the series and, as it turned
out, a much higher key than I had believed possible. I found
that court records did yield unpublished documents, that every
now and then I ran on a man or woman who said more or less
casually, "Why, we have a letter of Lincoln's written to father
in ——. Copy it if you wish." Occasionally I found a speech not
in the "Complete Works." By the time the work was put into
book form in 1899 I had an appendix of three hundred unpublished speeches and letters. This did not mean that none of them
had ever been in print. Many of them had appeared in newspapers or historical magazines. "Unpublished" meant uncol-
lected. On the whole this collection stood the scrutiny of experts
very well, though I think I was swindled in the case of at least
one document, a forgery by a man recommended to me by an
honest scholar who had used the man frequently for years.

Forgery was easy, so was pilfering of documents in those days,
so little attention did clerks give to their old papers, so glad were
they to get rid of them. There was frequently no objection to a
student carrying off anything that interested him. One of the
most important documents in the controversy over the legitimacy
of Lincoln's mother is now to be found in the Barton collection
which the University of Chicago bought. Mr. Barton probably
asked permission to take it home for examination, a common
enough practice in Illinois as well as in Kentucky, and forgot to
return it. Probably most of the legal documents in the private

Lincoln collections have been stolen. The original thief would have been horrified to have that harsh word applied to him. He simply put it into his pocket with or without permission, saying, "I'll just take this along."

But while I did get together some three hundred pieces I came nowhere near turning up all the letters and speeches then at large. I was under a time limit. Since I ended my search scores of items, some of value, have been published in one or another collection. I shall be surprised if, as time goes on, there does not turn up every now and then a genuine letter, though now more than ever caution must be taken in accepting a new piece. The forging of historical documents has become a lucrative trade.

From the beginning I did my best to reconstruct the physical surroundings of Lincoln's homes and activities. I was particularly interested in the setting of the Lincoln-Douglas debates, which I followed in their order; but it was not until I reached Galesburg, Illinois, where on October 7, 1858, the fifth debate was staged, that I found the stirring and picturesque material I sought in order to picture the scene of a debate. I was delighted that it should have been the fifth debate, which I have always considered the most important of the series, for it was in that that Lincoln brought his argument down to what to him was the crux of the whole matter, that is, that slavery was wrong and must be kept back or it would spread over the whole country.

The debate had taken place on the campus of Knox College on the east front of its historic Old Main, one of the most beautiful college buildings of that period in the Middle West.

I had the luck to find in Galesburg a helper who not only enthusiastically seconded my conviction that here was the place for the illustration which we wanted, but set out heartily to help me find material. This was John H. Finley, my old friend on the Chautauqua Assembly *Daily Herald*. Dr. Finley was now president of the college—"the youngest college president in the United States," he was popularly called, doing a piece of work which was winning him more and more recognition. It was through him that I was able to find the newspaper reports of the debate. It was through him that I was able to meet people who could give me recollections of the day.

The picture which resulted from our joint efforts was made by that excellent artist William R. Leigh, who did many of the illustrations for the series. It has had a continuing life, being reproduced again and again on the occasion of the commemorative celebrations of the debate which Dr. Finley inaugurated in 1896. It was at this celebration that Robert Lincoln made his first and only public address about his father.

The real fun of the Lincoln work, as well as some of the worthwhile results, came from setting myself little problems. I was curious, for instance, to know more of Lincoln as a speaker. Whenever I found an Illinois man who had been with him on the circuit or in public life I would bombard him with questions. He would tell me how Lincoln looked, what his voice was like, how he used stories. They all talked more about the Lincoln and Douglas debates than any other exhibit, but frequently would conclude by saying, "Well, those were good speeches, but they were nothing like the Lost Speech. That was the greatest thing Lincoln ever did." Or a man would begin by saying, "Well, you can never know much about him as a speaker, nobody can that never heard the Lost Speech."

It was, they said, a speech which so stirred his audience that the very reporters forgot to take their notes. Knowing reporters, I was skeptical about that, so I looked up some of them. They all told me that when Lincoln finally ended his speech they found themselves standing on, instead of sitting by their writing tables—and without a note!

Still I believed that somebody must remember something about the speech—enough at least to give an idea of the argument. Perhaps, I said to myself, I may pick up some of the phrases—get some real notion of it; so I went prowling about asking questions and finally learned that in the state of Massachusetts was a man who was said to have taken notes—a cool-headed man—a lawyer, not a reporter. His name was Henry C. Whitney. He knew Lincoln well, had travelled the circuit with him, had published a "Life on Circuit with Lincoln" with which I was familiar.

Of course there was nothing to do but look up Mr. Whitney, and that I did. To my great satisfaction I found he had a bunch of yellowed notes. He had always intended to write them up, he said; but when he tried it the result seemed so inadequate that he gave it up.

After much persuasion Mr. Whitney did get out a version of the Speech. When he turned it over to me I took it to the men in Illinois with whom I had talked and asked them what they thought of it. There were those who said, "It's impossible to write out that Speech." But there were others who said, "Yes, Whitney has caught the spirit, he has the argument, he even has many of the phrases, as of course he would have if he made notes."

The most emphatic and enthusiastic statement came from a man of importance—Joseph Medill, the editor of the Chicago *Tribune*. Mr. Medill had been one of the reporters at Bloomington in 1856 when the speech was made who found himself in the end on top of the table without a note! He thought Mr. Whitney's version was close to the original. Indeed, he wrote to Mr. McClure a long and interesting letter giving his recollections of the Convention. In that letter he said:

Mr. Whitney has reproduced with remarkable accuracy what Mr. Lincoln said, largely in his identical language and partly in synonymous terms. The report is close enough in thought and word to recall the wonderful speech delivered forty years ago with vivid freshness.

Well, that seemed to us reason enough for publishing Mr. Whitney's report along with the story of how I had found it, what the people who heard the speech in the first place said about it, both for and against. And that we did.

But out in Illinois there were a number of people who did not want to give up the tradition. The Lost Speech was the greater to them because it was lost. As long as it was lost you could make it bigger than any speech any man ever made, and nobody could contradict you. And so you will find those who claim that the Lost Speech is still lost. And of course you can take it or you can leave it.

More than once when I plumed myself on a "discovery" I encountered the loyalty of men to their legends. There was the Herndon story of Lincoln's failing to appear at the first wedding arranged for him and Mary Todd. I realized he rather lets his "historical imagination" loose in his description, but I never had questioned his story until by chance I mentioned it to one of the family, a woman who would have been there if there had ever been such a wedding ready. She froze me with her indignation. "Mr. Herndon made that story up out of whole cloth. No such thing ever happened." Amazed, I flew around to see what other men and women of the circle said. They all denied it. A sister of Mary Lincoln was particularly indignant because Mr. Herndon had put the bride in white silk. "Mary Lincoln never had a white silk dress until she went to Washington," she sputtered.

But in spite of all the documents and evidences I collected demolishing the episode, I reaped only sour looks and dubious headshakes. I had spoiled a good story or tried to. It still remains a good story. Every now and then somebody tells it to me. A biographer who tries to break down a belittling legend meets with far less sympathy than he who strengthens or creates one.

The most important piece of ghost writing I ever did came in the course of the Lincoln work—Charles A. Dana's "Recollections of the Civil War." Mr. Dana, at that time the active editor of the New York *Sun*, had had an exceptional war experience dating from 1862 to 1865 as assistant to Secretary Stanton. He

had spent much time in the field; he had been with Grant at Vicks-
burg, with Rosecrans and Thomas at Chattanooga, again with
Grant in the Peninsular Campaign. "The eyes of the government
at the front," Mr. Lincoln called him.

No man in the administration had had better opportunity of
judging Lincoln, particularly in relation to the conduct of the
war, and none was a better judge of character.

Could I get the whole story as far as it concerned Lincoln?
I hesitated to ask it. The truth was, I was afraid of Mr. Dana.
I knew him only on the editorial page of the New York *Sun*.
He was too clever, too quick-witted, too malicious for me to get
on with, I feared. They laughed at me at the office when I voiced
my qualms. Nobody was held higher there than Charles A. Dana.
He had been a customer of the McClure Syndicate from the beginning, and they believed in his professional integrity, admired
his detestation and relentless pursuit of fakers, honored and
tried to imitate his editorial motto, "If you see it in THE SUN
it's so."

"Why should you feel this way?" reproved Mr. Phillips. "Mr.
Dana is a gentleman."

"Nonsense! I'll take care of it for you," said Mr. McClure,
and he rushed to the *Sun* office. He did fix it and more, for, returning, he told me with glee that Mr. Dana was willing to give
his whole war story, that is if I would do the work and arrange
some practical plan for the interviews. The first step, of course,
was to find what Dana material, published and unpublished, was
in the war records. The editing of the records then under way
was in charge of J. Leslie Perry. Mr. Perry did not believe in
women fussing with history, particularly with Civil War history.
War was man's business.

"How can you understand it?" he shouted at me.

However, I insisted on my rights, and nobody could have been
more helpful when he considered a thing an obligation of his
official position. To the end Mr. Perry's chief satisfaction came

when he caught me slipping. "That's what comes from allowing a woman to write history," he would say jubilantly.

Between us we brought together a grist of Dana's dispatches and reports. I crammed on the campaigns, and by appointment appeared at the end of Mr. Dana's day, about four o'clock in the afternoon, for my first interview.

His desk was stripped of everything that pertained to the newspaper, but held a row of the latest books, not only in English but in three or four other languages, as well as a copy of the *Cosmopolis*, an ambitious and rather pretentious review in three or four languages issued for a short time in the late nineties.

Mr. Dana had already repented of his promise to Mr. McClure. "I am not interested in what I did in the past," he said irritably. "I am interested only in the present; I am trying to keep up with the world of today. I am studying Russian now—a very fascinating language. I don't want to bother with what I did in the Civil War. What do you propose?"

What I proposed was that he let me come to him with a stenographer and a set of prepared questions, say three times a week. He agreed, and for a good many weeks of the winter of '96 and '97 I went regularly to the *Sun* office after the paper was put to press. By the summer of 1897 I had my manuscript well in shape. Mr. Dana had never seen any of it. "Send me the proofs, I'll read them."

Publication was to begin in November of 1897. Mr. Dana went to London for the summer. I sent the proof of the first chapter over with a good many qualms, for it was all in the first person— "I" and "We." It came back with only a few verbal corrections— no comments. He was never to read more of his Recollections. The number of the magazine which carried the first chapter carried the notice of his death.

We published the entire story, and later the articles were put into a book, but with no credit to the ghost!

Taking it all in all it was the most impersonal job I ever had. I do not remember that Mr. Dana ever volunteered a word in all the many interviews I had with him except on the subject in hand, and that in answer to my questions. We never talked of the things which I knew he loved—pictures, orchids, poetry. It was a businesslike operation from start to finish. Probably it was his way of punishing me for being afraid of him.

Another and more important series which came out of the Lincoln work was Carl Schurz's "Reminiscences." Here I acted not as a ghost but as an editorial representative. Mr. Schurz had given me liberally for my story from his rich Lincoln experiences—the most important unpublished item being the part he played in helping Mr. Lincoln launch his plan for compensated emancipation.

As I reported these interviews the office became more and more convinced that here was a great series of reminiscences—just the kind of thing that Mr. McClure had hoped for when he first commissioned me to gather Lincoln material. Could Mr. Schurz be persuaded to write his reminiscences? When I broached the subject he almost immediately said: "No, no, I refused Gilder [Richard Watson Gilder, editor of the *Century*]. I cannot do it for anybody else."

But I felt so convinced that he ought to do it that I persisted in my begging, and finally he began to yield. The handsome sum *McClure's* was willing to pay had something to do with it, for Mr. Schurz was not a rich man and here was a chance to leave to his family this extra money. Once he had made up his mind to the task, he thoroughly enjoyed it; and no one could have been more anxious to use material to suit the needs of the magazine. Working with him was a joy. He was gay, companionable, full of anecdotes, frank in comment. I remember him best at his summer home at Lake George where it was necessary for me to go two or three times to settle some editorial point. Here you would hear him in the morning as he was getting ready for breakfast giving the Valkyrie cries, singing motive after motive of the Wagnerian operas, in a clear youthful voice. Sometimes he would spring up from the table where he was at work, and seating himself at the piano would improvise dashingly until the mood which had taken him from his desk passed; then back to his labor.

The house stood in the upper corner of a park of fifty or sixty acres of woodland—not overcleared—and open by winding paths down the hillside to the lake. Every turn, every rock had its name usually celebrating some Wagnerian scene, and as you passed Mr. Schurz would roll out the appropriate song. There never was a more lovable or youthful man of seventy than Carl Schurz.

The completion of the Life of Lincoln did not end my interest in the man. He had come to mean more to me as a human being than anybody I had studied. I never doubted his motives, and he never bored me. Still, whenever I have the opportunity I pick him up. The greatest regret of my professional life is that I shall not. live to write another life of him. There is so much of him I never touched.

ILLUSTRATIONS

*Esther Ann McCullough Tarbell and
Ida Minerva Tarbell, November 5, 1858*

Office staff of The Chautauquan, 1888: Miss Tarbell at left, sitting

At her desk in the McClure's office, 1898

First year of The American Magazine, 1907

From Lumière autochrome by Arnold Genthe, N. Y.

Miss Tarbell in her garden at her Connecticut farm, 1914

Photograph by Christian Duvivier

Red Cross Headquarters, Paris, France, 1919

© Jessie Tarbox Beals

Posing as a gardener, 1925

10

REDISCOVERING MY COUNTRY

THE four years I put in on "The Life of Abraham Lincoln" did more than provide me with a continuing interest. They aroused my flagging sense that I had a country, that its problems were my problems. This sense had been strong in my years on *The Chautauquan,* but the period following had dimmed it. Now I was beginning to ask myself why we had gone the way we had since the Civil War. Was there not enough of suffering and of nobility in that calamity to quiet the greed and ambitions of men, to soften their hates, to arouse in them the will to follow Lincoln's last counsels—"With malice toward none; with charity for all . . . let us . . . do all which may achieve and cherish a just and lasting peace among ourselves and with all nations." But greed and hate and indifference to the sufferings and rights of others had been rampant since the war. Did war as a method of righting wrongs so loosen the controls which man in times of peace establishes over himself that he is incapable of exercising the charity, the peaceful adjustments for which Lincoln called? Was there always after war an unescapable crop of corruption, of thirst to punish and humiliate and exploit the conquered? Must men go back where they had started, go back with controls weakened and burdened with a load of new and unexpected problems? True, this war had ended slavery as a recognized institution, given the black man legal freedom, but how about opportunity, discipline for freedom? And then again was a war necessary to destroy slavery? Was it not already doomed? Lincoln thought so. Doomed because it was showing itself unsound economically as well as because it outraged man's sense of justice and humanity. And how about the effect of this war on democracy? Were the problems it loosed less threatening to democratic ideals than slavery had been? Were they not possibly a more subtle form of slavery, more dangerous because less obvious?

A nice box of problems to tease me as I worked on Lincoln's life and out of the corner of the eye watched what was going on in the country. The number of things in America I was beginning to want to find out about was certainly dimming the things in France I had wanted to find out about. Unquestionably these new interests were helping to wean me from the plan on which I had settled. The process was painful. More than once I told myself that the sacrifice of my ambitions, of my love for Paris, for my friends there, was too much to ask of myself. I could never replace those interests and associations; but I was replacing them and suffering as I realized what was happening, revolting that nothing in my life seemed to last, to be carried through. By nature I was faithful. To give my time to new friends, neglect old ones in spite of never forgetting them, as I never did, was disloyal. I was beginning to repeat dolefully as well as more and more cynically, *"Tout lasse, tout casse, tout passe."*

Washington was helping in my weaning. The city as I knew it in the 1890's is lost in the Washington of the 1930's. The pivots on which it swings, the Capitol, the White House, were there then to be sure. So was the Washington Monument; but they stood by themselves, the near-by flanking unpretentious, often squalid. Today they are almost lost in the piles of marble heaped about them to accommodate the ambitions and creations of the last frantic twenty years. The town has stretched unbelievably to the northwest. Where once I knew wide lawns, wooded tracts, pleasant walks, are now acres upon acres of apartment houses and hotels. They have engulfed the delightful Woodley Lane where my friends the Hubbards lived in summer, and they have changed no less the quarter in which their fine town house stood—Connecticut Avenue where it merges into Dupont Circle.

Great houses were only just beginning then to find their way into the Circle. George Westinghouse had built there, so had Mrs. Leiter of Chicago. Old Washingtonians sniffed at their houses and their ways, laughed at Mrs. Leiter's "spinal staircase" as she was said to call it, and professed disgust at Mrs. Westinghouse's "reported" white velvet tablecloths. They resented the invasion of rich women attracted by the social possibilities of a diplomatic circle, of rich men attracted by the field for lobbying furnished by a Congressional circle.

But of this side of Washington I saw nothing. My social life was shaped largely by the continued kindness of Mr. and Mrs. Hubbard. I had become almost one of the family, was freely invited to meet their friends. Their circle was wide, including diplomats and statesmen and eminent visitors, though its core was the large group of distinguished scientists which made up the working forces of the Smithsonian Institution, the Agriculture Department, the Geological Survey, the Bureau of Mines, the Observatory. An important group they were, and nobody in town appreciated them more or took more pains to show his appreciation than Mr. Hubbard. Naturally the center of this group was Alexander Graham Bell, married to the Hubbards' daughter, Mabel.

The Bells lived across the Avenue from the Hubbards, and I soon had the good fortune to be welcomed there—a great privilege, for both Mr. and Mrs. Bell were rare persons. Mrs. Bell's story is well known, but it was only in seeing her with her husband and daughters that one could realize what a fine intellect and what an unspoiled and courageous character she had. She had been deaf and dumb from infancy, and Mr. Hubbard had determined to open life to her. Among the teachers of speech he brought to her was a young man then at Boston University— Alexander Graham Bell. Under his tutelage she made rapid strides, and the two young people learned to love one another. At that time Mr. Bell was giving his nights to trying to "make

iron talk." I once heard Mr. Hubbard say that when he found
Mr. Bell had made iron talk he told him he must develop his
telephone to a practical point or he could not have Mabel. Probably no other argument would have persuaded Alexander Graham
Bell, for he was the type of inventor whose interest flags when
he has solved his problem. Let somebody else take care of the
development. He would be off on a new voyage of discovery.

At the time I came into the circle Mr. Bell was, I think, the
handsomest and certainly the most striking figure in Washington. It was amusing to hear people discussing who was the handsomest man in town. There were various candidates—General
Miles, General Greely, Colonel John Foster; but while I conceded
they all had their points no one of them had the distinction of
Alexander Graham Bell, and no one of them certainly had the
gay boyish appetite for what he found good in life. He was more
like Massa Henry Watterson in that than anybody else I have
ever known, though the activities and interests of the two were
utterly different.

Mr. Bell's plan of living was modeled to suit himself. Often
he slept through the day when interruptions naturally came and
the telephone most often rang! If restless at night he played the
piano. Mrs. Bell could not hear, and the rest of the family, being
young and devoted, were never disturbed. He was up and began
his day around four to six. Often there were guests for dinner,
for everybody of note the world over who came to Washington
wanted to meet him. On Wednesdays after dinner there usually
gathered a group of scientists and public men to talk things over.
Mr. Bell was something to see at these dinners and gatherings,
the finest social impresario I ever saw in action, so welcoming,
appreciative, eager, receptive. I thought then I had never seen
anybody so generous about what others were doing. He loved to
draw out great stories of adventure and discovery and would
silence all talkers when once such narrating was started. Partly
this was because of Mrs. Bell, his intense desire that she enjoy

everything that was going on; and she did, thanks to the intelligent devotion of her daughters, Elsie and Marian, the first now the wife of Gilbert Grosvenor, one of the founders and the present editor of the *National Geographic Magazine,* the second the wife of David Fairchild, botanist and explorer, the organizer in the Agriculture Department of the work now known as the Division of Foreign Plant Exploration and Introduction—two men to whom the public owes big debts for services.

The most distinguished member of this Washington group of scientists after Mr. Bell was Professor Samuel Pierpont Langley, the head of the Smithsonian Institution, at that time agonizing over the problem of flying.

When I first met Dr. Langley in 1894 he was working on his air runner or aerodrome, a machine which, as I gathered from the talk I heard and did not too well understand, was to run on the air as an engine does on rails. He finally came out with a machine weighing about twenty-five pounds made up of a pair of rigid wings, twelve to fifteen feet across, and an engine which weighed not over seven pounds. It had cost him four years' work to develop the engine to that lightness. But would it fly? Could it be launched? Attempts were made from a houseboat down the river. These experiments were carried on with the utmost secrecy, for Dr. Langley was a taciturn man, proud, dignified, always awesome to me. He knew that there was a public that thought him a little touched in the head and wondered that the Government kept, as director of a great national institution, a man who held the crazy notion that one day people would fly, and who was willing to give his days and nights to proving it.

Dr. Bell took the most genuine and enthusiastic interest in Dr. Langley's experiments, was always present, I think, when an attempt to launch the air runner was made. I recall his disappointment when it fell, his rejoicing when it did finally fly. This was one day in May of 1896. I have heard him tell how suddenly the air runner rose to one hundred feet and flew in a big circle. It did not fall but made a perfect landing. Again it was launched and again it flew; and this time it went over the land and over the treetops, came back to the river and when its power was exhausted settled quietly on the water.

Inside that little circle at Dr. Bell's there was the consciousness of a great discovery, a certain solemnity that again it had been proved that labor, training, thought, patience, faith are not in vain.

Mr. McClure was as excited as any one of the Washington group over the news. He must immediately have an article from Dr. Langley himself, and I was commissioned to get it. I think perhaps it was a little strain on Dr. Langley's good will to have a young woman come to him and say: "Now we want the whole story of how you have done this thing, what it means; but no scientific jargon, please. We want it told in language so simple that I can understand it, for if I can understand it all the world can." Which, knowing me, he probably knew was true. He consented, and I had the privilege of talking with him occasionally about the article, of reading what he did and saying when necessary, "I don't see quite what this or that means," of seeing him docilely make it clear enough for me to understand. A year after the Langley contraption first flew we had in *McClure's Magazine* the whole story.

As a reward for my persistent effort to see that article come out to his satisfaction, he gave me what I think he considered the greatest treat he could give his friends. He took me to the Rock Creek Zoo after the crowds had gone and, with the help of the director, Dr. Baker, made the kangaroo jump and the hyena laugh.

But the public interest in his air runner, the fresh honors that now came to him did but little to wipe out the bitterness that ridicule had stirred in Dr. Langley. "There was a time," he said as he was going to England to take a degree which Oxford University (I believe it was) was giving him, "there was a time when

I should have been glad of this. It means little now." Yet he had his moments of strong emotion. Rarely have I been more moved than at a dinner at Mr. Hubbard's soon after the Greco-Turkish War began in 1897. A half-dozen men of seventy or thereabouts were at the table, among them Senator Hoar of Massachusetts, Major Powell, Edward Everett Hale, and Dr. Langley. They talked only of Greece and her helplessness before the Turk. They recalled the wave of sympathy which in their boyhood had swept over the country when the Turk attacked Greece. It was to Greece, said Senator Hoar, that he first gave money of his own, a long treasured twenty-five-cent piece. Dr. Hale and Dr. Langley fell to quoting Byron. Their voices shook as they declaimed,

> "The Isles of Greece, the Isles of Greece!
>
> .   .   .   .
>
> Earth! render back from out thy breast
> A remnant of our Spartan dead!
> Of the three hundred grant but three,
> To make a new Thermopylae."

"It was Byron," said Dr. Langley with an emotion of which I had thought him incapable, "who first stirred in me an enthusiasm for man's struggles for freedom, with a desire to join those who fight for it." He thought Byron first opened England's eyes to her duty to the oppressed of the Continent of Europe and at the same time opened the eyes of the Continent to the love of liberty, the sympathy with the helpless, in English literature. Certainly here was a Dr. Langley I had never before glimpsed.

This was not all of Washington I was seeing. As in Paris I set aside time for learning the city. How thin and young and awkward Washington seemed compared with the exhaustless life and treasures of Paris! Here was none of that wisdom of experience, that subtle cynicism, that pity and patience with men which made Paris like a great human being to me. Nor was there here the ripe charm of old palaces, quaint streets, hidden corners.

Everything was new, sprawling in the open. But if Washington had little to offer but promise it had that in abundance, and it did not know its own lacks. It was too full of pride in what it had done since John Adams moved into the White House and Congress into the Capitol. And then I had a problem to think about—the Washington Lincoln knew—and I went about with him from White House to War Department, up to the Congress, down to the Arsenal, into this and that hospital, up to the Soldiers' Home, over to Arlington. The pain and tragedy behind almost every step he took in the town dignified its unfinished streets, gave a meaning and a sanctity to its rawness. By such steps I told myself did Paris come through the centuries to be what she is.

But I did more than follow Lincoln about. I wanted to know the Washington of thirty years after Lincoln, and so I went to the Capitol when debates promised excitement, and I missed no great official show. When McKinley's inauguration came in 1896 I arranged to see it all. Once, I told myself, will do forever for an inauguration—as it has done. I began after breakfast and did not stop until the Inaugural Ball was far on its way. A fine colorful sightseeing experience, leaving a series of pictures which have never quite faded. Years later one of these pictures brought me a curious bit of minor political history. I was trying to persuade Richard Olney to write the story of the Venezuela message for *McClure's* and remarked that the first time I met him was at the McKinley Inaugural Ball. To my surprise he flushed.

"Outgoing Cabinet members are not expected to attend the Inaugural Ball of a new President," he said. (I hadn't known that, or of course I should not have spoken.) "But there was a reason for my presence. General Miles, then head of the Army, had come to me to say that there were rumors of an attempt on McKinley's life. 'Suppose that both he and Hobart should be assassinated before a new Cabinet is appointed,' he said. 'You would be Acting President. You must go to the Ball, walk with Mrs. McKinley, and stay until the end.' I didn't like the idea, but General Miles insisted; so I went. But the new President walked with his wife, and I had to hang around, conscious that more than one Republican was saying, 'What's Olney doing here?' "

What was behind General Miles' precaution, I never knew. The lives of presidents are always in danger, even in what we are pleased to call normal times, there being always plenty of grievances, real and fancied, to be squared. At the moment of the McKinley inauguration the despair and bitterness of many radicals over the defeat of Bryan were outspoken. The experience of the country with assassination in the thirty preceding years had been alarming. A man in General Miles' position charged with the safety of the heads of the government must keep in mind all possibilities. It would, of course, have been easy to assassinate the President and Vice President at the Ball. Given clever and determined conspirators, there would have been a chance to seize the government while a new President was being elected. But with a determined man like Olney on the ground, backed by a watchful and sufficient military guard scattered through the great Patent Office where the Ball was held, a temporary government could have been formed while the murderer was being manacled.

How General Miles would have enjoyed such a coup! In the first years of McKinley's administration I came to know him well, another one of the friendly acquaintances made in carrying out the varied tasks that came my way in my position as a contributing editor of *McClure's Magazine*. For several years popular interest in military affairs had been growing. There were several reasons: doubt of the efficiency of our army, talk of revolution, and particularly our strained relations with Spain.

Interest was still further excited in 1896 by the outbreak of the Greco-Turkish War, which, starting as a skirmish, soon grew until it looked as if it might involve all southeastern Europe, perhaps England, Russia. Obviously we should have an observer over there, and so in May General Miles and a staff started for the field. He studied the military organization of Turkey and of Greece, watched the armies lined up for battle, saw the end of the war. From Greece he and his staff went to London to represent the United States at Queen Victoria's Jubilee. Following that great show he had attended the autumn maneuvers of the greatest of then existing armies, those of Russia, Germany, and France.

Mr. McClure thought there was an important story in General Miles' observations, and I was commissioned to get it. But General Miles, willing and glad as he was to tell of his European experiences—he had never been abroad before—wanted to tell only of the sights he had seen, sights which had nothing to do with armies, their equipment, and their maneuvers. All that was shop for him. "They'll think I didn't see anything but soldiers and guns," he growled, "think I'm not interested in history and art. People don't know how wonderful Pompeii is, and I would like to tell them. A lot of them never heard of Alexander's sarcophagus—finest thing I ever saw. There are countries that would pay a million dollars to get it, and there's the Parthenon and Moscow and the Tower of London and the Louvre. There are the things I want to write about." And he was preparing to do it, as I saw by the stack of Baedekers, the volumes of the Britannica, the pamphlets and travel books on his desk. It took all my tact and patience to persuade the General that, whatever his interest, ours was centered only on military Europe.

In the course of this distasteful task I came to have a real liking for General Miles. He was as kindly and courteous a gentleman as I have ever known, and certainly the vainest. One of the real disappointments of his European visit was that the American uniform was so severe. There were hundreds of lesser ranks than himself on parade with three times the gold braid he was allowed. When it came to the Queen's Jubilee he revolted and had special epaulets designed. I was at Headquarters the day they arrived from London, and nothing would do but I must see them. He ordered the box opened, disappeared into an inner office and came back arrayed in all the glory the American Army allowed him.

I was working on the Miles articles on February 16, 1898, when the *Maine* blew up in Havana harbor. As no message came canceling my appointment with General Miles that morning I presented myself as usual though with some misgiving, for it seemed as if the very air of Washington stood still. At Headquarters there was a hush on everything, but the routine went on as usual. As we worked an orderly would come in with the latest report: "Two hundred fifty-three unaccounted for, two officers missing, ship in six fathoms of water only her mast visible, sir." Then a second report: "All but four officers gone, sir, and there are two hundred women up in the Navy Department." (The Army and Navy were in the same building in 1898.)

The General made no comment, but every now and then blew his nose violently, while his smart Chief of Staff, a gallant simple-minded officer with a bullet hole in his cheek, kept saying to himself: "Ain't it a pity! By Jove, ain't it a pity!"

Through the two months between the blowing up of the *Maine* and the declaration of war I vacillated between hope that the President would succeed in preventing a war and fear that the savage cries coming from the Hill would be too much for him, as they were in the end. I honestly believed then as I do now that he was doing his best, and this in spite of the fact that my heart was hot with resentment for what I considered his cowardly desertion of my Poland friends in 1893.

McKinley was patient, collected, surprisingly determined. Everybody indeed in the departments where the brunt must fall if war came seemed steady to me, as I watched things in my frequent visits to General Miles' Headquarters. Everybody was at his post, everybody except Theodore Roosevelt, Assistant Secretary of the Navy. He tore up and down the wide marble halls of the War and Navy Building—"like a boy on roller skates," a disgusted observer growled. More than once he burst into General Miles' office with an excited question, an excited counsel. Already he was busy preparing his Rough Riders for the war to be if he had his way. Already he saw himself an important unit in an invading army.

I remember this because it shocked me more than anything else I was noting. What chance had government in peace or war if men did not stay on their jobs? Was not fidelity to the trust committed to you a first obligation? And if Theodore Roosevelt felt—as he evidently did—that he was needed in the Army, did not good manners if nothing else require resignation? I was very severe on him in 1897, the more so because he had bitterly disappointed me in 1884 when he had refused to go along with the mugwumps in the revolt against Prohibitive Protection, refused and gone along with my particular political abomination, Henry Cabot Lodge. I had not been able to reconcile myself to him even when as a Police Commissioner of New York City he made his hearty and effective fight on the town's corruption.

The steadiness of General Miles and his staff in the weeks between the blowing up of the *Maine* and the breaking out of war with Spain raised my respect for Army training as much as Roosevelt's excited goings-on antagonized me. At the same time my contempt for the outpouring of Congress in a crisis was modified by almost daily association with one of its oldest members, the Senator from Massachusetts, George Frisbie Hoar.

When I had decided in 1894 that sufficient materials were at hand in Washington for the sketch *McClure's* wanted, to go with Gardiner Hubbard's Napoleon portraits, I went to live at a boarding house on I Street between Ninth and Tenth recommended by Mrs. Hubbard, chiefly because Senator and Mrs. Hoar lived there. The neighborhood had been not so long before one of the desirable residential sections of the town, but business and fashion were pushing well-to-do residents into Connecticut and Massachusetts avenues, into Dupont Circle and beyond. The fine old brownstone houses left behind were being used by trade and occasionally by owners, whose incomes had been cut or destroyed, as rooming or boarding houses. The head of the house into which I was received was a Mrs. Patterson, the widow of a once distinguished Washington physician. She and her daughter Elizabeth made of their home one of the most comfortable and delightful living places into which I had ever dropped. Such food! And best of all the Senator.

At this time Senator Hoar was close to seventy years of age. He had been in Congress for twenty-six consecutive years, seventeen of them in the Senate, and everybody knew that as long as he lived Massachusetts Republicans would insist on returning him. He embodied all the virtues of the classic New Englander and few of the vices. His loyalty was granite-ribbed; he revered the Constitution and all the institutions born and reared under it. He was proud of the United States, but his heart belonged to Massachusetts. In his mouth the name took on a beauty and an emotion which never ceased to stir me—Westerner that I was.

Combined with his patriotic loyalties was a passionate devotion to classic literature—Greek, Roman, English. He knew yards of Homer and Virgil, as well as of the greatest of the early English writers, and not infrequently at our Sunday morning breakfasts he would repeat long passages in his sonorous voice. This was the one hour in the week when the Senator laid aside all formality and became our entertainer. He never spoiled things by opinions on current events, but poured forth daily whatever came into his mind. We were a good audience, willing to sit until noon if he would talk. He claimed that it was Mrs. Patterson's codfish balls and coffee that put to flight all his cares and loosened his tongue. That Patterson Sunday morning breakfast was enough to put gaiety into any heart. Senator Hoar had already celebrated it in a widely circulated letter to a Pennsylvania editor who attacked him for never having done a stroke of useful work in his life and, what greatly amused the Senator, living in Washington on "champagne and terrapin!":

My dear man [he wrote the irate critic], your terrapin is all in my eye, very little in my mouth. The chief carnal luxury of my life is in breakfasting every Sunday morning with an orthodox friend, a lady who has a rare gift for making fish balls and coffee. You unfortunate and benighted Pennsylvanians can never know the exquisite flavor of the codfish, salted, made into balls and eaten on a Sunday morning by a person whose theology is sound, and who believes in all the five points of Calvinism. I am myself but an unworthy heretic, but I am of Puritan stock, of the seventh generation, and there is vouchsafed to me, also, some share of that ecstasy and a dim glimpse of that beatific vision. Be assured, my benighted Pennsylvania friend, that in that hour when the week begins, all the terrapin of Philadelphia or Baltimore and all the soft-shelled crabs of the Atlantic shore might pull at my trouser legs and thrust themselves on my notice in vain.

As we all knew, Senator Hoar had no money for "champagne and terrapin." He had sacrificed his law practice to public service, "getting a little poorer year by year." As a matter of fact he had no interest in making money. I never saw him more irritated than after taking a difficult case for which he was to get a fee of twenty-five thousand or thirty thousand dollars.

"Earning money is hateful to me," he said. "Never in all my life before have I undertaken a thing I did not want to do simply for money. Some things I like to do, believe that I can do better than I could do anything else. I never was such a donkey before. There are so many things I long to do; one of them is to learn Italian well enough to read Dante and Boccaccio and Ariosto in the original; and I want to commit Homer to memory. I would like to have my head *packed with Greek*."

The Senator's Sunday morning talks were rich with anecdotes of New England types. He had his antipathies—Margaret Fuller

Ossoli was one of them. He used to tell the story of an old Concord doctor who was called up in the night by a quavering voice outside his window asking, "Doctor, how much camphire can a body drink without its killing 'em?" "Who drunk it?" he asked. "Margaret Fuller." "A peck," snapped the doctor, shutting his window with a bang.

Dr. Mary Walker, who in her rather shabby man's attire was a familiar figure in those days, was a particular abomination. She made him "creepy," he said. Simply to mention her, I found, would dry up his talk. But the mention of Jonathan Edwards' name, although he particularly detested him, always loosened his tongue. "He was an inhuman cuss," he said one morning. "There is a true story of his riding through Northampton with a slave boy whom he had just bought tied to a cord and trotting behind the horse. 'Is thee doing as thee would be done by?' a woman of his faith called him, and Edwards said, 'I'll answer you some other time.' "

Senator Hoar rather enjoyed calling a man whose acts he disliked by hard names. Indeed he very much enjoyed salty words generally, and one morning ably defended them: " 'Dammit' is a useful word. It eases one's feelings." He also put up a strong argument for "whoppers." "They are," he contended, "a valuable weapon with the impertinent and the imbecile." There was much boyish mischief in him. He greatly admired our wholesome big-hearted Elizabeth, daughter of the house, her common sense and her gaiety, and loved to pinch her plump arm. He did it in the presence of us all and in spite of Mrs. Hoar's reproaches. "Do you know, Elizabeth," he said one evening as he followed us up the stairs from the dining room, "that it has taken nineteen hundred years of Christian civilization to produce a man who does not pinch a girl's pretty ankle when she is going upstairs ahead of him?"

In July, 1898, after Congress had adjourned Senator Hoar made up a party for a trip through the Berkshire Hills and I had the good fortune to be asked to join it. I had heard him talk much of his walking trips there in Harvard days with his favorite classmate, Francis Child: "as great a man at seventeen when he entered college," he said, "as when he died—a real genius." From the moment our little caravan left his home at Worcester the trip was like champagne to him. Trees, graveyards, epitaphs, views, the homes of the honored in this day and past days kept him busy. There was the Sheffield elm which we must stop to measure, the grave of Mumbet with the inscription his favorite Catharine Sedgwick had written for it; there was the best view of the Sleeping Napoleon on Cedar Mountain—this for me. Then we must spend the night at a certain inn on Mount Washington to give Elizabeth plenty of time to look up family graves and records. Her father had been born on Mount Washington, which was one of many reasons why the Senator admired her. He went with her to look up the graves and, returning late, said, "If we had not feared you would wait supper we would have stayed and been buried there."

I have certainly never known anyone for whom life at seventy was more joyous and full. He hated weakness, as well as everything that impaired his dignity, his self-reliance. He was a true untouchable and would fall into a rage if friend or stranger offered to assist him. "Unhand me," he thundered at a street car conductor who one day seized his arm to help him up the steps, and his wrath lasted until he had told us about the indignity at the dinner table. On this Berkshire trip a little accident happened to him which caused an explosion of the same nature. We were at an inn in the mountains, and after dinner had gone on to the lawn. The Senator was sitting on a rustic bench which gave way, turned him on his back, feet in the air. We all ran to assist him but were stopped in our tracks by a stentorian voice which roared, "I decline to be assisted."

But this was the Senator on a vacation, the Senator of our Sunday morning's breakfast. Take him when public affairs were

in a serious tangle, and he was glum, unapproachable. He suffered deeply over the trend to imperialism after the Spanish-
American War. To save Cuba from the maladministration of
Spain, to watch over her until she had learned to govern herself
seemed to him a noble expression of Americanism, but to annex
lands on the other side of the globe for commercial purposes
only, as he believed, was to be false to all our ideals. He had
the early American conviction that minding one's own business
was even more important abroad than at home. He wanted no
entangling alliances, and in those days following the treaty of
Paris he feared as never before for the country. Certainly there
were far fewer Sunday morning breakfast table talks. His greatest speech against the advancing imperialism was made in April
of 1900. At the head of the printed copy of his speech distributed by the Senate he placed these sentences:

No right under the Constitution to hold Subject States. To
every People belongs the right to establish its own government
in its own way. The United States can not with honor buy the
title of a dispossessed tyrant, or crush a Republic.

I was learning something of what responsibility means for a
man charged with public service, of the clash of personalities, of
ambitions, judgments, ideals. And it was not long before I was
saying to myself, as I had not for years, You are a part of this
democratic system they are trying to make work. Is it not your
business to use your profession to serve it? But how? That was
clearly now my problem. I could not run away to a foreign
land where I should be a mere spectator. Indeed, I was beginning to suspect that one great attraction of France was that
there I had no responsibility as a citizen. I must give up Paris.
Between Lincoln and the Spanish-American War I realized I
was taking on a citizenship I had practically resigned.

The war had done something to *McClure's* as well as to me.
In all its earlier years its ambition had been to be a wholesome,

enlivening, informing companion for readers, to give fiction, poetry, science of wide popular appeal—an ambition which it must be admitted opened the pages occasionally to the cheap, though it rarely excluded the fine. An eager welcome was given new writers. Indeed it was always a great day in the office when we thought a "real one" had reached us. While it fostered new writers it held on to the best of the old. It had touched public matters only as they became popular matters. Thus, when the Spanish-American War came it was quickly recognized that it yielded more interesting material than any other subject. There was a great war number and there was a continuous flow of war articles. *McClure's* suddenly was a part of active, public life. Having tasted blood, it could no longer be content with being merely attractive, readable. It was a citizen and wanted to do a citizen's part. It had a staff sympathetic with this new conception of the work. Mr. McClure had had in mind from the start the building of a permanent staff of good craftsmen, reporters on whom he could depend for a steady stream of contributions, as well as of editorial ideas. He wanted them versatile, flexible, as interested in the magazine as in themselves, capable of sinking themselves in a collective effort.

After I came in, the first to become such a permanent acquisition was Ray Stannard Baker. An article on the capture of John Wilkes Booth by Baker's uncle, Colonel L. C. Baker, written from personal reminiscences and documents, was submitted by Baker, then on the staff of the Chicago *Record.* It was "the General's" ideal of a *McClure's* article. Baker was urged to write more, and each piece emphasized the first impression. The year after his first appearance in the magazine, May, 1897, he joined the staff and became a regular contributing editor.

Baker was an admirable craftsman, as well as a capital team worker. He had curiosity, appreciation, a respect for facts. You could not ruffle or antagonize him. He took the sudden calls to go here when he was going there, with equanimity; he enjoyed the unconventional intimacies of the crowd, the gaiety and excitement of belonging to what was more and more obviously a success. He was the least talkative of us all, observant rather than garrulous, the best listener in the group, save Mr. Phillips. He had a joyous laugh which was more revealing of his healthy inner self than anything else about him.

When I learned a few years later that Baker was the author of the wise, homely, whimsical "Adventures in Contentment," "The Friendly Road" and other delightful essays under the nom de plume of David Grayson I said at once, "How stupid of me not to have known it! Haven't I always known that Baker *is* a David Grayson?" Few practical philosophers, indeed, have so lived their creed as Ray Stannard Baker, and none have had a more general recognition from the multitude of people in the country who, like him, believe in the fine art of simple living. It is a comforting and beautiful thing to have had as a friend and co-worker over many years so rare a person as Ray Stannard Baker.

By good fortune *McClure's* in this period happened on a reader of real genius—Viola Roseboro—the only "born reader" I have ever known. I found her in the office after one of my frequent jaunts after material. It was as a talker that I first learned to admire and love her. Her judgments were unfettered, her emotions strong and warm, her expressions free, glowing, stirring, and she loved to talk, though only when she felt sympathy and understanding. She loved to share books, of which she read many, particularly in the biographical field; she wanted none but the best—no imitation, no mere fact-finding. Her eagerness to let no good thing slip, her consciousness of the all too little time a human being has in this world to explore its riches made her rigid in her choice. An unsleeping eagerness to find talent and give it a chance, and secondarily, she said, to enrich the magazine, made every day's work with the unsifted manuscripts an adventure. If she found exceptional merit that was also suited to *McClure's* she might weep with excitement. And she stood to it till faith grew in those less sure of the untried. It was when *McClure's* was making a great hunt for a good serial that I saw her one morning bringing into the editorial sanctum Booth Tarkington's "The Gentleman from Indiana," tears celebrating the discovery as she cried, "Here is a serial sent by God Almighty for *McClure's Magazine!*"

This woman of unusual intelligence, loyalty and of truly Spartan courage was a precious addition to the crowd. Ill health, threatened blindness, have never lowered her enthusiasm, her ceaseless effort to find the best, to give the best. She is still doing it.

The most brilliant addition to the *McClure's* staff in my time was Lincoln Steffens. He had made himself felt in the journalistic and political life of New York City by a fresh form of reportorial attack. Young, handsome, self-confident, with a good academic background and two years of foreign life and observation, Steffens began his professional career unencumbered by journalistic shibboleths and with an immense curiosity as to what was going on about him. He was soon puzzled and fascinated by the relations of police and politicians, politicians and the law, law and city officials, city officials and business, business and church, education, society, the press. Apparently groups from each of these categories worked together, supporting one another, an organization close, compact, loyal from fear or self-interest or both. It was because of this organization, Steffens concluded, that graft and vice and crime were established industries of the city. Attacks from outraged virtue had slowed up the system at intervals ever since the Civil War, but never permanently deranged it. A few rascals might be exterminated, but they were soon replaced. The system had bred new rascals, grown stronger and more cunning with time. He set out to trace its pattern. Incredibly outspoken, taking rascality for granted, apparently never shocked or angry or violent, never doubtful of himself, only coolly determined to demonstrate to men and women of good will and honest purpose what they were up against and warn them that the only way they could hope to grapple with a close corporation devoted to what there was in it was by an equally solid corporation devoted to decent and honest government, business, law, education, religion. First as a reporter and later as the city editor of the *Globe*, Steffens stirred the town.

It was entirely in harmony with the McClure method of staff building that this able, fearless innocent should be marked for absorption. He was persuaded to take the editing of the magazine, now in its tenth year and steadily growing in popularity and influence. He was to be the great executive—the editorial head that would shift some of the burden from the shoulders of Mr. McClure and Mr. Phillips. But the machine was running smoothly even if with little outward excitement. Steffens made a brave effort to adjust himself to the established order, to learn the situation. Naturally he took Mr. McClure's meteoric goings and comings, his passionate and often despairing efforts to make his staff "see" what he did, his cries that the magazine was stale, dying, more seriously than those of us who had been longer together. He seems to have been bewildered by what went on in the excited staff meetings held whenever Mr. McClure came in from a foraging expedition. I had come to look on Mr. McClure's returns as the most genuinely creative moments of our magazine life. He was an extraordinary reporter; his sense of the meaning, the meat of a man or event, his vivid imagination, his necessity of discharging on the group at once, before they were cold, his observations, intuitions, ideas, experiences, made the gatherings on his return amazingly stimulating to me. Sifting, examining, verifying, following up, were all necessary. Mr. McClure understood that and trusted John Phillips to see that it was done, but he properly fought for his findings. In his "Autobiography" Steffens credits me with a tact in our editorial scrimmages which I do not deserve. It is true, as he says, that I was the friend of each and all, but what I was chiefly interested in was seeing the magazine grow in delight and in usefulness. I knew our excited discussions were really fertile. They also were highly entertaining.

It was in this unsatisfied seeking by Mr. McClure for more and more of contemporary life that Lincoln Steffens' chief contribution to it and to the political life of his period had its root. Mr. McClure's fixed conviction that great editing was not to be done in the office he finally applied to Steffens, who was bravely struggling there to become the great editor he had been called to be.

"You can't learn to edit a magazine in the office," Mr. McClure told him. "Get out, go anywhere, everywhere, see what is going on in the cities and states, find out who are the men and the movements we ought to be reporting."

And so Stef went for a month, to the Middle West mainly, constantly reporting back to the office in McClure fashion what he was finding. He combed the universities and the newspaper offices; he looked up politicians; he searched for writers, anything and everywhere which might possibly be grist to the greedy mill in New York.

One of the schemes on which he had been commissioned to check up was a series of articles on city and state governments. Almost at once he began to see larger and larger possibilities in the idea. There should be two series, he wrote the office, descriptions of the actual government of four or five typical cities and of as many states, humanized by studies of the men who ruled them or who were fighting the true rulers. A meeting with young district attorney Folk of St. Louis, then in the thick of a fight to reform his town, whetted his appetite. "If we take up the states," he wrote, "I would prefer to wait for William Allen White to write the articles. The cities will be more in my line. If I should be entrusted with the work I think I could make my name."

A few weeks later he was entrusted with the work. The result was "The Shame of the Cities" which, as he prophesied, made his name.

11

A CAPTAIN OF INDUSTRY
SEEKS MY ACQUAINTANCE

As STEFFENS' case shows there was always much fingering of a subject at *McClure's* before one of the staff was told to go ahead. The original hint might come from Mr. McClure's overflowing head and pocket, Mr. Phillips' notebooks, as much a part of him as his glasses, the daily mail, the chance word of a caller. We all turned in our pickings. They must concern the life of the day, that which was interesting people. An idea, once launched, grew until fixed on somebody; and, once started, it continued to grow according to the response of readers. No response—no more chapters. A healthy response—as many chapters as the material justified.

It was by this process that my next long piece of work came into being: "The History of the Standard Oil Company."

The deluge of monopolistic trusts which had followed the close of the Spanish-American War and the "return of prosperity" was disturbing and confusing people. It was contrary to their philosophy, their belief that, given free opportunity, free competition, there would always be brains and energy enough to prevent even the ablest leader monopolizing an industry. What was interfering with the free play of the forces in which they trusted? They had been depending on the Federal Antitrust Law passed ten years before. Was it quite useless? It looked that way.

There was much talk in the office about it, and there came to the top finally the idea of using the story of a typical trust to illustrate how and why the clan grew. How about the greatest of them all—the Standard Oil Company?

I suppose I must have talked rather freely about my own recollections and impressions of its development. It had been a strong thread weaving itself into the pattern of my life from childhood on.

I had come into the world just before the discovery of oil, the land on which I was born not being over thirty miles away from that first well. The discovery had shaped my father's life, rescuing him as it did thousands of others from the long depression which had devastated the eighteen-fifties. I had grown up with oil derricks, oil tanks, pipe lines, refineries, oil exchanges. I remembered what had happened in the Oil Region in 1872 when the railroads and an outside group of refiners attempted to seize what many men had created. It was my first experience in revolution. On the instant the word became holy to me. It was your privilege and duty to fight injustice. I was much elated when, not so long afterwards, I fell on Rousseau's "Social Contract" and read his defense of the right to revolt.

I had been only dimly conscious of what had happened in the decade following—the decade in which the Standard Oil Company had completed its monopoly. It was the effect on the people about me that stirred me, the hate and suspicion and fear that engulfed the community. I had been so deeply stirred by this human tragedy, as I have told, that I had made a feeble and ineffectual attempt to catch it, fix it in a novel.

The drama continued to unfold while I was abroad, came into our very household when a partner of my father's ruined by the complex situation shot himself, leaving father with notes. To pay them it was necessary in the panic of '93 to do what in his modest economy was unsound and humiliating—mortgage our home. While the personal tragedies came in my mother's letters, my brother wrote me vivid accounts of what was going on in the outside oil world, of the slow action of the Interstate Commerce Commission from which all independents had hoped so much, of businesses ruined while they waited for the decision; of the Ohio suit which drove the trust to reorganization, a legal victory which in no way weakened its hold or crippled its growth. Depressing as this was, I was elated by my brother's reports of the growing strength of a strongly integrated cooperative effort of producers, refiners, transporters, marketers, the Pure Oil Company. The only escape possible for those who would do independent business, he argued ably, was to build their own combination depending less on agitation, politics, legislation, more on sound business. Fight if necessary, but above all do business.

While I was still in Paris this clutter of recollections, impressions, indignations, perplexities, was crystallized into something like a pattern by Henry D. Lloyd's brilliant "Wealth Against Commonwealth." I had been hearing about the book from home, but the first copy was brought me by my English friend H. Wickham Steed, who, fresh from two years' contact with German socialism, took the work with great seriousness. Was not this a conclusive proof that capitalism was necessarily inconsistent with fair and just economic life? Was not socialism the only way out, as Lloyd thought?

I was more simple-minded about it. As I saw it, it was not capitalism but an open disregard of decent ethical business practices by capitalists which lay at the bottom of the story Mr. Lloyd told so dramatically.

The reading and discussions whetted my appetite; and when I came back to America in 1894, and heard anew in the family circle of what had been going on, my old desire to get the drama down seized me. Where were those notes I had made back in my *Chautauquan* days? Gathering dust in the tower room. I looked them up, saw that I had done well in choosing Pithole for my opening scene. Nothing so dramatic as Pithole in oil history. How many men it had made and ruined! But "the bottom had dropped out" in 1866. What was left of it now—1894? My brother and I drove over to see.

Thirty years before, Pithole had been a city of perhaps twenty thousand men and women with all the equipment for a permanent life. Now here were only stripped fields where no outline of a town remained. We spent a long day trying to place the famous wells, to fix my father's tank shops, so profitable while Pithole lasted, to trace the foundations of the Bonta House, which had furnished the makings of our home in Titusville. The day left us with a melancholy sense of the impermanence of human undertakings; and, more to the point, it showed me that if I were to reconstruct the town with its activities and its people, picture its rise and its fall, I must go back to records, maps, reminiscences; that I must undertake a long and serious piece of investigation before I began. But, given the material, how about my ability to make it live, to create the drama which I felt? One must be an artist before he can create—that I knew. I was no artist.

Mr. McClure's call to come on and write a life of Napoleon put an end to my hesitations; and, Napoleon done, there had been Lincoln and the Spanish-American War—no time to consider oil or even to rejoice over the final success of the integrated industry to which my brother had tied his fortune.

But here I was again faced with the old interest. The desire to do something about it, get down what I had seen, seized me. Was it possible to treat the story historically, to make a documented narrative? The more I talked, the more convinced I was that it could be done. But to tell the story so that people would read it was another matter. Mr. Phillips finally put it up to me to make an outline of what I thought possible. We couldn't go ahead without Mr. McClure's approval, and he was ill, in Europe with all his family.

"Go over," said John Phillips; "show the outline to Sam, get his decision." And so in the fall of 1890 I went to Lausanne in Switzerland to talk it over with Mr. McClure. A week would do it, I thought; but I hadn't reckoned with the McClure method.

"Don't worry about it," said he. "I want to think it over. Mrs.

McClure and you and I will go to Greece for the winter. You've never been there. We can discuss Standard Oil in Greece as well as here. If it seems a good plan you can send for your documents and work in the Pantheon." And he chuckled at the picture.

Almost before I realized it we were headed for Greece via the Italian Lakes, Milan and Venice. In Milan Mr. McClure suddenly decided that he and Mrs. McClure needed a cure before Greece and headed for the ancient watering place of Salsomaggiore. Here, in the interval of mud baths and steam soaks and watching such magnificent humans as Cecil Rhodes and his retinue recuperating from their latest South African adventure, we finally came to a decision. I was to go back to New York and see what I could make of the outline I had been expounding. Greece was to be abandoned.

Leaving Mr. and Mrs. McClure to finish their cure, I headed for New York to write what, as far as title was concerned, certainly looked like a doubtful enterprise for a magazine like *McClure's*: "The History of the Standard Oil Company."

"*McClure's* has courage." How often that remark was made after our undertaking was under way! But courage implies a suspicion of danger. Nobody thought of such a thing in our office. We were undertaking what we regarded as a legitimate piece of historical work. We were neither apologists nor critics, only journalists intent on discovering what had gone into the making of this most perfect of all monopolies. What had we to be afraid of?

I soon discovered, however, that, if we were not afraid, I must work in a field where numbers of men and women were afraid, believed in the all-seeing eye and the all-powerful reach of the ruler of the oil industry. They believed that anybody going ahead openly with a project in any way objectionable to the Standard Oil Company would meet with direct or indirect attack. Examination of their methods had always been objectionable to them. "Go ahead, and they will get you in the end," I was told by more than one who had come to that conclusion either from long observation or from long suffering.

Even my father said, "Don't do it, Ida—they will ruin the magazine."

It was a persistent fog of suspicion and doubt and fear. From the start this fog hampered what was my first business, making sure of the documents in the case. I knew they existed. Almost continuously since its organization in 1870 the Standard Oil Company had been under investigation by the Congress of the United States and by the legislatures of various states in which it had operated, on the suspicion that it was receiving rebates from the railroads and was practicing methods in restraint of free trade. In 1872 and again in 1876 it was before Congressional committees; in 1879 it was before examiners of the Commonwealth of Pennsylvania and before committees appointed by the legislatures of New York and of Ohio for investigating railroads. Its operations figured constantly in the debate which led up to the creation of the Interstate Commerce Commission in 1887; and again and again since that time the Commission had been called upon to examine directly or indirectly into its relations with the railroads.

In 1888, in the Investigation of Trusts conducted by Congress and by the State of New York, the Standard Oil Company was the chief subject for examination. In the state of Ohio, between 1882 and 1892, a constant warfare was waged against the Standard in the courts and the legislature, resulting in several volumes of testimony. The legislatures of many other states concerned themselves with it. This hostile legislation compelled the trust to separate into its component parts in 1892, but investigation did not cease; indeed, in the great industrial inquiry conducted by the Commission appointed by President McKinley, the Standard Oil Company was constantly under discussion, and hundreds of pages of testimony on it appear in the nineteen volumes of reports which the Commission submitted.

This mass of testimony—most, if not all, of it taken under oath—contained the different charters and agreements under which the Standard Oil Trust had operated, many contracts and agreements with railroads, with refineries, with pipe lines; and it contained the experiences in business from 1872 up to 1900 of multitudes of individuals. These experiences had exactly the quality of the personal reminiscences of actors in great events, with the additional value that they were given on the witness stand; and it was fair, therefore, to suppose that they were more cautious and exact in statement than are many writers of memoirs. These investigations, covering as they did all of the important steps in the development of the trust, included full accounts of the point of view of its officers in regard to that development, as well as their explanations of many of the operations over which controversy had arisen.

Aside from the great mass of sworn testimony accessible to the student, there was a large pamphlet literature dealing with different phases of the subject, as well as files of the numerous daily newspapers and monthly reviews, supported by the Oil Region, in the columns of which were to be found, not only statistics, but full reports of all controversies between oil men.

But the documentary sources were by no means all in print. The Standard Oil Trust and its constituent companies had figured in many civil suits, the testimony of which was in manuscript in the files of the courts where the suits were tried.

I had supposed it would be easy to locate the records of the important investigations and cases, but I soon found I had been too trustful. For instance, there was a Federal investigation of the South Improvement Company, the first attempt to make a hard and fast alliance between oil-bearing railroads and oil refiners, an alliance which inevitably would kill everybody not admitted, since by the contract the railroads not only allowed the privileged refiners a rebate on all their shipments, but paid them a drawback on those of independents. The railroads also agreed to give them full information about the quantity and the destination of their rivals' shipments. The Standard Oil Company as a monopoly had grown out of this pretty scheme.

Where could I get a copy of that investigation? More than one cynic said, "You'll never find one—they have all been destroyed." When I had located copies in each of two private collections I was refused permission to put my hands on them.

To be sure, I did by persistent searching find that so-guarded investigation in a pamphlet which is one of the three which are all I know to be in existence. I am not supposing that there are not others, for I quickly learned, when I was told that the entire edition of a printed document had been destroyed, to go on looking. Once a document is in print, somewhere, some time, a copy turns up, however small the edition. For instance, there was the important Hepburn investigation of the relations of railroads and private industries made by the State of New York in 1879. I could not find a copy in the Oil Region where I was working. The Standard had destroyed them all, I was told. At that time there was in the Public Library of New York City one of the ablest of American bibliographers—Adelaide Hasse. She had helped me more than once to find a scarce document.

"How about this Hepburn investigation?" I wrote Miss Hasse.

"Here in the Library for your use whenever you will come around." But she added: "Only one hundred copies were ever published. It is a scarce piece. I have known of a complete set selling for $100.00. It was understood at the time," she explained, "that one or two important railroad presidents whose testimony was given before the committee bought up and destroyed as many sets as they could obtain."

In the end all the printed documents were located. But there was the unprinted testimony taken in lawsuits. Had incriminating testimony been spirited away from the court files? Henry Lloyd made such an accusation in his first edition of "Wealth Against Commonwealth." It disappeared from a second edition.

I wrote to ask him, "Why?" "The testimony was put back after my book first appeared," he answered. I was particularly anxious to have the original of one of these documents, but when I came to look for it, it was not in the files. Where was it? How was I to locate it? And if I did succeed would there be any chance—to judge from past experience—that it would be turned over to me? I saw that I must have an assistant, someone preferably in Cleveland, Ohio, so many years the headquarters of the Standard's operations. It meant more expense, and I was already costing the office an amount which shocked my thrifty practice. But Mr. McClure and Mr. Phillips, being generous and patient and also by this time fairly confident that in the end we should get something worth while, told me to go ahead.

I had learned in my Lincoln work that an assistant, even if faithful and hard-working, may be an incumbrance when it comes to investigation. It needs more than accuracy; it needs enthusiasm for finding out things, solving puzzles—anybody's puzzles. I wanted a young man with college training, a year or two of experience as a reporter, intelligent, energetic, curious, convinced everything he was asked to do was important, even if he did not at the moment know why. He must get his fun in the chase—you in the bag. Also he must be trusted to keep his mouth shut.

I can recommend the technique I practiced in this case for finding my rare bird. From each of three different editors in Cleveland I asked the name of a young man whom he thought competent to run down a not very important-looking bit of information. To each of the names given me I wrote instructions from New York. I would be around soon to pick up the report, I told them, adding that I should prefer that he say nothing about the assignment.

When I went to Cleveland to view my prospects I found both number one and number two fine intelligent fellows. Their reports were excellent, but they had not the least interest in what they had done. I thanked them, paid them, and said, "Good day." The third young man came, short and plump, his eyes glowing with excitement. He sat on the edge of his chair. As I watched him I had a sudden feeling of alarm lest he should burst out of his clothes. I never had the same feeling about any other individual except Theodore Roosevelt. I once watched the first Roosevelt through a White House musicale when I felt his clothes might not contain him, he was so steamed up, so ready to go, attack anything, anywhere.

The young man gave me his report; but what counted was the way he had gone after his material, his curiosity, his conviction that it was important since I wanted it. I thought I had my man. A few more trials convinced me John M. Siddall was a find. He at that time was an associate of Frank Bray in the editing of *The Chautauquan*, the headquarters of which had been shifted to Cleveland from Meadville.

When Siddall once understood what I was up to he jumped at the chance—went to work with a will and stayed working with a will until the task was ended. He was a continuous joy as well as a support in my undertaking. Nothing better in the way of letter writing came to the *McClure's* office. In time everybody was reading Siddall's letters to me, whether it was a mere matter of statistics or a matter of the daily life in Cleveland of John D. Rockefeller, the head of the Standard Oil Company. If anything in or around Ohio interested the magazine the office immediately suggested, "Ask Sid." And Sid always found the answer. Mr. McClure and Mr. Phillips began to say, "We want Sid as soon as you are through with him." Sid saw the opportunity, and as soon as I could spare him in Ohio he joined the *McClure's* staff.

I had been at work a year gathering and sifting materials before the series was announced. Very soon after that, Mr. McClure dashed into the office one day to tell me he had just been talking with Mark Twain, who said his friend Henry Rogers, at that time the most conspicuous man in the Standard Oil group, had asked him to find out what kind of history of the concern *McClure's* proposed to publish.

"You will have to ask Miss Tarbell," Mr. McClure told him.

"Would Miss Tarbell see Mr. Rogers?" Mark Twain asked.

Mr. McClure was sure I would not ask anything better, which was quite true. And so an interview was arranged for one day early in January of 1902 at Mr. Rogers' home, then at 26 East Fifty-seventh Street. I was a bit scared at the idea. I had met many kinds of people, but this was my first high-ranking captain of industry. Was I putting my head into a lion's mouth? I did not think so. It had become more and more evident to me that any attempt to bite our heads off would be the stupidest thing the Standard Oil Company could do, its reputation being what it was. It was not that stupid, I told myself. However, it was one thing to tackle the Standard Oil Company in documents, as I had been doing, quite another thing to meet it face to face. And then would Mr. Rogers "come across"? Could I talk with him? So far my attempts to talk with members of the organization had been failures. I had been met with that formulated chatter used by those who have accepted a creed, a situation, a system, to baffle the investigator trying to find out what it all means.

My nervousness and my skepticism fell away when Mr. Rogers stepped forward in his library to greet me. He was frank and hearty. Plainly he wanted me to be at ease. In that way he knew that he could soon tell whether it was worth his while to spend further time on me or not.

Henry Rogers was a man of about sixty at this time, a striking figure, by all odds the handsomest and most distinguished figure in Wall Street. He was tall, muscular, lithe as an Indian. There was a trace of the early oil adventure in his bearing in spite of his air of authority, his excellent grooming, his manner of the quick-witted naturally adaptable man who has seen much of people. His big head with its high forehead was set off by a heavy shock of beautiful gray hair; his nose was aquiline, sensitive. The mouth, which I fancy must have been flexible, capable both of firm decision and of gay laughter, was concealed by a white drooping moustache. His eyes were large and dark, narrowed a little by caution, capable of blazing as I was to find out, shaded by heavy gray eyebrows giving distinction and force to his face.

I remember thinking as I tried to get my bearings: Now I understand why Mark Twain likes him so much. They are alike even in appearance. They have the bond of early similar experiences—Mark Twain in Nevada, Henry Rogers in the early oil regions.

"When and where did your interest in oil begin?" Mr. Rogers asked as he seated me—a full light on my face, I noticed.

"On the flats and hills of Rouseville," I told him.

"Of course," he cried, "of course! Tarbell's Tank Shops. I knew your father. I could put my finger on the spot where those shops stood."

We were off. We forgot our serious business and talked of our early days on the Creek. Mr. Rogers told me how the news of the oil excitement had drawn him from his boyhood home in New England, how he had found his way into Rouseville, gone into refining. He had married and put his first thousand dollars into a home on the hillside adjoining ours.

"It was a little white house," he said, "with a high peaked roof."

"Oh, I remember it!" I cried. "The prettiest house in the world, I thought it." It was my first approach to the Gothic arch, my first recognition of beauty in a building.

We reconstructed the geography of our neighborhood, lingering over the charm of the narrow ravine which separated our hillsides, a path on each side.

"Up that path," Mr. Rogers told me, "I used to carry our washing every Monday morning and go for it every Saturday night. Probably I've seen you hunting flowers on your side of the ravine. How beautiful it was! I was never happier."

Could two strangers, each a little wary of the other, have had a more auspicious beginning for a serious talk? For what followed was serious with moments of strain.

"What are you basing your story on?" he asked finally.

"On documents. I am beginning with the South Improvement Company."

He broke in to say: "Well, that of course was an outrageous business. That is where the Rockefellers made their big mistake."

I knew of course that Mr. Rogers had fought that early raid tooth and nail; and I also knew that later he had joined "the conspirators," as the Oil Region called them, in carrying out point by point the initial program. But I did not throw it up to him.

"Why did you not come to us at the start?" Mr. Rogers asked.

"It was unnecessary. You have written your history; besides, it would have been quite useless," I told him.

"We've changed our policy," he said. "We are giving out information." As a matter of fact Mr. Rogers may be regarded, I think, as the first public relations counsel of the Standard Oil Company—the forerunner of Ivy Lee—and I was, so far as I know, the first subject on which the new policy was tried.

In the close to two hours I spent that afternoon with Henry Rogers we went over the history of the oil business. We talked of rebates and pipe lines, independent struggles and failures, the absorption of everything that touched their ambition. He put their side to me, the mightiness of their achievement, the perfection of their service. Also he talked of their trials, the persecution (as he called it) by their rivals, the attack of Lloyd: "I never understood how Harper could have published that book. Why, I knew Harry Harper socially.

"There has always been something," he said a little ruefully.

"Look at things now—Russia and Texas. There seems to be no end of the oil they have there. How can we control it? It looks as if something had the Standard Oil Company by the neck, something bigger than we are."

The more we talked, the more at home I felt with him and the more I liked him. It was almost like talking with Mr. McClure and Mr. Phillips.

Finally we made a compact. I was to take up with him each case in their history as I came to it. He was to give me documents, figures, explanations, and justifications—anything and everything which would enlarge my understanding and judgment. I realized how big a contribution he would make if he continued to be as frank as he was in this preliminary talk. I made it quite clear to him, however, that while I should welcome anything in the way of information and explanation that he could give, it must be my judgment, not his, which prevailed.

"Of course, Mr. Rogers," I told him, "I realize that my judgments may not stand in the long run; but I shall have to stand or fall by them."

"Well," he said as I rose to go, "I suppose we'll have to stand it. Would you be willing to come to my office for these talks? It might be a little more convenient."

"Certainly," I replied.

He looked a bit surprised.

"Will you talk with Mr. Rockefeller?"

"Certainly," I said.

"Well," he said a little doubtfully, "I'll try to arrange it."

For two years our bargain was faithfully kept, I usually going to his office at 26 Broadway. That in itself at the start, for one as unfamiliar as I was with the scene and customs of big business, was an adventure. My entrance and exit to Mr. Rogers' office were carried on with a secrecy which never failed to amuse me. The alert, handsome, businesslike little chaps who received me at the entrance to the Rogers' suite piloted me unerringly

by a route where nobody saw me and I saw nobody into the
same small room opening on to a court, and it seemed never the
same route. I was not slow in discovering that across the court
in the window directly opposite there was always stationed a
gentleman whose head seemed to be turned my way whenever I
looked across. It may have meant nothing at all. I only record
the fact.

The only person besides Mr. Rogers I ever met in those offices
was his private secretary, Miss Harrison: a woman spoken of
with awe at that date as having a $10,000 salary, one who knew
her employer's business from A to Z and whom he could trust
absolutely. She radiated efficiency—business competency. Along
with her competency went that gleam of hardness which efficient
business women rarely escape. Miss Harrison appeared only on
rare occasions when an extra document was needed. She was as
impersonal as the chairs in the room.

We discussed in these interviews, with entire frankness, the
laws which they had flouted. I could not shock Mr. Rogers with
records—not even when I confronted him one day with the testimony he had given on a certain point which he admitted was
not according to the facts. He curtly dismissed the subject.
"They had no business prying into my private affairs." As for
rebates, "Somebody would have taken them if we had not."

"But with your strength, Mr. Rogers," I argued, "you could
have forced fair play on the railroads and on your competitors."

"Ah," he said, "but there was always somebody without scruples in competition, however small that somebody might be.
He might grow."

There it was, the obsession of the Standard Oil Company, that
danger lurked in small as well as great things, that nothing, however trivial, must live outside of its control.

These talks made me understand as I could not from the
documents themselves the personal point of view of independents
like Mr. Rogers who had been gathered into the organization

in the first decade of monopoly making. For instance, there was Mr. Rogers' reason for desiring the trust agreement made in 1882:

"By 1880," said Mr. Rogers, "I had stock in nearly all of the seventy or so companies which we had absorbed. But the real status of these companies was not known to the public. In case of my death there would have been practically no buyer except Mr. Flagler, Mr. Rockefeller, and a few others on the inside. My heirs would not have reaped the benefit of my holdings. The trust agreement changed this. The public at once realized the value of the trust certificate. That is, my estate was guarded in case of my death."

He often emphasized the part economies had played not only in building up the concern but in their individual fortunes— economies and putting their money back into the business. "We lived in rented houses and saved money to buy stock in the company," he told me once.

Only one who remembers, as I do, the important place that owning your own home took in the personal economy of the self-respecting individual of that day can feel the force of this explanation.

I was curious about how he had been able to adjust his well known passion for speculation with Mr. Rockefeller's well known antagonism to all forms of gambling.

"Didn't he ever object?" I asked.

"Oh," he said a little ruefully, "I was never a favorite. I suppose I was a born gambler. In the early days of the Charles Pratt Company, the company of which I was a member—I always carried on the speculations for the concern—Mr. Pratt said: 'Henry, I haven't got the nerve to speculate. I kicked all the clothes off last night worrying about the market.' 'Give me the money,' I told him, 'and I will furnish the nerve.' We simply raked in the money"—making a gesture with both hands. "And of course it came out of the producer."

"That is what my father always said," I told him. "One of the severest lectures he ever gave came from one of those booms in the market which sent everybody in the Oil Region crazy. I suppose you were responsible for it. I remember a day when the schools were practically closed because all the teachers in Titusville were on the street or in the Oil Exchange—everybody speculating. I was in high school; the fever caught me, and I asked father for $100 to try my luck in the market. He was as angry with me as I ever saw him. 'No daughter of mine,' he said, etc., etc."

"Wise man," Mr. Rogers commented.

"But it was not because he was so cautious," I said. "It was because he thought it was morally wrong. He would no more have speculated in the stock market than he would have played poker for money."

"I always play poker when the market is closed," commented Mr. Rogers. "I can't help it. Saturday afternoons I almost always make up a poker party, and every now and then John Gates and I rig up something. He'll come around and say, 'Henry, isn't it about time we started something?' We usually do."

All of these talks were informal, natural. We even argued with entire friendliness the debatable question, "What is the worst thing the Standard Oil Company ever did?" Only now and then did one of us flare, and then the other generally changed the subject.

"He's a liar and hypocrite, and you know it," I exploded one day when we were talking of a man who had led in what to me was a particularly odious operation.

"I think it is going to rain," said Mr. Rogers, looking out of the window with ostentatious detachment.

Mr. Rogers not only produced documents and arguments; he produced people with whom I wanted to talk. The most important was Henry Flagler, who had been in on the South Improvement Company, that early deal with the railroads which had started the Standard Oil Company off on the road to monopoly. There had always been a controversy as to who had suggested that fine scheme. Mr. Flagler was in it. What did he know? Mr. Rogers arranged that I talk with him.

Henry Flagler was not an acceptable figure even to Wall Street in those days. There were scandals of his private life which, true or not, his fellow financiers did not like. Bad for business. I found him a very different type from Henry Rogers. He, for instance, did not conceal his distrust of John Rockefeller. "He would do me out of a dollar today," he cried, off his guard, and with an excited smash of his fist on the table; and then, catching himself and with a remarkable change of tone: "That is, if he could do it honestly, Miss Tarbell, if he could do it honestly."

Mr. Flagler knew what I had come for, but instead of answering my direct questions he began to tell me with some show of emotion of his own early life, how he had left home because his father was a poor clergyman—$400 a year, a large family of children. He had not succeeded until he went into the commission business with Mr. Rockefeller in Cleveland. "And from that time we were prospered," he said piously. In the long story he told me, the phrase, "We were prospered," came in again and again. That was not what I was after. Their prosperity was obvious enough. Finally I returned with some irritation to the object of my visit.

"I see you do not know or are unwilling to say, Mr. Flagler, who originated the South Improvement Company; but this is certain: Mr. Rockefeller had the credit of it in the Oil Region. You know, yourself, how bitter the feeling was there."

"But, ah, Miss Tarbell," he said, "how often the reputation of a man in his lifetime differs from his real character! Take the greatest character in our history. How different was our Lord and Saviour regarded when he was alive from what we now know him to have been!"

After that, further questioning was of course hopeless, and until Mr. Rogers returned I sat listening to the story of how the Lord had prospered him. I never was happier to leave a room, but I was no happier than Mr. Flagler was to have me go.

Mr. Rogers produced Mr. Flagler and others of lesser importance. But although I referred to his semi-promise in our first interview to produce Mr. Rockefeller I found that after a few months there was no hope of this. If I hinted at it he parried.

Nearly a year went by after my first interview with Mr. Rogers before the articles began to appear. I rather expected him to cut me off when he realized that I was trying to prove that the Standard Oil Company was only an enlarged South Improvement Company. But to my surprise my arguments did not seem to disturb him. They had won out, had they not? He sometimes complained that I had been unnecessarily blunt or a bit vindictive, but he continued to receive me in friendly fashion and to give me, perhaps not all the help he might, but always something to make me think twice, frequently to modify a view.

But if he was not himself disturbed by what I was doing why did he continue the interviews? Gradually I became convinced it was because of his interest in my presentation of a particular episode in their history. It was a case in which Mr. Rogers and John Archbold, along with all of the members of the board of a subsidiary company, the Vacuum Oil Company of Rochester, New York, had been indicted for conspiring to destroy an independent refinery in Buffalo, New York.

In my opening interview with Mr. Rogers he with some show of feeling had told me he wanted me to get a correct and impartial version of this Buffalo case, as he always called it. There had been a break in his voice when with hesitation he said: "That case is a sore point with Mr. Archbold and me. I want you to go into it thoroughly. I have the reports of the testimony before the grand jury; it took me months to secure them. Of course in a sense I have no right with them. I told my children that if their father's memory is ever attacked this will serve to vindicate him. He must stand or fall in their estimation by that testimony."

At our second interview he produced the testimony before the grand jury, repeating again that of course he had no business with it but he had to have it. He would not allow me to take it away, and at his request I read the sixty or more pages in his presence. It seemed quite clear to me, as I told Mr. Rogers on finishing the reading, that his connection with the affair had been so indirect that there was no reason for his indictment, although it seemed equally clear to me that there was ample reason for the indictment of certain members of the Vacuum board. The judge was of that opinion, for he dismissed the indictment against Mr. Rogers and two of his fellow directors while sustaining that against the responsible operating heads of the concern.

I soon discovered that what Mr. Rogers wanted me to make out was that the three men who had founded the independent enterprise, all of them former employees of the Vacuum Oil Company, had done so for the sole purpose of forcing the Standard to buy them out at a high price; that is, that it was a case of planned blackmail. But the testimony certainly showed little evidence of that while it did show clearly enough that the managers of the Vacuum Oil Company, from the hour they had learned of the undertaking, had made deliberate and open attempts to prevent the Buffalo refinery doing business.

The more thoroughly I went into the matter—and I worked hard over it—the more convinced I was that, while there had been bad faith and various questionable practices on the part of members of the independent firm, they had started out to build up a business of their own. Also it was clear they had had hardly a shadow of success under the grilling opposition of the Standard concern. This included various suits for infringement of patents, all of which the Standard had lost. In course of the years of litigation four juries—two grand juries and two petit juries—gave verdicts against the Standard Oil Company.

Finally the independent concern was so shot to pieces by the continuous bombardment that it had to be put into the hands of a receiver. The Standard offered to settle for $85,000, and the judge ordered the acceptance. This made it the owner of the bone of contention.

I had a feeling that my final conclusion in the matter would probably end my relations with Mr. Rogers. I did not want to spring that conclusion on him, that is, I wanted him to know ahead of publication where I had come out. Although I had never allowed him to read an article before its appearance, that being part of the original compact, I broke my rule in this case. Promptly I received a letter asking me to call at 26 Broadway. He received me in his usual cordial way and told me he had gone over my article carefully, compared it with certain papers in his possession and had written me a letter in which he had stated his criticisms.

Handing me the letter, he said, "I think it will be a good plan for you to read that out loud, so that we can talk it over here."

I began to read, but broke off with the first sentence. Mr. Rogers had written that he appreciated my request that he should make the story correspond with his knowledge and opinion of the case.

"Mr. Rogers," I said, "if you will look at my letter you will see that I did not suggest that you make the article correspond with your opinion of this case. I am convinced that I cannot do that. I asked you to examine the article and see if I had made any errors in statement or had omitted any essential testimony on either side."

He smiled. "Never mind, go ahead," he said.

The letter was admirable, almost every point well taken. There was nothing which it was not proper for me to consider at least, and with certain of his points I said at once that I was willing to comply. The discussion of the letter finished, I inwardly breathed a sigh of satisfaction. We were going to part on friendly terms with neither of us having yielded our convictions.

But I had not counted on the resources of Henry Rogers in a matter in which he was deeply concerned, particularly one which touched his personal pride and aroused his fighting spirit. For as I was about to go he sprang on me an entirely new interpretation of the case. Not only was the suit of the independent refinery in which he had been indicted a continuation of the original blackmailing scheme, but the lawyers in the case had themselves been in the conspiracy. He laid before me a number of documents which he claimed proved it. The chief of these was the itemized report of the receiver. This report, he said, showed that the lawyers had taken the case knowing that if the Buffalo concern did not win there would be no fees, and showed that when the matter had finally been settled they had made what the receiver considered exorbitant claims for their services. There were five of them, and they finally were allowed some thirty thousand dollars.

"You can see," Mr. Rogers said as he pointed out these facts, "why they were so eager to convict us. They were making a raid on the Standard, and the bench was with them."

His charge that the bench was with them, he based on the fact that two of the lawyers originally in the case had later been elevated to the bench. They had not of course heard the case, but they had put their information and conclusions at the disposal of their successors.

I was startled by this sudden and sinister accusation and sat for some time with my head bent over the papers, forgetting his presence, trying to get at the meaning of the documents. Was there any other explanation than that which Mr. Rogers had given me with such conviction? Looking up suddenly for the first time in my experience with Mr. Rogers, I caught him looking at me with narrowed and cunning eyes. I took alarm on the instant.

"We are not the only ones, you see, Miss Tarbell."

"If this means what it seems to mean you are not. But I shall have to study these documents, Mr. Rogers; I shall have to consult a lawyer about the practice common in such cases."

"That will be all right," he said.

He was more exultant than I had ever found him. "I knew that paper would come in well some day. To get it I consented to our people buying the Buffalo refinery—we did not want it, but I wanted to get the receiver's reports and know just what had been done with the money we had paid them."

On the whole I had never seen him better pleased with himself than he was at that moment. His satisfaction was so great that for the first time in our acquaintance he gave me a little lecture for a caustic remark I had made. "That is not a Christian remark," he said. I contended that it was a perfect expression of my notion of a Christian.

"You ought to go to church more frequently," he said. "Why don't you come and hear my pastor, Dr. Savage?"

We parted on good terms after a discussion of our religious views and churchgoing practices, and he gave me a cordial invitation to come back, which I agreed to do as soon as I had studied the new angle in the Buffalo case.

Aided by a disinterested and fair-minded lawyer, I gave a thorough study to the documents; but do my best I could not convince myself that Mr. Rogers' contention was sound. It is not an unusual thing for lawyers to take cases they believe in, knowing that their compensation depends on their winning. Many clients with just cases would be deprived of counsel if they had to insure a fixed compensation, for not infrequently, as in the Buffalo case, all that a client has is involved in a suit. The practice is so common among reputable lawyers that it certainly cannot be regarded as a proof of a conspiracy, unless there is a reason to suppose that they have taken a case of whose merits they themselves are suspicious. There was no evidence that the counsel of the independent concern were not convinced from the first that they had a strong case. Their claims were large; but lawyers are not proverbial for the modesty of their charges and, besides, exorbitant charges can hardly be construed as a proof of conspiracy.

When I finally had written out my conclusion I sent a copy of it to Mr. Rogers, saying I should be glad to talk it over with him if he wished. He did wish—wrote me that he had new material to present. But before the date set for the meeting an article in our series was published which broke off our friendly relations.

In studying the testimony of independents over a period of some thirty years I had found repeated complaints that their oil shipments were interfered with, their cars side-tracked en route while pressure was brought on buyers to cancel orders. There were frequent charges that freight clerks were reporting independent shipments.

I did not take the matter seriously at first. The general suspicion of Standard dealings by independents had to be taken into consideration, I told myself. Then, too, I was willing to admit that a certain amount of attention to what your competitor is doing is considered legitimate business practice. I knew that in the office of *McClure's Magazine* we were very keen to know what other publishers were doing. And, too, there is the overzealous and unscrupulous employee who in the name of competition recognizes no rules for his game.

But the charges continued to multiply. I met them in testimony, and I met them in interviews. There was no escaping espionage, men told me. "They know where we send every barrel of oil. Half the time our oil never reaches its destination." I could scarcely believe it. And then unexpectedly there came to my desk a mass of incontrovertible proofs that what I had been hearing was true and more. As a matter of fact this system of following up independent oil shipments was letter-perfect, so perfect that it was made a matter of office bookkeeping.

"It looks sometimes," Mr. Rogers had said to me, "as if something had the Standard Oil Company by the neck, something bigger than we are."

In this case the something bigger was a boy's conscience. A lad of sixteen or seventeen in the office of a Standard plant had as one of his regular monthly duties the burning of large quantities of records. He had carried out his orders for many months without attention to the content. Then suddenly his eyes fell one night on the name of a man who had been his friend since childhood, had even been his Sunday-school teacher, an independent oil refiner in the city, a Standard competitor. The boy began to take notice; he discovered that the name appeared repeatedly on different forms and in the letters which he was destroying. It made him uneasy, and he began to piece the records together. It was not long before he saw to his distress that the concern for which he was working was getting from the railroad offices of the town full information about every shipment that his friend was making; moreover, that the office was writing to its representative in the territory to which the independent oil was going, "Stop that shipment—get that trade." And the correspondence showed how both were done.

What was a youth to do under such circumstances? He didn't do anything at first, but finally when he could not sleep nights for thinking about it he gathered up a full set of documents and secretly took them to his friend.

Now this particular oil refiner had been reading the *McClure's* articles. He had become convinced that I was trying to deal fairly with the matter; he had also convinced himself in some way that I was to be trusted. So one night he brought me the full set of incriminating documents. There was no doubt about their genuineness. The most interesting to me was the way they fitted in with the testimony scattered through the investigations and law-suits. Here were bookkeeping records explaining every accusation that had been made. But how could I use them? Together we worked out a plan by which the various forms and blanks could be reproduced with fictitious names of persons and places substituted for the originals.

It was after this material had come to my hands that I took the subject up with Mr. Rogers. "The original South Improvement Company formula, Mr. Rogers, provided for reports of independent shipments from the railroads. I have come on repeated charges that the practice continues. What about it? Do you follow independent shipments? Do you stop them? Do you have the help of railroad shipping clerks in the operation?"

"Of course we do everything we legally and fairly can to find out what our competitors are doing, just as you do in *McClure's Magazine*," Mr. Rogers answered. "But as for any such system of tracking and stopping, as you suggest, that is nonsense. How could we do it even if we would?"

"Well," I said, "give me everything you have on this point."

He said he had nothing more than what he had already told me.

As I have said, the article came out just before I was to see Mr. Rogers on what I hoped would be the last of the Buffalo case. The only time in all my relations with him when I saw his face white with rage was when I met the appointment he had made. Our interview was short.

"Where did you get that stuff?" he said angrily, pointing to the magazine on the table.

All I could say was in substance: "Mr. Rogers, you can't for a moment think that I would tell you where I got it. You will recall my efforts to get from you anything more than a general denial that these practices of espionage so long complained of were untrue, could be explained by legitimate competition. You know this bookkeeping record is true."

There were a few curt exchanges about other points in the

material, but nothing as I now recall on the Buffalo case. The
article ended my visits to 26 Broadway.

Nearly four years passed before I saw Henry Rogers, and
in that period exciting and tragic events had come his way.

There was the copper war. He and his friends had attempted
to build up a monopoly in copper to match that of the Standard
Oil Company in petroleum, the Amalgamated Copper Company.
A youngster, F. Augustus Heinze, had come into Montana, and
by bold and ruthless operation put together a copper company
of his own. The two organizations were soon at each other's
throats. It was a business war without a vestige of decency, one
in which every devious device of the law and of politics was re-
sorted to by both sides.

But Mr. Rogers had other troubles. He and his friends had
been engaged in organizing the gas interests of the East. They
had engineered stock raids which had been as disastrous to
Wall Street as to gambling Main Street. Such operations in the
past had never cost him more than a passing angry comment by
the public press. Now, however, came something damaging to
his reputation and his pride. It was a series of lurid articles by
a bold and very-much-on-the-inside broker and speculator—
Thomas Lawson of Boston. For nearly two years Lawson published monthly in *Everybody's Magazine* under the admirable
title "Frenzied Finance" circumstantial accounts of the speculation of the Rogers group and what they had cost their dupes.
That story cut Mr. Rogers' pride to the quick. He is said to
have threatened the American News Company with destruction
if it circulated the magazine.

Taken all together the excitement and anger were too much for
even his iron frame and indomitable spirit, and in the summer
of 1907 he suffered a stroke which put him out of the fight for
many weeks. When he came back it was at once to collide with
the Government suit against the Standard Oil Company, and
soon after that with the "rich man's panic" of 1907, a panic for

which his old enemy in copper, F. Augustus Heinze, was largely responsible.

Early in November, when the panic was still raiding the banks and the millionaires of the country, I stood one day at a corner on Fifth Avenue waiting for the traffic to clear. Suddenly I saw an arm waving to me from a slowly passing open automobile, and there was H. H. Rogers smiling at me in the friendliest way.

When I reported the encounter at the office Mr. Phillips at once said:

"Why not try to see him? If he'll talk about what is going on, what a story he could tell!"

But would he see me? I was a little dubious about trying. Still the greeting and the smile seemed to mean that at least he harbored no ill will. Suppose, I said, he is sufficiently subdued to go over with me his exciting life. What a document of big business in the eighties and nineties he could produce if he would put down his recollections with the frankness with which he had sometimes talked to me! It seemed worth trying for, and I asked for an appointment. I had not made a mistake. Mr. Rogers was harboring no ill will. I was promptly invited to come to his house. He greeted me heartily. I found him physically changed, stouter, less sinewy, but quite as frank as ever. He told me of his stroke; he spoke bitterly of what he called the Roosevelt panic as well as of Roosevelt's interference with the business of the Standard Oil Company. He gave me my cue when he began to talk about the early days of the Oil Region. "There is a whole chapter," he said, "that has not been written, that from '59 to '72."

We were getting on swimmingly when our interview was cut short by a card handed him—Joseph Seep, the head of the Standard Oil Purchasing Agency. It amused him greatly that Mr. Seep should have come in while I was there.

"Now you'll have to go," he said, and he put me out by a circuitous route. As at 26 Broadway callers were not to see one another.

As we came into a dark hall he turned on the light. "You see we have to economize now," he said laughingly. Our good-bye was cordial. "We'll talk about this again," he said. "Call up Miss Harrison in a week or ten days, and we'll make an appointment."

The appointment was never made. The coming months were too difficult for Mr. Rogers. His vast business affairs continued complicated; the legend of his invincibility in the market was weakened. Moreover, such was the bitterness of the Standard Oil Company over the Government suit that I doubt if he or his associates would have considered it wise for him to talk to me. They probably thought he had talked already too much to too little purpose. They—and he probably—never understood how much he had done to make me realize the legitimate greatness of the Standard Oil Company, how much he had done to make me understand better the vastness and complexity of its problems and the amazing grasp with which it dealt with them.

Their complaint against me, Mr. Rogers' complaint, was that I had never been able to submerge my contempt for their illegitimate practices in my admiration for their genius in organization, the boldness of their imagination and execution. But my contempt had increased rather than diminished as I worked.

I never had an animus against their size and wealth, never objected to their corporate form. I was willing that they should combine and grow as big and rich as they could, but only by legitimate means. But they had never played fair, and that ruined their greatness for me. I am convinced that their brilliant example has contributed not only to a weakening of the country's moral standards but to its economic unsoundness. The experience of the last decade particularly seems to me to amply justify my conviction.

I was never to see Mr. Rogers again, for in May of 1909 he suddenly died—two years before the Supreme Court dissolved the Standard Oil Company.

12

MUCKRAKER OR HISTORIAN?

It was inevitable that my visits to 26 Broadway should be noised among critics and enemies of the Standard Oil Company curious about what *McClure's* was going to do. It was not infrequent for some one on the independent side to say with a wise nod of the head: "Oh, they'll get around you. You'll become their apologist before you get through." It was quite useless for me to insist that I was trying to be nobody's apologist, that I was trying to balance what I found. At least two people of importance whose experiences I was anxious to hear from their own lips refused to see me. I learned later that Henry D. Lloyd had written them after he learned I was seeing Mr. Rogers that they had better not talk, better not show me their papers, that inevitably I should be taken in.

Now I had already talked with Mr. Lloyd, already had help from him, but the Rogers association evidently upset him for a time. My first article seemed to reassure him, for he wrote me at once on its appearance: "I read your first installment of the story of the Standard Oil Company with eager curiosity, then intense interest and then great satisfaction." He seems to have divined at once where I was heading.

The suspicion of my relations with 26 Broadway cut me off for some two years from one of the most interesting independent warriors in the thirty years' struggle. This was one Lewis Emery, Jr., whom I had known from childhood. He had grown up in the oil business, side by side with H. H. Rogers; he had been a producer and a refiner as well as one of the powerful factors in building up the Pure Oil Company, the integrated concern in which my brother was carrying on. From the start Mr. Emery had fought the Standard's pretensions, individually and collectively, politically and financially. He had a gift for language — a marvelous vituperative vocabulary—and he had no restraint in using it. He was a feature of almost every investigation, every lawsuit, a member of every combination of producers and refiners. Where he was, there were sure to be lively exchanges between him and the representatives of the other side. His particular abomination was John Archbold, vice president of the Standard Oil Company, a person as free with charges and epithets as Lewis Emery himself.

"You are a liar," he shouted one day in an investigation when Mr. Emery had made an exaggerated charge.

Joseph H. Choate was Mr. Archbold's lawyer.

"There, there, Mr. Archbold!" he said. "We'll put Mr. Emery on the stand and convict him of perjury."

Without noticing Mr. Choate's remark Mr. Emery called across the table, "Young man, if this table wasn't so wide I would tweak your nose for that."

Such exchanges were not infrequent.

Henry Rogers, who really liked Lewis Emery, was always trying to calm him down. "Can't you stop this, Lew?" he said one day. "Come with us, and it will be better for you. There is no hope for you alone, but with us there is a sure thing."

Mr. Emery, who told me of this offer, said: "Henry, I can't do it even if I wanted to. They would mob me in the Oil Region if I went back on them."

They would not have mobbed him, but they would have done what would have been worse for a man of his temperament, his passion for free action whether wise or unwise—they would have ostracized him.

The most tragic effect I had seen in my girlhood of "going over to the Standard," as it was called, was partial ostracism of the renegade. When a man's old associates crossed to the other side of the street rather than meet him, when nobody stopped him on the street corner to gossip over what was going on, few men were calloused enough not to suffer. It was worse than mobbing. The Oil Region as a matter of fact never mobbed any man so far as I know, though it did occasionally destroy property and once at least hung Mr. Rockefeller himself in effigy.

By this time Lewis Emery had fought his way to a substantial position in the oil world; but to the end he prided himself on being a victim. When he finally talked to me after he learned from Mr. Lloyd that the embargo against me had been raised, he said, with what seemed to me considerable satisfaction: "I have been tortured. I am a wounded man because of them, and I hate them."

In spite of this he was getting a good deal out of life. He was a rich man, and he was making the most of his money. He never let money stifle his personality. His success in being himself was in striking contrast to that of most of the successful oil men of that day whom I knew. Most of them, independent and Standard, submitted to an application of veneer, a change of habits which destroyed much of their natural flavor. They took little part in politics and social agitation; they remained regular in all things; they made their investments only in sure enterprises. You knew always where to find them. But not so Lewis Emery, Jr. He continued to wear his clothes naturally, to go on his own erratic way. He threw himself into political movements, wise and unwise, and he never lost his pioneering spirit. After he was seventy years old, as a final fling, he took on a gold mine in Peru, a gold mine which was reached by climbing mountains and descending narrow paths cut out of rock, crossing swaying rope bridges— approaches fit only for the most daring mountain climbers. Yet there he was when nearly eighty charging up and down those mountains and trotting his mule across those bridges when younger men led their mules and crept.

The degree to which he was reconciled to me after two years of ostracism was proved by his annual invitation to come along to Peru with his party. And I would have gone and told the story of his mine as he wanted me to do if it had not been for the pictures he sent me—those pictures of unprotected swaying bridges suspended from mountain side to mountain side, hundreds of feet above the rushing rocky streams. I had not the head for that, and so gave up what would have been, I am sure, one of the most amusing adventures that ever came my way.

Not a few of the personal experiences in gathering my materials left me with unhappy impressions, more unhappy in retrospect perhaps than they were at the moment. They were part of the day's work, sometimes very exciting parts. There was the two hours I spent in studying Mr. John D. Rockefeller. As the work had gone on, it became more and more clear to me that the Standard Oil Company was his creation. "An institution is the lengthened shadow of one man," says Emerson. I found it so.

Everybody in the office interested in the work began to say, "After the book is done you must do a character sketch of Mr. Rockefeller." I was not keen for it. It would have to be done like the books, from documents; that is, I had no inclination to use the extraordinary gossip which came to me from many sources. If I were to do it I wanted only that of which I felt I had sure proof, only those things which seemed to me to help explain the public life of this powerful, patient, secretive, calculating man of so peculiar and special a genius.

"You must at least look at Mr. Rockefeller," my associates insisted. "But how?" Mr. Rogers himself had suggested that I see him. I had consented. I had returned to the suggestion several times, but at last was made to understand that it could not be done. I had dropped his name from my list. It was John Siddall who then took the matter in hand.

"You must see him," was Siddall's judgment.

To arrange it became almost an obsession. And then what seemed to him like a providential opening came. It was announced that on a certain Sunday of October 1903 Mr. Rockefeller before leaving Cleveland, where he had spent his summer, for his home in New York would say good-bye in a little talk to the Sunday school of his church—a rally, it was called. As soon as Siddall learned of this he begged me to come on. "We can go to Sunday school; we can stay to church. I will see that we have seats where we will have a full view of the man. You will get him in action."

Of course I went, feeling a little mean about it too. He had not wanted to be seen apparently. It was taking him unaware.

Siddall's plan worked to perfection, worked so well from the start that again and again he seemed ready to burst from excitement in the two hours we spent in the church.

We had gone early to the Sunday-school room where the rally was to open—a dismal room with a barbaric dark green paper with big gold designs, cheap stained-glass windows, awkward gas fixtures. Comfortable, of course, but so stupidly ugly. We were sitting meekly at one side when I was suddenly aware of a striking figure standing in the doorway. There was an awful age in his face—the oldest man I had ever seen, I thought, but what power! At that moment Siddall poked me violently in the ribs and hissed, "There he is."

The impression of power deepened when Mr. Rockefeller took off his coat and hat, put on a skullcap, and took a seat commanding the entire room, his back to the wall. It was the head which riveted attention. It was big, great breadth from back to front, high broad forehead, big bumps behind the ears, not a shiny head but with a wet look. The skin was as fresh as that of any healthy man about us. The thin sharp nose was like a thorn. There were no lips; the mouth looked as if the teeth were all shut hard. Deep furrows ran down each side of the mouth from the nose. There were puffs under the little colorless eyes with creases running from them.

Wonder over the head was almost at once diverted to wonder over the man's uneasiness. His eyes were never quiet but darted from face to face, even peering around the jog at the audience close to the wall.

When he rose to speak, the impression of power that the first look at him had given increased, and the impression of age passed. I expected a quavering voice, but the voice was not even old, if a little fatigued, a little thin. It was clear and utterly sincere. He meant what he was saying. He was on his own ground talking about dividends, dividends of righteousness. "If you would take something out," he said, clenching the hand of his outstretched right arm, "you must put something in"—emphasizing "put something in" with a long outstretched forefinger.

The talk over, we slipped out to get a good seat in the gallery, a seat where we could look full on what we knew to be the Rockefeller pew.

Mr. Rockefeller came into the auditorium of the church as soon as Sunday school was out. He sat a little bent in his pew, pitifully uneasy, his head constantly turning to the farthest right or left, his eyes searching the faces almost invariably turned towards him. It was plain that he, and not the minister, was the pivot on which that audience swung. Probably he knew practically everybody in the congregation; but now and then he lingered on a face, peering at it intently as if he were seeking what was in the mind behind it. He looked frequently at the gallery. Was it at Siddall and me?

The services over, he became the friendly patron saint of the flock. Coming down the aisle where people were passing out, he shook hands with everyone who stopped, saying, "A good sermon." "The Doctor gave us a good sermon." "It was a very good sermon, wasn't it?"

My two hours' study of Mr. Rockefeller aroused a feeling I had not expected, which time has intensified. I was sorry for him. I know no companion so terrible as fear. Mr. Rockefeller, for all the conscious power written in face and voice and figure, was afraid, I told myself, afraid of his own kind. My friend Lewis

Emery, Jr., priding himself on being a victim, was free and happy. Not gold enough in the world to tempt him to exchange his love of defiance for a power which carried with it a head as uneasy as that on Mr. Rockefeller's shoulders.

My unhappiness was increased as the months went by with the multiplying of tales of grievances coming from every direction. I made a practice of looking into them all, as far as I could; and while frequently I found solid reasons for the complaints, frequently I found the basic motives behind them—suspicion, hunger for notoriety, blackmail, revenge.

The most unhappy and most unnatural of these grievances came to me from literally the last person in the world to whom I should have looked for information—Frank Rockefeller— brother of John D. Rockefeller.

Frank Rockefeller sent word to me by a circuitous route that he had documents in a case which he thought ought to be made public, and that if I would secretly come to him in his office in Cleveland he would give them to me. I knew that there had been a quarrel over property between the two men. It made much noise at the time—1893—had gone to the courts, had caused bitterness inside the family itself; but because it was a family affair I had not felt that I wanted to touch it. But here it was laid on my desk.

So I went to Cleveland, where John Siddall had a grand opportunity to play the role of sleuth which he so enjoyed, his problem being to get me into Mr. Rockefeller's office without anybody suspecting my identity. He succeeded.

I found Mr. Rockefeller excited and vindictive. He accused his brother of robbing (his word) him and his partner James Corrigan of all their considerable holdings of stock in the Standard Oil Company. The bare facts were that Frank Rockefeller and James Corrigan had been interested in the early Standard Oil operations in Cleveland and had each acquired then a substantial block of stock. Later they had developed a shipping business on the Lakes, iron and steel furnaces in Cleveland. In the eighties they had borrowed money from John D. Rockefeller, putting up their Standard Oil stock as collateral. Then came the panic of '93, and they could not meet their obligations. In the middle of their distress John Rockefeller had foreclosed, taking over their stocks, leaving them, so they charged, no time in which to turn around although they felt certain that they would be able a little later, out of the substantial business they claimed they had built up, to pay their debt to him. Their future success proved they could have done so.

I could see John Rockefeller's point as I talked with his brother Frank. Frank Rockefeller was an open-handed, generous trader —more interested in the game than in the money to be made. He loved good horses—raised them, I believe, on a farm out in Kansas; he liked gaiety, free spending. From his brother John's point of view he was not a safe man to handle money. He did not reverence it; he used it in frivolous ways of which his brother did not approve. So it was as a kind of obligation to the sacredness of money that John Rockefeller had foreclosed on his own brother and his early friend James Corrigan. He was strictly within his legal rights and within what I suppose he called his moral right.

But the transaction left a bitterness in Frank Rockefeller's heart and mind which was one of the ugliest things I have ever seen. "I have taken up my children from the Rockefeller family lot. [Or "shall take up"—I do not know now which it was.] They shall not lie in the same enclosure with John D. Rockefeller."

The documents in this case, which I later analyzed for the character sketch on which we had decided, present a fair example of what were popularly called "Standard Oil methods" as well as what they could do to the minds and hearts of victims.

The more intimately I went into my subject, the more hateful it became to me. No achievement on earth could justify those methods, I felt. I had a great desire to end my task, hear no more of it. No doubt part of my revulsion was due to a fagged brain. The work had turned out to be much longer and more laborious than I had had reason to expect.

The plan I had taken to Mr. McClure in the fall of 1890, which we had talked over in Salsomaggiore, Italy—I still have notes of our talk on a yellow piece of the stationery of the Hôtel des Thermes—called for three papers, possibly twenty-five thousand words. But before we actually began publication Mr. Phillips and Mr. McClure decided we might venture on six. We went through the six, and the series was stretched to twelve. Before we were through we had nineteen articles, and when the nineteen were off my hands I asked nothing in the world but to get them into a book and escape into the safe retreat of a library where I could study people long dead, and if they did things of which I did not approve it would be all between me and the books. There would be none of these harrowing human beings confronting me, tearing me between contempt and pity, admiration and anger, baffling me with their futile and misdirected power or their equally futile and misdirected weakness. I was willing to study human beings in the library but no longer, for a time at least, in flesh and blood, so I thought.

The book was published in the fall of 1904—two fat volumes with generous appendices of what I considered essential documents. I was curious about the reception it would have from the Standard Oil Company. I had been told repeatedly they were preparing an answer to flatten me out; but if this was under way it was not with Mr. Rockefeller's consent, I imagined. To a mutual friend who had told him the articles should be answered Mr. Rockefeller was said to have replied: "Not a word. Not a word about that misguided woman." To another who asked him about my charges he was reported as answering: "All without foundation. The idea of the Standard forcing anyone to sell his refinery is absurd. The refineries wanted to sell to us, and nobody that has sold or worked with us but has made money, is glad he did so.

"I thought once of having an answer made to the McClure articles but you know it has always been the policy of the Standard to keep silent under attack and let their acts speak for themselves."

In the case of the Lloyd book they had kept silent, but only because Mr. Rockefeller had been unable to carry out his plans for answering. What he had proposed was a jury of the most distinguished clergymen of the day to consider Mr. Lloyd's argument and charges. Certain clergymen invited refused unless there should be a respectable number of economists added to the jury. That, apparently, Mr. Rockefeller did not see his way to do, and the plan was abandoned. So far as I know Mr. Lloyd's book was never answered by the Standard Oil Company.

But I wanted an answer from Mr. Rockefeller. What I got was neither direct nor, from my point of view, serious. It consisted of wide and what must have been a rather expensive anonymous distribution of various critical comments. The first of these was a review of the book which appeared in the *Nation* soon after its publication. The writer—one of the *Nation's* staff reviewers, I later learned—sneered at the idea that there was anything unusual in the competitive practices which I called illegal and immoral. "They are a necessary part of competition," he said. "The practices are odious it is true, competition is necessarily odious." Was it necessarily odious?

I did not think so. The practices I believed I had proved, I continued to consider much more dangerous to economic stability than airing them, even if I aired them in the excited and irrational fashion the review charged. As I saw it, the struggle was between Commercial Machiavellism and the Christian Code.

The most important of the indirect answers was an able book by Gilbert Holland Montague. It separated business and ethics in a way that must have been a comfort to 26 Broadway.

As soon as published, Mr. Montague's book became not exactly a best seller but certainly a best circulator—libraries, ministers, teachers, prominent citizens all over the land receiving copies with the compliments of the publisher. Numbers of them came back to me with irritated letters. "We have been buying books for years from this house," wrote one distinguished librarian, "and never before was one sent with their compliments. I understand that libraries all over the country are receiving them. Can it be that this is intended as an advertisement, or is it not more probable that the Standard Oil Company itself is paying for this widespread distribution?"

The general verdict seemed to be that the latter was the explanation.

Some time later there came from the entertaining Elbert Hubbard of the Roycroft Shop of East Aurora, New York, an essay on the Standard extolling the grand results from the centralization of the industry in their hands.

I have it from various interested sources that five million copies were ordered printed in pamphlet form by the Standard Oil Company and were distributed by Mr. Hubbard. They went to schoolteachers and journalists, preachers and "leaders" from the Atlantic to the Pacific. Hardly were they received in many cases before they were sent to me with angry or approving comments. For a couple of years my birthday and Christmas offerings were sure to include copies of one or the other of these documents with the compliments of some waggish member of the McClure group.

I had hoped that the book might be received as a legitimate historical study, but to my chagrin I found myself included in a new school, that of the muckrakers. Theodore Roosevelt, then President of the United States, had become uneasy at the effect on the public of the periodical press's increasing criticisms and investigations of business and political abuses. He was afraid that they were adding to the not inconsiderable revolutionary fever abroad, driving people into socialism. Something must be done, and in a typically violent speech he accused the school of being concerned only with the "vile and debasing." Its members were like the man in John Bunyan's "Pilgrim's Progress" who with eyes on the ground raked incessantly "the straws, the small sticks, and dust of the floor." They were muckrakers. The conservative public joyfully seized the name.

Roosevelt had of course misread his Bunyan. The man to whom the Interpreter called the attention of the Pilgrim was raking riches which the Interpreter contemptuously called "straws" and "sticks" and "dust." The president would have been nearer Bunyan's meaning if he had named the rich sinners of the times who in his effort to keep his political balance he called "malefactors of great wealth"—if he had called them, "muckrakers of great wealth" and applied the word "malefactors" to the noisy and persistent writers who so disturbed him.

I once argued with Mr. Roosevelt that we on *McClure's* were concerned only with facts, not with stirring up revolt. "I don't object to the facts," he cried, "but you and Baker"—Baker at that time was carrying on an able series of articles on the manipulations of the railroads—"but you and Baker are not *practical.*"

I felt at the time Mr. Roosevelt had a good deal of the usual conviction of the powerful man in public life that correction should be left to him, a little resentment that a profession outside his own should be stealing his thunder.

This classification of muckraker, which I did not like, helped fix my resolution to have done for good and all with the subject which had brought it on me. But events were stronger than I. All the radical reforming element, and I numbered many friends among them, were begging me to join their movements. I soon found that most of them wanted attacks. They had little interest in balanced findings. Now I was convinced that in the long run the public they were trying to stir would weary of vituperation, that if you were to secure permanent results the mind must be convinced.

One of the most heated movements at the moment was the effort to persuade the public to refuse all gifts which came from fortunes into the making of which it was known illegal and unfair practices had gone. "Do not touch tainted money," men thundered from pulpit and platform, among them so able a man as Dr. Washington Gladden. The Rockefeller fortune was singled out because about this time Mr. Rockefeller made some unusually large contributions to colleges and churches and general philanthropy. "It is done," cried the critics, "in order to silence criticism." Frequently some one said to me, "You have opened the Rockefeller purse." But I knew, and said in print rather to the disgust of my friends in the movement, that there was an unfairness to Mr. Rockefeller in this outcry. It did not take public criticism to open his purse. From boyhood he had been a steady giver in proportion to his income—10 per cent went to the Lord—and through all the harrowing early years in which he was trying to establish himself as a money-maker he never neglected to give the Lord the established proportion. As his fortune grew his gifts grew larger. He not only gave but saw the money given was wisely spent; and he trained his children, particularly the son who was to administer his estate, to as wise practice in public giving as we have ever had. That is, it did not take a public outcry such as came in the early years of this century against the methods of the Standard Oil Company to force Mr. Rockefeller to share his wealth. He was already sharing it. Indeed, in the fifteen years before 1904 he had given to one or another cause some thirty-five million dollars.

If his gifts were larger at this time than they had ever been before, his money-making was greater. If they were more spectacular than ever before, it may have been because he thought it was time to call the public's attention to what they were getting out of the Standard Oil fortune. At all events it seemed to me only fair that the point should be emphasized that it had not taken a public revolt against his methods to force him to share his profits.

I could not escape the controversies, hard as I tried. Nor could I escape events, events which were forcing me against my will to continue my observations and reports. My book was hardly published before it was apparent that the oil field which it had covered and which for so long had been supposed to be the only American oil field of importance was soon to be surpassed by those in the Southwest. The first state to force recognition of the change on the country at large was Kansas, where suddenly in the spring of 1905 there broke out an agitation as unexpected to most observers as it was interesting to those who knew their oil history. Kansas, we old-timers told ourselves, was duplicating what the Oil Creek had done in 1872. It was putting on a revolt. How had it come about?

For a number of years "wildcatters" with or without money had been prospecting for oil in the state. Only a modest production had rewarded them at first, but in 1904 oil suddenly poured forth in great quantities. On the instant Kansas went oil-mad, practically every farmer in the state dreamed of flowing wells. As soon as it was proved that Kansas was to be a large field the Standard took charge. It leased, drilled, and, most important, it threaded the state with its pipe-line system. No sooner was oil proved to be on a farmer's land than the pipe-line people were there caring for it at market rates. But they began not only to develop and handle scientifically and efficiently, but quite as scientifically and efficiently they began to get rid of all the small fry that in the early days of small wells had been refining and marketing. They would take all the oil that Kansas could produce, they said, but on their own terms: they wanted no interference.

As soon as this became clear to Kansas the state rose in revolt. The Populists, who for six years now must needs grumble in a corner, came out to inveigh with all of their old fervor against the trust. Women's clubs took it up, political parties took it up. A program was developed, the gist of which was that Kansas would take care of its own oil. Bills were introduced into the legislature calculated to control railroad rates, pipe-line rates, competitive marketing. To the joy of the Populists and to the horror of the conservatives a bill for a state refinery was presented by the governor himself. Kansas had a hemp factory in the state penitentiary not doing so badly. Why should not the penitentiary run an oil refinery, too? The legislature agreed to do it.

The excitement grew and so attracted the attention of the country that the office concluded that I must go out and see what I could make of it. I did not much want to go, not only because of my desire to free myself of the subject but because my heart was too heavy with personal loss to feel enthusiasm for any task. In the spring of 1905 my father had died after a long slow illness. To me he had always been everything that is summed up in the word "dear." Modest, humorous, hard-working, friendly, faithful in what he conceived to be the right, he loved his family and friends and church, and asked only to serve them. His business associates held him as a man of honor and a gentleman.

Father's death for a time darkened my world. Later I began to realize that the dearness of him was to remain as a permanent thing in my life. But in 1905 this sense of continued companionship was something which came slowly out of a dark sea of loss. So it was with a heavy heart that I went to see what was happening in Kansas.

First I wanted to see with my own eyes if the fields I had been hearing about were as rich as advertised; so I spent some ten days driving about southeastern Kansas and northeastern Oklahoma, then just coming in with the promise of great wells. It was about as exciting a journey as I ever have made. It was on one of these trips I saw my first dust storm. Driving in a buckboard behind two spirited horses across a practically unbroken prairie, my companion suddenly looked behind him. "Jehoshaphat!" he shouted. "Wrap your head up." I turned to see the sky from horizon to zenith filled with dark rolling clouds. It was not from fire. What was it? "A dust storm," my companion cried.

Quickly and expertly he prepared to take it. He loosened the checkreins of the horses, and the spirited animals evidently knowing what they were in for dropped their heads as low as they could hold them and leaned up against each other. We wrapped ourselves as closely as we could and, like the horses, clung to each other. The storm did not last long, but it was pretty awful while it did. The air was thick, you could not breathe. But it passed, and I was ordered to shake myself out. I found that I was almost engulfed with a fine black dust, that it was packed close to the hubs of the wheels of our buckboard. It was ten days before I got rid of that dust, for it was ten days before I had a real bath. The dust had turned the primitive water supplies into a muddy liquid quite impossible to drink and hopeless for cleansing.

The wonder of it was that the real discomforts counted not at all at the time. I had joined an eager, determined, exultant procession of wildcatters and promoters, of youths looking for their chance or seeking adventure for the first time, tasting it to the full.

Nothing so great as this Kansas and Indian Territory field had ever been known. Every well was to be a gusher, every settlement a city. On every side they were selling town lots and stock in oil companies. One of the most irresponsible stock-selling schemes I have ever known, I happened on in one of these trips. Two anxious-faced boys were going about among experienced oilmen begging them for oil leases, preferably oil leases on which there was a proved well. The lads had come as sightseers and had been caught in the wild excitement of the region. Everybody had a scheme to make himself and his friends rich. Why not they? And largely as a joke they had sent out a flamboyant letter offering stock in a mythical oil field. The letter had gone to scores of innocents in the East, and in answer schoolteachers, clergymen, and women with little or no money had poured in subscriptions.

If there had been few subscriptions they would have been able to return them, but here they were when I saw them with literally a suitcase full of checks and money orders and not a foot of land leased, and in the excitement there was practically no land to be had. They must either get a lease or go to the penitentiary, they concluded. Hence their alarm, their pitiful begging of older men to help them out of the predicament into which their irresponsibility had plunged them.

It was not long before I found I was being taken for something more serious than a mere journalist. Conservative Standard Oil sympathizers regarded me as a spy and not infrequently denounced me as an enemy to society. Independent oilmen and radical editors, who were in the majority, called me a prophet. It brought fantastic situations where I was utterly unfit to play the part. A woman of twenty-five, fresh, full of zest, only interested in what was happening to her, would have reveled in the experience. But here I was—fifty, fagged, wanting to be let alone while I collected trustworthy information for my articles—dragged to the front as an apostle.

The funniest things were the welcomes. The funniest of all was at the then new town of Tulsa, Oklahoma. I had arrived late at night in what seemed to me a no man's land, and after considerable trouble had found a place in a rough little hostelry where I was so suspicious of the look of things that I moved the bureau against the lockless door. I am sure now that I was as safe there as I should have been in my bed at home.

I had registered, of course, and the next morning before I had finished my breakfast I was waited on by the editor of the local newspaper, who took me to his office, a barnlike structure next door, for an interview. Almost immediately a handsome youth in knickerbockers and high laced boots came hurriedly in.

"I think I ought to tell you, Miss Tarbell," he said with a grin, "that you are in for a serenade."

"A serenade," I said, "what do you mean?"

"Well," he said, "the Tulsa boomers have been making a tour of cities to the north. Their special train has just come in; they want something to celebrate, and, learning that you were in town they are sending up the band to welcome you. They want a speech."

I had never made an impromptu speech in my life. I was horrified at the idea. "You must get me out of this," I begged of my gallant but very amused informer.

"No," he said, "there is no way to escape. Here they are."

And there they were—a band of thirty or forty pieces, several of the players stalwart Indians.

I had to face it, and for once in my life I had a happy idea. "Go buy me two boxes of the best cigars that are to be had in town." And I shoved a bill into his hand. "Go quickly."

And then the band began. Not so bad, but so funny. There I was standing on the sidewalk with all the masculine inhabitants of Tulsa—so it seemed to me—packed about, some of them serious and some of them highly delighted at my obvious consternation. I had not guessed wrong about the cigars. They preferred them to a speech, I saw as I passed around the circle distributing them to the players. What was left I gave to the bodyguard which had assembled to back me up. A compliment I have always treasured was given by one of the Indians, as he watched me disposing of my goods: "He all right." Still more flattering it was as I went around in Tulsa that day to meet gentlemen who had fat cigars tied with little red ribbons in their buttonholes, and to have them point gaily to them as I passed.

But the serenade was not the end of the celebration. That afternoon I was taken out in a barouche—the only one in the countryside, I was told—the band behind, and paraded up and down the distracted streets of Tulsa. A day or two later when

I went on my journey, it was with a seatful of candy, magazines, books, flowers, everything that the community afforded for a going-away present. I never had been before nor have been since so much the prima donna.

But all this was preliminary to the real task of finding out what was happening in Kansas, outside of the production of oil. The legislation already passed was intended to make the Standard Oil Company the servant of the state. But I had long ago learned it was one thing to pass laws and another thing to enforce and administer them. How were they getting on?

I went first to see the governor—E. W. Hoch—a humorless and honest man. It was he who had sponsored the state refinery. I found him impressed by what he had done, but a little doubtful about how things were going to come out. He was opening his mail when I went in and he showed me letters nominating him for the Presidency. He had been receiving many of them, he said. It was obvious they came from radical socialists rejoicing over the encouragement that he was giving to the public ownership of industry. He liked the applause but did not like the source. He was no socialist, he protested to me. He was a firm believer in the competitive system. The state refinery was a "measuring stick."

He had wanted to settle definitely just what the profits of the refinery business in Kansas were. Nobody knew except experts, and they wouldn't tell. A first-class oil refinery would settle for all time the cost of refining Kansas oil and force the sale at a reasonable price. He was not trying to drive private industry out of the state. He merely wanted to force private industry to be reasonable—the private industry being of course the Standard Oil Company.

Governor Hoch and the state as a whole were soon feeling the effect of the letdown which always follows an exciting legislative campaign, particularly for the winner. Not since the early nineties had Kansas enjoyed so rousing a time. And now it was over and they had to come down to business. But could they get down to business? Could they administer the new laws? Meetings were being held, half in jubilation over the successful legislation, half in anxiety about the next step. I was asked to come and speak at one of them.

I was no speaker, but I could not let them down. Moreover, because of my familiarity with past exciting experiments on the part of indignant oil independents I realized better than they did, so I thought, the hard pull they had before them.

"Your problem now," I told them, "is to do business. As far as laws can insure it you have free opportunity; but good laws and free opportunity alone do not build up a business. Unless you can be as efficient and as patient, as farseeing as your great competitor—laws or no laws, you will not succeed. You must make yourselves as good refiners, as good transporters, as good marketers, as ingenious, as informed, as imaginative in your legitimate undertakings as they are in both their legitimate and illegitimate."

My speech was not popular. What they wanted from me was a rousing attack on the Standard Oil Company. They wanted a Mary Lease to tell them to go on raising hell, and here I was telling them they had got all they could by raising hell and now they must settle down to doing business.

"You have gone over to the Standard Oil Company?" said one disgusted Populist.

I saw I had ruined my reputation as the Joan of Arc of the oil industry, as some one had named me. But there were hard-headed independent legislators and business men in the state who consoled me, "You are right, we must learn to do business as well as they do."

One immediate national effect of the Kansas disturbance was to arouse the legislatures of other oil-producing states in the Southwest to enact laws not unlike those of Kansas, though I do not remember that a state refinery was sponsored anywhere else.

There was a wide demand that Congress place the pipe-line system under the Interstate Commerce Commission, subject it to the same restrictions as interstate rails, but most important was the fine popular backing the row gave the trust-busting campaign of Theodore Roosevelt, now President of the United States. He had begun his attack on big business by putting an end to the first great holding company the country had seen—the Northern Securities Company. He had followed this by a bill establishing a department for which people had been asking for a decade or more, that of Commerce and Labor, including a Bureau of Corporations with power to examine books and question personnel. Congress at first shied at the measure, but Mr. Roosevelt thundered, "If you do not pass it this session I will call an extra session." And they knew he would.

Ironically enough it was the Standard itself that broke the reluctance of Congress. The proposal had shocked it out of its usual discretion. There never was an organization in the country which held secrecy more essential to doing business. Breaking down the walls behind which it operated was not to be tolerated. It seems to have been the peppery John Archbold who took charge of the fight against the bill, using all the political influence of the company, which was considerable at that moment.

Roosevelt soon learned something of what was going on—it is not certain how much; and when he saw his measure in danger he gave out the statement that John D. Rockefeller had wired his friends in the Senate, "We are opposed to any antitrust legislation—it must be stopped."

The last thing in the world that John D. Rockefeller would have done was to send such a telegram to anybody. Probably Mr. Roosevelt knew that; but somebody in the Standard was passing on such a word, and Mr. Rockefeller was the responsible head of the organization. His name did the work. Congress passed the bill in a hurry. The Bureau of Corporations was speedily set up, an excellent man at its head—James Garfield.

The first task assigned it by the President was an investigation of the petroleum industry.

This investigation reported in 1906 that the Standard Oil Company was receiving preferential rates from various railroads and had been for some time. One of the most spectacular business suits the country had seen up to that time followed. The Standard was found guilty by Judge Kenesaw Landis, the present arbitrator of the manners and morals of national baseball, and a punishment long known as the "Big Fine"—twenty-nine million dollars—inflicted. The country gasped at the size of the fine, but not so the Bureau of Corporations. My correspondent there contended that over eight thousand true indictments had been found, and that the maximum penalty would have amounted to over a hundred and sixty million dollars!

But even the twenty-nine million dollars, so modest in the view of the Bureau of Corporations, was not allowed to stand, for in 1908 Judge Peter Grosscup of the Circuit Court of Appeals in Illinois upset it. Roosevelt was angry. "There is too much power in the bench," he told his friends.

But by this time the Government had under way another and a much more serious line of attack, from which Roosevelt was hoping substantial results. Back in 1890 the Congress had enacted what was known as the Sherman Antitrust Law, a law making illegal every contract and combination restraining trade and fostering monopoly. The Government was now seeking to apply this law to the Standard Oil Company. Was it not the first industry to attempt monopoly? Had it not been the model for all the brood?

Such a suit was no new idea. Independent oilmen had long talked of it, and in 1897 they had been ready to go ahead when at the last moment the lawyer to whom they had entrusted their case was taken suddenly ill and died. It must have seemed to the energetic Lewis Emery, Jr., who had been engineering the attack that the Lord himself had "gone over to the Standard."

Ten years went by, and then in September, 1907, the United States of America began suit against the Standard Oil Company of New York *et al.* There were months and months of hearings. If I had been a modern newspaper woman I could have made a good killing out of that long investigation, for more than one editor asked me to analyze the testimony as it came along or give my impressions of the gentlemen who appeared on the witness stand. But I had no stomach for it; I never attended a public examination though I of course read the published testimony with care.

I knew well enough that the time would come when, if I did my duty as a historian, I must analyze the suit; but that must be after it was ended and a sufficiently practical test had been made of the decision. It would be a long time, I told myself, before I should be obliged to take up the story where I had left it.

13

OFF WITH THE OLD
—ON WITH THE NEW

TWELVE years had gone by since I tied myself, temporarily as I thought, to the McClure venture. To my surprise, the longer I was with the enterprise the more strongly I felt it was giving me the freedom I wanted, as well as a degree of that security which makes freedom so much easier a load to carry. Here was a group of people I could work with, without sacrifice or irritation. Here was a healthy growing undertaking which excited me, while it seemed to offer endless opportunity to contribute to the better thinking of the country. The future looked fair and permanent.

And then without warning the apparently solid creation was shattered and I found myself sitting on its ruins.

Looking back now, I know that the split in the McClure staff in 1906 was inevitable. Neither Mr. McClure nor Mr. Phillips, the two essential factors in the creation, could have done other than he did. The points at issue were fundamental. Each man acted according to an inner something which made him what he was, something he could not violate.

Back of the difficulty lay the fact that at this time Mr. Mc-Clure was a sick man. The hardships of his youth and early manhood, the intense pressure he had put on himself in founding his enterprises had exhausted him. For several years he had been obliged to take long vacations, usually in Europe with his family, his staff carrying on his work in his absence. The enterprises were bringing him larger and larger returns and more and more honor; but that was not what he most wanted. He wanted to be in the thick of things, feel himself an active factor in what was

254

doing. Above all he wanted to add to what he had already achieved, to build a bigger, a more imposing House of McClure.

"What he wanted was more money," I have heard men comment.

They were wrong. I have never known a man freer from the itch for money as an end than S. S. McClure. Money for him meant power to do things, to build, to help others. On his way up he had gathered about him a horde of dependents with whom he was always ready to share his last dollar. He was reckless with money as with ideas.

In these years when he was practically living in Europe, though returning regularly to the United States, his chief interest was not in what his enterprises were accomplishing, but in adding something bigger than they were or could be. Only by doing this could he prove to himself and to his colleagues that he was a stronger and more productive man than ever. Nothing else would satisfy him.

His passion to build, to realize his ambitions, made him careless about laying foundations. What he did usually had the character of improvisation, frequently on a grand scale, sometimes merely gay spurts of fancy. I was myself caught in one of the latter when Mr. McClure in London suddenly ordered me in Paris to drop whatever I was doing and to hurry into Germany to collect material for an animal magazine.

Animals were an abiding interest with *McClure's*. Rudyard Kipling laid the foundation in the Jungle tales. After that great series few were the numbers that did not have an animal in text and picture. It was as much a passion as baseball was to become in the latter days with *The American Magazine*.

I spent a lively month visiting zoos, interviewing animal trainers and hunters and keepers, buying books and photographs, turning in what I considered a pretty good grist of materials and suggestions. What became of it, I never knew, for I never heard

a word of it after I came back to America. The only remnant I
have now of that month is a powder box of Dresden china bought
at the showrooms of the factory of the crossed swords, it being
my practice when on professional trips to use my leisure seeing
the town, guidebook in hand, and buying all the souvenirs my
purse permitted.

It was in 1906 that Mr. McClure brought home from one of
his foraging expeditions the plan which was eventually to wreck
his enterprises. He had it cut and dried ready to put into action.
Without consultation with his partners he had organized a new
company, the charter of which provided not only for a *McClure's
Universal Journal,* but a McClure's Bank, a McClure's Life Insurance Company, a McClure's School Book Publishing Company, and later a McClure's Ideal Settlement in which people
could have cheap homes on their own terms. It undertook to combine with a cheap magazine—which it goes without saying was
to have an enormous circulation with the enormous advertising
which circulation brings—an attempt to solve some of the great
abuses of the day, abuses at which we had been hammering in
McClure's Magazine. He proposed to do this by giving them a
competition which would draw their teeth.

By the time Mr. McClure got around to explaining his plan
to me and asking my cooperation he had worked himself up to
regarding it as an inspiration which must not be questioned.
It seemed to me to possess him like a religious vision which it
was blasphemy to question. Obsessed as he was, he was blind and
deaf to the obstacles in the way. I am sure I hurt Mr. McClure
by telling him bluntly and at once that I would never have anything to do with such a scheme.

In a recently published letter Lincoln Steffens tells how he
saw Mr. McClure's plan. To him it was not only "fool" but "not
quite right." Certainly it was not right. As organized, it was a
speculative scheme as alike as two peas to certain organizations
the magazine had been battering.

The tragedy of the situation was that Mr. McClure did not see and could not understand the arguments of his associates that his plan was not only impossible but wrong. This failure of judgment was, I am convinced, due to his long illness. The mental and physical exhaustion from which he was suffering, and which he could not bring himself to understand or accept, explains the unwisdom of this undertaking, his contention that it was an inspiration, his stubbornness in insisting that it be accepted and set to work. Human reason has little influence on one who believes he is inspired.

The members of the staff were little more than outsiders when it came to the final decision. It was up to John Phillips to accept and do his utmost to aid in the grandiose adventure or patiently to wait while persuading the General that it was not the mission of the McClure crowd to reconstruct the economic life of the country, that we were journalists, not financial reformers. I think no man ever tried harder to keep another from a suicidal undertaking; and certainly no man could have been firmer from the start in his refusal to go along.

The struggle went on for six months, and no two men ever tried more honestly to adjust their differences; but they were irreconcilable. It came to a point where one or the other must sell his interest in the magazine. It was Mr. McClure who bought out his partner.

Although *McClure's Magazine* is no longer on the newsstands, it does occupy a permanent place in the history of the period that it served, because it worked itself into the literary and economic life of the country.

It was a magazine which from the first put quality above everything else and was willing to chase checks around town in order to pay for it. For those who collect Kipling there are the first publications of many of his rarest poems, short stories, and such distinguished serials as "Captains Courageous" and "Kim." Here first appeared Willa Cather and O. Henry.

It was a magazine which backed regardless of expense, one might say, the investigations and reports of men like Ray Stannard Baker and Lincoln Steffens. For twelve years it encouraged with liberality and patience the work of which I have been talking in this narrative.

Mr. McClure had two editorial policies when it came to getting the thing he felt was important for the Magazine. First, the writer must be well paid and the expense money be generous. Second, and most important of all, he must be given time. He did not ask that you produce a great serial in six months. He gave you years if it was necessary. I spent the greater part of five years on "The History of the Standard Oil Company." I was what was called a contributing editor; that is, I turned in suggestions as they came to me in my work around the country. I did occasional extra articles that seemed to be in my line. I read and took part in editorial counsels, but it was recognized that all the time I demanded should be given to the serial. I know of no other editor and no other publisher who has so fully recognized the necessity of generous pay and ample time, if he were to get from a staff work done according to the best editorial standard, and worthy of the magazine and the writer.

When it was finally decided that Mr. Phillips was to sever his long relation to *McClure's* several members of the editorial staff resigned, including Ray Stannard Baker, Lincoln Steffens, John Siddall, the efficient young managing editor Albert Boyden, and myself. We could not see the magazine without Mr. Phillips.

The last day we left the office, then on Twenty-third Street near Fourth Avenue, some of us went together to Madison Square and sat on a bench talking over our future. We were derelicts without a job.

But not for long.

There was then in New York, though it was not generally known, a magazine group which wanted a change. The magazine was very old—long known as *Frank Leslie's Illustrated*

Monthly, recently changed to *The American Magazine.* Its owner was Frederick L. Colver; its editor, Ellery Sedgwick (afterward editor of the *Atlantic*); its publisher, William Morrow (afterward the founder of William Morrow & Company, the book publishing house). Mr. Colver approached Mr. Phillips: "Why don't *you* take it over?"

Finally in council assembled, our editorial group together with David A. McKinlay and John Trainor of the McClure business department, decided to incorporate the Phillips Publishing Company and buy *The American Magazine.* With what we could put in ourselves and money from the sale of stock to interested friends, we secured funds for the purchase and sufficient working capital.

We left *McClure's* in March: six months later, October, 1906, appeared our first issue. The announcement shows how seriously we took ourselves, as befitted people who had seen something in which they deeply believed go to pieces. We had been too cruelly bruised to take anything lightly, but luckily we were able to make two additions to our staff, each man with a vein of humor not to be dried up or muddled by any cataclysms—William Allen White and Finley Peter Dunne (Mr. Dooley).

We had known Mr. White in the *McClure's* office since the day of his famous editorial, "What's the Matter with Kansas?" After that came his Boyville stories, two or three of which *McClure's* published, and then at intervals studies of political situations and political figures. It was not long before he began to come to New York. He was a little city-shy then, or wanted us to think so. As I was one of the official entertainers of the group, it occasionally fell to me to "take him by the hand," as he put it, and show him the town. I could have hardly had a more delightful experience. He judged New York by Kansas standards, and New York usually suffered. His affection and loyalty for his state, his appreciation and understanding of everything that she does—wise and foolish—the incomparable journalistic style in

which he presents her are what has made him so valuable a national citizen. His crowning achievement among the many to be
credited to him has been remaining first, last, and always the editor of the Emporia *Gazette*. A staunch friendship had sprung
up between Mr. White and Mr. Phillips, and it was natural
enough that he interested himself in the new venture.

As for Peter Dunne, we went after him and rather to my surprise he came along, taking a desk in our cramped offices and
appearing with amazing regularity. At this time he was some
forty years old—the greatest satirist in my judgment the country has yet produced. He had a wide knowledge of men and their
ways. There was no malice in his judgments, but a great contempt for humbuggery as well as for all forms of self-deception
devoted to uplifting the world. However, he felt kindly towards
our ardent desire to improve things by demonstrating their unsoundness and approved our unwillingness to use any other tools
than those which belonged legitimately to our profession. He
came out strongest in his contributions to the department of editorial comment, which Mr. Phillips had introduced under the
head of "The Interpreter's House." We were all supposed to
contribute whatever was on our minds to this department. Mr.
Phillips and Mr. Dunne did the censoring and dovetailing. I did
not often make "The Interpreter's House," much to my chagrin.
Dunne said, "You sputter like a woman," which I fear was true.
If it had not been for him the first Christmas issue of "The Interpreter's House" would have been bleak reading. We had each
of us broken forth in lament for the particular evil of the world
which was disturbing us, offering our remedies.

It seems to me [wrote Dunne, editing our contributions] that
we are serving up a savory Christmas number . . . a nice present
to be found in the bottom of a stocking . . .
You cannot go to the Patent Office in Washington and take
out a patent that will transform men into angels. The way upward, long and tedious as it is, lies through the hearts of men.

It has been so since the founding of the Feast. Nothing has been proved more clearly in the political history of the race than this, that good will to men has done more to improve government than laws and wars.

. . . Let us close down our desks for the year. If you want to find me for another week I will be found in the wonderful little toy shop around the corner.

That editorial broke the tension which had made me think this was no time to go home for Christmas. I went.

Peter Dunne hated the pains of writing. His labor affected the whole office—sympathy with what he was going through, fear that his copy would not be in on time, eagerness to see it when it came, to know if it was "one of his best." But Peter's work was never what he thought it ought to be, and he sought forgetfulness.

Indispensable on the new editorial staff, seeing Peter through his birth pains, keeping the rest of us at our tasks, nursing new writers, making up the magazine, was Albert Boyden. He had come fresh from Harvard to *McClure's* and had at once made himself a place by his genius for keeping things going and his gift for sympathetic friendliness. It was a combination which became more valuable and irresistible as time went on. Bert was everybody's friend, whether editor, artist, or writer. "One can have friends, one can have editors," Ray Stannard Baker was to write later, "but Bert was both."

He was of the greatest value to the *American* in bringing together writers and artists who were attaching themselves to the new magazine. Bert was so fond of us all that he could not endure the idea that we did not all know one another, and he made it his business to see that we had at least the opportunity. He lived on the south of Stuyvesant Square, four flights up. There was no one in all that circle of distinguished contributors who did not welcome the chance to climb those stairs to Bert's dinners and teas. And what a group of people came! They are recorded in his guest book: Booth Tarkington, Edna Ferber, Stewart Edward White, his wife and his brother Gilbert, Julian and Ada Street, the Norrises, the Rices and Martins of Louisville, Joe Chase, Will Irwin, and a dozen more, along with visiting celebrities, politicians, scientists, adventurers. What talk went on in that high-up living room! What wonderful tales we heard!

Bert was so much younger than the rest of us, so full of enthusiasm and hope, so much more vital and all-shedding, that it is still to me incredible that he should have left this world so much earlier than I. He died in 1925, but he lives in a little book which J. S. P. edited in his memory. How proud Bert would have been of that! "There is nobody like J. S. P.," he used to say. Many of his big circle of friends contributed their recollections of him. I have never known another person in my life for whom quite such a book could have been written.

In spite of the gay unity of our group, the vigor and steadiness with which it began and continued its operation, I had suffered a heavy shock. I know now I should not have taken it as well as I did (and inwardly that was nothing to boast of) if it had not been cushioned by an engrossing personal interest. I had started out to make a home for myself.

I had already made three major attempts to establish myself —first in Meadville, then in Paris, then in Washington—and all had failed. When in 1898 it became evident that if I were to remain on the *McClure's* staff I must come to New York, I was in no mood to adopt a new home town. New York might be my writing headquarters, but Titusville should be home. Finally I would return there, I told myself. But Titusville was five hundred miles away. There were no airplanes in those days. The railroad journey was tedious and expensive, week-ending was impossible. I soon grew weary of the week-end makeshifts of a homeless person in a city. I wanted something of my own. And at last by a series of circumstances, purely fortuitous, I acquired forty acres and a little old house in Connecticut.

I had meant to let the land and the house run to seed if they wanted to. I had no stomach, or money, for a "place." I wanted something of my very own with no cares. Idle dream in a world busy in adding artificial cares to the load Nature lays on our shoulders.

Things happened: the roof leaked; the grass must be cut if I was to have a comfortable sward to sit on; water in the house was imperative. And what I had not reckoned with came from all the corners of my land: incessant calls—fields calling to be rid of underbrush and weeds and turned to their proper work; a garden spot calling for a chance to show what it could do; apple trees begging to be trimmed and sprayed. I had bought an abandoned farm, and it cried loud to go about its business.

Why should I not answer the cry? Why should I not be a farmer? Before I knew it I was at least going through the motions, having fields plowed, putting in crops, planting an orchard, supporting horses, a cow, a pig, a poultry yard—giving up a new evening gown to buy fertilizer!

Seeing what I was in for and fearing lest I should do as so many of my friends had done—go in deeper than my income justified, find myself borrowing and mortgaging in order to carry out the fascinating things I saw to do—I laid down a strict rule which I have followed ever since, and which I recommend to people of limited incomes who acquire a spot in the country, and want it to be a continuous pleasure instead of a continuous anxiety. I resolved that I would spend only what I could lay aside from income, that I would divide this appropriation into three parts—one for the land, one for the house, one for furnishing. As the budget was very small it meant that a thousand things that I wanted to do went undone, and still are undone. But it meant also that I had little or no financial anxiety.

If the call of the land had been unexpected and not to be denied, even more unexpected and still less to be denied was the call of the neighborhood. I was not long in learning that in the houses I could see in valley and on hillside centered the most genuine of human dramas, tragic and comic.

After the land and its background, the greatest gift of God to us ("us" including my niece Esther) was our nearest neighbors Mr. and Mrs. G. Burr Tucker, at the side of whose house swung a sign, "Antiques for Sale."

But it was as neighbors, not as customers Mr. and Mrs. Tucker regarded us from the start. When Burr was not over helping us settle he was watching what was going on from his front porch. I have never had more pungent, salty, faithful friends. They had spent most of their lives on the corner, not always selling antiques. Mrs. Tucker had taught in the schoolhouse at the top of the hill for twenty-nine years, and Burr had had a varied and picturesque career as a salesman of pumps, fruit trees, any gadget that seemed to be useful to his country neighbors.

Not long before we moved in he had discovered by accident that there were people in the outside world who bought old spinning wheels, ancient chairs, ancient pottery. Burr knew the contents of every garret and woodshed for twenty miles around, and when he made his discovery he began systematically to buy them out. By the time I arrived on the scene he had an established business.

Not knowing whether we were going to like our new acquisition well enough to make it permanent, Esther and I had decided to furnish out of a department store basement. But in looking over Burr's miscellaneous assortment my eye fell on an old-fashioned melodeon, charming in line, its bellows broken but easy to repair—$10. I couldn't resist it, and so I became almost from the first day a customer of my nearest neighbor. It was a great day when Burr went "teeking," as they called the hunt for treasures. We would watch for his return, and when his white horse and wagon loaded high with loot appeared down the road we were on the ground as soon as he was.

Not only did the immediate vicinity yield rich and exciting

material, but a little distance away there were people from the world we knew. There were the friends who had first shown me the country—Noble and Ella Hoggson, up the Valley, the center of a jolly and interesting group known as the "Valley Crowd." A mile or so away was one of the most interesting women in the literary world of that day—Jeannette Gilder, sister of Richard Watson Gilder, a lively writer and editor.

Perhaps no woman in her time carried to more perfection the then feminine vogue for severe masculine dress: stout shoes, short skirt, mannish jacket, shirt, tie, hat, stick. They were the last word in style. They suited her as they did few, for she was large of frame, with strong, bold features and a fine swinging gait; but the masculinity was all on the surface. Esther came home one day shouting with laughter: "Miss Gilder is a fake. She wears silk petticoats and is afraid of mice."

Soon after I acquired my farm the countryside was stirred by the news that Mark Twain was building only eight or nine miles away from us. Everybody seemed to know what was happening with the building, the settling, the life going on. That was partly because of our omnivorous curiosity and partly because Mark Twain was a friendly neighbor. He every now and then gave a great party, sending the invitations around by our peripatetic butcher, a member of one of our first families, a gentleman as well as a good tradesman.

I have a few treasured recollections of days when Jeannette Gilder and I drove over to tea or lunch with Mark Twain, heard great stories of the doings in his new home. It was from him that I heard the story of the famous burglary; it was from him I heard the story of one of the best practical jokes ever played— when Peter Dunne and Robert Collier sent him an elephant.

Not only was all this fun and excitement and novelty shared by my niece and those of my family who came to see what we were so excited about, but every member of the *American* staff sooner or later appeared at the farm to look us over. From the start our chief counselor had been Bert Boyden, who six months after I had taken the first option on the place had insisted on accompanying me to see whether I had better take it up.

Bert looked at the oaks, he looked at the gay little stream that ran across the land, and without hesitation said, "Buy it." And buy it, I did. Having had a part in the purchase, Bert superintended henceforth all changes. He approved my plan of budgeting. He helped me select the wallpapers which were hung; he was interested in the larder for the winter.

In the summer when his family was at a distance J. S. P. came often to discuss the perplexities of the magazine and rest himself from the commotion of the office. The Norrises came, and Kathleen named my pig. Who but Kathleen would have called him "Juicy"? He looked it, fat as butter. The Siddalls came often, for in the summer we kept their famous cat, "Sammy Siddall." The Rices, the Martins, the Bakers—all came to look on that rough land and shell of a house and wonder, I suspect, how I could be happy with anything so simple, be satisfied with no more pretentious plans than I had.

Among those who came in those early days was one who has left a crimson streak across the history of his time—Jack Reed. Jack, just out of Harvard, was giving half-time to the *American,* half-time to writing. We would invite him for the week end but he was never at the station when we drove over to find him. Likely he had missed his train, taken a freight—that was more fun. And late in the evening he would come walking over the hilltop demanding food and a bed, and we would sit long hearing the adventures of his day.

It was on one of these trips that Jack found near by a natural amphitheater. Before he had left he had planned to buy the place and worked out in detail a Greek theater. He started towards New York on foot, expecting to raise the money from friends en route. "I was all ready to put up money," one of them told me not many years ago.

But when Jack was back at his desk in New York he forgot the theater—I never heard of it afterwards. That was the delightful creature Jack Reed was, up to the time that he discovered what is called life. He took it hard. Now his bones lie under a tomb in Moscow, one of the martyrs to Lenin's great vision of the communal life.

All this was good for me, cushioned the shock I had suffered, convinced me that at least I had gotten my hands on something permanent, a fundamental factor in my future security—a home —a home capable of feeding me if the worst came to the worst. But while it was good for me it was not so good for my work on the magazine.

I had believed I could work better in the quiet of the country, but I was discovering that the country was more exciting than the town and the office as I knew it. Its attractions were proving too much for the difficult task which had been assigned me in the planning for the first year of the *American*. The task was nothing less than to write a history of the making of our tariff schedules from the Civil War on. It had been a natural enough selection for me after the experience with the history of the Standard Oil Company for the tariff was quite as much a matter of popular concern at the moment as the trust had been in 1900. There was a growing demand for revision. How could we get into the fight? A subject must be found for me. How about the tariff? Was a historical treatment possible? I thought so; at least I so despised the prohibitive tariff that I was willing to try if the magazine was willing to back me.

I suppose most of us have had at various periods of our life homemade remedies for the economic ills we see about us. When I was a girl in high school I looked on an eight-hour day of productive labor for everybody as the way out. I was much less worried by the hardships the long day brought working people than the mental and moral deterioration I imagined suffered by people who did not work. Idleness, not labor, was the scourge of the world. For me the eight-hour day was a save-the-idle day!

Before I left *The Chautauquan* I had concluded that there was a trilogy of wrongs—all curable—responsible for our repeated depressions and our poorly distributed wealth: discrimination in transportation; tariffs save for revenue only; private ownership of natural resources. I was still of that opinion when, largely by accident, I had my chance to strike at number one in my trilogy. Could I by the method I had followed in that case, and the only one I knew how to use, present a plausible argument against Number Two?

What had particularly aroused me was the way tariff schedules were made, the strength of what we now call pressure groups —the powerful lobbies in wool and cotton and iron and sugar which for twenty-five years I had watched mowing Congress down like a high wind. There was no concealment of the pressure. The lobbyists went at it hammer and tongs and battered down opposition with threats, bribes, and unparalleled arrogance. By these tactics they had overcome Mr. Cleveland's famous tariff message of 1886, had passed the outrageous McKinley bill of 1890, had ruined the Wilson bill of 1893, had defeated the promise of McKinley and Dingley and Aldrich to lower duties in 1896, and had substituted the highest and most distorted schedules the country had yet seen. But it looked in 1906 as if the Day of Judgment was near, and I asked nothing better than to be on the jury.

I went into it blindly—on faith, certainly not on knowledge— and I had a handicap that I was far from realizing at the time: that was that, while in the case of the Standard Oil I had spent my life close to the events, the tariff and its makers had never touched my life. This was something that I had read in a book.

Another handicap was that my indignation was directed towards legal acts. Congress had adopted these schedules, under coercion if you please, but still it had adopted them. The beneficiaries had the sanction of law. It was a different case from challenging railroad discriminations, which were forbidden by law.

As I worked on the *Congressional Record* and related documents I looked up men still living who had had a part in the struggle on one side or the other. There were many of them scattered around the country, now out of Congress for the most part, but not averse to talking. As a rule I got little from them. The fight which seemed to me so important was a dead issue to them. They had lost or won. It was all part of a game. Fresh from reading the daily discussions in the *Record*, curious about this or that man or argument, I found them hazy, often not particularly interested. There was little of the righteous indignation which I thought I found in their recorded speeches. Had that been political, instead of righteous, indignation? I began to think so.

It was Grover Cleveland who put heart in me. He had lost none of his righteous indignation over the aid prohibitive tariffs were giving certain trusts, none of his alarm over the growing disparity between industry and agriculture they were fostering. He felt deeply the wrong of the prices they were inflicting on the farmer, the professional class, the poor. I got nothing but encouragement from him for the review I had planned.

Luckily I already had a pleasant working relation with Mr. Cleveland. It had come about in my last two years on *McClure's*, when my chief editorial task had been trying to persuade him that it was his duty to write his reminiscences for us, incidentally offering myself as a ghost if he felt that he needed one.

As his letters to me at this time show he was not entirely unfriendly to the project:

I want to do the thing; and yet I am afraid the difficulties in the way of doing it are fundamental and inexorable. You see the project requires me to exploit myself and my doings before the public. I do not see how I can do this, though I am terribly vain and often bore my friends privately by tiresome reminiscence. And yet I cannot but think that there are incidents and results in my career, which by their narration might be of service in stimulating those who aspire to good citizenship—"and there we are." This latter consideration hints of duty; but then comes the fear that what seems to me duty is a mere fantastic notion, and thereupon the old disinclination resumes its sway.

. . . .

I have frequently thought no one could help me so much as you; and it has seemed to me more than once that you and I might possibly "cook up something" in a summer vacation's freedom from distractions.

Nothing came at this time, 1904, of the "Tarbell-Cleveland fantasy," as Mr. Cleveland gaily dubbed it, and two years later the project was dismissed, but in a letter so friendly that I cannot resist quoting from it:

I do not believe a man who has turned the corner of sixty-nine years, is any less vain and self-satisfied than when he was a youth. At any rate here I am, in this sixty-nine predicament, delighted with the generous things you say of me in the goodness of your heart, and more than halfway deluding myself into the notion that I deserve them. I want to be very sensible and hard-headed in this affair; but in any event I am entitled to rejoice in your good opinion of me, and your hearty wishes for my welfare and happiness.

I thank you from the bottom of my heart for them; and I shall gratefully remember them as long as I live. Somehow I have an idea that you know me well—and surely I need not afflict myself with the fear of vanity if I have found a friend in you.

With those letters in my files I felt free, when I undertook the tariff work for the *American*, to ask Mr. Cleveland to talk to me about the making of his tariff message in 1886, and the failure of the Wilson bill in 1893. He was most generous, and when I had completed my story of the two episodes I asked him to read the manuscript and give me a candid judgment and of course his corrections and his suggestions. The chief suggestion that he made showed a sensitiveness to his literary style in public documents which I had not suspected. Charming letter writer as Mr. Cleveland was, in his public documents he was ponderous. I must have enlarged a little on this, for I find this paragraph in his letter with which he sent back the proofs:

I have ventured to suggest a little toning down of your characterization of my style—thinking perhaps you would be willing to make an alteration to please me if for no other reason. You know we are all a little sensitive on such a point.

There was another paragraph in that letter which touched me deeply:

Your article has caused me to feel again the greatest sorrow and disappointment I have ever suffered in my public career—the failure of my party to discharge its most important duty and its fatuous departure from its appointed mission.

But lean as heavily as I dared on Mr. Cleveland, work as I would and did on the tariff debates of Congress (I can wish my worst enemy no greater punishment than reading them in full), I could not put vitality into my narrative. It was of the *Congressional Record*—it was secondhand.

It was the making of the Payne-Aldrich bill in 1909 that finally gave a certain life to my narrative. Here was something belonging to the present, not something of the past. By all the signs Theodore Roosevelt should have been the St. George to lead in the revision the public was calling so loudly for, particularly after the panic of 1907. Few of his party leaders paid attention.

"Are not all our fellows happy?" Speaker Joseph Cannon asked as the demand for revision became louder.

Roosevelt himself heard it, but frankly said to his intimates that he did not know anything about the tariff. He did not and he would not take the time to learn. He hammered at the effects of privilege, pursued "malefactors of great wealth," but was not willing to do the hard studying of the causes which produced the malefactors.

Mr. Taft, who followed Roosevelt, had no choice. The platform on which he was elected called "unequivocally" for tariff reform, and as soon as he was inaugurated he called a special session to do the work. My chagrin was great when I realized at once that all the ancient technique I had been trying to discredit was repeating itself. It is, I told myself, the same old circus, the same old gilded chariots, the same old clowns. So far as arguments were concerned they might have been taken from the hearings of '83, of '88, of '93, of '96. Figures were changed, and nobody could deny that these figures of growth were impressive; but they came from interested men.

"They are incapable of judging," Mr. Carnegie told the committee. "No judge should be permitted to sit in a cause in which he is interested; you make the greatest mistake in your life if you attach importance to an interested witness."

The process which "Sunset" Cox back in the seventies characterized as "reciprocal rapine"—buying votes for the schedule their constituents wanted by voting for schedules they could not justify—was in full swing.

Never was the tariff as the "cause of prosperity" worked harder. It was the answer of the prohibitive protectionist to the charge that the tariff was a tax. In all the early years they had called it so—a tax to produce revenue, encourage new industries, protect higher wages, a better standard of living. But Mr. Cleveland had called it boldly "a vicious, inequitable, illogical tax," and illustrated his adjectives tellingly. The effect of his attack was so disastrous that the supporters of prohibitive duties went into a huddle to find a new name. "The cause of prosperity" was the euphemism they produced.

A repeater that had figured in every tariff bill was the answer of the priests of the dogma to the argument that the poor should

be considered. According to the pictures they drew there were
no poor in the United States. This refusal to recognize poverty
was no more discouraging in the making of the bill of 1909 than
the indifference to the effect high tariffs were having on the cost
of the necessities of life. In this they ran true to historical prece-
dent. From the time the business man took charge in the late
seventies any attempt to call the attention at hearings to what
a duty would do to the price of a necessity of life was ignored
or jeered.

Justice Brandeis, then plain lawyer Brandeis, was before a
committee considering the Dingley bill.

"And for whom do you appear?" he was asked.

"For the consumer," he answered.

The committee, chairman and all, laughed aloud, but they
were good enough to say, "Oh, let him run down."

This old indifference to the effect of higher prices on the living
of the poor stirred me to the only article in my series which
seemed to "take hold." I called it, "Where Every Penny Counts."

The worth-while thing, from my point of view, was that it
reached women. "I never knew what the tariff meant before,"
Jane Addams wrote me.

Here was something which touched those in whom she was
interested—wage earners. She knew from actual contact what
the increase of a cent in the price of a quart of milk, a spool of
thread, a pound of meat, meant to working girls with their six
or eight dollars a week. She knew that every penny added to
the cost of their food, clothes, or coal gave less warmth, less covering. It was not difficult to show that what they were trying to
do in Washington in the making of the Payne-Aldrich bill was
just that—a tariff that would add to the cost of things that must
be had if people were to live at all.

To my deep satisfaction this effort to make the new tariff bill
in the good old way was promptly met by a rousing challenge
from a group of progressive Republican Senators, men who had

been largely responsible for forcing the promise to reform into the party platform. When they discovered that there would be no reform if the lobbyists and their friends in Congress could prevent it, they crystallized into one of the most vigorous and intelligent fighting bands that had been seen for many years in Congress. Insurgents, they were called.

The leader in the revolt, interested in railroad reform rather than the tariff, was La Follette of Wisconsin. Others were Beveridge of Indiana, Cummins and Dolliver of Iowa, Borah of Idaho, and Bristow of Kansas. They were already familiar figures at the *American* along with certain members of the House, particularly the salty and peppery William Kent of California —Phillips, Baker and Steffens being in frequent communication with them.

The most brilliant and witty, as well as the most thoroughly informed of the tariff insurgents was the amiable Senator Dolliver from Iowa—twenty years in Congress—always regular—always stoutly supporting the tariff bills turned out by the committee.

"What ails you now?" I asked him.

"Well," he said, "I had been going on for twenty years taking practically without question what they handed me; but these alliances between the party and industrial interests have at last set me thinking. I began to understand something of the injustice that was being done to the consumer. And then we promised to reform the tariff."

When the insurgents divided up the schedules for study, Schedule K—wool—the most difficult and the most important politically, fell to Senator Dolliver. He found he had been voting for years for duties which, when he sat down to read the schedule, he could not understand. He discovered they were a mixture of tricks, evasions, and discriminations—intended to be so, he believed. He determined to master them.

And master them he did by months of the severest night work. He pored over statistics and technical treatises. He visited mills and importing houses and retail shops. He sought the aid of experts, and in the end he knew his subject so well that he went onto the floor of the Senate without a manuscript and literally played with Schedule K, and incidentally also with Senator Aldrich, who was said to fly to the cloak room whenever Senator Dolliver rose to speak. When he had finished his clean, competent dissection, Schedule K lay before the Senate a law without principles or morals; and yet, just as it was, the Senate of the United States passed it, and the President of the United States signed it, and it went on the statute books.

Why? Neither Mr. Taft nor Mr. Aldrich defended the wool schedule which made the bill odious. They both were frank in explaining that it was politically necessary, not at all a question of the fairness of the schedule, but a question of what powerful interests demanded. The wool interests could defeat the bill if they did not get what they wanted.

My conviction about the inequity of Schedule K was so strong that when the *Outlook* published a long defense of it, plainly an advertisement but not so marked, I protested in a personal letter to its vociferous contributing editor, Theodore Roosevelt, with whom by this time I was on fairly friendly terms. Just what I said in my letter about the *Herald* which so stirred his wrath I do not remember, but his answer to my comment is so typically Rooseveltian in temper and reasoning that I think it should be preserved:

May 6, 1911

Oh! Miss Tarbell, Miss Tarbell!

How can you take the view you do of the Herald! You compare it with the Tribune. It is perfectly legitimate to compare the Tribune with Mr. Watterson's paper, the Courier-Journal. Honest people could agree or disagree about those two papers. Personally I think that during the last thirty or forty years the Tribune has been infinitely more helpful to good causes than the Courier-Journal, but, as I say, people can differ on such a subject; and I should be very glad to meet at any time either Henry Watterson or Whitelaw Reid. But to compare either one of them with the Herald is literally and precisely as if I should compare either the American Magazine or The Outlook with Town Topics.

Having expressed his opinion of the *Herald*, he proceeded to an elaborate specious explanation of the matter which had so stirred my ire that I had protested to him.

Now as for what you say about The Outlook's publishing "The Truth about K." In the first place, I admit at once that the title, the type, and the placing of this advertisement *did* make it look to many readers like an editorial article. We used the same title, type and placing that had been used for similar articles for twenty years; but our attention was subsequently called to the fact, to which you now call my attention, i.e., that some people were misled in the matter; and in consequence we at once abandoned this twenty years' custom. From now on, every article of the kind will appear under the heading of "Advertising Department" or "Advertising Section," so that there cannot be any possible mistake in the future. As for the publication of the article itself, I most emphatically think that it was not only justifiable, but commendable. The Outlook publishes continually letters from people upholding policies or views with which The Outlook diametrically disagrees. (For example, The Outlook has on several different occasions published letters taking a very dark view of my own character and achievements, whether at San Juan Hill or elsewhere.) This particular article by Spencer I should have been glad to see published in the regular section of the Outlook as putting forth his side of the case, just as I am now trying to secure publication in The Outlook of an article from the North Western farmers giving their side of the case against Canadian reciprocity. Spencer's article, however, was too long, and such being the case, as I say, I was not merely willing but glad to see it put in. (I did not know it had been put in, of course, until long after it had appeared; but when I did see it, I was glad that it had been put in.) Probably you know that on April 8th The Outlook editorially took up this question, stated that the American Woolen Company was entirely justified in printing their article as an advertisement, and that The Outlook violated in no degree the ethics of journalism in admitting the advertisement to its pages and expressed its total disagreement with the views expressed in the article. I would have gone further than this; I would have stated that The Outlook did not violate the ethics of journalism, but rendered a great and needed service as an example in showing its willingness to accept the statement of a case with which it did not agree, to put it in exactly as it was written, and then itself to comment with absolute freedom, as it has done, upon the arguments made in the advertisement. Let me repeat that if The Outlook had had space, which it unfortunately did not have, I should have been glad to see Spencer's article inserted, not as an advertisement, but as a communication signed by Spencer, and avowedly stating his side of the case.

Sincerely yours

THEODORE ROOSEVELT

I felt that I had won my case with Mr. Roosevelt's assurance that henceforth "every article of the kind would appear under the head of "Advertising Department."

When the Payne-Aldrich bill was finally passed with Mr. Taft's and Mr. Aldrich's brutally frank explanations, I was done with the tariff as a subject for further study and writing. Four years later came the Democratic effort to make a revision. I had only the most casual interest. It was the same old method. They might make a better bill, I told myself, but there never could be a fair one as long as tariffs were set by a Congress under the thumb of people personally interested.

One thing seemed to me clear which is still clearer now, the combined prohibitive tariff industries were digging their own grave. Foreign markets they had to have; but they refused to buy from those to whom they wanted to sell. What the gentlemen did not realize was that by this procedure they were practically forcing nations not naturally industrial to copy their methods, industrialize themselves. These nations soon were succeeding with such skill that in spite of the boosting of the tariff again and again the foreigners continued to undersell us.

But the prohibitive protectionists were building a future competitor threatening to be stronger than foreign trade. This in the realm of politics. There had been no more hearty and conscienceless supporters of prohibitive tariffs than certain groups of organized labor, conspicuously the Amalgamated Steel and Iron Workers under John Jarrett. They were not a numerous body, but with the cry of the full dinner pail they were able to back the demands of the employers. They had a body of votes that no political party dared defy. But in teaching organized labor the power of political pressure the industrialists gave them a weapon that they did not see might one day be turned against themselves.

Back in the eighties one of the wisest and soundest economists we have produced, David A. Wells, said in substance of the victory of the tariff lobbies: "This is a revolution. It will take another revolution to overthrow the leadership now established by business men."

I felt after the bill of 1909 that there was nothing for an outsider like me to do but wait for that revolution.

I felt this so deeply that when President Wilson invited me to be a member of the Tariff Commission he formed in December, 1916, I refused. I was pleased, of course, that Mr. Wilson thought me fit for such a place. I knew that I should find the associations interesting. The dean of tariff students in the United States— Dr. Taussig of Harvard—was the chairman. To be under him would be an education that would be worth the taking, but I did not hesitate.

First, there was my personal situation—my obligations. I had no right to give up my profession for a connection of that sort, in its nature temporary. Then I realized my own unfitness as Mr. Wilson could not. I had had no experience in the kind of work this required. I was an observer and reporter, not a negotiator. I am not a good fighter in a group; I forget my duty in watching the contestants. But primarily there was my hopelessness about the service the Tariff Commission might render. Its researches and its conclusions, however sound, would stand no chance in Congress when a wool or iron and steel or sugar lobby appeared. A Tariff Commission was hamstrung from the start.

Of course it was not only my interest and work on the tariff that had led Mr. Wilson to offer me the position. He was looking about for women to whom he could give recognition. He was an outspoken advocate of suffrage and wanted to use women when he thought them qualified.

Jane Addams pleaded with me to accept "for the sake of women," but I did not feel that women were served merely by an appointment to office. Women, like men, serve in proportion to their fitness for office, to the actual fact they have something to contribute. I had no enthusiasm for the task, did not even respect it greatly. I believed, too, that harm is done all around by undertaking technical jobs without proper scientific training. The cause of women is not to be advanced by putting them into positions for which they are untrained.

The press comments on the idea of a woman on this commission were not unfriendly, as far as I saw them; but they were a little surprised and, as I was to find later, protests were made to Mr. Wilson. My friend Ray Stannard Baker, working on the Wilson papers, came across an answer of the President on December 27, 1916, to one protesting gentleman which I am not too modest to print:

As a matter of fact, she has written more good sense, good plain common sense, about the tariff than any man I know of, and is a student of industrial conditions in this country of the most serious and sensible sort.

14

THE GOLDEN RULE IN INDUSTRY

I was done with the tariff, but it was out of the tariff that my next serial came—born partly of a guilty conscience! In attempting to prove that in certain highly protected industries only a small part of a duty laid in the interest of labor went to labor I had taken satisfaction in picturing the worst conditions I could find, badly ventilated and dangerous factories, unsanitary homes, underfed children. But in looking for this material I found, in both protected and unprotected industries, substantial and important efforts making to improve conditions, raise wages, shorten hours, humanize relations.

My conscience began to trouble me. Was it not as much my business as a reporter to present this side of the picture as to present the other? If there were leaders in practically every industry who regarded it not only as sound ethics but as sound economics to improve the lot of the worker, ought not the public to be familiarized with this belief?

At that moment, and indeed for a good many years, the public had heard little except of the atrocities of industrial life. By emphasizing, the reformers had hoped to hasten changes they sought. The public was coming to believe that the inevitable result of corporate industrial management was exploitation, neglect, bullying, crushing of labor, that the only hope was in destroying the system.

But if the practices were not universal, if there was a steady, though slow, progress, ought not the public to recognize it? Was it not the duty of those who were called muckrakers to rake up the good earth as well as the noxious? Was there not as much driving force in a good example as in an evil one?

280

The office was not unfriendly to the idea. As a matter of fact *The American Magazine* had little genuine muckraking spirit. It did have a large and fighting interest in fair play; it sought to present things as they were, not as somebody thought they ought to be. We were journalists, not propagandists; and as journalists we sought new angles on old subjects. The idea that there was something fundamentally sound and good in industrial relations, that in many spots had gone far beyond what either labor or reformers were demanding, came to the office as a new attack on the old problem. Mr. Phillips, always keenly aware of the new and significant, had his eye on the movement, I found, and was willing to commission me to go out and see what I could find.

This was in 1912, and for the next four years I spent the bulk of my time in factories and industrial towns. The work took me from Maine to Alabama, from New York to Kansas. I found my material in all sorts of industries: iron and steel in and around Pittsburgh, Chicago, Duluth; mines in West Virginia, Illinois, and Wisconsin; paper boxes and books and newspapers everywhere; candy in Philadelphia; beer and tanneries and woodwork in Wisconsin; shirts and collars and shoes in New York and Massachusetts. I watched numberless things in the making: turbines and optical lenses, jewelry and mesh bags, kodaks and pocketknives, plated cutlery and solid silver tea services, Minton tableware and American Belleek, cans and ironware, linen tablecloths and sails for a cup defender, furniture I suspected was to be sold in Europe for antiques, and bric-a-brac I knew was to be sold in America as Chinese importations, railroad rails and wire for a thousand purposes, hookless fasteners and mechanical toys. I seemed never to tire of seeing things made. But do not ask me now how they were made!

I never counted the number of factories I visited. Looking at the volume in which I finally gathered my findings, I find there are some fifty-five major concerns mentioned; but these were those which in my judgment best illustrated the particular point I was trying to make. There were many more.

My visits had to be arranged beforehand. I took pains to make sure of my credentials, but I soon discovered that my past work served me well. The heads of the industries and many workmen were magazine readers, liked to talk about writers and asked all sorts of curious questions about men and women they had become acquainted with in *McClure's* and the *American:* Kipling, Baker, Steffens, Will White, Edna Ferber, just coming on at that time. There was often considerable asperity at the top when I presented my letters of introduction. They set me down as an enemy of business; but again and again this asperity was softened by a man's love of Abraham Lincoln. He had a habit of reading everything about Lincoln that he could put his hands on, collected books, brought out my "Life" to be autographed. That is, while I was *persona non grata* for one piece of work, another piece softened suspicion and opened doors to me.

My first move in a factory was to study the processes of the particular industry. Machines were not devils to me as they were to some of my reforming friends, particularly that splendid old warrior Florence Kelley, then in the thick of her fight for "ethical gains through legislation." To me machines freed from heavy labor, created abundance. That is, I started out free of the inhibition that hate of a machine puts on many observers. I think because of this I was better able to judge the character of a factory, to see its weak as well as its good points. I was able to understand what the enemy of the machine rarely admits: that men and women who have arrived at the dignity of steady workers not only respect, but frequently take pride in, their machines.

Again, I gave myself time around these factories. The observer who once in his life goes down for half a day into a mine or spends two or three hours walking through a steel mill, naturally revolts against the darkness, the clatter, the smoke, the danger. As a rule he misses the points of real hardship; he also misses the satisfactions. As my pilgrimage lengthened, I became more and more convinced that there is no trade which has not its devotee.

"Once a miner, always a miner." "Once a sailor, always a sailor." One might go through the whole category.

"Why," I now and then asked miners, "do you stay by the mine?"

"I was brought up to it." "I like it." "Nobody bothers you when you are working with a pick." "Nice and quiet in the mines."

"But the danger!"

"No worse than railroading." "My brother got killed by a horse last week."

In the end I came to the conclusion that there was probably no larger percentage of whose who did not like the work they were doing than there is in the white-collar occupations. In the heavy industries particularly, I found something like the farmer's conviction that they were doing a man's job. It made them contemptuous of white-collar workers.

I spent quite as much time looking at homes as at plants. The test I made of the industrial villages and of company houses was whether or no, if I set myself to it, I could make a decent home in them. I found even in the most barren and unattractive company districts women who had made attractive homes. There was the greatest difference in home-making ability, in the training of women for it. The pride of the man who had a good housekeeper as a wife, a good cook, was great. I do not remember that a man ever asked me to come to his house unless he considered his wife a good housekeeper. I remember one so proud of his home that he took me all over it, showing with delight how his Sunday clothes, his winter overcoat, the Sunday dress of his little girl, were hung on hangers with a calico curtain in front to keep them clean. His housekeeper, in this case a mother-in-law, confided to me in talking things over that night that in her judgment the reason so many men drank was that the women did not know how to keep house.

Visiting with the family after the supper dishes were cleared away, I managed to get at what was most important in their lives. After steady work it was the church. After minister or priest, the public-school teacher was the most trusted friend of the household. In many places, however, I found her authority beginning to be divided with the company nurse, for the company nurse was just being added to industrial staffs. Many of my reforming friends felt that in going into a factory and taking a salary a nurse was aligning herself with the evil intentions of the corporation, but the average man did not feel that way. She helped him out in too many tight places.

As to the relation of workmen to their union—for often they belonged to a union—I concluded that in the average industrial community it was not unlike that of the average citizen to his political party and political boss.

Both the union and the employer seemed to me to be missing opportunities to help men to understand the structure of industry, perhaps because they did not themselves understand it too well, or sank their understanding in politics. Both union and employer depended upon one or another form of force when there was unrest, rather than education and arbitration. In doing this they weakened, perhaps in the end destroyed, that by which they all lived.

The most distressing thing in mills and factories seemed to me to be the atmosphere of suspicion which had accumulated from years of appeal to force. I felt it as soon as I went into certain plants—everybody watching me, the guide, the boss, the men at the machines.

But to conclude that because of this suspicion, this lack of understanding, which keeps so many industries always on the verge of destruction, there were no natural friendly contacts between the management and the men is not to know the world.

I found that practically always the foreman or the boss, sometimes the big boss, in an industry had come up from the ranks.
In various industrial towns I found the foreman's family or the
superintendent's family living just around the corner, and his
brother, perhaps his father, working in the mine or the mill. He
was one in the family who had been able to lift himself. Nor
did it follow that there was bad blood between a "big boss" and
the head of a warlike union. I had been led to believe they did
not speak in passing. I had supposed that, if Samuel Gompers
and Judge Gary met, they would probably fly at each other's
throat; but at the Washington Industrial Conference in 1919,
standing in a corridor of the Pan-American Building, I saw the
two approaching from different directions. They were going to
pass close to me. I had a cold chill about what might happen.
But what happened was that Mr. Gompers said, "Hello, Judge,"
in the friendliest tone and Judge Gary called cheerfully, "Hello,
Sam." And that was all there was to it. Later, when I was to
see much of Judge Gary, trying to make out what the famous
Gary code meant, and how it was being applied, we talked more
than once of Samuel Gompers and his technique. The Judge
had great respect for him as a political opponent, as well he
might.

It is hard to stop talking when I recall these four years, drifting up and down the country into factories and homes. The
contrast between old ways and new ways was always before me.
Many a sad thing I saw—nothing more disturbing than the
strikes, for I managed to get on the outskirts of several and follow up the aftermath, which was usually tragic.

There was the ghastly strike in certain fertilizer plants at
Roosevelt on the Jersey coast. I followed it through to its unsatisfactory end. Rival labor and political bodies fought each
other for days while the men with drawn and hopeless faces
loafed in groups in saloons or on doorsteps.

"All going to the devil while their unions fight," said the

woman who gave me my meals in the only boarding house in the desolate place. "I am for the union, but the union does not know when they go into a strike which they can avoid what they are doing to men. It turns them into tramps. They leave their families and take to the road. It is better that they leave. I think the women often think that, so they won't have any more babies. No, the union does not see what it does to men. But what are the men going to do when things were like they were in this place? You know what their wages were. You know what a hellish sort of place this is. What are they going to do?"

It was the men who saw industry as a cooperative undertaking who gave me heart. I do not mean political cooperation, but practical cooperation, worked out on the ground by the persons concerned. The problems and needs of no two industrial undertakings are ever alike. For results each must be treated according to the situation. The greatest contributions I found to industrial peace and stability came when a man recognized that a condition was wrong and set out to correct it.

There was Thomas Lynch, president of the Frick Coke Company of Westmoreland County, Pennsylvania. Tommy Lynch had swung a pick before John Lewis did and, like Lewis, had risen by virtue of hard work and real ability, from one position to another—one to become the head of a group of mines, the other to become the head of a group of miners. But no union could keep up with Tommy Lynch in the improvements he demanded for his mines and miners. It was he who originated the famous slogan "Safety First." When I talked with him about rescue crews he swore heartily, "Damn rescue work—prevent accidents."

Tommy Lynch's work did not end in the mine. He had a theory that you could not be a good worker unless you had a good home. He literally lifted some seven thousand company houses, which he had inherited from an old management, out of their locations between high mountains of lifeless slag and put them onto tillable land, gave every woman water in her kitchen and a plot of land for a garden.

In 1914, when I was first there, out of 7,000 homes 6,923 had gardens. And such gardens! It took three days for Mr. Lynch and two or three other distinguished gentlemen to decide on the winners of the nine prizes given for the finest displays. They were estimating that the vegetable gardens yielded $143,000 worth of vegetables that year. I went back to see what they were doing with those gardens in the middle of the late depression. There were even more of them, and they were even more productive. Knowing what the garden meant, the miners had turned to the cultivation with immense energy. The company had plowed and fertilized tracts of untilled land near each settlement, and the men were raising extra food for the winter. Many of these miners were selling vegetables in the near-by town markets.

Believing as I do that the connection of men and women with the soil is not only most healthy for the body but essential for the mind and the soul, these gardens aroused almost as much thankfulness in my heart as the safety work.

But Tommy Lynch could not have worked out his notions of safety and gardening without the cooperation of the miners, even if it was sometimes begrudging.

Then there was Henry Ford attacking the problem which most concerned his plant, labor turnover—in his case something like 1200 per cent. He had come into the industrial picture with his minimum wage of five dollars a day just before I began my work. In May of 1915 I set up shop for ten days in a Detroit hotel in order to study what he was doing. The days I spent in and around the Ford factory; nights, tired out with observations and emotions, I came back to a hot bath and dinner in bed, talking my findings into a dictaphone until I fell off to sleep.

Connections had not been hard to make. There was then at the head of Ford publicity an experienced and able gentleman who realized that articles in *The American Magazine* on the Ford plant, whether favorable or not, were good for the concern, and who saw to it that I had every chance. Mr. Ford himself was my first important objective. He saw me in his big office looking down on the plant, a plant then employing eighteen thousand men. At the first glimpse of his smiling face I was startled by the resemblance to the picture of the young Lincoln which had played such a part in the launching of the Lincoln articles in *McClure's*. It was the face of a poet and a philosopher, as in the young Lincoln there was a young Emerson.

Like a poet and a philosopher, Henry Ford was unhurried. He was no slave to his desk. I saw it practically abandoned when he was wrestling with the successor to Model T. "Mr. Ford does not often come in," my conductor told me. "He is wandering through the factories these days. We never touch his desk."

He was boyish and natural in off hours. Coming into the private lunchroom for officers at the plant, where I judged a place was always left for him, I saw him throw his long right leg over the back of the chair before he slid leisurely into the seat.

"I have got an idea," he said. "People complain about the doors of the car—not convenient. I am going to put a can opener into every car from now on and let them cut their own."

He delighted in the flow of Ford jokes, wanted to hear the latest, to see it in the house organ.

When he saw me, it was he who did the talking, and he seemed to be straightening out his thoughts rather than replying to my questions. When I asked him his reasons for mass production he had a straight-away answer.

"It is to give people everything they want and then some," he said. And then he went on to enlarge in a way I have never forgotten.

"There's no reason why everybody shouldn't have everything he needs if we managed it right, weren't afraid of making too much. Our business is to make things so cheap that everybody can buy 'em. Take these shears." He picked up a handsome pair of large shears on his desk. "They sell for three or four dollars, I guess. No reason you couldn't get them down to fifty cents. Yes, fifty cents," he repeated as I gasped. "No reason at all. Best in the world—so every little girl in the world could have a pair. There's more money in giving everybody things than in keeping them dear so only a few can have them. I want our car so cheap that every workman in our shop can have one if he wants it. Make things everybody can have—that's what we want to do. And give 'em money enough. The trouble's been we didn't pay men enough. High wages pay. People do more work. We never thought we'd get back our five dollars a day; didn't think of it; just thought that something was wrong that so many people were out of work and hadn't anything saved up, and thought we ought to divide. But we got it all back right away. That means we can make the car cheaper, and give more men work. Of course when you're building and trying new things all the time you've got to have money; but you get it if you make men. I don't know that our scheme is best. It will take five years to try it out, but we are doing the best we can and changing when we strike a snag."

What it simmered down to was that if you wanted to make a business you must make men, and you must make men by seeing that they had a chance for what we are pleased to call these days a good life. And if they are going to have a good life they must not only have money but have low prices.

There was much more, I soon found, than five dollars a day and upwards that was behind the making of men at Ford's. There was the most scientific system for handling mass production processes that I had ever seen. Tasks were graded. A workman was given every incentive to get into higher classes. But I was not long at Ford's before I discovered that it was not this system, already established, it was not the five dollars, it was not the flourishing business, it was not advertising—deeply and efficiently and aggressively as all these things were handled—which at the moment was absorbing the leaders of the business. It was what Mr. Ford was calling "the making of men." It was a thoroughly worth-while and deeply human method. Mr. Ford knew that, do all you can for a man in the factory—a short day, higher wages, good conditions, training, advancement—if things are not right for him at home he will not in the long run be a good workman. So he set out to reorganize the home life of the men.

It was done by a sociological department made up at that time of some eighty men all taken out of the factory itself, for Mr. Ford's theory was then that, no matter what you wanted done, you could always find somebody among the eighteen thousand "down there," as he called it, that was qualified. So they had selected eighty for social service work and these men were doing it with a thoroughness and a frankness which was almost as important as the five dollars a day had been.

"Paternal" was the adjective generally applied to the Ford method; but one of the interesting things about Mr. Ford is the little effect a word has on him. Call a thing what you like, it is the idea, the method, that he is after. If that seems to him to make sense, you may have your word—it doesn't trouble him.

So they went energetically about their determination to add to what they were doing for the making of men inside of the factory a thorough overhauling of the men's lives outside. There were certain things that were laid down as essential. You had to be clean—cleanliness had played no part in the lives of hundreds of these men. But when they did not get their "big envelope" and asked why, they were told it was because their hands were dirty, they didn't wash their necks, didn't wear clean clothes. Ford's men must be clean. Already it had made an astonishing difference in the general look of the factory. And this cleanliness was carried by the sociological department into the home. The men must be kept clean, and the women must do their part.

Many of the women as well as the men were discovering for the first time the satisfaction of cleanliness. "Feels good," said a working woman to me, reluctant but thorough convert according to my conductor. "Feels good to be clean."

They were enemies of liquor, and no man who drank could keep his place. But he was not thrown out: he must reform. And some of the most surprising cures of habitual drunkenness that I have ever come across I found in the Ford factory in 1915.

There was a strong sympathy throughout the factory for derelicts. There were four hundred men in Ford's when I was there who had served prison terms. Nobody knew them, but each had his special guardian; and no mother ever looked after a child more carefully than these guardians looked after their charges.

In this social work Mr. Ford was constantly and deeply interested. As nearly as I could make out, there was nothing of which they all talked more.

I dined one night with four or five of the officers, including Mr. Ford, and while I had expected to hear much about mass production and wage problems the only thing I heard was, "How are you getting on with Mary?" "How about John?" "Do you think we can make this housing scheme work?" That is, what I was discovering at Ford's was that they were not thinking in terms of labor and capital, but in terms of Tom, Dick, and Harry. They were taking men and women, individuals, families, and with patience and sense and humor and determination were putting them on their feet, giving them interest and direction in managing their lives. This was the Henry Ford of 1916.

But work like that of Tommy Lynch and Henry Ford depended upon individual qualities of a rare and exceptional kind, also upon the opportunity to test ideas. Neither Lynch nor Ford was willing to let bad situations, a stiff problem alone. It challenged their wits, particularly when it concerned men in mine and factory. They were not hampered by dogmas or politics.

They did things in their own way, and if one method did not work tried another; and both had a rare power to persuade men to follow them. They were self-made, unhampered products of old-fashioned democracy, and both were thorns in the flesh of those who worked according to blue prints, mechanized organizations or the status quo. But the success of both with the particular labor problems they tackled was the answer to critics.

Only how could men of lesser personality, lesser freedom of action, and lesser boldness in trying out things follow? They could not. They had to have a more scientific practice if they were to achieve genuine cooperation in working out their problems. And what I was seeing in certain plants, as I went up and down the country, convinced me it had come in the Frederick Taylor science of management.

I had first heard of Taylor in the *American Magazine* office. John Phillips had sensed something important on foot when he read that Louis Brandeis, acting as counsel for certain shippers in a suit they had brought against the railroads, had told the defendants that they could afford lower rates if they would reorganize their business on the lines of scientific management which Frederick Taylor had developed. They could lower rates and raise wages.

"And who is Frederick Taylor?" asked Mr. Phillips. "Baker, you better find out."

And so Frederick Taylor had come to know the *American* group, and he had given to the *American*, much to our pride, his first popular article explaining what he meant by scientific management. In the following letter Mr. Taylor tells a protesting friend why he gave it to us:

I have no doubt that the Atlantic Monthly would give us a better audience from a literary point of view than we could get from the American Magazine. But the readers of the Atlantic Monthly consist probably very largely of professors and literary men, who would be interested more in the abstract theory than in the actual good which would come from the introduction of scientific management.

On the other hand, I feel that the readers of the American Magazine consist largely of those who are actually doing the practical work of the world. The people whom I want to reach with the article are principally those men who are doing the manufacturing and construction work of our country, both employers and employees, and I have an idea that many more persons of that kind would be reached through the American Magazine than through the Atlantic Monthly.

In considering the best magazine to publish the paper in, I am very considerably influenced by the opinion I have formed of the editors who have been here to talk over the subject; and of these Ray Stannard Baker was by far the most thorough and enthusiastic in his analysis of the whole subject. He looked at all sides in a way which no other editor dreamed of doing. He even got next to the workingmen and talked to them at great length on the subject. I cannot but feel, also, that the audience which reads the work of men of his type must be an intelligent and earnest audience.

Mr. ———, who has just been here, suggested that among a certain class of people the American Magazine is looked upon as a muckraking magazine. I think that any magazine which opposed the "stand-patters" and was not under the control of the moneyed powers of the United States would now be classed among the muckrakers. This, therefore, has no very great weight with me.

Taylor believed like Henry Ford that the world could take all we could make, that the power of consumption was limitless. "To give the world all it needs is the mission of industry," he shouted at me one day I spent with him at Boxley (his home near Philadelphia)—shouted it with many picturesque oaths. I have never known a man who could swear so beautifully and so unconsciously.

Mr. Taylor's system in part or whole had been applied in many factories which I visited in my four years. You knew its outward sign as soon as you entered the yard. Order, routing,

were first laws, and the old cluttered shops where you fell over
scattered material and picked your way around dump heaps were
now models of classified order. A man knew where to find the
thing he needed, and things were placed where it took the fewest
steps to reach them.

Quite as conspicuous as the physical changes in the shop was
the change in what may be called its human atmosphere. Under
the Taylor System the business of management was not only
planning but controlling what it planned. Management laid out
ahead the day's work for each man at his machine; to him they
went with their instructions, to them he went for explanations
and suggestions. Office and shop intermingled. They realized their
mutual dependence as never before, learned to respect each other
for what they were worth. Watching the functioning, one realized men had come to feel more or less as Taylor himself felt:
that nothing of moment was ever accomplished save by cooperation, which must be "intimate and friendly." Praised once for
his work on the art of cutting metal he said a thing all leaders
would do well to heed:

"I feel strongly that work of any account in order to be done
rightly should be done through true cooperation, rather than
through the individual effort of any one man; and, in fact, I
should feel rather ashamed of any achievement in which I attempted to do the whole thing myself."

Nothing was more exciting to me than the principles by which
Taylor had developed his science. They were the principles he
had applied to revolutionary discoveries and inventions in engineering. I made a brief table of them. They make the best code
I know for progress in human undertakings:

1) Find out what others have done before you and begin
where they left off.

2) Question everything—prove everything.

3) Tackle only one variable at a time. Shun the temptation
to try more than one in order to get quick results.

4) Hold surrounding conditions as constant and uniform as possible while experimenting with your variable.

5) Work with all men against no one. Make them want to go along.

There is enduring vitality in these principles and there is universality. They are as good for battered commonwealths as for backward disorganized industries. Think what it would mean in Washington today if all the experimenters began where others had left off, if no demonstrated failure was repeated, if theory was held to be but 25 per cent of an achievement, practice 75, if one variable at a time was experimented with, if time were taken for solutions and above all if everybody concerned accepted "intimate and friendly" cooperation as the most essential of all factors in our restoration.

This hunt for practical application of the Golden Rule in industry left me in much better spirits than my studies of transportation and tariff privileges. The longer I looked into the latter the deeper had been my conviction that in the long run they would ruin the hope of peaceful unity of life in America. They seemed to me inconsistent with democracy as I understood it and certainly inconsistent with my simple notions of what made men and women of character. Were we not getting a larger and larger class interested only in what money would buy? Particularly did I dislike the spreading belief that wealth piled up by a combination of ability, illegality, and bludgeoning could be so used as to justify itself—that the good to be done would cancel the evil done. What it amounted to was the promotion of humanitarianism at the expense of Christian ethics; and that, I believe, made for moral softness instead of stoutness.

But there was nothing soft about the experiments I had been following. Where they succeeded, it was by following unconsciously in general Taylor's stiff principles. Patient training, stern discipline, active cooperation alone produced safety, health, efficient workmen, abundance of cheap honest output. I had faith in these things. They were the foundation of genuine social service. All desired goods followed them as they became part of the nation's habit of life, reaching down to its lowest depths.

Many of my reforming friends were shocked because the one and only reason most industrial leaders gave for their experiments was that it paid. Generally speaking, the leaders were the kind who would have cut their tongues out before acknowledging that any other motive than profit influenced them. Certainly they sought dividends; but they believed stability, order, peace, progress, cooperation were back of dividends. That industry which paid must, as Mr. Ford said, "make men." That the right thing paid, was one of their most far-reaching demonstrations. Men had not believed it. They were proving the contrary; so in spite of the charge of many of my friends that I was going over to the enemy, joining the corporation lawyer and the company nurse, I clung to the new ideals. What I never could make some of these friends see was that I had no quarrel with corporate business so long as it played fair. It was the unfairness I feared and despised. I had no quarrel with men of wealth if they could show performance back of it untainted by privilege.

Sometimes I suspected that the gains I set forth as practical results of this experimenting inside industry were resented by those who had been working for them for years through legislation, organization, agitation, because they had come about by other methods than theirs and generally in a more complete form than they had ventured to demand. But that the idealists had been a driving force behind the new movement inside industry was certain. Their method could not do the thing, but it could and did drive men to prove it could be done.

My critics who charged me with giving comfort to the enemy did not see that often this enemy disliked what I was trying to do even more deeply than my so-called muckraking. Indeed, he took those pictures of new industrial methods and principles as a kind of backhanded muckraking—indirect and so unfair.

It threw all established methods of force into a relief as damaging as anything I ever had said about high duties and manipulations of railroad rates.

Whatever challenges my new interest aroused, however confused my own defense of it was, I knew only that I should keep my eye on it and report any development which seemed to me a step ahead. That, of course, was counting on continued editorial sympathy in the *American*. But hardly had I finished my book before that sympathy was cut off by a change in ownership.

The change was inevitable, things being as they were in the magazine world after 1914. The crew who had manned our little ship so gallantly in 1906 when we left *McClure's* had lost only one of its numbers. A few months after we started Lincoln Steffens withdrew. He objected to the editing of his articles, demanded that they go in as he wrote them. The same editorial principles were being applied to his productions that were applied to those of other contributors. They were the principles which he himself had been accustomed to applying and to submitting to on *McClure's*. The editorial board decided the policy could not be changed and accepted Steffens' resignation.

Back of his withdrawal, as I saw it, was Steffens' growing dissatisfaction with the restrictions of journalism. He wanted a wider field, one in which he could more directly influence political and social leaders, preach more directly his notions of the Golden Rule, which certainly at that time was his chosen guide.

Certainly it was the creed of the *American*. It had always been John Phillips' answer to our fervent efforts to change things, "The only way to improve the world is to persuade it to follow the Golden Rule."

I suppose Steffens had heard of the Golden Rule, but I am certain he had never thought about it as a practical scheme for improving society. It seemed to me, at the time, that it came to him as an illumination, and for some years he held tight to it, preaching it to political bosses, to the tycoons of Wall Street, the Brahmins of Boston, confronting them with amazing frankness and no little satisfaction with their open disregard of its meanings. He became greatly disillusioned finally by discovering that men were quite willing to let their opponents act upon the Golden Rule but much less so to be governed by it themselves.

My first realization that Steffens was struggling with the problem which confronted us all—that is, whether we should stick to our profession or become propagandists—was one day when I looked up suddenly to find him standing by my desk more sober, less certain of himself than I had ever seen him.

"Charles Edward Russell has gone over to the Socialist party," he said. "Is that not what we should all be doing? Should we not make *The American Magazine* a Socialist organ?"

I flared. Our only hope for usefulness was in keeping our freedom, avoiding dogma, I argued. And that the *American* continued to do.

In the years that were to come, wars and revolutions largely occupied Steffens. Wherever there was a revolution you found him. He wrote many brilliant comments on what was going on in the world. When he came back from Russia after the Kerensky revolution he was like a man who had seen a long hoped-for vision.

"I have looked at the millennium and it works," he told me.

It was to be the practical application of that Golden Rule he had so long preached. But to my mind the Russian Revolution had only just begun. The event in which he saw the coming of the Lord I looked on as only the first of probably many convulsions forced by successive generations of unsatisfied radicals, irreconcilable counterrevolutionists. When I voiced these pessimistic notions to Steffens he called me heartless and blind.

But there were other forces working against the type of journalism in which we believed. We were classed as muckrakers, and the school had been so commercialized that the public was beginning to suspect it. The public is not as stupid as it sometimes seems. The truth of the matter was that the muckraking school was stupid. It had lost the passion for facts in a passion for subscriptions.

The coming of the War in 1914 forced a new program. It became a grave question whether, under the changed conditions, the increased confusion of mind, the intellectual and financial uncertainties, an independent magazine backed with little money could live. In undertaking the *American* we had all of us put in all the money we could lay our hands on. We had cut the salaries of *McClure's* in two, reduced our scale of living accordingly, and done it gaily as an adventure. And it had been a fine fruitful adventure in professional comradeship. We had made a good magazine, and we were all for making a better one and convinced we could do it. "I don't think," Ray Baker wrote me not long ago, "that I look back to any period of my life with greater interest than I do to that—the eager enthusiasm, the earnestness, and the gaiety!" But we had come to a time when under the new conditions the magazine required fresh money, and we had no more to put in.

The upshot was that in 1915 the *American* was sold to the Crowell Publishing Company. The new owners wanted a different type of magazine, and John Siddall, who had been steadily with us since I had unearthed him in Cleveland as a help in investigating the Standard Oil Company, was made active editor. Siddall was admirably cut out to make the type of periodical the new controlling interests wanted. I have never known any one in or out of the profession with his omnivorous curiosity about human beings and their ways. He had enormous admiration for achievement of any sort, the thing done whatever its nature or trend. His interest in humankind was not diluted by any desire to save the world. It included all men. He had a shrewd conviction that putting things down as they are did more to save the world than any crusade. His instincts were entirely healthy and decent. The magazine was bound to be what we call wholesome. Very quickly he put his impress on the new journal, made it a fine commercial success.

Gradually the old staff disintegrated. Peter Dunne went over to the editorial page of *Collier's*—Bert Boyden went to France with the Y.M.C.A.—Mr. Phillips remained as a director and a consultant—Siddall would hear of nothing else. "He is the greatest teacher I have ever known. I could learn from him if I were making shoes," he declared. And years later when, facing his tragic death, he was preparing a new man to take his place he told him solemnly, "Never fail to spend an hour a day with J. S. P. just talking things over."

As for me it was soon obvious there was no place for my type of work on the new *American*. If I were to be free I must again give up security. Hardly, however, had I acted on my resolution before along came Mr. Louis Alber of the Coit Alber Lecture Bureau, one of the best known concerns at that time in the business. Mr. Alber had frequently invited me to join his troupe, and always I had laughed at the invitation: I was too busy; moreover I had no experience, did not know how to lecture. Now, however, it was a different matter. I was free, and I might forget the situation in which I found myself by undertaking a new type of work. Was not lecturing a natural adjunct to my profession? Moreover, Mr. Alber wanted me to speak on these New Ideals in Business which I had been discussing in the magazine, and he wanted me to speak on what was known as a Chautauqua circuit, a kind of peripatetic Chautauqua. Perhaps my willingness to go had an element of curiosity in it, a desire to find out what this husky child of my old friend Chautauqua was like.

At all events I signed up for a seven weeks' circuit, forty-nine days in forty-nine different places.

15

A NEW PROFESSION

IT WAS not until my signed contract to speak for forty-nine consecutive days in forty-nine different places was laid before me that I realized I had agreed to do what I did not know how to do. I had never in my life stood on my feet and made a professional speech. To begin with—could I make people hear? I felt convinced that I had something to say, and so did my sponsors—but to what good if I could not be heard? What was this thing they called "placing the voice"? I went to my friend Franklin Sargent of the American Academy of Dramatic Arts, told him of my predicament. After a first test he agreed with me that I did not know how to use my voice, and that unless I could learn I was letting myself in for a bad failure.

Mr. Sargent was good enough to take me on as a pupil, uninteresting a one as I must have been. He began by putting me on the simplest exercises but with severe instructions about keeping them up. I went about my apartment day and night shouting "Ma, Me, Mi, Mo," "Ba, Be, Bi, Bo." I learned that the voice must come from the diaphragm, and that the diaphragm must be strong to throw it out for an hour at a time. Regularly every morning and every night, lying on my back with books on my stomach, I breathed deeply until I could lift four or five volumes.

By the time the circuit opened in July I knew theoretically how to use my voice; but I soon found that to do it without now and then getting it into my throat, making horrible noises and throwing myself into nervous panics, I must be more conscious of it than was good for my method of handling my material. Indeed, it was not until my second year of speaking that I could count on my voice for the hour of the performance. I never came to a point where I did not have to ask that a glass of water be put within reach—just in case. I found a glass of water a safety device if my attention was distracted for a moment and I lost my line of argument. I could pick it up, pretend to drink, change my position, regain poise.

So much for my voice. I knew how to make people hear what I was saying. Now as to material. I was to talk on the same subject day after day. That is, I was supposed to make daily the same speech. I was afraid of a memorized speech. A lecture experience of my old friend George Kennan was largely responsible for that. After he had published his classic work on Siberia Mr. Kennan took his story to the lecture platform. He wrote his lecture with characteristic care—memorized it and repeated it night after night on the long tours he made. It was an admirable lecture, one of the most moving I ever heard.

In telling me of his platform experiences Mr. Kennan dropped this warning: "In giving a memorized lecture one must be very careful that no two sentences end with the same words. In my lecture on Siberia I unwittingly used five or six identical words to end different sentences—one near the opening, the other near the closing of my talk. One night when perhaps I was unusually tired, instead of picking up what followed the first sentence I picked up the words that followed the second. That is, I was ending my lecture when I had only just begun it. I saved myself, but after that I always took care that there were no two sentences in my talk with identical, even similar endings."

My memory is a tricky and unreliable organ—never properly trained, never held resolutely to its job. I should have been afraid to trust it on a lecture platform. Moreover, I realized that, since I was no orator and never should be, my only hope was to give the appearance of talking naturally, spontaneously. I put together what seemed to me a logical framework and decided to drape it afresh every day, never to begin with the same words, to use fresh illustrations, to think aloud, experimenting. I soon discovered a fresh beginning every day was too much to ask of myself under the conditions of travel. I found it foolish, too, for if I had struck an opening that arrested attention, why change it for one that might not? I soon found that illustrations which were all right in an article did not serve with an audience. The line of argument which I would have followed in an article became more effective on a platform if switched. That is, as it turned out, although I was giving the same lecture every day, it was never quite the same. I worked on it constantly; and that is what kept my interest. I think, because always I found however tired I might be, however much I despised myself for undertaking to do what I more and more realized I did not know how to do, I always was interested in my subject, talking as if it was something of which I had never talked before. It was that personal interest in my material which carried me through.

I had not given a thought in advance to the physical aspect of my undertaking. I had known that every day for forty-nine days I was to speak in a different place; I knew that meant daily traveling, but that had not disturbed me. I had always prided myself that I was superior to physical surroundings. I had not been long on the Chautauqua Circuit before I was realizing that they played an enormous part in my day. I found I was inquiring about the town to which we were headed: "How about the hotel? Are there bathrooms? If so, am I to get one?"

I was uneasy about the table—the ideas of cooking and serving—and at night about the noises, the drafts and other unmentionable worries. To my amazement the bed in which I was to sleep soon was taking an altogether disproportionate place in my mind. It is a fact that, when the circuit was over and I came to tell its story, I could draw a diagram of any one of the rooms in which I had slept, giving the exact location of the bed in relation to windows and doors and bathroom. I remembered these beds when I did not remember the hotel.

To my surprise I found myself deeply interested in the physical life of the circuit, so like the life of the circus. We performed in tents, and our outfit was as gay as ever you saw—khaki tents bound in red, with a great khaki fence about, pennants floating up and down the streets, and within, order, cleanliness, and the smartest kind of little platform and side dressing rooms.

Naturally I had no little curiosity about my traveling companions. Scoffing eastern friends told me that there would be bell ringers, trained dogs, and Tyrolese yodelers. I found no such entertainment, but I could hardly have fallen in with pleasanter company. A quintette of young people whose business it was to sing for three-quarters of an hour before my afternoon lecture and for a like period before the evening entertainment, proved to be the gayest, kindest, healthiest of companions. They were hard workers, seriously interested in pleasing their audiences. They knew not only how to work, but how to live on the kind of junket that I had undertaken. In other words, here was a group of five young people who were doing what to me was very unusual, in a thoroughly professional way. The seventh member of our party, the evening entertainer, Sydney Landon, had had long experience on the circuit. He was doing his work exactly as a good writer or a good lawyer would do his. I saw at once that what I had joined was not, as I had hastily imagined, a haphazard semi-business, semi-philanthropic, happy-go-lucky new kind of barnstorming. It was serious work.

In starting the Chautauqua work I was not conscious that there was a large percentage of condescension in my attitude. My first audience revealed my mind to me with painful definiteness, and humbled me beyond expression. It was all so unlike anything that I had had in my mind. I was to speak in the evening and arrived at my destination late and after a rather hard day. It was a steel town—one which I had known long years before. The picturesqueness of the thing struck me with amazement. Planted on an open space in the straggling, dimly lighted streets, where the heavy panting of the blast furnaces could be clearly heard, I saw the tent ablaze with electric lights, for, if you please, we carried our own electric equipment. From all directions men, women, and children were flocking—white shirtwaists in profusion, few coats, and still fewer hats. And there were so many of them! I felt a queer sensation of alarm. Here in the high-banked tiers were scores upon scores of serious faces of hardworking men. I had come to talk about the hopeful and optimistic things that I had seen in the industrial life of the country; but face to face with these men, within sound of the heavy panting of great furnaces, within sight of the unpainted, undrained rows of company houses which I had noticed as I came in on the train, the memory of many a long and bitter labor struggle that I had known of in that valley came to life, and all my pretty tales seemed now terribly flimsy. They were so serious, they listened so intently to get something; and the tragedy was that I had not more to give them. This was my first audience. I never had another that made so deep an impression upon me.

I had not been long on the Circuit before I realized that my audience had only a languid interest in my subject, that what they were really interested in, wanted to hear and talk about, was the War, then ending its second year. But I could not talk about the War. Nothing had ever so engulfed me as in a black fog, closed my mouth, confused my mind. Chiefly this was because of the apparent collapse of organized efforts to persuade or to force peaceful settlements of international quarrels. These had taken so large a place in the thinking and agitating of the liberal-minded with whom I lived that I had begun to delude myself that they were actually strong enough to prevent future wars. Largely these efforts were the result of the revulsion the conflicts of the nineties had caused; the Boer War, the Greco-Turkish War, the Spanish War. People who wanted to live in peace wrote books, talked, organized societies—national and international. Jane Addams stirred the English-speaking world by her "Newer Ideals of Peace." William H. Taft, Elihu Root, leading public men, educators, combined in one or another society advocating this or that form of machinery.

And while this was going on Theodore Roosevelt was doing his best to counteract it by his bold talk of war as a maker of men, the only adequate machine for preparing human beings for the beneficent strenuous life he advocated.

What was the *American Magazine* to do about it? It seemed to us that we ought to find some answer to Theodore Roosevelt. Certainly we could not do it by promoting organized efforts; certainly not by preaching. We must prove him wrong.

In 1910 our attention was turned to what seemed a possibly useful educational effort against war, inaugurated at Stanford University by its president, David Starr Jordan. I knew Dr. Jordan slightly. His argument for opening the channels of world trade in the interest of peace had helped keep up my spirits when laboring against the tariff lobbies that so effectively closed them. What were they doing in Stanford? It was decided that I go out and see; at least there might be material for an article or two. Early in 1911 Dr. Jordan arranged that I spend a few weeks at the university. He was very cordial, meeting me at Los Angeles, where I arrived low in mind and body from an attack of influenza.

There was to be a peace meeting that night—Dr. Jordan was to speak. They had announced me, and when I refused to get out of my bed they took it as proof of indifference to the cause. The truth was that the idea of speaking extemporaneously was at that time terrifying to me; ill too, I could not, or perhaps would not, rally my forces. I would rather be regarded as a sneak than attempt it.

But Dr. Jordan understood and laughed off my apology, and together we made a leisurely trip to Palo Alto. He was a delightful companion when he felt like talking, as he often did! There was nothing which did not interest him. Looking out of the car window, he talked not of peace at all but of birds and trees and fishes and Roosevelt and the recent earthquake.

At Palo Alto I found that the most exciting course then offered to the students was the six weeks on war and peace which I had come to study. The big assembly room was packed for all the public lectures. Among the advanced students following the course were several who have since made names for themselves: Bruce Bliven, Robert L. Duffus, Maxwell Anderson.

There was considerable intensive work on special themes. One student was collecting war slogans; another, making a comparison of declarations of war, each of which called God to witness that its cause was just. Another student was compiling tables showing the yearly increase in the costs of armament in the twenty years from 1890 on; another, the economic losses through the devastations caused by war; and so on. All interesting and useful material.

But, study the work as closely as I could, I could not for the life of me lay my hands on that definite something which the *American* needed. Finally I took my discouragement to Dr. Jordan, and together we planned collaboration on a series of articles to be called "The Case Against War." Dr. Jordan in his autobiography, "The Days of a Man," tells of our scheme and what became of it; "crowding events permitted war to frame its own case."

In August, 1914, all of the machinery on which peace lovers had counted collapsed. The Socialists in a body in every country took up arms; so did organized labor, so did the professional advocates of peace.

It was not only this collapse of effort that had stunned me. From the hour war was declared I had a sense of doom quite inexplicable in so matter-of-fact a person. We should go in; of that, I felt certain. After we did go in John Siddall more than once recalled how in August of 1914, when a party of us were dining at the then popular Hungarian Restaurant on Houston Street, I had said that before the thing was ended the United States, the world, would be in.

"You are a prophet," Siddall would laugh.

But I was not a prophet. It was the logic of my conviction that the world is one, that isolation of nations is as fantastic as isolation of the earth from the solar system, the solar system from the universe.

All this made a species of Fabian pacifist of me. I was for anything that looked to peace, to neutrality, but it was always with the hopeless feeling that one simply must do what one can if the house is on fire.

I could not share the hate of Germany, in spite of my profound devotion to France, my conviction that Germany had believed a war of conquest essential to realize what she called her destiny, that she had been consciously preparing for it, that she thought the Day had come when she could venture it.

The awful thing seemed too big for hate by puny humans, and I was amazed and no little shocked soon after the outbreak when, visiting my friend John Burroughs at Squirrel Lodge in the Catskills, I found him whom I had always regarded as an apostle of peace and light in a continuous angry fever against all things German. Woodchucks were troubling his corn, and every morning he went out with his gun. "Another damned Hun," he would cry savagely when he returned with his dead game.

Time did not cure John Burroughs' wrath, for in December, 1917, he pledged himself in an open letter published in the New York *Tribune* never to read a German book, never to buy an article of German make. But John Burroughs was not the only one of my supposedly gentle-souled friends who felt this serious necessity to punish not only now but forever.

I was too befogged to hate or to take part in the organizations looking to ending the War which sprang up all about, and which I felt so despairingly were all futile.

There was Mr. Ford's Peace Ship. Mr. Ford had startled me one day in the spring of 1915, when in Detroit I was observing his methods for making men, by saying suddenly: "You know I am rather coming to the conclusion that we ought to join the Allies. If we go in we can finish the thing quickly. And that is what should be done. As it is now, they will fight to a finish. It ought some way to be stopped, and I see no other way."

Six months later Mr. Ford called me up at my home in New York and asked if I would not come to his hotel: he and Miss Addams wanted to talk with me. Of course I went at once.

It is curious how sometimes, when one steps inside a door without knowing what is behind it, one senses caution. The door was open to Mr. Ford's suite—nobody in sight, no answer to my ring; but I could hear voices and followed them to a room at the end of the hall. Mr. Ford was standing in the corner facing me. Before him were two rows of men—reporters, I knew.

"Here, boys, is Miss Tarbell—she will go with us," he called.

"Go where, Mr. Ford?" I asked.

"Oh," he said, "we are chartering a Peace Ship. We are going to Europe and get the boys out of the trenches by Christmas."

I had a terrible sinking of heart. "Oh, Mr. Ford, I don't think I could go on such an expedition!"

"Come with me and we will convince you."

And he led me into a room where Madame Rosika Schwimmer and my old friend Fred Howe were talking—Jane Addams was not there.

"Tell Miss Tarbell what we are going to do. We want her to go along." And he went back to the reporters.

I put in one of the most difficult hours of my life. Madame Schwimmer argued ably; so did Mr. Howe; and all that I could say was, feeling like a poor worm as I said it, "I can't see it."

When Mr. Ford came back and they told him, "She can't see it," I tried to explain my doubts. He listened intently and then very gently said, "Don't bother her—she'll come."

On top of this interview came a long telegram followed by a longer letter, both signed by Henry Ford. I doubt now if he ever saw either of them. Certainly the signature at the foot of the letter is not his. I am putting them in here, long as they are, because they are important in the history of the Peace Ship, and so far as I know have never been printed. Here they are:

November 24, 1915

Will you come as my guest aboard the Oscar Second of the Scandinavian American Line sailing from New York December fourth for Christiania, Stockholm and Copenhagen? I am cabling leading men and women of the European Nations to join us enroute and at some central point to be determined later establish an International Conference dedicated to negotiations leading to a just settlement of the War. A hundred representative Americans are being invited among whom Jane Addams, Thomas A. Edison and John Wanamaker have accepted today. Full letter follows. With twenty thousand men killed every twenty four hours, tens of thousands maimed, homes ruined, another winter begun, the time has come for a few men and women with courage and energy irrespective of the cost in personal inconvenience, money sacrifice and criticism to free the good will of Europe that it may assert itself for peace and justice with the strong probability that international disarmament can be accomplished. Please wire reply.

November 27, 1915

Dear Miss Tarbell:—

From the moment I realized that the world situation demands immediate action, if we do not want the war fire to spread any further, I joined those international forces which are working toward ending this unparalleled catastrophe. This I recognize as my human duty.

There is full evidence that the carnage, which already has cost ten millions of lives, can and is expected to be stopped through the agency of a mediating conference of the six disinterested European nations, Holland, Denmark, Sweden, Norway, Switzerland, Spain, and the United States.

Envoys to thirteen belligerent and neutral European governments have ascertained in forty visits that there is a universal peace desire. This peace desire, for the sake of diplomatic etiquette, never can be expressed openly, or publicly, until one side, or the other, is definitely defeated, or until both sides are entirely exhausted.

For fifteen months the people of the world have waited for the governments to act; have waited for governments to lead Europe out of its unspeakable agony and suffering and to prevent Europe's entire destruction. As European neutral governments are unable to act without the cooperation of our government, and as our government, for unknown reasons, has not offered this cooperation, no further time can be wasted in waiting for governmental action.

In order that their sacrifice may not have been in vain, humanity owes it to the millions of men led like cattle to the slaughter house, that a supreme effort be made to stop this wicked waste of life.

The people of the belligerent countries did not want the war. The people did not make it. The people want peace. It is their human right to get a chance to make it. The world looks to us, to America, to lead in ideals. The greatest mission ever before a nation is ours.

This is why I appealed to you, as a representative of American democracy, in my telegram of the twenty-fourth. It is for this same reason that I repeat my appeal to you and urge you to join a peace pilgrimage.

Men and women of our country, representing all of its ideals and all of its activities, will start from New York on the 4th of December aboard the Scandinavian-American Steamship Oscar II. The peace ship that carries the American delegation will proceed to Christiania, where Norway's valiant sons and daughters will join the crusade. In Stockholm, the ship's company will be reinforced by the choicest of Sweden's democracy. The crusade will then go on to Copenhagen, where further harbingers of peace will be foregathered.

These various groups will add such momentum to the crusade that when the pilgrims reach The Hague, with its achievements of international justice and comity, the moral power of the peace movement will be irresistible. In The Hague we hope to meet delegations from Switzerland and from Spain.

From all these various delegations will be selected a small deliberative body which shall sit in one of the neutral capitals. Here it will be joined by a limited number of authorities of international promise from each belligerent country. This International Conference will frame terms of peace, based on justice for all, regardless of the military situation.

This International Conference will be an agency for continuous mediation. It will be dedicated to the stoppage of this hideous international carnage and further dedicated to the prevention of future wars through the abolition of competitive armaments.

In case of a governmental call for an official neutral conference before the Peace Ship departs from New York, or even reaches European shores, our party will continue on its mission, rejoicing that the official gathering has materialized. We will then place our united strength solidly behind those entrusted by the governments to carry on the peace negotiations.

In The Hague the members of the Peace Pilgrimage will dissolve. Accommodations will be provided for each one back to his home. It is impossible to determine the exact length of time the pilgrimage will take. Six weeks, however, should be allowed.

I respectfully beg of you to respond to the call of humanity and join the consecrated spirits who have already signified a desire to help make history in a new way. The people of Europe cry out to you.

Information about the meeting place in New York, the hour of sailing, the amount of luggage, your accommodations, etc., will be sent as soon as we have your reply. I should appreciate it if you would telegraph your affirmative decision. Will you send it to the Hotel Biltmore, Suite 717, New York, our temporary headquarters.

Yours for peace
HENRY FORD.

I have no copies of my replies, but I know the gist of them must have been a heavy-hearted "I can't do it, Mr. Ford."

The night after my visit to the hotel Miss Addams called me up, and for a half-hour we argued the matter on the telephone. All I could say was: "If you see it you must go, Miss Addams. I don't see it and I can't. It is possible that standing on the street corner and crying, 'Peace, Peace,' may do good. I do not say that it will not, but I cannot see it for myself."

We were to talk it over in the morning, but that night they took her to Chicago, hurried her into a hospital. She was very ill. Jane Addams did not go on the Peace Ship.

Years after, I asked her, "Would you have gone if you had not been ill?"

"I certainly should," she said. "There was a chance, and I was for taking every chance."

She always took every chance when it was a matter of human relief. And if she had gone things would have been different on the Peace Ship, for she and not Madame Schwimmer would have been in command. She saw quite clearly the managerial tendencies of Madame Schwimmer, but she saw also her abilities. She was not willing because of doubts to throw over a chance to strengthen the demand for peace, and she undoubtedly trusted to her own long experience in handling people to handle Madame Schwimmer. But she did not go.

It was a tragedy of hasty action, of attempting a great end without proper preparation. Mr. Ford would never have attempted to build a new type of automobile engine as he attempted to handle the most powerful thing in the world—the unbridled passions of men organized to come to a conclusion by killing one another.

The Peace Ship was a failure; but so were the under-cover official efforts the President and his sympathizers then steadily pushed. Things grew blacker. The day when we would go in seemed always nearer to me. In February of 1916 my depression was deepened by hearing Mr. Wilson himself admit it. My friends Secretary and Mrs. Daniels had been so gracious as to include me among their guests at the Cabinet dinner they were giving in honor of the President and the new Mrs. Wilson.

We were all standing in the Daniels drawing room waiting their arrival. I was talking so interestedly with somebody that

I had forgotten what it was all about, when I was conscious of a distinguished pair in the doorway. It took me an instant to remember what we were there for, and that this was the President and his lady. How they looked the part!

At the dinner table the President was gay, telling stories, quoting limericks. Later, when it came my turn to talk to him and I told him how charming I had found Mrs. Wilson's animation and lively wit, he rather eagerly fell to talking of her and, to my amazed delight, of the difficulties of courting a lady when each time he calls the house is surrounded by secret service men!

Dropping his gaiety, he told me a little of the situation at the moment. "I never go to bed without realizing that I may be called up by news that will mean that we are at war. Before tomorrow morning we may be at war. It is harder because the reports that come to us must be kept secret. Hasty action, indiscretion might plunge us into a dangerous situation when a little care would entirely change the face of things. My great duty is not to see red."

I carried away from that dinner a feeling of the tremendous difficulty, of the tremendous threat under which we lived, and of a man that had steeled himself to see us through. It strengthened my confidence in him.

But of all this I could say nothing on my Chautauqua circuit, even when I began to realize that, more than anything else, these people were interested in the War.

One of the most convincing proofs I received of this came from things I overheard at night. We ended our circuit with a siege of terrific heat—the kind of heat that made sleep impossible. The best room you could get was generally on the second-floor front. You pulled your bed to the window, and lay with your head practically out; but if you could not sleep you would certainly be entertained, for on the sidewalks below there would gather, around nine-thirty or ten, a little group of citizens who had come downtown after supper "to see a man." Shopkeepers, laborers, traveling men, lawyers, and occasional preachers and hotel keepers would sit out talking war, preparedness, neutrality, Wilson, Hughes, for half the night.

"Look at them," said a talkative Congressional candidate. "Four years ago I could have told how practically every one of the men in this town would vote in November. I can't do it today. Nobody can. They are freed from partisanship, as I could never have believed. They are out there now thrashing over Wilson and Hughes, and not 25 per cent of them know which it will be when election day comes."

More and more I came to feel that you could count on these people for any effort or sacrifice that they believed necessary. One of the most revealing things about a country is the way it takes the threat of war. Just after we started, the call for troops for Mexico came. It seemed as if war were inevitable. There was no undue excitement where we traveled, but boys in khaki seemed to spring out of the ground.

I shall never forget one scene, which was being duplicated in many places in that region. We were in an old mountain town in Pennsylvania. Our hotel was on the public square, a small plot encircled by a row of dignified, old-fashioned buildings. In the center stood a band-stand, and beside it a foolish little stone soldier mounted on an overhigh pedestal—a Civil War monument. We were told that on the square at half-past nine in the evening a town meeting would be called to say good-bye to the boys who were "off to Mexico on the ten-thirty." "How many of them?" I asked. "One hundred and thirty-five," was the answer. And this was a town of not over twenty-eight hundred people.

As the hour approached, the whole town gathered. It came quietly, as if for some natural weekly meeting; but a little before ten o'clock we heard the drum and fife, and down the street came a procession that set my heart thumping. Close beside the City Fathers and speakers came a dozen old soldiers, some of them in faded blue, two or three on crutches, and behind them the boys, one hundred and thirty-five of them—sober, consciously erect, their eyes straight ahead, their step so full of youth.

The procession formed before the little stone soldier, who somehow suddenly became anything but foolish; he took on dignity and power as had the boys in rank—boys whom, if I had seen them the day before, I might have called unthinking, shiftless, unreliable. The mayor, the ministers, a former Congressman, all talked. There was a prayer, the crowd in solemn tones sang "My Country, 'Tis of Thee." There was a curt order; the procession re-formed; the old soldiers led the way, and the town followed the boys to the "ten-thirty."

Nothing could have equaled the impression made by the quietness and the naturalness of the proceedings. Beside the continuous agitations and hysteria to which the East had treated us in the last two and a half years, this dignity, this immediate action, this willingness to see it through, gave one a solemn sense of the power and trustworthiness of this people. It was a realization that I should have been willing to pay almost any price to come to. Certainly it more than paid me for my forty-nine nights in forty-nine different beds.

Eight months later this impression of the steadiness of the people under the threat of war was deepened. After my Chautauqua circuit, which I had supposed to be a temporary adventure, the lecture bureau asked to book me for a month of lyceum work, most of it in the Middle West. Late in January of 1917 I started out.

I was on the road when the break with Germany came. Our evening papers of February 3rd had the digest of the President's speech to Congress. The next Sunday morning there was the full text. I went out to walk early that morning, and one of the first things I saw was a lively row in front of a barber shop. Inquiring, I found that a big Swede had expressed sympathy with the

Kaiser, and was being thrown into the street. At the hotel, my chambermaid, the elevator boy, the table waiter, did not wait for me to introduce the subject. Everybody was talking about what the break meant—war of course. They were ready, they said.

As the days went on, I found that was the opinion of everybody. One morning I landed at a railway junction town, with no train until late afternoon. It was a forlorn place at any time, but deadly now, with the thermometer around twenty below. A friendly ticket agent warned me that the only hotel was no place for ladies, and sent me off into the territory beyond the railroad shops to a dingy-looking house which, he said, was kept by a woman who was clean and decent. It was anything but inviting on the outside, but travelers who are choosers are poor sports. The woman gave me a room and, following the only wisdom for the lecturer who would keep himself fit, I went to bed. It was four o'clock in the afternoon when I came down. The woman of the house, whom I had found in the morning rubbing out clothes, was in a fresh gingham dress, sitting in the living room reading the Chicago *Tribune*. Beside her lay a copy of the *Record Herald*. I found that this woman since the beginning of the trouble in Europe had been reading full details in these admirably edited newspapers. She had not been for a war, she said, until they went back on their word.

"That settled it for everybody out here. Now," she said, "there is nothing else to do."

I do not know how often I heard those words in the days that followed. When the President said of America in closing his address to Congress on April 2, 1917, "God helping her she can do no other," he was only expressing that to which the majority of the people of the West, as I heard them, had made up their minds.

Closely watching, I personally felt utterly remote. There was nothing for me to do. In the pandemonium of opinion nothing I could say or do would hinder or help, and so I went on with my daily rounds.

I was speaking at a big dinner in Cleveland early in April when a telegram was handed to me, signed by the President. It appointed me a member of what he called the Woman's Committee of the Council of National Defense.

I did not know what the appointment meant, but when your Government is trying to put through a war, whether you approve or not, I had long ago concluded that as for me I would do whatever I was asked to do. And so I sent at once an acceptance of what I took as an order. Two weeks later I received my first instructions. They came from the head of the committee, Dr. Anna H. Shaw.

16

WOMEN AND WAR

WHAT is it all about? That is what we asked ourselves when on May 2nd, answering the call of our chairman Dr. Anna Shaw, we met in Washington. And where were we to sit? We were but one of many anxious, confused, scrambling committees for which a place must be found. Our predicament was settled by finding a room somewhere on Pennsylvania Avenue—a dreary room with a rough table and not enough chairs to go around. My first contribution to winning the War was looting chairs from adjacent offices. My success gave me hope that after all I might be at least an errand boy in the war machine.

It was not long, however, before the Woman's Committee was a beneficiary of the civilian outbreak of patriotic generosity which had swept Washington. "You may have our house, our apartment," people cried. A fine and spacious old house close to Connecticut Avenue facing the British Embassy was offered us, a much more comfortable and dignified headquarters than I think we expected under the conditions. We remained there throughout the War.

But what were we there for? The Administration had called us into being. What did it expect of us? It was quickly obvious that what it wanted at the moment was an official group to which it could refer the zealous and importuning women who wanted to "help," the various organizations already mobilizing women for action. Considerable rivalry had developed between them, and it was certain to become more and more embarrassing. Our committee had been cleverly organized to spike this rivalry, including as it did the presidents of the leading national groups of women: the National Suffrage Society, the Women's Federation of Clubs, the National Women's Council, the Colonial Dames, the National League for Women's Service. Everybody in the list represented something except myself. I was a lone journalist with no active connection with any organization or publication. I was conscious that that was against me in the committee though apparently it had not been in the minds of President Wilson and Secretary Baker.

We were not an independent body, but one of the many subsidiaries of the Council of National Defense, the managing head of which was the present president of the American Telephone and Telegraph Company, Walter Gifford—a man of intelligence, sense, amazing self-control and patience. This I had reason to know, as I frequently represented the committee before him.

The fact that we had to go to men for orders irritated Dr. Shaw from the start. She felt we ought to be able to decide for ourselves what women should do, or at least she, the head of the committee, should sit on the Council of National Defense. I think Dr. Anna never quite forgave the Administration for subjecting us to the directions of man, whose exclusive authority in world affairs she had so long disputed.

Our mandate had been to consider women's defense work for the nation. But what were we to do with the results of our consideration, our recommendations? Our conclusion was that we must find a way to get them to the women of the country. To do that, we must coordinate the various agencies represented in our body, enlist others, create a channel for the Government's requests and orders. It meant organization. Here we were strong, for Dr. Shaw and Carrie Chapman Catt were the most experienced and successful organizers of women in the country. Moreover, they could command not only the organizations which they had created but, through their partners on the committee, other great national groups. To me the way that organization came into existence so quickly and so quietly was magic, unaccustomed as I was to organization in any form. It was not long before every state, every county, practically every community, had a branch of the Woman's Committee of the Council of National Defense. Before the year was up there were states which in twenty-four hours after receiving our requests could pass them down to their remotest corner.

From the start the committee worked—Dr. Anna saw to that. She and Mrs. Catt settled down in Washington. For myself I canceled two book contracts, determined to do what I could, indefinite as the task seemed. We met regularly; we kept office hours; we were keen to make something of our job.

The committee took it for granted that we were to handle the food problem already looming so large. By midsummer we had our organizations everywhere, planting and hoeing. On top of this came dehydration, and we had many hot discussions about the best method. I remember a morning when the committee gave itself over to reminiscences of helping grandmother string apples for drying, of the way mother dried corn and berries.

Then came canning—the larder was to be full. We were pretty well under way and rather proud of ourselves, thinking this was a special job, when Herbert Hoover came back from feeding Europe and was put at the head of the American Food Administration in a building of his own, practically a dictator of the food of America. Obviously Mr. Hoover was the one man in the world who could properly manage the huge and many-sided job; but it caused considerable heartburning in the Woman's Committee that gardening and canning and drying should not be left entirely to us. Were we not already in the field? Had we not an organization which was rapidly extending to the last woman in the country? Were they not digging and planting and canning and saving? But in spite of Dr. Anna's bristling opposition we were soon put in our place, made an auxiliary. It fell to me to act as liaison officer, which amounted to nothing more than finding out at food headquarters what they wanted from women and passing it on.

What we soon had contrived to become, thanks largely to Dr. Anna and Mrs. Catt, was a free channel through which we could pour speedily and uninterruptedly any request which came to us from any department of the war machine. We developed a disciplined army with other things to do than knitting and bandage making, gardening and canning, essential and important as these were.

Our most useful service, as I see it, was a growing activity in preventing the machinery of daily life from rusting in the storm of war. Take the women going in droves into industry. For the most part they were as untrained as the boys drafted into the Army, as willing as these to take it, throw themselves away.

Jane Addams had said to me at the beginning of the War: "Everything that we have gained in the way of social legislation will be destroyed. It will throw us back where we were twenty-five years ago."

That did not seem to me to be necessary nor indeed to be the way things were already going. Take this woman in industry for whom Miss Addams was especially alarmed. Recruiting for munition factories had been pushed before we went into the War by the National League for Woman's Service, of which Maude Wetmore, a member of the Woman's Committee, was chairman. As early as March, 1917, the league was at work in the Department of Labor. Soon after war was declared the President and the Secretaries of War and Labor called for general support of labor laws for women as well as for men. Mrs. J. Borden Harriman was soon made chairman of a committee on women in industry of the Council of National Defense. About the same time our committee created a department to handle the problem and was given a tenth member from the ranks of organized women— Miss Agnes Nestor of Chicago, a leader in the glove workers' union. We were a little concerned about the new appointee, but Miss Nestor from the start was one of the most useful members of the committee—wise and patient in understanding all problems though naturally concentrated chiefly on her own, which were grave enough, because of the rapid multiplication of agencies with their unavoidable rivalries and jealousies.

The determination not only to protect woman in her new capacity but educate her, thrust her ahead, was strong. Representatives of organized women met in Kansas City in June demanding new standards for war contracts. The upshot was that Florence Kelley was made a member of the Board of Control of Labor standards for Army Clothing. Things went rapidly after that. A woman's division was created in January in the United States Employment Service with Mrs. H. M. Richard at its head. About the same time Mary Van Kleeck was made head of a woman's branch in the Ordnance Service and our Agnes Nestor, who had by this time become generally recognized for her intelligence and steadiness, was appointed on the newly formed advisory council to the Secretary of Labor in war labor legislation.

Agnes Nestor and Mary Anderson, the present head of the Women's Bureau of the Department of Labor, demonstrated as I had never seen it the education to be had in a labor organization which seeks by arbitration and more arbitration and still more arbitration to improve its situation without weakening the industry by which it lives, one that appeals to force only as a last resort, never as a mere threat.

What all this amounts to is that through the activities of women in and out of industry there was a steady clarification and strengthening of our position.

The chief service of the Woman's Committee in the matter was seeing that full information of what was going on was sent broadcast. Miss Nestor's reports reached women in quarters where labor standards had probably never been heard of. In our bulletins we kept up a constant stream of news items of what women were doing in industry not only in this country but in others. To make our vast horde conscious of the needs of sisters at the machine, eager to support what the Government had decided was right and just for her protection, was our aim. We did our part in proving that even in war determined women can not only prevent backward movements but even move forward.

Similar to what we did for the woman in industry was the help we were able to give to the Children's Bureau. Julia Lathrop, its head, told us how its work was falling behind: playgrounds in many places given up, maternity work shut down. Could we help to stem this backward flow? We turned our machinery at once to the support of the bureau. Women in districts where its work had never been known were aroused to establish nursing centers, look after maternity cases, interest themselves afresh in what was happening to children. It was a work of education as well as of renewal.

Julia Lathrop told me one day just before the committee went out of existence that the work of her bureau had been extended more in the few months that we had been promoting it than it could have been with their machinery in as many years.

As the effectiveness of our national channel began to be understood, naturally enough all sorts of requests came to help out in putting over this or that scheme, to grant favors for this or that friend. While the majority of such efforts were entirely legitimate, there were some of dubious character.

I recall an amusing illustration of the latter. Just after war began to take its toll the Gold Star Mothers were organized, and our committee was asked to prepare an official arm band with a gold star or stars. The idea had not been noised about before a gentleman high in the counsels of the nation came to us with the request that we make the badge not of black as decided but purple—purple velvet. His reason was that a friend of his, a manufacturer of velvet, had on hand some thousands of yards of purple velvet which he would like to dispose of. We did not see our way to change our choice of color and material.

A request which led to a peck of trouble for me came from the two persons in the country I least expected to look to us for help—Loie Fuller and Sam Hill, friends of Queen Marie of Rumania. If I remember correctly they wanted us to bring her over in the interest of the Allied cause. We compromised by promising to send her a message of sympathy. I was commissioned to see that it was properly illuminated, and through my affiliation with the Pen and Brush Club of New York, a group of women writers and artists, a really beautiful parchment roll was turned out. We were so pleased with it that we had one made for Queen Elisabeth of Belgium.

But how were we going to get them to the Queens? Mr. Gifford of the Council was unsympathetic. No one would have dared suggest to Mr. Lansing that the State Department interest itself. The War Department could not be expected to carry them. Those messages lay about the Woman's Committee for weeks a burden and finally a joke, a burden and a joke which was thrown on my shoulders when in January of 1919 I went to Paris for observation for the *Red Cross Magazine*. Surely in Paris there would be some way of delivering them. It was Robert Bliss of our Embassy who came to my help in the case of Queen Marie, and much to my relief passed the roll on—to a representative of the Rumanian Government, I understood, although I never had any diplomatic assurance that it really landed on the desk of the Queen.

As to the message to Queen Elisabeth, Mrs. Vernon Kellogg, who was *persona grata* with the Queen, was in Paris and, knowing that she was going back to Brussels, I hastened to her with my roll, told her my predicament, begged her to take it off my hands, which she kindly did. And that was the last I heard of the messages to the Queens.

By the end of our first year I was persuaded that the making of a permanent Federal agency lay in the Woman's Committee.

I took my notion to the Secretary of the Interior, Franklin Lane, who had proved a helpful friend of the committee in moments of strain.

"Why," I asked, "could not the present Woman's Committee be continued after the War in the Department of the Interior? Why could it not be put under a woman assistant secretary and used as a channel to carry to women in the last outposts of the country knowledge of what the various departments of the Government are doing for the improvement of the life of the people? You know how limited is the reach of many of the findings of the bureaus of research, of their planning for health and education and training? Why not do for peace what we are doing for war?"

Secretary Lane was interested, but in the committee itself there was little response. Dr. Anna pooh-poohed it. It was too limited a recognition. What she wanted was a representative in the Cabinet, and she was unwilling to take anything else.

It is possible that Dr. Anna did not want to encourage ideas concerning women from a woman as lukewarm as I had always been in the matter of suffrage. She wanted a committee as actively interested in pushing ahead the cause of votes for women as it was in defense work, in protecting women and children. From her point of view the cause was as vital as protecting women in industries, indeed essential to that problem.

There was only one other woman on the committee as lukewarm as I in the matter of suffrage, and that was one of our most valuable and distinguished members—Mrs. Joseph Lamar of Atlanta, the widow of Justice Lamar of the Supreme Court of the United States. Mrs. Lamar and I saw eye to eye as a rule in the work of the committee, and we both felt it should keep out of suffrage work. Not so easy for old-time national leaders like Dr. Anna and Mrs. Catt, with militant suffragists picketing the White House, begging for arrest; but they showed admirable restraint. Indeed, I believe that restraint to have been in the long run the soundest politics. It certainly helped in bringing both Houses of the Congress to accept the Nineteenth Amendment in the early summer of 1919, giving nation-wide suffrage to women.

Dr. Anna's attitude towards me was quite understandable. She was familiar with and resented, as she told me quite frankly, certain activities of mine which had conflicted with both her convictions and her arguments—activities which had been a surprise and a regret to many of those whose opinions I valued highly.

I had always resented the pains that militant suffragists took to belittle the work that woman had done in the past in the world, picturing her as a meek and prostrate "doormat." They refused, I felt, to pay proper credit to the fine social and economic work that women had done in the building of America. And in 1909, after we took over the *American Magazine*, I burst out with a series of studies of leading American women from the Revolution to the Civil War, including such stalwarts as Mercy Warren, Abigail Adams, Esther Reed, Mary Lyon, Catharine Beecher, the fighting antislavery leaders—not omitting two for whom I had warm admiration, if I was not in entire agreement with them, Elizabeth Cady Stanton and Susan B. Anthony.

I thought I made a pretty good showing, but I found it was not welcome. And on top of that I settled my position in the minds of Dr. Anna and many of her friends by a series of little essays which I finally brought together under the title of "The Business of Being a Woman." That title was like a red rag to many of my militant friends. The idea that woman had a business assigned by nature and society which was of more importance than public life disturbed them; even if it was so, they did not want it emphasized.

Feeling as I did, I could not fight for suffrage, although I did not fight against it. Moreover, I believed that it would come because in the minds of most people democracy is a piece of machinery, its motive power the ballot. The majority of the advocates for women's suffrage saw regeneration, a new world through laws and systems; but I saw democracy as a spiritual faith. I did not deny that it must be interpreted in laws and systems, but their work deepens, broadens, only as the spirit grows. What I feared in women was that they would substitute the letter for the spirit, weaken the strategic place Nature and society had given them for keeping the spirit alive in the democracy, elevating it to the head of the procession of life, training youth for its place. But what chance had such ideas beside the practical program of the suffragist?

My arguments again had no emotional stuff in them. They carried no promise of speedily remaking the hard life most women were living, had always lived. The suffragists pictured a society renewed, regenerated, stripped of corruption and injustice, all done by a single stroke—giving votes to women. They would never betray the trust—the old fiction to which they held so tenaciously that women are by nature "better" than men and need only the chance in politics to clear society of its corruption. I could not agree.

It is not to be wondered that Dr. Anna suspected me, had a certain resentment at my being a member of her committee. In spite of all this, as the months went on she and I became better and better friends. She was so able, so zealous, so utterly given to her cause that I had always had genuine admiration for her. Now I found her a most warm-hearted and human person, as well as delightfully salty in her bristling against men and their ways.

An event in the history of our committee was a grand evening gathering in one of Washington's theaters. We all sat in state on the platform, and in the boxes were several members of the Cabinet with President Wilson himself, for a part of the evening at least. Dr. Anna made a capital speech, little antimasculine chips flying off her shoulder every now and then, to the particular delight of the President.

"Dr. Anna," I told her the next day, "you are one of the most provocative women I have ever known, an out-and-out flirt." But we were good enough friends by this time for her to laugh. I am not sure but she was a bit flattered.

When the work of the committee was over and she was sending out her final report, thanking each of us officially for our part in what I always think of as her achievement, she included in mine a hand-written personal letter which I shall always treasure as a proof of the bigness and the beauty of the nature of this splendid woman.

Evidently she remembered how she had sputtered at me sometimes. "You talk too much, Miss Tarbell." True—I always do if I have a listening audience. "I hate a lukewarm person," she declared when I persisted in balancing arguments. She did; she had never known for a moment in her life the frustration, the perplexities of lukewarmness.

But now she wrote thanking me for what she called "my consideration and kindness" toward what she called her "blunders and mistakes." Just what she meant, I do not know. It was enough for me that she should end with "sincere and affectionate regard"—enough because I knew she understood what I had never put into words, that for her I had never had anything but a sincere regard—a regard which our associations had turned to real affection.

The only professional work I did in this period was a few weeks of lecturing, a contract which I had made before we went into the War.

I have spoken of the quietness and steadiness with which people through the country seemed to me to be taking the call for troops in 1916 when I was on the Chautauqua circuit—of the conviction I had as I saw them in the Middle West on the declaration of war in April of 1917, that they had already made up their minds, were ready to go.

But I confess I was unprepared for what I everywhere met early in 1918, traveling chiefly in the South, the Middle West, and the Southwest. The country was no longer quiet, no longer reflective. On every street corner, around every table, it was fighting the War, watchfully, suspiciously, determinedly. All the paraphernalia of life had taken on war coloring; the platforms from which I spoke were so swathed in flags that I often had to watch my step entering and leaving. I found I was expected to wear a flag—not a corsage. At every lunch or dinner where I was a guest all declarations were red, white, and blue.

When you are on a lecture trip one of your few resources is the newsstand. I had the habit of searching the postal-card racks for local points of interest—local celebrations. But now all these had disappeared. The racks were filled with pictures of soldiers in all of their scores of operations, humble and otherwise —not only on parade, but on "spud duty." There were thrilling pictures of cavalry charges, of marches across country, of aeroplanes directing field maneuvers, touching scenes in hospitals, cheering ones of games, endless sentimental ones to be sent to the boys.

A change had come over the literature of the newsstands. Serious magazines I had never before seen in certain southwestern towns were there now. "Anything that pertains to patriotism is a good seller," a railroad station news agent told me. "Why, look at the books we carry!" And there they were, Hankey, Empey, Boyd Cable, disputing attention with "Slashaway, the Fearless," "Gunpowder Jim," "The Mystery of Demon Hollow."

The libraries of scores of towns made a specialty of war books. At Council Bluffs—an old, large, rich, and cultivated town of course—I found on an open shelf beside the librarian's desk Hazen's "Modern European History," John Masefield's "Gallipoli," "The Old Front Line," André Chéradame's essays, Hueffer's "Between St. Denis and St. George," and a score of others. They all showed signs of much reading.

As for the newspapers, they were given over to the war. It was my duty to make sure that they were giving the releases of our committee fair attention. They were—the local women were attending to that. Editors might and did grumble because Washington was swamping them with information and suggestions which often they felt were "old stuff," repetition; but they sweated to do their part.

The editorial attitude was not characterized by excessive respect for great names, particularly if the great name was that of an enemy. I was in Texas when the Zimmermann note was given out by the President. Nothing could have been more amusing than the contemptuous attitude of the average Texan citizen whom I met. Some of the country newspapers did not even take the trouble to print the gentleman's name, but called him "Zim." You received the impression that a German-Japanese attack on our Southwest border would be a very simple matter for Texans to clean up. All they asked, I was told, was for Uncle Sam to keep his hands off. They would take care of it. There was little anger but much contempt.

Everywhere the boys were the absorbing interest. In the Southwest and along the Atlantic coast I practically lived with them. They crowded every railroad station, hustled into every train. There was rarely a night that I was not wakened by their demanding beds in already overflowing sleepers. Troop trains passed you en route, all sorts of slogans scribbled in chalk on the cars. From wherever they came they were sure to announce that they were bound for Berlin.

It is of course beside the truth to say that all young soldiers were big and cheerful and spirited and brave; but the total impression was certainly one of bigness, of freedom, and of exultation in the enterprise. One came to have a fierce pride in them, an impatience of any criticism of what they did, a longing to fight for them, since one could not fight beside them.

Crossing the Apache Trail in March of 1918, we picked up three silent, rough youths who had come from somewhere out of the desert, and were making for camp to enlist. They were fascinating traveling companions, shy, watchful, suspicious, discovering for the first time the ordinary arrangements of railroad life. I remember a wonderful young savage with whom I traveled for a day. We were depending on eating houses for food and woke up to find our train six hours late. This meant no breakfast until possibly eleven o'clock. Of course the boy was famished. He ate ravenously and then bought right and left sandwiches, pie, hard-boiled eggs, an armful of packages. You could almost hear him saying to himself, "They are not going to catch me again." They had put one over on him, but next time he would be ready for them.

The interest of the boys in what was before them was unflagging. They were not afraid to talk about the worst. When the *Tuscania* went down, those bound for sailing points were not fazed in the least by the danger of the passage; but more than once I felt that the tragedy had whetted their desire to get at the enemy.

The interest of older men in the young soldier was inexhaustible. They were like the little boys in that. Little boys could not resist a soldier. It was startling to see a baby of three years slip away from his mother, walk down the aisle to where a soldier boy was sitting, watch him silently with wide-open eyes, get a little bolder, stretch out his hand and stroke his clothes, get a little bolder still and ask him if he might put on his cap.

Soldier or not soldier, however, the men talked war, talked it all the time when they were not reading their newspapers. How the news filtered to them in certain remote spots, it was hard to understand. In crossing the Apache Trail I was startled to see a man rise from the desert, as it seemed, and ask if we had any more news about "them big guns," if anybody had found out "how they do it." We gave him all the papers we had, and the passengers freely aired their theories of the mystery.

With the inexhaustible interest went a fierce determination to see that every suggestion of the Government was carried out.

When the Third Liberty Loan opened I was traveling in a section where there were many German settlers.

"What is their attitude?" I asked a woman active in the work of our committee.

"We have but one family in this town," she said. "After being waited on by five of our leading citizens they took $10,000 of Liberty Bonds."

I do not know whether these citizens carried ropes in their hands when they made the call, but I did see in one town a detachment of citizens parading with ropes on the pummels of their saddles and banners marked "Beware."

It had been agreed by all concerned that I talk on what was doing in Washington as I had been seeing it. Now and then I was "lent" by my sponsor to aid in a drive of one kind or another. Once I spoke from the platform of "Oklahoma Billy Sunday," a picturesque and highly successful revivalist who patterned his campaigns after those of his great namesake. A liberty loan drive was on, and no gathering, not even a revival, certainly not a lecture, was allowed in the town which did not share its time with the grim banker heading the local committee. He opened the meeting and left me shivering with what might happen to those who differed with him about the size of their purchase. Then came boisterous singing and praying, broken to let me tell my story. How dull and uninspired it sounded, sandwiched between this goading and inflaming!

I realized more and more as I went on that I did not really know much more of my subject than they did in Bisbee, Arizona, or Little Rock, Arkansas, so persistently did they tap every source of information; but I certainly knew fewer things that were not so. It was inevitable that, stirred to their depths by the continuous flow of all this young life towards the battle fields of Europe, they should "see red," hate, suspect. I could neither give them the inside information they craved nor stir them to the hate of which they had absolute need, I sometimes felt, to keep up their courage.

"Are you a pacifist?" a stern citizen on a Missouri railway platform asked me one morning as I was leaving a town where I had spoken the night before, and where I had deplored the will to hate I was sensing.

"Well," I parried, "I am for winning this war."

"Did you sign this?" He pulled out a prewar list of names, a peace society list where my name appeared. It was headed by Jane Addams—"that woman," he called her.

"I am proud to be classed with 'that woman,'" I said indignantly. "She is one of the world's greatest, and if the world could or would have heeded her counsels you boys would not be dying in France."

There was no time for argument or arrest, for my train came. I took it, followed by the black looks of more than one listener.

But it was the boys that were doing this. They had given of their blood, and their hearts went with the gift. They were all like an old fellow that I heard cry out one day, "I can't bear to think of one of Ours gettin' hurt."

It would be idle of course to pretend that in the territory over which I traveled between the break with Germany and the Armistice—in twenty-five different states, something like twenty-five thousand miles—there were no indications of revolt; but, as I saw them, they were infrequent and never in public. Now and then I came upon a man or woman who dared to say to me when he had me in a corner: "I am a pacifist. We must find another way." With which I so heartily agreed. But that man or woman would not have said that on the street corner without danger to his life.

People generally did not have much interest in what was to happen after the War was ended. They took it for granted that Germany would be driven back. That was what they were working for. But how the adjustments were to be made—that did not deeply concern them. What they wanted was to have it over and get the boys back. That done, they were willing to forget, pay the bill—but there must be no more of this senseless business in the world. Even the most violent occasionally confided that to you.

All these observations—of which I talked, I am afraid too much, to the members of the committee when I came back—strengthened my conviction that, whatever it cost, there was no doubt that the country would insist on seeing it through. That conviction was never stronger than when the Armistice was suddenly signed.

17

AFTER THE ARMISTICE

THE War was over and the United States was setting the brakes on its war machinery, setting them so hurriedly in some cases that they created situations almost as destructive as war. There was nothing left now for the Woman's Committee of the Council of National Defense but to clean up and move out. Dr. Anna stayed by while an admirable executive secretary and a small clerical force put things into order, reported what had been done, thanked everybody for his or her cooperation.

By the end of the year my desk had been cleared and I was preparing for a new job, to go to France for the *Red Cross Magazine*. My old editor, John S. Phillips, had been in charge there for some months, making a really significant and stimulating journal. He wanted a fresh eye on the rehabilitation work the organization was carrying on in France. He thought I might furnish it. I agreed to try.

Crossing the ocean in January, 1919, gave one some notions of what war had done to the accustomed orderly procedure of life. I was to sail to Bordeaux at a fixed hour; but no ship as yet went on time, though passengers were expected to arrive on time and to sit for hours as we were locked in the waiting room at the dock. At least it gave you an opportunity to eye as a whole those who were to be your fellow passengers. Everybody on my ship was evidently connected with some problem of restoration, the most interesting being the French bent on rehabilitating families they feared were stripped of everything. They were even taking food. As we waited a woman who guarded two enormous hams explained to me that her mother had begged her to bring a *jambon*. She had not had a *jambon* for so long. It was a new idea to me. I knew that sweets would be welcome to my friends, and I had armed myself with chocolates and bonbons; but a *jambon!* Why should I not take one to my dear Madame Marillier? Securing a permit to leave the dock, I hunted up a neighboring market and after much negotiation persuaded a wholesale dealer to sell me a ham, almost as big as I was. It was a problem to get it into the ship, but it was more of a problem to get it off, get it to Paris. I had queer ideas of what I might need in the way of luggage, and in my equipment was a pair of enormous saddlebags into which I had thrown high boots, heavy blankets, sweaters, woolen tights and hose—just in case. Crowding them all into one bag, into the other I put my *jambon.* In the long and tedious railroad journey from Bordeaux to Paris, I was packed in with a group of fine serious young Quakers going over to help a reconstruction project, and that terrible piece of luggage jumped from the rack and almost brained one of my companions. I cannot recall all the adventures of that ham, but I know that I was never more relieved than when I laid it at the feet of my old friend.

"What in the world?" she exclaimed (or its equivalent). And Seignobos said, "Oh, these Americans."

I was not long in Paris before I felt keenly that many of the French were saying, "Oh, these Americans!" We seemed to swarm over everything, to absorb things. At least this was true in the quarters where, at the urgency of my friends Auguste Jaccaci and William Allen White, I had gone to live—the Hôtel de Vouillemont just off the Place de la Concorde.

Walking down the Rue de Rivoli to the Red Cross Headquarters was like walking the streets of Washington in the vicinity of the governmental departments active in the prosecution of the War. All the familiar faces seemed to have been transported to Paris, as indeed great numbers of them had. Mingling with them were officers and men on leave, many seeking desperately to drown ghastly memories in any form of pleasure that would bring forgetfulness, more of them intent on sightseeing, buying gifts to take home. I found the pleasantest duty my Red Cross uniform brought me in Paris was when stalwart doughboys accosted me. "Say, sister, won't you help me find something to take home to my mother—my girl?" Before we were through with the shopping I had the family history but never a word about the war—that was done with. They wanted to forget it and go home. They resented the delay.

"We have paid our debt to Lafayette. Now who in hell do we owe?" This was the legend I saw once on a camion crossing the Place de la Concorde. I was told it was torn down by a scandalized officer and forbidden to be used in the future. But it expressed the doughboy's opinion, as I got it, better than anything else I saw or heard.

Not only the scenes in my quarter but the conditions of living shattered all my preconceived notions of hardship. I had been prepared for hardtack, but once at Vouillemont I found that if I took the trouble to market and bring in my purchases I could supplement the unbalanced meals with almost anything I wanted. The prices were high to be sure—sixteen cents each for eggs—two to four dollars a pound for butter—a dollar and a half for a little jar of honey. Many extras could be bought more cheaply at the American Commissariat. William Allen White was buying at the Commissariat the prunes on which he seemed principally to live, but marketing gave me the opportunity I wanted for finding out what the alert Parisian shopkeepers were thinking and saying. I sounded out that opinion daily until it was cut off by the conviction running through the town that America no longer sympathized fully with the French, that she was not going to force Germany to pay the sixty-five billion dollars the people felt they should have.

The Americans living around the Place de la Concorde assured me that Paris was not changed; not for them perhaps, but when I went among my old French friends, most of whom had stuck it through the War, changes stared me in the face. I had hurried to my old quarter on the Left Bank. Great gaps in the circle around the Panthéon and in the Boulevard Saint-Michel skirting the Luxembourg told the story of what the quarter had endured. The *laiterie* where once I had bought eggs and milk and cheese was gone, the space carefully boarded. I hunted among the neighbors for the cheerful Madame whom I had so enjoyed. She had died with the building, they told me.

There were little neglects in the once carefully kept apartments of my friends that affected me all out of proportion to their importance. The door into Madame Marillier's *chambre à coucher* would not close.

"Nothing has been mended in Paris, you know, now for three years," my friend explained.

It was literally true: nothing painted, nothing mended, little replaced. Craftsmen and tradesmen were in the trenches or in their graves. So many of those whom once you had known, the people who had served you or had been your comrades, were in their graves. Madame Marillier, pointing to a long roster of names on her desk in the salon, said: "Look, these are our dead. Read them. You will remember some of the names." And I did, men whom I had known twenty-five years before, and whose brilliant talk I had listened to at her Wednesday night dinners.

They could not bring back their dead; but after all the horror life was to go on, and they were bravely doing their best to give it something of its character before the War.

One thing they were counting on was the return to their homes and to the museums of their treasured *belles choses*. When I went out to dinner with French acquaintances who had possessed beautiful things, often pictures catalogued as national treasures, empty frames stared from the walls. The canvases had been cut out and sent to a safe place, generally somewhere in the South; but they would soon have them back, and that would help.

Not only in Paris but wherever invasion was threatened there had been an immediate effort to hustle the best loved treasures out of reach. At Amiens, they told me, they had "sent away" the famous *L'Ange pleurant*. It was back when I was there in March, and people were coming from all the towns near by to see it, to gloat and weep over it.

I was concerned with the fate of the "pretty girl of Lille" that exquisite wax bust attributed by some to Leonardo da Vinci; and when I made Lille my headquarters for a few days I at once made inquiries. The gallery was closed, but there had just been received many boxes of pictures which the Germans were carrying off when stopped on their retreat. The authorities were not adverse to having an accredited journalist see with his own eyes what had happened, and I was permitted to visit the gallery. The boxes were there standing against the wall, still unopened, and on each was clearly printed the name of the picture and of the German museum to which it had been assigned—beautiful evidence of the amazing efficiency with which the Germans had conducted their looting.

"Why, there," I said as I went about, "there is the 'pretty girl of Lille'!"

The curator winked at me. "Do you think so?" he said. "That is what the German Emperor thought when he went through the museum. It is a replica. The pretty girl is in a safe place and she will stay there until I am sure they won't come back." ("They" was the term I heard almost universally applied to the Germans in the devastated regions.)

Everywhere was the same joy over the safety and the return of their *belles choses*. I think I have never been in a group where gratitude mingled with sorrow was stronger than when my friend Auguste Jaccaci, who had been in Paris throughout the War at the head of the beautiful work for Belgian and French children lost or orphaned by the War, asked me to go with him to the opening of a room in the Louvre, closed of course through the dark period. It was one of the smaller galleries, but in it had been gathered new possessions, things bought in the War, others left by wills, a collection of choicest pieces. They were welcomed by the leading connoisseurs of the city: the directors of the Louvre and the Luxembourg, a few artists, a few great ladies. Everybody was in black and went about with unsmiling but touching appreciation, hardly believing, it seemed to me, that again he or she was free to rejoice in beauty. It was like coming home after the long funeral of a beloved member of a family.

But I was more concerned with the everyday conditions under which humble people were living, particularly in the territory so lately occupied. That was where the Red Cross could now be of the most practical help, it seemed to me. It took but little looking about to see that nothing we could provide would come amiss, either to those who had been caught and so remained through the War or to those who were now coming back, generally under the protest of the authorities.

I had not imagined that a bombardment could so strip a community, a countryside, of all the little conveniences of life. At Lens—once a great manufacturing and mining town, now a vast mass of red brick dust, hardly a wall left—I went about looking for signs of life, for I had been told that a few people had weathered the horror and were to be found living underground. Coming on what seemed to be a path running over a pile of debris, I followed it into an opening; and there, in what was left of a basement, sat a woman sewing. There was a fire on the hearth. She got up to greet me—a child ran out, a little girl with tousled head, dirty and ragged. "You must pardon the way we look. We have been here for many months. We haven't a comb. No pins, nothing. But we are happy they have gone."

Every now and then I came upon little groups who had found shelter in enemy trenches throughout the War. In a small town southeast of Laon, in the region occupied at the beginning of the War and held until the final retreat, I came upon a half-dozen children who had been brought up in the trenches. A couple of French sisters had come back to the region and were trying to civilize them. "You have no idea," they told me, "how difficult it is to teach them to use handkerchiefs." This was an apology for running noses. But, if ignorant of all civilized ways, these youngsters were remarkably healthy. They had had the food of the invaders, and they had lived in the earth very much like young animals. While they knew nothing of books they knew everything about war: guns, batteries, shells, uniforms. On the latter they had positive ideas. They had never seen a Red Cross uniform before, and they criticized it openly: "pas chic"—by which I suppose they meant "bungling." And I must confess mine was.

Continually as I went about I asked myself how it could be that every pin, every needle, every spool of thread, every comb, had gone. Larger articles you understood, but these little things! The silence of the devastated regions was even more perplexing than this stripping. I drove to the Belgian border several times, and it was a long time before I could make out why it was so still. Finally it occurred to me that I saw and heard nothing alive, no cat, no dog, no hen. All these creatures had completely disappeared. And when they began to be brought back the rejoicing was like that of the return of the beautiful things to the cities. One would live again perhaps.

At Vic-sur-Aisne where the American Committee for Devastated France was carrying on its fine practical work, among the many, many, things it was doing was attempting to restock with poultry. The daughter of an eminent New York family had an incubator in her bedroom where she told me she soon hoped to have a flock of chicks. The day that I was there a hen which had been imported laid an egg. It was an event in the countryside. I saw peasant women wipe away tears that day as they looked at that hen and her egg. They would live again.

I shared this feeling later when spring began to come, and in going over torn battlefields I saw the primroses. One day I heard a skylark sing and sing until it came out of the blue and dropped like a stone to the ground. It was like a voice of promise from heaven.

What saved one's reason within this immense devastation—so completely, incredibly horrible—was the intelligent and energetic way in which restoration was going on. Highways had been opened from Paris to Lille and on to Brussels. They included such shattered towns as Albert, Arras, Béthune, Lens, Armentières. I could go comfortably, and did, to Ypres, Cambrai, Saint-Quentin, Laon, Rheims—to all important points in northeastern France and along the border. It was when you disobeyed orders and explored unopened territory that you got into trouble. I tried Messines Ridge and landed in a shell hole. It took twenty small Annamese, located by my doughboy chauffeur at work on a clean-up job a mile or so away, to lift out our car and carry it a quarter of a mile to something like safety. The angry berating of an English officer—the English being responsible in that territory—still rings in my ears.

The most heartening sight was the steady, slow redemption of the mutilated land. As a rule the job of clearing away the first layer of war debris was given to German prisoners and soldiers from French colonies. It was a horrifying mess of abandoned tanks, artillery, guns, shells, hand grenades—not all duds, unhappily, as daily accidents demonstrated. With the debris cleared away, the heavy task of leveling the land followed. It was often deeply riddled, as over the Chemin des Dames, where the underpinning of hard white limestone lay shattered on the top—the soil far below. After the leveling came the tractors plowing the land, and finally the seeding. Along the highways outside of most of the big wrecked towns I saw between Paris and Lille were short stretches in one or another stage of this orderly redemption.

French, English, and Americans were all connected with the restoration. What really mattered, I felt, was the work of the French: first, it was their business; then, they understood their people—what they could and could not expect them to do. They were most successful in getting individuals to do the things they had always done in the way they had always done them. The American workers, marvelous as they were, wanted to reform the French modes of life. They were keen on sanitation and chintz curtains; the Frenchmen were keen on community tractors; the Frenchwomen, on community sewing machines.

After I had seen one little group of Frenchwomen gathered by an energetic duchess in a wing of her battered château making over old clothes for ragged refugees, who had had literally nothing new for years, I thought I knew what the Red Cross could best do for the devastated regions.

The Red Cross had on hand at the end of the war millions of garments, the output of thousands of little sewing and knitting circles scattered from ocean to ocean and from Great Lakes to Gulf. Innumerable shirts, drawers, pajamas, scarfs, sweaters, were piled in storehouses—the most extensive that I saw being at Lille. My cry was: "Turn them over to the French sewing circles so rapidly forming and if possible send a sewing machine with them. You can be sure that the Kalamazoo pajamas, the Topeka shirts, everybody's sweaters, will be refitted for children and men and women who at present have not a decent shirt to their backs, or decent drawers to their legs." A desultory distribution was already making, but I wanted it general and systematic. It was consoling to have found at least one thing, obvious as it was, which I felt I could energetically back.

Practical help was the more worth while because so intelligently turned to use. The few returning to the towns from which they had been driven often showed amazing resourcefulness and courage. They wanted to rebuild their homes, set up their shops; but when they came to the town where they once had lived it frequently was impossible to find the spot which they supposed they owned. At Cantigny, an utterly devastated flat ruin the day I saw it, a Frenchman and his wife appeared and quietly went about trying to locate the site of their home. They went away in disagreement as to where their street had run.

At Péronne I talked with a carpenter who had set up his shop. He told me he had had difficulty in finding his old location, but he thought he was on the right spot—at least the authorities told him he might settle there. By pulling scaffoldings from tumble-down houses and bringing in corrugated iron from near-by trenches he had made himself a waterproof shelter, arranged a workbench and already was earning a little money helping the authorities here and there in the cleaning up. A piece of constructive work he had taken on was salvaging doors. Here he had found a solid doorframe, there a panel; and, putting these together, he was producing a stock. He was certain it would not be long before he would have customers for them.

All this put heart in me in the same way the first primrose, the first skylark, had done. There was an indomitable something in men then, as there was in nature, something that made them live and grow.

Paris and the Peace Conference taxed my faith more severely than the devastated regions. My brother back in the United States wrote me that the job the Conference seemed to have set itself was as big as creating the world. Men were not big enough for that, and one was aghast that they felt so equal to it—or, if not that, were willing to give the impression of feeling equal.

What scared me was that so many battered people accepted this notion of what the Conference could and would do. From all over the globe they brought their wrongs and hopes and needs to be satisfied. Many of them also brought along ideas for the making and running of the new world—ideas in which they felt the quality of inspiration. The success of the Conference would depend in the mind of each of these suppliants, upon his getting what he was after.

But at the very outset they were balked by their failure to

reach the one man who they believed had not only the will but the power to satisfy their grievances and hopes—the Messiah of the Conference, Woodrow Wilson.

There was always somebody in the complex and all-embracing organization of the Conference to hear, sift, report their case; but again and again they could get no notion of what was happening to it. Insistence on an answer, on knowing how things were going, often closed doors which at first had welcomed them. I felt this deeply in the case of the Armenians. My interest in them had been aroused by a delegation at the Hôtel de Vouillemont. In the number was a woman with one of the most beautiful and tragic faces that I had ever looked on. It was not long before this woman was putting her case before me in excellent English, for she had had all the advantages of a European education. She and her companions had all suffered from the cruel and relentless atrocities which had paralyzed their country. Now their hope was that the United States would take the mandate for Armenia. Before I realized it I had become a determined advocate of that solution of their problem. I feel sure that, if we had gone into the League of Nations, I should have felt called to work for a mandate for Armenia.

The saddest thing was to see the gradual fall of their hopes, to know the day had come when, whatever had been the original reception, they could no longer get the ear of principals or experts. Balfour was said to have shouted at an aide as he threw the memoranda of the Armenians in the corner: "Do not bring me another of these things at this Conference. I know all I want to know about this cause, and I will not read any more memoranda."

Something of this kind was happening in delegation after delegation, and as hope went out of the suppliants resentment took its place. Soon many of the disappointed were joining the no small number that from the start had come to Paris, so far as I could see, to do their best to ruin the Conference. From every country came political opponents of the chosen delegates and of the settlements which they were seeking; from no country were there more of these than from the United States, and certainly from no country were there so many whose chief weapon was malicious gossip.

There was nothing for these political malcontents to do but talk, and that they did whenever they could find a listener—in cafés, on street corners, at French dinner tables—dinner tables becoming more and more unsympathetic as it began to be rumored that the full measure of punishment they asked was not to be given Germany. These groups naturally absorbed the bewildered people who were getting no answer to their supplications, who were being put off from day to day. It was easy to persuade them that the Peace Conference was a failure.

What startled me as the days went on was the passing of the will to peace which had been strong, even taken for granted at the start. Hate was replacing it. Again and again I recalled in those days a shrine I had once seen in Brittany called "Our Lady of the Hates"—one of those frank realistic shrines where symbolic figures portray the devils which torment men and prevent peaceful living. That shrine haunted my dreams when the confusion and bitterness seemed daily more confounded.

The social revolutionists at the Peace Conference never reached the point of building barricades as I had seen them do in Paris twenty-five years before; but they did make it rather lively on May 1st and inconvenient for many people who wanted to do their part in keeping the world moving in an orderly fashion— their humdrum part of delivering milk, looking after the sick, keeping things clean. They threatened such dire calamity if they were not allowed to meet and obstruct circulation in certain central places that the Government, usually stupid in such matters, shut down on their ambition so completely that of course they collected in these forbidden places and did their best to cause bloodshed.

I remember one young thing who thought the time had come and meant to be in the center of carnage. She went out early in the morning and posted herself on the steps of the Madeleine and sat there all day in a state of honest, genuine enthusiasm ready to sacrifice herself as well as everybody in sight. But there was no real fray—only some discouraging little street rows, with theatrical attempts to make capital out of them, and a few pitiful dead, little useful people with dependents taking a holiday and eager to see.

It was a great day for American doughboys. They had been ordered to stay indoors, to give up their firearms, and to do nothing that in any way would invite disaster. Their answer was like that of the would-be revolutionist for they streamed by hundreds over the monuments and cannon of the Place de la Concorde. There was not a monument or a point of vantage around that Place that any human being could climb to that was not occupied by these youths. If there was to be a revolution, they were going to be there to see it break out.

That which contributed more than anything else, it seemed to me at the time, to the suspicion and commotion around the Peace Conference was that it fed the onlookers (the press included) so little actual information to chew on. The delegates and committees sat behind closed doors, only spoke when a conclusion was reached, a document adopted. The public wanted to sit in a gallery and hear the discussions leading to conclusions and documents, and—being shut out—speculated, gossiped, believed the worst, spread false and damaging reports.

It took out its resentment by creating a four-headed monster—Wilson, Clemenceau, Lloyd George, and Orlando—preparing to dragoon the world into a fresh crop of unholy alliances and commitments and to refuse justice to multitudes of small and weak peoples and causes. It was prepared beforehand to doubt whatever the Conference did.

In the confusion and discouragement the one concrete thing I found was the International Labor Conference. At the beginning of the century one of the hopes of pacifists like Dr. Jordan, Jane Addams, and their associates had been the International Association for Labor Legislation, organized in 1900. It had been carried on without much help from labor itself until the War came; then labor set up a loud demand for international action. The undertaking added to that Americanization of the Place de la Concorde and the Rue de Rivoli which had struck me on my arrival. Many men and women I had known when I was working editorially and otherwise on labor relations turned up. It was like home to see Mr. Gompers barging up and down the Rue de Rivoli and to run onto Mary Anderson and Rose Schneiderman in the garden of the Tuileries.

I was lucky enough to fall in at the start with Dr. James T. Shotwell, the active head of the labor committee of the American delegation. Dr. Shotwell's intelligence and patience were of the utmost help, I have always felt, in getting the final agreement adopted, early in April in a full session. Certainly it was due to his generous explanations that I was able to follow what was going on.

At the same time I had the satisfaction of finding old-time French friends interested and active in the undertaking—most important of these Albert Thomas, who from the start was one of the vital influences in the Conference. Then my old friend Seignobos was actively interested. Shotwell in his "At the Paris Peace Conference" describes him as "a little old man, talking fast and furiously, very well satisfied with our labor business, which he seems to hold in higher regard than we do." Seignobos did hold it in high regard, hoped much for its future. I suspect he too was glad to find something in the complicated peace negotiations he could put his hands on, see through.

One of the most unexpected of my experiences in these days was the revival of past episodes in my life. The friends I had known so well in Paris back in the nineties, such as had escaped death or disability, were constantly turning up in important positions. Most influential among them all was the Englishman Wickham Steed, now the editor of the London *Times*, a person who ranked with ambassadors, but who was good enough to take notice of his old Latin Quarter friends.

Another of my intimates of those days was Charles Borgeaud, who had come up from Geneva with the Swiss plan for a confederation of nations, a sound and excellent document, which I suppose was filed away with the multitudes of plans which flooded the Conference in those days. I was so excited by seeing about me so many of these old acquaintances and friends that I attempted to get them together for lunch one day—Seignobos, Madame Marillier, Steed, Louis Lapique, all that I could put my hands on. The result gave me a melancholy sense of what twenty-five years can do, particularly a twenty-five years ending in such a catastrophe as they had all been going through, to take the edge off once keen friendships.

A more satisfactory revival of past and gone associations came from meeting numbers of former professional friends who were filling one or another post. Here were William Allen White and Auguste Jaccaci; here was Ray Stannard Baker, the head of the American press delegation, one of the few Americans having an easy entree to the President himself, conducting his difficult post with fine judgment and an absolute fairness which silenced the tongues of some of the most bumptious and political-minded correspondents.

"How can you bully so straight a chap as Ray Baker?" a correspondent anxious for a special privilege said disconsolately in my hearing one day.

There were hours when it seemed like a gathering in the office of the old *American Magazine*, so natural and intimate it was.

But these hours were not very many. My business was to furnish at least an article a month for the *Red Cross Magazine* and to follow the progress of the efforts to bring about a peace settlement including a league of nations. There were days when it seemed to me an inexplicable confusion, a bedlam; but, as a matter of fact, as the days went on I became satisfied by studying the communiqués, following the press conferences, reading the reliable English and French papers and the daily digests of what the papers of the United States were saying (posted at our press quarters), that a practical plan for international cooperation was taking form and that gradually more and more of the delegates of the thirty-one nations represented were consenting to it. To get something they would all sign seemed to me creative statesmanship of the highest order. For each of these nations had problems of its own, political, economic, social, religious, which must be considered before its representative dared sign. Thirty-one varieties of folks back home sat at that peace table, and they all had to be heard. In final analysis it was the failure patiently to listen to the political objections coming from the United States and trying openly to meet them which kept us out of the largest and soundest joint attempt the world had ever seen, to put an end to war. For that is what I believed the Covenant of the League of Nations to be when I heard the final draft read and adopted at the Plenary Session of the Conference on April 28.

But no one could have studied the truly august assembly adopting the Covenant without realizing the threats to its future in its make-up. They lay in the certainty of a few that the problem was solved—there would be no more wars. President Wilson, the noblest and the most distinguished figure of them all, seemed to believe it. But there were men putting down their names who did not believe it, who sneered as they signed; and still more dangerous were the stolid ones who accepted without knowing what it meant. Clemenceau had told his people what the Covenant meant—"sacrifices," sacrifice for all; he was the only man at the Peace Conference whom I heard use the word, and yet the key to the peace of the world is sacrifice, sacrifice of the strong to meet the needs and urges of the weak. If the League of Nations, led as it has been by the great satisfied nations, had grappled with that truth at the start, it is possible we should not now be seeing signatories take up war to satisfy their needs and urges.

These doubts weighed heavily upon me as I left the Plenary Session. But in the group of exultant Americans who that day saw the world made over I had no desire to voice them. There was only one of my friends to whom I could confide my fears—that was Auguste Jaccaci, a doubting Thomas with profound faith in some things (I never quite made out what): beauty and a directing God, I think. The night after the signing of the Covenant, Jac and I sat long in troubled silence over our coffee and *petit verre*, for neither of us could believe that the signing of a paper by however many nations could in itself bring immediate peace to the world.

Still I believed with all my heart in the attempt. My business now as a journalist and a lecturer, I told myself, was to explain the intent of the Covenant, what it set out to do, also to warn that it must be given time to work out its salvation.

Before leaving America for the Peace Conference I had signed a contract to go for ten weeks of the summer of 1919 on a Chautauqua circuit in the Northwest. By this time I had an understanding with my sponsors that I should be allowed to talk on what I had seen and heard at the Peace Conference. I now hurried home to fill that contract. I had hardly landed before I realized how bitter was the political attack on the Covenant. Would audiences in the Northwest listen to its defense?

But I did not allow this worry to intrude itself into my lecturing. In fact it was not in me to worry, once on the road, for I quickly discovered I was making what would probably be the most interesting trip of my life. And so it turned out. The country was incredibly exciting and of endless variety. I joined a circuit already ten weeks old in northern Utah. We skirted the

Great Salt Lake and traveled from one Mormon settlement to another. It amuses me now to remember how surprised I was to discover that Mormons were like Gentiles, that I at once felt towards them exactly as I did towards different religious sects at home. True, the attempt of taxi drivers, hotel clerks, baggage-men, to convert me when they caught me idle in their vicinity was a bit disconcerting at first, but I soon began to expect it and to find interest in their arguments.

After Utah came the lava country of southern Idaho along the Snake River. We climbed over the mountains into Oregon, went down the Columbia, over to the sea, up the coast to Portland, Tacoma, Seattle. We were in the Yakima apple country and in the berry fields of Puyallup, and everywhere in cherry orchards, such cherries as I had never imagined.

For a week we junketed around Vancouver Sound in primitive little steamers. We pitched our tents in lumber towns built on stilts, crossed fire-devastated mountains into the Coeur d'Alene region of northern Idaho, where one still heard reverberations of the labor struggles which had so agitated us on *McClure's* and the *American*. Then Montana—miles of plateaus and plains, the air thick with smoke, the earth sprinkled with ashes, for the mountains were on fire.

This magnificent and varied country carried with it a varied and compelling human story. Each new town turned up some bit of human tragedy or comedy. These people were pioneers, or pioneers once removed. They knew all the dangers, the hardships, the defeats, and conquests of pioneering. Their talk was of what they or their fathers had lived and seen. Whatever it had been, their hope was unquenchable. Every town we entered was the finest in the Northwest, the finest even when you knew that shift-ing trade and industry was cutting the very feet out from under it.

This was the land of Borah, but never in all those ten weeks, talking on the League of Nations, did I receive from press or individuals anything but respectful hearing. I was the first person who had come into their territory from the Peace Conference, and they wanted to hear all I had to give. They would do their own appraising.

As the days went by, I sensed a growing bewilderment at the fight against the League. These people had listened for years to people they honored urging some form of international union against war. They had heard Dr. Jordan and Jane Addams preaching a national council for the prevention of war, President Taft advocating a league to enforce peace. In many of the towns there had been chapters of these societies.

On our circuit there was a superintendent who reminded me every time we met that back in the 1890's he had spent practically all his patrimony going about the Northwest preaching a league of nations. It irked him, he said, that I should be receiving money for talking what he twenty-five years before had talked without price, purely for love of the cause. And no wonder!

With such a background, was it strange that many people in the Northwest should have been puzzled that the Congress of the United States was seemingly more and more determined that we should not join this first attempt of the civilized world to find substitutes for war in international quarrels?

Seeking reasons for this refusal, I felt the one which had most weight with people was the guarantee that France was asking from England and the United States to come to her aid in case of unprovoked attack by Germany, that is, a guarantee which was to remain in force until the League of Nations was a going concern.

I found that most people were against this. They wouldn't run the risk of having to help France again. I was for granting the guarantee provisionally and for a limited period. I believed such a guarantee would quiet what I felt to be one of the real dangers of the after-war situation, the near hysteria of France. Americans proud of their generous part in saving France from what looked to them like calculated annihilation said: "Why these hysterics? The War is over. The nations are going to enforce peace. The devastated region is to be restored at Germany's expense. Forget it."

How could America understand the years of horror France had just suffered, the devastation of centuries of loving labor, the wiping out of three and a half million of her best youth? And most serious of all perhaps, how could America realize what France so clearly realized, that the Great War was but the latest expression of centuries of determination on the part of Central Europe to reach the sea? It must have an ocean front even if this could be obtained only by crossing the dead body of France.

I had spent some hours at Châlons-sur-Marne just before I returned. Nobody in that town was so alive to me as Attila. Fifteen hundred years before, he had led the forces of Central Europe so far and had been stopped; but Central Europe had come back again and again, driven by the urge for the sea. Again and again France had saved herself, but she knew now she could never do it without the help of those who believed her culture one of the earth's great possessions. She must have guarantees. But how could the United States understand that centuries of experience were behind France's fear? They had not met Attila at Châlons-sur-Marne—I had.

All of this I talked in more or less detail until in midsummer my lips were closed for two weeks by William Jennings Bryan. Mr. Bryan for many years had been the brightest star of the Chautauqua platform. The management of the circuit liked to introduce him for whatever time he could give and they afford. It meant that the regular performer must either step down or divide his period. The evening was the proper hour for Mr. Bryan, for only then could the men come. Now I spoke in the evening. "Cut your time to forty minutes, and go on a half-hour earlier," were my instructions. I, of course, obeyed.

Now Mr. Bryan was presenting a two-hour discussion of what he considered the ideal political Democratic platform at that moment. In his planks he included joining the League of Nations but turning down the guarantees to France. At our first joint appearance he rose to condemn guarantees an hour after I had pleaded for them. When he was told of the conflict of opinion he at once looked me up, and in effect told me that I must not present views opposed to his on a platform where he was speaking. He in no way tried to influence my opinion, only to shut it off. I insisted that it was good for the audience to hear both sides. "The audience came to hear me," said Mr. Bryan; "it is important they know my views." He did not want them confused as they might be, he said, if I began the evening by airing mine.

Of course Mr. Bryan did not say, "You are of no political importance, and I am of a great deal," but that was what he meant. It was quite true, and I bowed for the time being to the demands of politics, but only for the moment. The two weeks over, I began again to talk guarantees with more interest on the part of my audience because of what Mr. Bryan had been saying and also, I suspect, less agreement.

By the time the circuit ended, the League was in a bad way in Congress. A bitter partisan war had broken out and Woodrow Wilson ill, his Scotch stubbornness the harder because of his illness, would not budge an inch. It was a sickening thing to watch. The only consolation was that the rest of the world wanted peace enough to make the sacrifices and run the risks a League undoubtedly demanded.

Wilson's enemies gloated: he was beaten, stripped of his glory; the world would forget him, was already forgetting him. They were wrong.

In the months that followed the final collapse of the League as far as the United States was concerned, I was much in Washington; and nothing I saw was more moving than the continual quiet popular tributes to Woodrow Wilson. On holidays and Sundays groups were always standing before his home, watching for a glimpse of him. Let him enter a theater and the house rose to cheer, while crowds waited outside in rain and cold to see him come out—cheer him as he passed.

On November 11, 1921, the body of America's Unknown Soldier was carried from the Capitol where it had lain in state to its grave in Arlington—a perfect ceremony of its kind. The bier was followed by all we had of official greatness at that moment: President Harding and his Cabinet, the Supreme Court, the House, the Senate, officers of the Army and Navy, and General Foch our guest of honor. At the end, following all this greatness but not of it, came a carriage. As the packed ranks between which the procession had passed in silence saw its occupants, Woodrow Wilson and Mrs. Wilson, a muffled cry of love and gratitude broke out, and that cry followed that carriage to the very doorway of their home. It was to be so until he died. He was the man they could not forget.

They will not forget him in the future. He is the first leader in the history of society who has treated the ancient dream of a peaceful world as something more than wishful thinking, the first who was willing to stake all in drawing the nations of the world together in an effort to make that "just and lasting peace among ourselves and with all nations" for which Abraham Lincoln pleaded.

In Paris in 1919 Woodrow Wilson actually persuaded the leaders of the majority of the earth's nations to help him build and set up a machine for such a peace. The complaint is that it has not done all it attempted. But how can any person who knows anything of man's past efforts to create machinery for the betterment of his life suppose that this, the most ambitious international undertaking ever made, would from the start run without friction or breakdown, would never need overhauling, even rebuilding?

That is not in the nature of things. The League has lived for eighteen years now. Its weaknesses have developed with experience, so has its usefulness. Its services to the world have been innumerable if not spectacular. If its failures have been spectacular, they have not destroyed the structure; rather they have demonstrated certain points at which it must be rebuilt.

The world will not forget the man who led in this effort to achieve enduring peace. That is what I was saying in those bitter days and have been saying in all the melancholy ones since.

18

GAMBLING WITH SECURITY

My TEN weeks of daily talking on the Peace Conference and the Covenant of the League of Nations ended the War for me. Also, it forced me to consider anew the problem of security. It was nearly four years now since I had put an end to it by severing my connection with *The American Magazine*. But the years had been so full of the War, the scramble to do something that somebody thought was needful, and at the same time to keep the pot boiling, that I had not realized what had happened. It meant for me, as I now saw, the end of an economic era.

I sat down to take stock. Here I was sixty-three with only a small accumulation of material goods. I must work to live and satisfy my obligations. To be sure I had my little home in Connecticut which in the fifteen years since I had acquired it had not only grown increasingly dear to me; it had also taken on an importance which I had not foreseen. It had become the family home. Here my mother had come to pass the last summers before her death in 1917; here my niece Esther had been married under the Oaks; here my niece Clara and her husband Tristram Tupper, battered by war service, had come in 1919 to live in our little guest house. Here Tris had written his first successful magazine story. Here their two children passed their first years. Near by, my sister had built herself a studio to become her home. A hundred associations gave the place a meaning and dignity which I had never expected to feel in any home of my own, something that only comes when a place has been hallowed by the joys and sorrows of family life.

I had carried out my original intention of never letting it become a financial burden; so, adrift as I now was, I not only could afford my home but felt that it was the strongest factor in my scheme of security, for here I knew I could retire and raise all the food I needed if free lancing petered out.

I was quite clear about the work I wanted to do. It was to continue writing and speaking on the few subjects on which I felt strongly, and of which I knew a little. These subjects had made a pattern in my mind. If men would work out this pattern I felt that they would go a long way towards ending the world's quarrels, quieting its confusions. First and most important were the privileges they had snatched. I wanted to see them all gradually scrapped, cost what it might economically. They were a threat to honest men, to sound industry, to peaceful international life.

I wanted to help spread the knowledge of all the intelligent efforts within and without industry and government, to put an end to militancy, replace it with actual understanding. And then I wanted to do my part towards making the world acquainted with the man who I believed had best shown how to carry out a program of cooperation based on consideration of others— that was Abraham Lincoln.

There was a man, I told myself, who took the time to understand a thing before he spoke. He knew that hurry, acting before you were reasonably sure, almost invariably makes a mess of even the best intentions. He wanted to know what he was about before he acted, also he wanted all those upon whom he must depend for results to know what he was about and why. Whatever he did, he did without malice, taking into account men's limitations, not asking more from any one than he could give. More than anybody I had studied he applied in public affairs Frederick Taylor's rules for achievement of which I have spoken above. The more people who knew about Lincoln, the more chance democracy had to destroy its two chief enemies, privilege and militancy. I proposed to take every chance I had to talk about him.

This was the program on which I was so set that I was willing to follow it even if it did take away from me the comforts of a regular salary.

Giving up the salary troubled me less than finding myself without the regular professional contacts which I had so enjoyed for twenty years, and on which I found, now I was free, that I had come to depend more than I would have believed.

Not belonging to an editorial group meant that when I dropped my pen at lunch time I no longer could join a half-dozen office mates full of gossip of what the morning had brought: the last Tarkington manuscript; something of Willa Cather's; a letter from Kipling; that new person from Louisville, George Madden Martin, with a real creation, Emmy Lou; that new person from Wisconsin, Edna Ferber, with a bona fide human being in hand, Emma McChesney; or it might be Dunne's last "Dooley," or Baker's last adventure in "Contentment," or gossip from the last man in Washington, perhaps direct from the White House, and always surely from our liberal friends in Congress. This was the stuff of our lunch-table talk. We gloated or mourned, and our eyes were always on what was coming rather than what had been.

I no longer had an office next door to these friends. My study had become my workshop. Now I must pay my own secretary's bill, my own telephone calls, buy my own stationery. I gasped when I found what these extras amounted to. Freedom, I saw, was going to be expensive as well as lonesome.

However, for nineteen years I have kept to my decision. How little I have contributed to my program in these nineteen years! The chief piece of writing I planned to do I have never finished. That was bringing "The History of the Standard Oil Company" up to date. I had dropped the story in 1904, but the dissolution of the company in 1911 left me with the melancholy conviction that sooner or later I should have to estimate the trial and put down how the new set-up was working. I talked two or three times with George Wickersham, the Attorney General who brought the suit, and he always cautioned me not to hurry, to let the decision have a chance to work out. I think we decided that about ten years would do it. But the War put a different face on oil. It suddenly became a matter for government control. It was no longer a private business. It was life and death for the Allies. Oil was as necessary to them, Clemenceau wrote to Wilson, as the blood of men. Everything that rolled or sailed or flew must have it. The great struggle of the nations with navies, England at the head, to command oil at its source, followed the War. The earth was ransacked for it in a terrific predatory hunt. In this effort of the nations to command oil supplies great names arose challenging that of Rockefeller— Sir Henri Deterding, Marcus Samuel, William Knox D'Arcy. The Standard Oil Company no longer ruled the oil world. There were the Royal Dutch and the Shell making up finally the Royal Dutch Shell; there was the Anglo-Persian. All of the dramatic and frequently tragic goings-on had to settle down into something like orderly procedure before the history I had in mind could be written.

The time came, along in 1922, when Mr. Wickersham said, "You had better go at it." But it was not Mr. Wickersham's dictum that hurried me to undertake to tell the story of what had happened since 1904. It was an entirely unexpected piratical attack on the two-volume edition of the history which had been exhausted for some time. My publisher, wisely enough, was waiting for the promised third volume before reprinting. When it became known in the trade that the book was no longer on the market a report was spread that the Standard Oil Company had bought and destroyed the plates, and the price soared. Down in Louisiana Huey Long paid one hundred dollars for a set, so I was told.

As I frequently received inquiries as to where the books could be found or where a purchaser could be found for a set, I turned the correspondence over to my secretary, a canny woman, who established a trading relation with a dealer in old books; and the two of them were in a fair way to do a nice little business when their hopes were blasted by the appearance in a New York bookstore of an entirely new edition of the work—a cheap edition, selling for five or six dollars. My publishers made an immediate investigation and found that it had been printed in England, probably from German plates.

As the third volume was not ready, there was nothing for the publisher to do but reprint the two, which he very promptly did. On the appearance of the reprint the pirated edition disappeared from the market. This episode set me to work promptly at the third volume.

But I needed a financial backer if the work was to be put through promptly. I found it unexpectedly in the editor-in-chief for whom the first two volumes had been written—S. S. McClure. *McClure's Magazine*, which had been suspended for a few years, had been revived, Mr. McClure in charge. He felt that bringing Standard Oil history up to date was a logical and might be an important feature for the periodical.

For me there was satisfaction in trying to revive the old editorial relations. I had always missed the gaiety and excitement Mr. McClure gave to work, and, too, I had always felt a little anxious about what I suspected was happening to him in a group which, even if it was made up of the very best of the town—men and women of ability and loyalty, naturally eager to prove that they could make a *McClure's Magazine* as good as ever had been made or better—could not, I was convinced, understand Mr. McClure, get out of him what he had to give like his old partner and friend John S. Phillips. So I was willing to give all I had to help in the revival of the old periodical.

I had my book well in hand, some twenty thousand words written, when the new *McClure's* was suspended and the third volume on the Standard Oil Company was cast out before publication had begun.

Perhaps it was just as well, both for *McClure's* and for me. Repeating yourself is a doubtful practice, particularly for editor and writer. I feel now there was no hope of my recapturing the former interest in the former way. The result would have smelt a bit musty. Indeed, though I hate to admit it, I think there has been a slight mustiness about all I have done in the nineteen years since I started "on my own"—that is, not on assignment—built as it has been on work done before the Great War.

Left with twenty thousand words on hand and no editor, I was obliged to make a quick turn in the interest of security and took on the first piece of work that offered. For one reason or another I have never been able to return to that third volume and it looks now as if it were a piece of work for my ninth decade since it failed to mature in the seventh and eighth!

If I failed to carry out my plan for tracing the maneuvers of the master monopoly after the Government had taken it apart in 1911 and after it adapted itself to the new and extraordinary situations forced by the Great War, I did trace what could be done in a corporation whose parts all had been built more or less on privilege, and which itself enjoyed high tariff protection, when a man took hold of it who believed that ordinary ethics did apply to business. This study was shaped around the life of Judge Elbert H. Gary.

It was no idea of mine, this life of Gary, and when it was proposed to me by that energetic and resourceful editor Rutger Jewett I promptly said, "No." But Mr. Jewett was insistent. He had talked the matter over with Judge Gary, who had told him he would open his records and answer my questions if I would do the book.

That meant, I supposed, that he had confidence in my ability to be fair-minded, whatever my suspicions. His judgment was formed on my handling of certain efforts to improve and humanize the conditions of labor in the mills, factories, and towns of the United States Steel Corporation. The Corporation under his direction had been a pioneer in safety and sanitation work. It had developed a pension system, improved communities, improved its housing, built schools and hospitals where there was no community to take care of these needs. It was the broadest, soundest record that I had found in my gathering of material for the articles *The American Magazine* had published under the title of "The Golden Rule in Business." I knew from my talks with Judge Gary that there was nothing going on in the Steel Corporation in which he was more deeply interested.

Moreover, I knew he was a man I could talk with freely. More than once, when he as spokesman of the Corporation was under attack for arbitrary dealings with labor, I had gone to him for his side of the case; and although I might not agree, and frequently did not, I always came away enlightened and with a rather humiliated feeling that I had shown myself an amateur in a conversation where he was very much the expert.

But was I equal to finding out the truth of things in this enormous industrial labyrinth which he ruled? Moreover, if Judge Gary had been an industrial plunderer, should I be willing so to present him? I had no heart for a repetition of my experience with H. H. Rogers.

Another reason for hesitation was that I knew if I did undertake it, and was as fair as I knew how to be, I should at once be under suspicion by groups with whose intentions for the most part I sympathized. They were unwilling to consider Gary in any light save that of Scapegoat Number One. An attack —yes—they would welcome it. An attempt to set down his business life as he had actually lived it—no. That was whitewashing.

Finally I took the matter to Judge Gary himself. "I do not know that I want to write your life," I told him. "If I find practices which seem to me against public policy as I understand it I shall have to say so. I appreciate your efforts to make working conditions for labor as good as you know how to make them, but it does not follow that I can stand for your financial policies. It is not your humanitarianism but your ethics I suspect."

"Well," Judge Gary laughed, "if you can find anything wrong in our doings I want to know it. I had George Wickersham in here for a year or more going over the whole set-up telling me what he thought we ought not to do, and I followed every suggestion he made. The Government has had its agency here for two years examining our books, and they gave us a clean bill of health. The Supreme Court has refused to declare us a monopoly in restraint of trade. Do your worst, and if you find anything wrong I shall be grateful."

I felt more of an amateur than ever after that. I also concluded that it would be sheer cowardice on my part to refuse the job which I really needed. I had not been long at my task, however, before I was heartened by the certainty that, from the formation of the Corporation, Judge Gary had made a steady and surprisingly successful fight to strip the businesses which he was putting together of certain illegal privileges, as well as to set up an entirely new code of fair practices—the Gary Code, it was jeeringly called in Wall Street.

Orders went out neither to ask nor to accept special favors from the railroads. Full yearly reports of the financial condition of the Corporation, whether good or bad, were sent out. These reports reached the public as early as they did the directors themselves, putting an end to the advance information which many insiders were accustomed to using for stock selling or buying. Various forms of predatory competition were attacked from the inside. Judge Gary not only laid down his code, he followed it up, preached it zealously to his board.

Another unheard-of innovation was his support of President Theodore Roosevelt's attempts to control business. It had become an axiom of Big Business to fight every effort of the Government to inspect or regulate. When Gary took the opposite course, applauded Roosevelt's efforts, declared that he was doing business good, doing him good, he was treated as a traitor by many colleagues.

Well, this seemed to me as good business doctrine as I had come across in any concern—much better, more definite and practical as a matter of fact than I got from most corporation critics. But how far was this followed up in practice? Before I was through I made up my mind that Judge Gary's code was applied just as completely and as rapidly as he could persuade or drive his frequently doubting and recalcitrant associates to it. But that took time, took frequent battles. Indeed, more than once he had come close to losing his official head, fighting for this or that plank in his platform. The Gary Code and the effort to put it into practice reconciled me to my task.

Judge Gary was an easy man to work with because he was so interested in following his own story. He had been too busy all his life to give attention to the route by which he had come. Now he enjoyed the looks back. Finding that he was willing to take literally his promise to open records and answer questions, I laid out a little plan for covering his life chronologically. It pleased him, for he was the most systematic of men. It gave him delight to remember. "How a man's mind unravels!" he exclaimed one day when he had suddenly recalled something long forgotten.

Our interviews were carried on always at 71 Broadway. He kept his appointments exactly. Rarely did he keep me waiting, and if by necessity he did he always apologized. If I came late I was made to feel clearly that that was a thing not to be done.

While Judge Gary was prepared to be frank in his talks with me he was not prepared to be misquoted. He evidently had learned that even with the best intentions a reporter may distort what a man has said out of all resemblance to what he meant. He

guarded against this by always having at our interviews a secretary who took down in shorthand all that he said, all that I
said. I made longhand notes, dictating them as soon as I went
back to my desk. I do not remember that a question of misunder-
standing of meaning ever came up.

Convinced that the Gary Code was genuine, not mere window
dressing for the public, nothing interested me more than how a
man in his fifties who had been for twenty years a successful
corporation lawyer was willing to preach to Wall Street as he
had done. I finally concluded the truth to be that Elbert Gary
had never outgrown his early bringing up. He had never gotten
over a belief in the soundness of what he had learned in Sunday
school and of what later he had taught through most of his manhood in Sunday school. The difference between him and some
of his fellows in business brought up in the same way was that
he insisted that the Sunday-school precepts of honesty, consideration for others, fair play, should be preached on week days as
well as Sundays, in the board room as well as the church. If he
ever sensed that his preaching was both comic and irritating to
Wall Street—which I doubt—he never gave sign of such a per-
ception.

I soon found that I need not hesitate to bring him all sorts
of criticisms of his doings as I unearthed them in studying the
public's reactions to the Steel Corporation's operations. They
never fretted or irritated him; rather he enjoyed analyzing them
for my benefit. He never dismissed radical opinions as nonsense.
In the year I was working with him there was never a public
radical meeting in New York—and there were a good many of
them that year—that he did not read all the speeches, and comment on them intelligently and with good humor.

"We must know about these things," he said. "We must know
all about Lenin, all about Mussolini. They are great forces; they
are trying new forms of government." His knowledge prevented
him from being scared.

Above all Gary enjoyed stories of his struggles to establish his own preeminence and his own code in the Steel Corporation. At the start he had several of the strong men in the Corporation against him; but he had won out, and it gave him the greatest satisfaction to show me letters of congratulation, to quote former opponents as saying, "You were right, I was wrong." Particularly he enjoyed the very good terms on which he stood with Theodore Roosevelt, whose unpopularity in Wall Street surpassed even that of the second Roosevelt.

He still talked with emotion of the decision of the Government to bring suit against the Steel Corporation under the Sherman Law. He thought he had satisfied it that the Steel Corporation was not a monopoly in restraint of trade, that it was what Mark Twain called a good trust; and when the Attorney General's office decided that there might be a question about the quality of this goodness Gary was terribly disturbed. There were advisers who thought he ought to try to settle the suit outside, but he would not have it so. The Government had doubts, and he must satisfy them. He believed that the law did not apply to the Steel Corporation; he believed that the Corporation was not contrary to a sound business policy, a menace to the country. That must be settled once for all. Of course he was jubilant over the outcome: it justified his conviction.

Judge Gary had done a great job, and he knew it; but, interestingly enough, it never made him pompous. As a matter of fact he was simple, natural, in talking about it. Along with this really simple enjoyment of his own conflict he had a nice kind of dignity and a carefulness of conduct which were not entirely natural to him. To be sure he had always been a good Methodist, a good citizen, a hard-working lawyer; but at the same time in all these earlier years he had led what was then called a gay life. He had liked a fast horse, liked to hunt and see the world. He was curious about all kinds of human performances, looked into them whenever he had the chance. When he became the head of the Steel Corporation he could no longer sing in the choir—he had to go to the Opera and sit in a box. He no longer drove fast horses. He wanted to fly, and the board of the Steel Corporation passed an ordinance against it—too dangerous. When he traveled it was more or less in state, and he couldn't slip out with a crowd of men at the stopping places to see the town.

It was hard on him, but he felt deeply that he owed it to the Steel Corporation to be above reproach. Not a little of this carefulness was due, I think, to the effect on the public, the exhibits that several of the new steel men had made of themselves after the Corporation was formed in 1901 and their offices were centered in New York. They were rich beyond their wildest dreams. The restrictions of the home towns were gone, and they broke loose in a riotous celebration which scandalized even Mr. Morgan. Gary joined in nothing which approached orgies. He was too hard a worker and always had been, and he saw with distress the effect the high living of certain of the steel men was having on the public. It was a danger, he felt, equal to the speculation in steel stock by officers of the corporation. To counteract it he gradually became more and more a model of correctness.

I came out of my task with a real liking for Judge Gary and a profound conviction that industry has not produced one in our time who so well deserves the title of industrial statesman. But I had to pay for saying what I thought. Under the heading of "The Taming of Ida M. Tarbell" my favorite newspaper declared that I had become a eulogist of the kind of man to whom I was sworn as an eternal enemy. But Judge Gary was not the kind of captain of industry to which I objected. On the contrary, he was a man who, at the frequent risk of his position and fortune, had steadily fought many of the privileges and practices to which I had been objecting.

However, one is judged largely by the company one keeps.

Judge Gary belonged to an industrial world where the predatory, the brutal, the illegal, the reckless speculator constantly forced public attention. That there was another side to that world, a really honest and intelligent effort in the making to put an end to these practices, few knew or, knowing, acknowledged. I could not complain. I knew how it would be when I started. But I must confess that more than once, while I was carrying on my work, I shivered with distaste at the suspicion I knew I was bringing on myself. The only time in my professional life I feel I deserve to be called courageous was when I wrote the life of Judge Gary.

My active interest in the industrial life of the country brought me unexpected adventures. The most instructive as well as upsetting was serving on a couple of those Government conferences which twentieth century Presidents have used so freely in their attempts to solve difficult national problems. An Industrial Conference called by President Wilson for the fall of 1919 was the first of these. Mr. Wilson felt clearly at the end of the War that our immediate important domestic problem was to establish some common ground of agreement and action in the conduct of industry. What he wanted evidently was a covenant by which employer and employee could work out their common problems as cooperators, not as enemies. There was need of action, as any one who remembers those days will agree. The whole labor world was in an uproar, and one of the periodical efforts to organize the steel industry was under way. Mr. Gompers, the head of the American Federation, sponsoring the strike, had had little or no sympathy with a contest at the moment but had been pushed into it by the adroitness of the radical elements boring from within throughout the War.

"These disturbances must not go on. It should be possible to make plans for a peaceful solution," Mr. Wilson said.

And so a Conference was called. In spite of my refusal to serve on his Tariff Commission, President Wilson had evidently not given me up. As a matter of fact our acquaintance and mutual confidence had grown during the War.

He now named me as one of four women representatives, the others being Lillian Wald, head of the Nurses' Settlement in New York City, Gertrude Barnum, assistant director of the investigation service of the United States Department of Labor, and Sara Conboy of the textile workers' union.

The Conference was an impressive and exciting body of some fifty persons divided into three groups representing the public, labor, the employers. I, of course, sat in the first group, where I found as my colleagues a bewildering assortment of men from various ranks of life. There were Dr. Charles Eliot, Charles Edward Russell, John D. Rockefeller, Jr., Judge Gary, John Spargo, Bernard Baruch, Thomas L. Chadbourne, Jr., and a score or more less known to the public, though not necessarily less influential.

At the head of the labor group was Samuel Gompers. Among his colleagues were some of the most experienced labor leaders in the country.

The members of the employer group were chosen from among men who had been particularly helpful in directing their industries during the War.

There were many interesting characters on the body. Two that I particularly enjoyed were Henry Endicott, who with the Johnsons had established the famous shoe towns near Binghamton, New York, and a delightful pungent character from Georgia—Fuller E. Callaway—who in twenty years had built up from scratch mills and a village with homes and schools—everything to give life and a chance to hard-working mill people. Mr. Callaway's story of what he had done in Georgia was one of the very few joyous contributions to a gathering doomed to be a dismal failure.

A body could have scarcely had a heartier welcome from the public than we did. People seemed to feel we should find a way to end the fighting; that was what we were there for, Secretary of Labor Wilson told us in his keynote speech. If we could produce a document which would secure the rights of all those concerned in an industry, it would find a place in the hearts of men like the Magna Charta, the Bill of Rights, the Declaration of Independence, the Constitution of the United States and the Emancipation Proclamation. He brought us all to our feet—all save a few who were too interested in political strategy to entertain a high purpose.

We were there to plan for the future of industry. But almost at once we discovered that it was not peace or the future of industry that was in Mr. Gompers' mind. Also, we discovered that the master politician of the body was Mr. Gompers. We were hardly organized before he called upon us to appoint a committee to report on the steel strike.

Dr. Charles Eliot, outraged, rose in all his very genuine majesty and reminded the body that we were not there to attend to the troubles of the present but to plan that such troubles might be avoided in the future. But the steel strike was on the table, and we left it there when we disbanded, a menace and an irritation.

It was not Mr. Gompers' resolution, however, which ruined the Conference. It was the inability of the representatives of labor and employers to agree on a definition for collective bargaining. The Conference as a whole contended that such a definition must be a leading plank in the platform we were there to make, but there were to be many other planks. Committees were at once formed to frame them. Almost every member of the Conference, too, had some particular resolution that he wanted to incorporate. I know I did. But most of us never found an opportunity to present our notions. Collective bargaining and what it meant were always getting in our way. The employer group and a considerable number of the public group believed that the definition which the labor group offered meant a closed shop. Judge

Gary openly charged this. But labor was quite as strong in its suspicion that the definition which came from the employer group encouraged company unions, at that moment flourishing in numbers that alarmed them. Suspicion governed both groups.

This went on for two weeks; then Secretary Lane, the acting chairman of the Conference, appealed to a very sick President, and from his bed Woodrow Wilson begged us not to allow division on one point to destroy our opportunity:

At a time when the nations of the world are endeavoring to find a way of avoiding international war [he wrote], are we to confess that there is no method to be found for carrying on industry except in the spirit and with the very method of war? Must suspicion and hatred and force rule us in civil life? Are our industrial leaders and our industrial workers to live together without faith in each other, constantly struggling for advantage over each other, doing naught but what is compelled?

My friends, this would be an intolerable outlook, a prospect unworthy of the large things done by this people in the mastering of this continent; indeed, it would be an invitation to national disaster. From such a possibility my mind turns away, for my confidence is abiding that in this land we have learned how to accept the general judgment upon matters that affect the public weal. And this is the very heart and soul of democracy.

But it was too late. The labor body walked out, except a few railroad men, wise and experienced in negotiations. A group of employers followed them. It was defeat. There was nothing for the President to do but disband the Conference. He did ask, however, that the public group of some twenty-five carry on. Now this group included a number of extraordinarily able men. From them had come some of the wisest and broadest suggestions that had been placed before the Conference. They could have presented an impressive program, but they had been outmaneuvered. They lost heart; they refused to go on. The only remarks I made at that Conference, bewildered as I had been by the political maneuvering, were when I saw the public group prepared for the cowardly business of denying the President's request. "Let us stick to it, do our best, make some report," I pleaded.

But I do not think anybody heard me. I had an impression as I talked that most of them were calculating when they could get a train to New York.

My next adventure in Government service came two years later as a member of President Harding's Unemployment Conference. The country had been caught in the first great postwar depression, and nobody was ready for it. Nobody knew, indeed, how widespread the unemployment was. Mr. Harding called a conference to deal with the problem without attempting to find out. The result was that on one hand you had an opposition belittling the numbers, on the other hand you had the responsible sponsors of the Conference probably exaggerating them. Nobody knew. And how easy it would have been to find out, by the same method the country had used in the War when, by a co-operative effort, the number of draftable men was counted in twenty-four hours at a limited expense!

This was an impressive Conference because of the make-up, and it was a mighty well conducted Conference: the chairman, Secretary of Commerce Hoover, kept it in hand from the start— and this in spite of the fact that there were all the elements of conflict found in the Industrial Conference and some extra, for here we had rivalry between the labor groups themselves, particularly that thorny problem of trade jurisdiction. But Mr. Hoover was enormously skillful, and we came out with a program which, if it had been carried out with the machinery which the Conference devised, would have brought the country to 1929 in a very different state of preparedness.

After our dismissal I put together in a lecture what I conceived to be the practical conclusion of the Conference. As my text I used one of the first principles laid down, "The time to act is before a crisis becomes inevitable." This text was an official and authoritative recognition of the unpalatable fact that business always moves in cycles—that a boom will be followed by a slump, that common sense demands preparedness.

How prepare? The Federal Government, state, county, community down to the smallest, was to have in reserve plans and money for work it wanted done that was not absolutely essential at the moment. When a slump started, this reserve was to be called out.

Private industry was by no means let off. In good times it was to lay up a surplus with which to keep plants and laboratory alive and ready for action as soon as there was a return of orders. The employee was to be protected by employment insurance. The individual householder was to keep back certain needed repairs and improvements for the day of need. That is, everybody was to be ready with his life preserver.

For two years I talked with the conviction of one who has a scheme he believes sound, and I was listened to with more or less enthusiasm, until it was obvious the slump was passing. It was a bad dream well over—good times had come. Why lay plans for the future? By 1926 there were no longer audiences to listen to a talk on preparing for unemployment. Apparently everybody, even President Hoover, who had been the all-efficient chairman of the Conference, forgot all about the program.

On the whole my little excursions into public service were discouraging and disillusioning; but they did convince me that I was right when I gave as one of my reasons for not going on to President Wilson's Tariff Commission the fact that I was not fitted for the kind of work a commission or conference requires.

I was an observer, a reporter. What interested me was watching my fellow members in action: the silent wariness of Secretary Hoover; the amused and slightly contemptuous smile of Charlie Schwab when he heard a woman had been put on the coal committee; the unwillingness of representatives of rival mining unions to do anything to relieve the immediate suffering of West Virginia miners, sufferings so useful in their campaigns; the stubborn look on the faces of those who fought over jurisdiction in an effort to reach an adjustment which would permit hungry men to take up work waiting for them; the quick political line-up; the clever political plays; the gradual fade-out of the objective, its replacement by party ambitions.

All together it was a revealing study of the reason there is so little steady progress in the world. These failures joined to the refusal to have anything to do with the League of Nations put an end to my hope that the War had taught us much of anything. We were not ready for the sacrifices necessary for peace, nor had we grasped the natural methods by which things grow. We believed we could talk, petition, legislate, vote ourselves into peace and prosperity. We had not learned that toil and self-control are three-fourths of any achievement, and that toil and self-control begin with the individual.

I went on with my talking in these years with a troubled mind. Continue this way, and we would destroy democracy. We had allowed, often encouraged, groups of self-interested individuals to have their way. That meant transformations in government machinery, new types of leaders, a multiplication of the children of privilege we had always so feared, the substitution of humanitarianism for ethics, sympathy for justice.

I was discouraged, but I never lost faith in our scheme of things. I never came to believe that we must change democracy for socialism or communism or a dictatorship. You do not change human nature by changing the machinery. Under freedom human nature has the best chances for growth, for correcting its weaknesses and failures, for developing its capacities. It is on these improvements in men that the future welfare of the world depends. So I believed, and so I argued as I went about, though sometimes, I confess, with a spirit so low that my tongue was in my cheek.

Such was my growing disillusionment when in 1926 I was asked to go to Italy to report on the Fascist State of Benito

Mussolini, now four years in power, a scandal to the democracies at which he openly jeered, but an even greater one to the Socialists and Communists who once had thought him on the way to being the strongest radical leader in Europe.

I knew little of what had gone on in Italy after the end of the War. I knew the parliamentary system had broken down; I knew there had been two years of guerrilla warfare after the Peace Conference, a period in which it was nip and tuck whether the next ruler of Italy would be Communist or Fascist. The Fascists under their leader Mussolini had won out. I had been amazed, and had never ceased to be amazed, that the dramatic march on Rome which ended in changing a parliamentary form of government into a dictatorship had been carried out without bloodshed. An astonished world had seen tens of thousands of unorganized and in part unarmed men march from every point in Italy to Rome, call for Mussolini, get him by order of the King and then march home again—not a brick thrown, not a head broken. It was the most amazing transfer of government I had known of.

But I had never given much attention to what had followed. I had never asked myself if it was inevitable that a dictator should arise in Italy. I had never asked who was this man Mussolini or what was this corporate state which was emerging.

Uneasy as I was over the way things were going in the United States, I vaguely felt when I was asked to go look all this up that possibly there were lessons there. Possibly I might learn something from Italy's experience about the process by which manacles are put on free government. However, the real reason I went to Italy was because I was offered so large a sum that I thought I could not afford to refuse.

My friends did their best to discourage my going. Down in Washington a worried undersecretary who gave me my passport and letters of introduction told me pessimistically that I probably should be arrested.

"But why?" I asked.

"Well, that is what is happening now to all our Americans. They drink too much, talk too much. The chief reason, as far as we can make out, is that they have to arrest them because they are attacking the government. We do the same thing here now and then, you know."

In Paris my best friends, among them Mr. Jaccaci, so much of an Italian that he talked the dialects of several provinces, told me with all seriousness that I should be searched. I must not carry letters to members of the opposition, nor books hostile to Mussolini. Now I was armed with things of that sort, collected in Washington, New York, and Paris. I did not propose to give them up without a struggle.

I was told I should find no newspapers excepting those sympathetic to the regime—a serious handicap, as I always count largely on newspapers. I must always use the Fascist salute. I took this so seriously that I practiced it in my Paris bedroom. I must not speak French. I was counting on that, as I speak no Italian. That is, I started off to Italy with a large collection of "don'ts" coming from people I considered informed. If I had not had a natural dislike of giving up an undertaking I never would have carried out my assignment.

However, at the end of the first day in Rome, a very exciting day, I awakened to the fact that nobody had searched my bags for incriminating documents, that I had talked French all day, and that I hadn't noticed anybody using the Fascist salute, and, most important, that I had found at every newspaper kiosk all the French and English papers side by side with the Italian. It gave me confidence. As a matter of fact in the four to five months that I was in Italy I did practically what I had planned to do, and nobody paid any attention to me. My mail was never interfered with, so far as I know. That is, none of the dire prophecies of interference to which I had listened at the start came true.

I do not mean to say it was always easy to get to the people with whom I wanted to talk; more than once, when I succeeded, I found the person fearful of quotation. I do not mean to say that I found no revolts. Down in Palermo, in corners of Milan and Florence and Turin, as a matter of fact almost everywhere, I ran across bitter critics of the new regime such as I hear every day in this year of 1938 of the President of the United States; but on the whole even good parliamentarians were accepting Mussolini. "He has saved the country," men told me. "We don't accept his methods, we don't believe in dictatorship; but it is better than anarchy."

Making my headquarters at Rome, I went over the country fairly well, particularly the industrial sections. I visited Turin with its hydroelectric developments, its great Fiat factory, its artificial silk, all plants of the first order. I spent some days in Milan, visited the great Pirelli plant, at the moment making underground cables for Chicago. I saw what was left of the co-operatives at Bologna. I climbed into that plucky little independent Republic of San Marino. Mussolini had been there just before I arrived. They were all for him. He worked and made people work. That is what had made San Marino.

I went south into Calabria, over into Sicily—always looking for the effects of the new regime on the life of the people. There was no doubt sensible things were going on—redemption of land, extension of water power, amazing efforts at wheat production; and the people were accepting the regime with understanding, realists that they were.

The first thing that springs to my mind now when I recall those months in Italy is a long procession of men, women, and children bent in labor. They harvested fields of rice, wheat, alfalfa, laying grain in perfect swaths; they sat on the ground, stripping and sorting tobacco leaves. Tiny girls, old women crowded narrow rooms, embroidering with sure fingers lovely designs on linen, fine and coarse; they cooked their meals before all the world in the narrow streets of Naples; they carried home at sunset from the terraces or slopes of mountains great baskets of grapes, olives, lemons—young women straight and firm, their burdens poised surely on their heads, old women bent under the weight on their backs. They drove donkeys so laden that only a nodding head, a switching tail were visible; they filled the roads with their gay two-wheeled carts, tended sheep, ran machines, sat in markets, spun, weaved, molded, built—a world of work.

Mingled with these pictures of labor were equally vagrant ones of these same men and women at play: holiday and Sunday crowds filling the streets, the roads, the cinemas, the dancing pavilions, the squares of little towns that traced their history back clearly more than two thousand years. In those squares, gay with flags and streamers and light and booths, in the evenings, throngs held their breath as to the notes of soft music the lithe figures of the ropewalkers passed high overhead with slow and rhythmic steps.

It was hard to realize when I looked on them that six years earlier these same people had been as badly out of step as they were perfectly in step at the present moment, that instead of rhythmic labor, there was a clash of disorder and revolt. Men and women refused not only to work themselves, but to let other people work. Grain died in the fields, threshing machines were destroyed, factories were seized, shops were looted, railway trains ran as suited the crew. Sunday was a day, not of rest, amusement, prayer, but of war; fêtes were dangerous, liable to be broken up by raids. Instead of the steady balance, orderly action, so conspicuous today, were the disorganization, anger, violence of a people unprotected in its normal life: a people become the prey of a dozen clashing political parties and not knowing where to look for a Moses to lead it out of their Egypt. How could it be, one asked, that in so brief a time a people should drop its clubs and pick up its tools?

There was only one answer: Mussolini. Already he was a

legend, a name everywhere to conjure with. I used it myself after I had talked with him, on scared gentlemen to whom I had letters of introduction, and who feared quotation: "But Mussolini saw me—talked with me." Nothing too much trouble after that.

But what kind of man was this dictator?

"You must go and see Mussolini," our able and friendly Ambassador Henry P. Fletcher told me one morning while I was working on the Embassy's voluminous records of what had gone on in Italy since the end of the War. I balked.

"I am not ready with the questions I want to ask him."

"Oh," said Mr. Fletcher, "just go down and have a chat with him."

With my notion of Mussolini gathered largely from English and American as well as hostile Italian sources, the word seemed utterly incongruous. Could one chat with this bombastic and terrifying individual who never listened, told you what to think, to say? Impossible. But of course I went.

The most exciting and interesting hour and a half I spent in Italy was in an anteroom watching twoscore or more persons who were waiting to be received, watching them go in so scared, come out exultant, go in inflated, come out collapsed. There was no one of them but was anxious, even the Admiral of the Fleet then at Ostia. He walked nervously about while he was waiting, adjusting his uniform, and when his turn came strode in as if marching in a parade.

Nothing I saw in Italy, as I have said, was more interesting to me. Though I must confess that all the time there was an undercurrent of nervousness. What I was afraid of was that my French would go to pieces, provided he gave me a chance to speak at all—of which I had a doubt. What if I should forget and say "vous" instead of "votre excellence"? Should I be shot at sunrise?

It was all so different from what I had anticipated. I must have misread and misheard the reports of interviews to have had such an unpleasant impression of what was waiting me. As I crossed the long room towards the desk Mussolini came around to meet me, asked me to take one of the two big chairs which stood in front of his desk—and, as he seated me, was apologizing, actually apologizing, in excellent English for keeping me waiting. As he did it I saw that he had a most extraordinary smile, and that when he smiled he had a dimple.

Nothing could have been more natural, simple, and courteous than the way he put me at my ease. His French, in which he spoke after his first greeting, was fluent, excellent. I found myself not at all afraid to talk, eager to do so. If he had not been as eager, I think I should have done all the talking, for luckily at once we hit on a common interest—better housing. His smiling face became excited and stern. He pounded the table.

"Men and women must have better places in which to live. You cannot expect them to be good citizens in the hovels they are living in, in parts of Italy."

He went on to talk with appreciation and understanding of the various building undertakings already well advanced, some of which I had seen in different parts of the country. He talked at length of the effect on women of crowded, cheerless homes. "A reason for their drinking too much wine sometimes," he mused.

He was particularly interested in what prohibition was doing to working people in the United States. "I am dry," he said, "but I would not have Italy dry [sec]." And he amused me by quickly changing sec to seche. "We need wine to keep alive the social sense in our hard-working people."

Altogether it was an illuminating half-hour, and when Mussolini accompanied me to the door and kissed my hand in the gallant Italian fashion I understood for the first time an unexpected phase of the man which makes him such a power in Italy. He might be—was, I believed—a fearful despot, but he had a dimple.

I left Italy, my head alive with speculations as to the future of the man. There was a chance, and it seemed to me a very good one, that he would be assassinated. Three dramatic attempts were made on his life while I was there, attempts known to the public. There may have been others, the authorities kept quiet. As I was sailing there came a rash attack on him at Bologna, the assassin being torn to pieces, so it was said, by an enraged crowd. For months after my return I watched my morning paper for the headline, "Mussolini Assassinated."

Of course there was a chance—so far as I could see, it was what Mussolini himself believed he could realize—to bring Italy to an even keel economically, by thrift, hard work, development of resources and by a system of legitimate colonization in the parts of the earth where he could obtain land, by treaty or by purchase.

And there was a third possibility to one at all familiar with the course of dictators in the world, particularly with the one with whom you instinctively compare Mussolini—Napoleon Bonaparte—that the day would come when he would overreach himself in a too magnificent attempt, an attempt beyond the forces of his country and so of himself, and he would finally go down as Napoleon went down.

Are Ethiopia and the alliance with Franco and the rebels of Spain to be to Mussolini what Spain and Russia were to Napoleon?

I was glad to breathe the air of the United States. It was still free, whatever our follies. There was at that moment no dictator in sight—no talk of one. But it was not Mussolini or the Corporate State which mattered to us: it was what was back of them. Why had parliamentary government broken down in Italy, the Italy of Garibaldi, of Cavour, Victor Emmanuel? Why had a dictator been able to replace it with a new form of government? Could this happen in the government of Washington and Lincoln? Those were the questions of importance to Americans. There was where there was something to learn.

19

LOOKING OVER THE COUNTRY

My CHIEF consolation in what I looked on as the manhandling
of democratic ideals and processes in all ranks of society, public
and private, was Abraham Lincoln. In spite of his obvious limitations and mistakes he had won the biggest battle for freedom
we have yet had to fight. He had done it by taking time to figure
things out, by sticking to the conclusions he had reached so long
as, and no longer than, they seemed to him sound, by squaring
his conduct always with what he conceived to be just, moral
principles. The more I knew of him, the better I liked him and
the more strongly I felt we ought as a people to know about how
he did things, not ask how he would solve a problem tormenting
us, but how he would go to work to solve it.

Feeling as I did and do about him, I have kept him always
on my workbench. There has never been a time since the War
that I have not had a long or short piece of Lincoln work on
hand. The result has been five books, big and little, and a continuous stream of articles, long and short.

The only fresh water in this Lincolnian stream was in a book
I called "In the Footsteps of the Lincolns." Beginning with the
first of the family in this country—Samuel, who came in 1637—
I traced them mile by mile from Hingham, Massachusetts, where
Samuel started, down through Massachusetts, New Jersey, Pennsylvania, the Shenandoah Valley, the wilderness of Kentucky,
southwestern Indiana, into Illinois, to the final resting place. I
ran down the records that had been left behind, copied the in-
scriptions on gravestones, went over houses in which they had
lived, looked up the families into which they had married, the
friends they had made. When I finished my journey I felt that

I had quite definitely and finally rescued the Lincolns from the ranks of poor white trash where political enemies had so loved to place them.

I have the satisfaction of knowing that this seven-generation pilgrimage of the Lincoln family has been added to the itineraries which enthusiastic students include in the cult of Lincoln now growing so strong in this country. I have never had an honor which pleased me more than a certificate from this group naming me Lincoln Pilgrim Number One.

My conviction that we needed in all our difficulties to familiarize ourselves with good models, sound laboratory practices led me to publish in 1932 a life of Owen D. Young. Mr. Young had impressed me as being just what I called him, "A New Type of Industrial Leader." And how we needed one! I had first heard of him in connection with what was called the President's Second Industrial Conference. After what I regarded as the cowardly retreat of the members of the President's first conference Mr. Wilson had called a second with the same objective, a distinguished body of men, among them Owen D. Young.

The sessions of this conference were all secret—a contrast to the noisy publicity which had surrounded the first gathering, and which had been partly responsible for its failure, the political-minded conferees being able in this way to speak to the country when they made speeches to their fellows—a privilege they valued more than trying to understand and cooperate with their fellows.

It was not long before I began to hear rumors of the satisfactory way the second conference was going and to hear the name of Owen D. Young as the man who as much as anybody else was leading to a broad, fair program of recommendations. His fairness, based on his experience in industrial relations, came as a surprise to not a few of the members of the conference, for Mr. Young represented the General Electric Company.

Secretary Wilson, who was then at the head of the Federal

Labor Department, declared that Mr. Young had no fear and no prejudice as a conferee, that he worked with an open mind. Attorney General Gregory said of him that there was no man on the conference who was so progressive in his philosophy of industrial relations. These opinions from the inside of the conference, followed by its admirable published report, with which I learned Mr. Young had had much to do, set me to following his work in labor matters so far as it reached the public.

I was deeply impressed by the showing he made as a negotiator on the Dawes and Young committees called to settle the thorny problem of what reparations Germany should make to the Allies —the first sitting in 1924 and the second, in 1929—Mr. Young being the chairman of the latter.

He proved himself a negotiator of unusual quality. He knew the facts. He kept his head under all circumstances. He had the warmest kind of human sympathies as well as what one of his colleagues called "a superior emotional sensitiveness," which made him steer clear of danger points before anybody else realized that they were near.

Such were the qualities, I told myself, needed in a leader to handle the infinitely difficult tangle in labor relations that was more and more disturbing industry.

All I could do was to say so in print, and that I tried to do in a book that came out in 1932 and had the misfortune to collide with a Presidential boom for Mr. Young which misguided friends were cooking up contrary to his wishes. It was the last thing that he wanted. He had the good sense to see that there were vastly important things for the good of the public to be done inside his industry. He wanted to go on with them. He was doing a good job and should have been left with it, I felt. But numbers of admirers and interested politicians continued to cry for him for President until finally Mr. Young came out flat-footed to say that under no circumstances would he accept a nomination.

But here was my book coming out while this outcry was going

on, and naturally enough political-minded reviewers took it as intended for a campaign biography. The point I had been try- ing to make, that here was somebody with rare ability to lead in the labor struggle, was entirely lost. I still believe that if we could have had him active in these past years so disheartening for peaceful industrial relations, the years which have set back so far the hope of genuine understanding cooperation inside in- dustry, we should have been saved the peck of trouble that we are now in.

It was out of the stuff gathered in these various undertakings that I was depending for security. But the return from the books and articles of a free lance is more or less uncertain, particularly when they come in so sober a form as mine and are always shaped to fit a self-made pattern.

I saw that I must have an annual sure if modest money crop, and I found it from 1924 on in lyceum work. My two seasons on the Chautauqua platform had encouraged the lecture bureau to add me to its list of "talent," and it was arranged that I go out from four to six weeks a year beginning around Lincoln's birthday when dinners and celebrations called for speakers, and running on into March—usually five engagements a week, the local committees choosing the subject from the half-dozen I of- fered.

These bookings covered the country from North to South and East to West, long and erratic journeys. Frequently I occupied two different beds a night, and now and then three. It was brutal, exhaustive business, but I learned to climb into an upper berth without a fuss, to sleep on a bench if there was no berth, to re- joice over a cup of hot coffee at an all-night workmen's lunch counter, to warm my feet by walking a platform while waiting for a train. By the end of the first season I had developed a stoical acceptance of whatever came. This, I argued, saved nerv- ous wear and tear. I think now a certain amount of indignant protest, useless as it would have been, might have put more zest into my travel, as well as my talking.

It was not only hard but lonesome business. From the day I started out I felt myself a detached wanderer, one who had laid aside personality and become a cog in the mechanism called a lecture bureau. My one ambition was to fill the specifications of the schedule and have it over with. It was not until I said good-bye to the last committee and was headed home that I felt the joyful rush of reviving personality.

This is putting an unfair face on my experiences. These long railroad journeys, these nights waiting in dreary stations were not without their rewards. I carry no more beautiful pictures in my mind than those flashed on me riding across this country: glittering snow mountains with stars hanging over them as big as a moon; miles of blossoming redbuds rising from the mist along an Oklahoma stream; the lovely rounded forms of the Ozark Mountains stretched as in sleep across Missouri; amethyst deserts; endless rolling prairies yellow with wheat or white with snow. These journeys took me at one time or another into every state in the Union, and there is no one of them in which some bit of remembered beauty does not take the curse off the almost universal disorder, even squalor of their towns and cities as I saw them going in and out by rail.

These long rides, these night waits, brought unforgettable looks into human lives. Strange how travelers will confide their ambitions, unload their secrets, show their scars to strangers. Never have I been more convinced of the supreme wisdom of the confessional of the Catholic Church than by the confidences poured into my ears in these brief and accidental meetings. Memorable and poignant though these experiences are of the country's beauty as well as of its human tragedy and comedy, they are little more than a blur. The rapid and crowded succession of events left no time to follow up, digest, get at the meaning, the solution. This was particularly tantalizing when it came to the actual filling of the engagement, for here you were for a time in close contact with a few people, your committee, and you had an hour or more facing an audience representative of a community.

The committee represented authority. It was my business to follow its instructions, please it if I could. Its chairman was the first person I sought on arrival—that is, the first after checking up on how and when I was to get away from the place at which I had just arrived.

To be sure, I had careful routing, but was the train by which I was ordered to leave still running? Had there been a flood or blizzard or accident to make a detour necessary? Sometimes it was an exciting detour. More than once I had to go fifty or a hundred miles by car over flooded or snowbound roads which the pessimistic declared impassable, and which only an adventurous youth for a good round sum would undertake to negotiate. In one of these hold-ups I traveled two hundred miles in a freight car behind an engine, the first to go over the snowbound road in a week. More than once on these exciting detours I felt that probably I should not come out alive; but I always did and always found, however late my arrival, my audience was waiting me. As a matter of fact those little adventures were highly stimulating after hours and hours of the benumbing comfort of trains.

When I knew how I was to get away, I looked up the committee. So far as I was concerned, the point at which I most frequently found a serious conflict in a committee was the subject on which I was to talk. That was supposed to have been settled— I had their letter for it. But not everybody wanted me to talk on so-and-so. Usually I found it was because somebody feared I might be too radical. They didn't want anything said on their platform which would antagonize the well-to-do conservative sponsors of the course or encourage the town's social and economic rebels.

I remember times when, after an exciting discussion behind the scenes, I stood in the wings waiting for the signal to come onto the platform while behind me the discussion went on. Only at the last moment did the chairman say begrudgingly, "Well, talk on so-and-so." But the chief objector meeting me after the lecture said, "I would so much have preferred to have heard you on so-and-so."

But the indecision of the committee was not the only trying experience before I was actually on my feet and at my job. There was the introduction. You never knew exactly what was to happen. As a matter of fact the introduction should and frequently does give opportunity for repartee, for anecdote—an easy way for putting yourself at once on terms of friendliness with your audience. But I was never happy at that kind of thing. On the Chautauqua circuit the fashion has been for the speaker to go out as soon as the music was over, take his stand and begin. Nobody said, "This is So-and-So who will speak on so-and-so." Nobody told them anything about you—you stood up and said your piece.

The ritual on the lyceum platform was different. There they made the most of me, as a rule. It sometimes seemed to me that each successive committee had a different way of presenting me. Sometimes I marched out with the master of ceremonies, a man or woman, and was placed in an armchair while the chairman made remarks about me which were often bewildering. I have been introduced as the author of George Kennan's Siberian books and of Edna Ferber's Emma McChesney stories. I have heard a long explanation of why I had never married. Once I was called a notorious woman by the speaker, he evidently thinking that the word was flattering. Often I had a bodyguard made up of important women of the community—a tribute to my sex.

One of the most peculiar fashions, as well as the most trying, was having a scene arranged behind the drop curtain. The stage was turned into a pleasant sitting room, and a half-dozen of the leading women of the town in their best gowns were seated about in informal fashion. When we were all ready the curtain went up. There would be music, and then the chairman would tell them who I was, and why I was supposed to be worth their attention. While this was going on the audience was locating the different persons of importance on the stage and criticizing the setting and the costumes.

One going as a lecturer to the most remote parts of the country that support a lecture course may think he will be a treat, but if he has any sensibility he will soon discover that, far from that, he usually has a critical audience. It is interested in what he has to say, treats him with courtesy and respect; but it has also had experience with scores of lecturers in past years and compares his matter and his manner with theirs. I have been in towns in the Middle West where they had heard Thackeray and Dickens read, had listened to Emerson and Bronson Alcott, and had heard every popular lecturer in all the years since their day.

Your real opportunity to judge of the intelligence and alertness of the community comes while you are speaking. Look for an hour or more into the faces of a group of men and women who, whatever they may think of you, are courteous enough to give you their attention, and you know soon what certain individuals think of what you are saying. Always I found myself speaking to someone who I knew heartily disagreed with me, someone I felt I would like to convince. Always I knew that there was a man waiting to challenge me. Usually these challenges came from Socialists or Single Taxers. If an opportunity was given to ask questions after my talk (something which I always encouraged), they were the first on their feet. The community knew them and knew what their questions would be, and frequently laughed at them. But a really good audience enjoys seeing a speaker heckled a bit and the speaker, if he is really interested in his business, is glad to take the heckling. I know nothing better for a lecturer who is going over the same arguments night

after night than to know that there will probably be somebody
in his audience who will seize the first opportunity to pick on
a weak point, challenge his generalization, his facts. If that
happens you always go away from your lecture better equipped
than you came to it.

In the twelve years in which I regularly made an annual lecture trip—I gave up the work in 1932, finding it too much for
my strength—in all those twelve years I everywhere found the
liveliest absorption in national policies. People told you how
they felt about an undertaking, how it was working out in
their particular community—important, for here you had the
test of the pudding in its eating. It was what I saw of the work-
ings of prohibition in the 1920's that drove me to do one of
the most unpopular things I ever did—that was to tell bluntly
how I saw it working in hotels from one end of the land to the
other, disheartening evidences of its effect on the young, the
unexpected dangers it brought to a woman traveling alone at
night, both in stations and on trains. I set down what I had seen
over a wide range of territory, what I had heard from the mouths
of men and women who had been ardent prohibitionists, and
who were appalled by the things that were happening particularly to youth in their own communities.

I had never been a prohibitionist in principle. My whole theory for the improvement of society is based on a belief in the
discipline and the education of the individual to self-control and
right doing, for the sake of right doing. I have never seen
fundamental improvements imposed from the top by ordinances
and laws. I believed that the country was gradually learning
temperance. But if prohibition could be made to work I was willing it should be tried. But what I saw in these years had led
me by 1928 to feel that something unexpected and very disastrous was going on, and that it must be faced, not hidden. It
was the most important observation that my crowded lecture
days yielded, but as I say it brought me bitter criticism and

now and then an intimation from some indignant woman of power and parts that I had sold myself to the liquor interests. One lady even intimated that if she had known that my pen was for sale she would have bid for it. This kind of criticism, however, is one of the things that one who says what he thinks must be prepared to meet. It is very difficult to believe that those who disagree with you are as convinced of the right of their point of view as you are, that they are not being bribed or unduly influenced, have no selfish purpose as you are sure you have not.

Two generalizations topping all others came out of this going up and down the land in the years between 1920 and 1932. The first is the ambition of our people to live and think according to what they conceive to be national standards. They adopt them whether they suit their locality or not, and often in adopting them destroy something with individuality and charm. For the traveler it begins with the hotel, spick and span, and as like as two peas to the one in A-ville—B-ville—and so on. Over the way is a sturdy stone building dating from the days of the coach and four. You may sigh for its great rooms and for a sight of the old lithographs sure to be on the wall, but you know it is run down. The town cannot support two, and it prefers the smart and comfortable commonplace to modernizing its fine old inn.

Look out your hotel window and you will see opposite a smart little dress shop, a duplicate of one you have been seeing everywhere you have halted, a duplicate of many a one you have seen on New York avenues. Next door is a standardized beauty parlor, and the pretty girl who waits on you at the table, the daughter probably of some solid and self-respecting townsman, has the latest coiffure and blood-red nails. She is struggling to look as she supposes girls do in Chicago or New York.

When the committee takes you out to drive it is to show their one high building, a high building on a prairie with limitless land to occupy, or a country club as fine as the one in the nearest city. The pride is in looking like something else, not themselves. The growth of this progress in imitation can be traced in the change that has come over the local postal card. All my life I have been a buyer of postal cards, largely on account of my mother, to whom I always sent pictures of the localities through which I was passing. Mother died in 1917, but up to this day I rarely go through a station that I do not say to myself, "I must find a card for Mother"—and turn away with a pang. In the years between 1920 and 1932 the postal card grew steadily less interesting. Once there were pictures of a near-by fort, the earliest house, a local celebrity, a rare view, but now it is all of high buildings and new blocks. They give of course the pictures of the Zoo and the parks, and even the Zoo and the parks pride themselves, like the country club, on their resemblance to those of the nearest large city.

The growing evidence that nationalization is blotting out local individuality, destroying the pungent personality of sections, states, communities, struck me with new force after the months I spent in Italy in 1926. In Italy I had found that, however deeply unionism might be written in the hearts of some men, you were a Roman, a Perugian, a Venetian, a Neapolitan before you were an Italian. The long arm of Fascism was reaching into the provinces and the towns, but it did not as yet disturb their ways of life. Mussolini had shown, up to that date, rare knowledge of his Italians. He had left them their ways. Sure of them, they did not worry so much about the change in government. Most of them could see about them the proofs of two thousand years of change; they could show you records and scars of a long succession of emperors, kings, consuls, dictators. It did not seem to make a vast difference to them what the government was if they could go on being themselves.

Perhaps our national ambition to standardize ourselves has behind it the notion that democracy means standardization. But standardization is the surest way to destroy the initiative, to benumb the creative impulse above all else essential to the vitality and growth of democratic ideals.

The second of my two generalizations was slower in its making. It came when I began to scratch below the surface of the imitative life so conspicuous. Then I found a stable foundation of people who stayed at home and went about their business in their own way and without much talking. These were people who in spite of droughts and dust storms stuck to their farms, making the most of good years, saving enough to carry them through the evil ones, adding a little, year by year, to their possessions in town and country, supporting schools, churches, and incidentally lecture courses. They were people who believed in freedom to work out their own salvation and asked from the state nothing more than protection in this freedom. It was the business of government, as they saw it, to keep off the plunderers and let them alone.

Democracy to them was not something which insured them a stable livelihood. It was something which protected them while they earned a livelihood. If they failed it was their failure. If the Government did not protect them from transportation plunderers, manipulations of money, stock gambling in goods which they raised to feed the world, it was the Government's failure. Then they had the right to change the Government, hold it up to its duty. That was their political business.

This was about what I found, the country over. When once I had learned to look beyond the restless imitative crowd, to hunt out people who were going about their business steadily, and for the most part serenely, I began to breathe more freely and to say: "Well, perhaps, after all, the men and women of this country as a whole do know what they are about. They do know what democracy means, and in the best way that they can under many hampering circumstances they are trying to live it."

Some such conclusion I always brought back with me from

my annual swings around the country, my dozens of nights in dozens of different places—the high spot of which always was the hour of searching the faces of the men and women who came to listen to what I had to say, and who, I knew, sized me up for just about what I was worth. I might be fooling myself but not them.

20

NOTHING NEW UNDER THE SUN

HERE then is the record of my day's work still unfinished at eighty. Nobody can be more surprised than I am that I am still at work. Looking forward at life at thirty, forty, fifty, sixty, generally finding myself tired and a little discouraged, having always taken on things for which I was unprepared, things which were really too big for me, I consoled myself by saying, "At seventy you stop." I planned for it. I would burrow into the country, have a microscope—my old love. I knew by this time that was not the way for me to find God, but I expected to have a lot of fun watching the Protozoa and less anguish than watching men and women.

But I discovered when seventy came that I still had security to look after. I could make it by seventy-five, I thought. But I did not. And I have come where I am with a consciousness that, so long as my head holds out, I shall work. More important, I am counting it as one of my blessings. In spite of the notion early instilled into me that the place of the aged is in the corner resignedly waiting to die, that there is no place for their day's work in the scheme of things, that they no longer will have either the desire or the power to carry on, I find things to do which belong to me and nobody else.

It is an exciting discovery that this can be so. Old age need not be what the textbooks assure us it is. Shakespeare is wrong. Cicero, dull as he is in comparison, is more nearly right. More, it can be an adventure. My young friends laugh at me when I tell them that, in spite of creaking joints and a tremulous hand, there are satisfactions peculiar to the period, satisfactions dif-

898

ferent from those of youth, of middle life, even of that decade of the seventies which I supposed ended it all.

I have been finding it a surprising adventure, if frequently disillusioning and disturbing, to review my working life, to pick out what seems to be the reason for my going here and not there, for thinking this and not that. It has been a good deal like renewing acquaintance with a friend I had not seen since childhood. Probably the reason for this is that I have never stopped long enough after any one piece of work to clean up, valuate what I had done. Always a new undertaking was on my table before I was finished with what went before. Packing boxes and letter files of badly classified material still clutter up my small space with the physical evidence of the incompleteness of every piece of work I have undertaken.

This explains why telling my story has been so full of surprises. "I did not realize I felt that way," I have told myself more than once. "I had forgotten I did that." "I cannot imagine why I thought that."

I took on self-support at the start that I might be free to find answers to questions which puzzled me. After long floundering I blundered into man's old struggle for the betterment of his life.

My point of attack has always been that of a journalist after the fact, rarely that of a reformer, the advocate of a cause or a system. If I was tempted from the strait and narrow path of the one who seeks for that which is so and why it is so, I sooner or later returned. This was partly because of the humor and common sense of my associates on *McClure's* and *The American Magazine*, and partly because the habit of accepting without question the teachings and conventions of my world was shattered when in girlhood I discovered that the world was not created in six days of twenty-four hours each. That experience aroused me to questioning, qualifying even what I advocated, which no first-class crusader can afford to do.

I have never had illusions about the value of my individual contribution! I realized early that what a man or a woman does is built on what those who have gone before have done, that its real value depends on making the matter in hand a little clearer, a little sounder for those who come after. Nobody begins or ends anything. Each person is a link, weak or strong, in an endless chain. One of our gravest mistakes is persuading ourselves that nobody has passed this way before.

In our eagerness to prove we have found the true solution, we fail to inquire why this same solution failed to work when tried before—for it always has been tried before, even if we in our self-confidence do not know it.

We are given to ignoring not only the past of our solutions, their status when we took them over, but the variety of relationships they must meet, satisfy. They must sink or swim in a stream where a multitude of human experiences, prejudices, ambitions, ideals meet and clash, throw one another back, mingle, make that all-powerful current which is public opinion—the trend which swallows, digests, or rejects what we give it. It is our indifference to or ignorance of the multiplicity of human elements in the society we seek to benefit that is responsible for the sinking outright of many of our fine plans.

There are certain exhibits of the eighty years I have lived which particularly impress me. Perhaps the first of these is the cyclical character of man's nature and activities. If I separate my eighty years—1857 to 1937—into four generations, examine them, compare my findings, I find startling similarities in essentials. Take the effort to create, distribute, and use wealth. How alike are the ups and downs that have marked that effort!

I was born in the year of a major panic. The depression which followed it was smothered in war. That war over, quickly there followed in 1866 a serious depression—world-wide. In 1873 came a major panic. When this first period came to an end in 1877 the country was still deep in the clutch of the unhappy depression which followed that panic.

Each of my three successive generations beginning in 1877, 1897, 1917, has featured a "major" panic followed by five to seven years of depression. Then has come·a brilliant short-lived recovery ending in what we euphoniously call today a recession.

My fifth generation, just opening, promises well to duplicate its predecessor. If I live ten years longer I no doubt shall see another major panic, and one still more difficult for the productive individual or group to handle because the practice of following the provident ant's example and storing up in the good time reserves to meet the bad has been made a political offense.

Each generation repeats its leaders. Each sees men endowed with superior inventiveness, energy, and genius for business, inspired by love of power and possession, launch selfish schemes—Carnegies, Rockefellers, Goulds. If each of these strong men left something sinister behind, each also contributed to higher living standards and hurried on the nationalization of the country. The public without whom they could not have lived a day saw in their greedy grandiose undertakings whatever was for its benefit, and took it while ordering its government to control whatever was sinister.

And while they built and served and exploited, other men endowed with far greater idealism than practical sense planned new forms of government, new laws, advertised panaceas, all guaranteed to produce security and justice. Each generation has had its Henry George, its Bellamy, its Bryan, intent on persuading mankind that he had found the way, could lead men to the good life.

In each generation employer and employee have faced the decision—war or cooperation. If war has been the answer in the majority of cases, there have always been those who have gone ahead building up a great mass of evidence of what men inspired by good will, free from suspicion and self-interest, can do in industry by patient cooperative experiments.

Side by side with these exhibits have gone magnificent governmental attempts to correct abuses, to make man's life in the Republic freer, securer, more just, efforts to carry out the avowed purpose of the government we started a hundred and fifty years ago. And these efforts are alike in essentials—the New Deal of Franklin Roosevelt, the New Freedom of Woodrow Wilson, the Square Deal of Theodore Roosevelt, the fight for a larger freedom of opportunity of Grover Cleveland, the struggle to wipe out slavery of Abraham Lincoln.

Again and again in these generations have we seen the great airship of democracy lift from the ground, stagger, gather itself together, soar, sail, while those who had chosen the pilot and loaded in his cargo watched the flight with confidence and exultation. This time their dream had come true.

But the ship has always come back, its journey unfinished, and doubters have jeered at those who believed in it, cried out that it would never fly, that freedom, equal opportunity were only foolish fancies; men, they gloated, function only under strong single rulers. Dictatorship alone makes efficient government—national power and glory. The state, not the individual, is the end.

There is no denying that these repeated failures or half-successes have made cynics of many who have had a hand in the flights, or at least been sympathetic watchers.

It has been sickening to see hopes grow dim under the hammering of reality, to see a generation lose its first grand fire and sink into apathy, cynicism. One asks oneself if man has the staying power ever to realize his ideals. One is inclined when this hour of futility comes to agree with Arthur Balfour that human life is but a disreputable episode on one of the minor planets. As far as I am concerned that smart and cynical estimate never could stand a good night's sleep.

If I find little satisfaction or hope in examining and comparing one by one my four successive generations, I find considerable in looking at them as a whole. When I do that, I see not a group of cycles rolling one after another along a rocky and uneven road but a spiral—the group moves upward. To be sure it is not a very steady spiral, but I am convinced that is the real movement.

Could there be greater evidence that this is true than that the world as a whole has today come to conscious grips over that most fundamental of problems: Shall all men cooperate in an effort to make a free, peaceful, orderly world, or shall we consent that strong men make a world to their liking, forcing us to live in it? more than that, train us to carry it on?

It is well that the issue should be clear, so clear that each of us must be forced to choose.

Even more hopeful, if not so clear to many people, is the increasing knowledge that we are getting of man as an individual and as a mass, coming to us particularly from men of science. What we have yet to find out, apparently, is what we can expect of man under this or that circumstance, what words and what promises stir him, what persuades him to cooperation or to revolt, why he follows a particular type of leader at a particular time and how long he can be counted on. Once we know better what we can get out of man under particular circumstances we can plan our action with something like the certainty with which the electrician plans his machine. He knows the nature of the current, what it will do and not do. He puts no strain on it which experiment has proved fatal.

When we reach that knowledge and control of human forces we shall know why the League of Nations works so badly, why we have before us the terrible and apparently uncheckable shambles of Spain and China, why an intolerable outbreak of racial and religious prejudice should shame us at this period of our history, why we must be prepared to meet the savage out-

breaks of men and peoples still contemptuous of contracts, un-
amenable to ideals of honor, peace, and conciliation.

One consolation in any effort to socialize and democratize our
plans of life is that the mass of men want a simple world. In
every country they ask little more than security, preferably of
their own making, freedom to build in the way they like so far
as possible. They will follow any system or any leader that
promises them that. Politicians would do a better job for men
if they wrote fewer constitutions, devised fewer automatic cures,
gave more attention to disciplining and training common men
and women the world over to honest labor, to cooperation with
their fellows, to sacrifice when necessary, keeping alive in them
their natural spark of freedom.

How are we going to do it? That is the gravest question we
face. In 1921 I went to Washington to report Secretary Hughes'
Conference on the Limitation of Armaments. It seemed to me
that I had better do some preliminary reading on the problems,
so I went to a wise man at the Carnegie Endowment for International Peace for advice. He turned out to be a philosopher.

"First," said he, "read 'Don Quixote': he will tell you what
they cannot do. Then read Aesop's Fables: that will tell you
what they can do. But above all read the King James Version
of the Bible, which tells you that peace on earth is promised
only to men of good will."

There you have it. If we want peace we must make men of
common sense, knowing what can be done and what cannot be
done, also men of good will.

How are we to do that? I see no more promising path than
each person sticking to the work which comes his way. The
nature of the work, its seeming size and importance matter
far less than its right relation to the place where he finds himself. If the need at the moment is digging a ditch or washing
the dishes, that is the greatest thing in the world for the moment.

The time, the place, the need, the relation are what decide the value of the act.

It is by following this natural path that new and broader roads open to us, moments of illumination come. There is the only reliable hope of the world. It takes in all of us but puts it up hard to each of us to fit the day's work into the place where we stand, not crowding into another's place: no imitation, no hurry, growth always, knowing that light and power come only with growth, slow as it is.

Madame Curie so saw it. Asked what a woman's contribution to a better world should be, she replied that it began at home, then spread to those immediately connected, her immediate friends, then the community in which she lived; and if the work proved to meet a need of the world at large it spread there. But the important thing was the beginning, and that beginning, Madame Curie insisted, was in the home, the center of small things.

Work backed by such a faith makes life endurable. I doubt if I could have come into my eighties with anything like the confidence I feel in the ultimate victory of freedom, the ultimate victory of man's self-respect, if I had not groped my way through work into some such faith.

I know I should find this end of life less satisfactory if it were not a working end, conditioned as it must be by certain concessions to years, easements necessary if I am to keep vigor for my two or three hours a day at my desk and, once accepted, becoming more and more enjoyable.

No one can imagine what a satisfaction it is to me to find that I need not go to conferences and conventions and big dinners. That job belongs to youth. It alone has the appetite, the digestion, the resilience for the endless talk and late hours of those functions, also the confidence that salvation is to be reached through them.

Still more satisfactory is the acceptance of the fact that I have not the strength to run about on trains and give lectures. That, too, is the job of young people, and the best I can hope for them in carrying it on is that they will learn as much about people as I think I did. The humility which that will engender will be all to their good.

A discovery which has given me joy, and which had something of the incredible about it, is the durability of friendship born at any period in one's life. I have enlarged in this narrative only on professional friendships, those that belong legitimately to my day's work, but this discovery does not cover them alone but all the range from childhood to now.

Circumstances, time, separations, may have completely broken communication. The break may have been caused by complete divergence of opinion, differences as grave as those which caused the breaking up of our old McClure crowd, as grave as the ghastly separations that war brings; but you pick up at the day when the friendship was—not broken but interrupted.

One of the most beautiful personal demonstrations I have had of this unbreakable quality in friendship was a birthday party which S. S. McClure gave Viola Roseboro, John Phillips, and myself when he was seventy-eight, and I close to it. Miss Roseboro had stayed with Mr. McClure when the rest of us left him. That had never made a rift in anybody's relations with her, and now we all sat down together as once we had sat down in the old St. Denis, the old Astor, the old Holland House—lunching places that marked the stages by which *McClure's* worked itself successively into better quarters, went uptown. And we talked only of the things of today, as we always had done. We sat enthralled as in the old years while Mr. McClure enlarged on his latest enthusiasm, marveling as always at the eternal youthfulness in the man, the failure of life to quench him.

One of my great satisfactions has been a revival of curiosity. I lost it in the 1920's and early 1930's. Human affairs seemed to me to be headed for collapse. War was not over, and men were taking it for granted it was. The failure of the hopes of previous generations had taught us nothing. The sense of disaster was strong in me. What I most feared was that we were raising our standard of living at the expense of our standard of character. If you believed as I did (and do) that permanent human betterment must rest on a sound moral basis, then our house would collapse sooner or later.

It was taking a longer view, looking at my fifty years as a whole, that revived me. I thought I saw a spiral, was eager to prove it.

Once more I am curious. It is an armchair curiosity—no longer can I go out and see for myself; but that has its advantages. It compels longer reflection, intensifies the conviction that taking time, having patience, doing one thing at a time are the essentials for solid improvement, for finding answers. Perhaps, I tell myself, I may from an armchair find better answers than I have yet found to those questions which set me at my day's work, the still unanswered questions of the most fruitful life for women in civilization, the true nature of revolutions, even the mystery of God. It is the last of the three which disturbs me least. The greatest of mysteries, it has become for me the greatest of realities.

）

INDEX